0
10
20
30
FINLAND
Helsinki
Leningrad
Oslo
Stockholm
Tallinn
ESTONIA
Riga
LATVIA
LITHUANIA
Kaunas
Moscow
U. S. S. R.
ORTH
EA
Copenhagen
EAST
GERMANY
Berlin
Amsterdam
Bonn
ssels
Warsaw
POLAND
Prague
CZECHOSLOVAKIA
Kiev
Odessa
Munich
Vienna
Budapest
AUSTRIA
HUNGARY
RUMANIA
Bern
Trieste
Belgrade
Bucharest
YUGOSLAVIA
BULGARIA
Sofia
Istanbul
Rome
ALBANIA
Tirane
Athens
DITERRANEAN
SEA
60
50
40
10
20

INTERNATIONAL STUDIES

of the

Committee on International Relations

University of Notre Dame

INTERNATIONAL STUDIES

of the

Committee on International Relations

University of Notre Dame

The Fate of East Central Europe: Hopes and Failures of American Foreign Policy
Edited by STEPHEN D. KERTESZ

German Protestants Face the Social Question
WILLIAM O. SHANAHAN

Diplomacy in a Whirlpool: Hungary Between Nazi Germany and Soviet Russia
STEPHEN D. KERTESZ

Soviet Imperialism: Its Origins and Tactics
Edited by WALDEMAR GURIAN

Pan-Slavism: Its History and Ideology
HANS KOHN

The Foreign Policy of the British Labour Government
M. A. FITZSIMONS

Christian Democracy in Italy and France
MARIO EINAUDI *and* FRANCOIS GOGUEL

Bolshevism: An Introduction to Soviet Communism
WALDEMAR GURIAN

Europe Between Democracy and Anarchy
FERDINAND A. HERMENS

(*Out of Print*)

The Soviet Union: Background, Ideology, Reality
Edited by WALDEMAR GURIAN

The Catholic Church in World Affairs
Edited by WALDEMAR GURIAN *and* M. A. FITZSIMONS

THE FATE

OF EAST CENTRAL EUROPE

Hopes and Failures

of American Foreign Policy

THE FATE OF EAST CENTRAL EUROPE

Hopes and Failures

of American Foreign Policy

Edited by STEPHEN D. KERTESZ

UNIVERSITY OF NOTRE DAME PRESS

1956

Library of Congress Catalog Card Number 56-9731

NOTRE DAME, INDIANA

PREFACE

THE political importance and present plight of East Central Europe has inspired this symposium on *The Fate of East Central Europe: Hopes and Failures of American Foreign Policy*. For the present it would seem that the least we can do for the captive nations behind the Iron Curtain, as well as for ourselves, is to reconstruct carefully the record of the past and to examine the methods and results of Communist conquest, so as to facilitate the laying out of a better future for the subjugated nations. In harmony with these objectives the symposium deals with American foreign policy in the area, treating in short compass the recent history of the captive nations, as well as the cases of Finland and Austria, two more-fortunate countries on the periphery of the Soviet Empire, and Yugoslavia, which occupies a somewhat unique position.

The Introduction brings together some of the major questions dealt with in detail in the various chapters and mentions certain problems of a general nature not discussed elsewhere.

Part One analyzes the principal aspects of American foreign policy toward East Central Europe from the earliest period to the present time. The second chapter attempts the formidable task of condensing the history of American foreign policy from the nineteenth century until the second World War. In the third chapter American and Allied policies during the second World War are set forth; this chapter is of central importance, for wartime decisions determined the postwar fate of East Central Europe. The fourth chapter deals with the new era of American foreign policy which began with the Truman Doctrine and the Marshall Plan. While these latter policies proved highly successful in many parts of the world, they were ineffective in "Russia's Europe," where American and British endeavors to support the Yalta pledges and later the human rights clauses of the peace treaties were doomed because of the uncooperative attitude of the Soviet Union.

The postwar history of individual countries in East Central Europe and the effect of several American policies upon their fate, together with the special actions of American policy in the various countries, appears in Parts Two and Three. It seemed appropriate to include accounts of Finland and East Germany, although neither of these nations is actually situated in East Central Europe. The authors of the chapters dealing with the fate of individual countries worked according to the same directives, but, because of the greatly differing national backgrounds and courses of events in these various countries, unity of approach was not always feasible. American foreign policy asserted itself—or failed to assert itself—both in the context of American-Soviet relations and in political, economic, and cultural developments within the East Central European states. There was not much to be said about the few and mostly futile American diplomatic moves in countries enslaved by Soviet agents at the close of hostilities. In their postwar history there came a time after which only political organizations subservient to the Soviet Union were tolerated, and from this time onward American diplomatic moves were virtually paralyzed. In more fortunate countries, such as Austria and Yugoslavia, American diplomacy had more leeway and achieved tangible results.

To supplement the history of general political and social developments in East Central Europe, Part Four examines the economic problems between the Soviet and non-Soviet worlds and touches upon economic trends in the captive countries. Part Five offers a glimpse into a more desirable future, outlining some ideas for a free East Central Europe.

Early versions of chapters 1, 3, 4, 17, and 18 were presented and discussed at a conference held at Notre Dame on February 11, 1955 under the joint efforts of the Committee on International Relations and the Center for Soviet and East Central European Studies. The chapters were written from information available in the spring and summer of 1955, and most of them were updated from the galley proofs.

Bibliography, chronologies, and basic data concerning individual countries will be published in a companion volume. This will include the more important documents and data concerning sovietization and communization of the countries figuring in Part Two of the present volume and also documents characteristic of international political developments affecting the countries included in Parts Two and Three.

The editor takes this opportunity to express to all contributors his sincere thanks for their cooperative spirit, which greatly facilitated the integration of the symposium. His task was further alleviated by the cooperation of Professor M. A. Fitzsimons, Director of Publications of the Committee on International Relations, and Professor A. S. Ryan of the Notre Dame English Department, both of whom kindly advised him in editorial problems and are responsible for numerous stylistic improvements. I am grateful to my research assistants and especially to Donald J. Carbone, whose industry and resourcefulness were always forthcoming. Bernard Browne and Paul Corscadden prepared the index.

Stephen D. Kertesz

with both the more important documents and their respective [illegible] and enumeration of the countries' [illegible] in Part Two of the present volume, and also documents reflecting all international political developments affecting the countries included in Parts Two and Three.

The editor takes this opportunity to express to all contributors his sincere thanks for their cooperative spirit, which greatly facilitated the compilation of the symposium. The [illegible] was increased by the cooperation of Professor M. A. [illegible], Director of Publications of the Committee on [illegible], and Professor A. S. Ryan of [illegible] [illegible] of whom [illegible]

[illegible] valuable improvements [illegible] assistants, and especially to Donald [illegible] industry and resourcefulness were always [illegible] Michael Browne and Paul [illegible] prepared the index.

Stephen D. Kertesz

CONTENTS

Chapter 1

Introduction

STEPHEN D. KERTESZ

THE UNITED STATES has seldom had a comprehensive foreign policy for East Central Europe. Usually no such policy seemed necessary. To Americans the East Central area of the Continent was a faraway region, remote from the national interest. The prevailing American attitude toward that area of Europe was largely sentimental, rooted in the memories of immigrant citizens. Sentiment, happily, required no long-range planning, specific political objectives, or concrete political backing.

On occasion, certain general principles of American foreign policy had been applied. The American Government repeatedly protested against religious and other persecutions. Throughout the nineteenth century the American public watched with sympathy the struggle of oppressed peoples, such as the Poles and Finns and Hungarians. During the Hungarian war of independence in 1848–49 the United States decided to recognize Kossuth's regime as a *de facto* government, but the combined force of the Austrian and Russian armies destroyed independent Hungary before an American representative could reach the country, and the American gesture came to naught.

Beginning in the 1880's, several million East Central Europeans came to the United States, to be absorbed into the American population without coercion. They considered it a privilege to become American citizens and contributed with their blood, labor, and ingenuity to making the American Republic a strong force for freedom and a symbol of a better future for men everywhere.

Firm as was the new allegiance of the people who emigrated to the United States, their continued interest in their former homelands was not without significance, especially during the first World

War. Poles and Czechs and representatives of other nationalities at that time sought American support for their national objectives. The American attitude was of great importance for the fate of East Central Europe. The problems involved nonetheless seemed to be of incidental rather than of major interest to President Wilson and other high officials of the United States. They concentrated on general world problems. Then too, the English-speaking powers have naturally been more at ease in dealing with maritime regions, whose problems are relatively familiar, than with large, almost landlocked continental areas. The complicated nature of ethnic factors and the emotions involved were especially baffling. The leading part taken by President Wilson in the closing period of the war and at the Paris Peace Conference, a role which benefited some of the nations of East Central Europe, was followed in the 1920's and 1930's by virtual American withdrawal from European politics.

It is true that during this period cultural and economic intercourse greatly increased between the United States and most of the East Central European states. Because the American nation had become the chief creditor of the world, American loans and investments were an important factor in the economic life of East Central Europe. The new economic power of the United States was a link of some consequence, as was also the impact of certain outstanding American universities and the expanding activities of the Rockefeller Foundation and other private philanthropic enterprises. But all these efforts took place through a variety of channels, in a rather haphazard way, and were not paralleled by a positive American policy in the area.

Meanwhile, isolation, the neutrality legislation of the latter 1930's, and above all the military weakness of the United States had encouraged the conquest-minded totalitarian regimes in Europe and Asia. The lack of an assertive American foreign policy before the second World War had its effect on the course of events in the countries in East Central Europe. Wartime inter-Allied decisions and the westward advance of the Red Army sealed their fate.

Timetable and Methods of Soviet Conquest

The Nazi domination of East Central Europe caused great disruption and suffering in that area of the Continent, but it was succeeded in 1944–45 by a Russian occupation which has proved even more destructive. With the possible exceptions of Albania and Yugoslavia, no Communist government could have been established in East Central Europe without the actual or potential threat of the Red Army, and it was under its pressure that the Communist revolution was imposed. In Yugoslavia, Western assistance was the decisive factor in strengthening the Communist-led guerilla movement. Tito himself did not openly advocate a Communist regime for Yugoslavia during the war but in his program promised pure democracy without coercion, the inviolability of private property, and no revolutionary social changes. His vigorous fight against the Nazi foe was a major unifying force. The people rallied around him through the Communist-front organization called the "National Liberation Front." In Albania, Tito's assistance was instrumental in the victory and consolidation of the Communist regime. In Poland, Eastern Germany, Czechoslovakia, Hungary, Rumania, and Bulgaria, the Moscow-trained Communist organizers followed the Red Army. They seized the key power positions with the help and under the protection of the occupying Russian Army and manipulated the political transformation of each country.

The Russians in 1945 could have established subservient Communist dictatorships in all the "liberated" countries, but probably because of the Yalta Declaration on Liberated Europe and other tactical considerations connected with international and internal politics the moment was believed to be inopportune. A gradual procedure was adopted. Instead of attempting to introduce the Soviet system in one sweeping move, the Communist Party under the leadership of Moscow-trained Communists permitted in each country the establishment of a coalition government. In setting up these regimes the aim was to give formal compliance to the Yalta Declaration and, for the moment, to satisfy popular feelings in the respective countries.

Communists dominated the coalition governments from the very beginning. They organized the police and seized other key positions of power. They directed the execution of radical agrarian reforms and dominated the so-called people's courts. Later they eliminated the independent leaders of the non-Communist parties; eventually these leaders were driven into exile, imprisoned, or killed. Then a few intimidated politicians or disguised Communists were proclaimed as representatives of some of the non-Communist splinter parties and the "coalition" continued. The final step was introduction of the one-party system, followed by establishment of the so-called people's democracies, which, in the words of the veteran Hungarian Communist leader Mátyás Rákosi, are "in a position to establish a proletarian dictatorship without the Soviet form, because they can base themselves on the great Soviet Union."

There were differences in the timetables and methods of Communist conquest, but the general pattern for a variety of situations remained the same. In countries occupied by the Red Army, courage and determination could not change the Moscow-dictated course of events. This pattern was not fully applied and failed in one instance. Finland's peripheral and isolated geographical location beyond the main street of Soviet expansion gave her a special position. Though Finland fought two wars against the Soviet Union, she was not occupied by the Red Army. In the postwar period the Finns' traditional courage and firm but cautious determination again prevailed over internal subversion, threats, and external pressure. Thus Finland has so far avoided the fate of a Communistic puppet dictatorship although she is in the mouth of the Soviet mammoth. On the other hand, in the case of the three Baltic states—Latvia, Lithuania, Estonia—it was not necessary for the U.S.S.R. to employ the usual ceremonious procedure, and after the war these countries reassumed the status of Soviet republics, which the U.S.S.R. had initially imposed on them in 1940.

Three East Central European states—Poland, Czechoslovakia, and Yugoslavia—belonged to the victorious camp at the end of the war and became original members of the United Nations. In these states Communist actions differed somewhat from Communist actions in Albania and in such former Axis satellites as Bulgaria, Rumania, and Hungary. The armistice agreements burdened the latter nations with heavy reparations deliveries and other economic obligations. During the armistice period they lived under the strict political and military control of the Russian-led Allied Control Commissions. These international bodies were used by the Russians as tools of Soviet policy whereby, in cooperation with the occupying Red Army and the local Communist parties, the political transformation of the satellites was engineered. Soviet tactics also were adapted to geographical factors, to specific inter-Allied agreements, and generally to the local conditions in each country. Important considerations, for example, were the proportion of Communists, of fellow travelers, and of actual or potential anti-Communist elements among the various East Central European peoples, together with the religious and social conditions and, not the least, the strategic importance of each country.

Despite special agreements concluded at Yalta stipulating coalition regimes and free elections in Poland and Yugoslavia, in both countries Communist regimes were installed from the beginning, and free elections were never held. In Polish politics the chief factor was, and remains, the "liberating" Red Army; no matter how unpopular or unwise Communist actions have been, Russian bayonets have supported them. In Poland, in the adjacent East Germany, and in the lower region of the Danube, Russia has vital strategic interests. The Red Army, entrenched in the North German plain with solid bases in Poland, points its sword toward Western Europe. At the same time the Soviet Union urges the neutralization of Germany. Rumania and Bulgaria, situated on the shore of the Black Sea, are part of the road to Istanbul, and in Rumania are the Ploesti oil fields. In such regions Soviet action was prompt and inexorable. As for Yugoslavia, the basic difference between Marshal Tito's regime and that of other Communist-dominated states has been that during and after the war Tito had time to build an independent party machinery and to organize the Yugoslav army, police, and public services without Russian control. This made possible his break with Stalin in 1948 and has meant a measure of independence for Yugoslavia ever since, although his internal regime remains as repugnant to the Yugoslav people as do the Communist regimes to the peoples of the other captive nations.

In contrast with the Yugoslav, Bulgarian, Rumanian, and Polish developments, the Soviet Union tolerated relatively free elections in the westernmost Danubian countries. In point of time the Hungarian elections preceded the others and had great international repercussions. The Western democracies considered the resounding Communist defeat in the Budapest municipal elections (October 7, 1945) and in the general elections in Hungary (November 4, 1945) as evidence that free elections were possible under Russian occupation. The Smallholders Party obtained an absolute majority in both elections, while the Communists polled only 17 per cent of the total vote in the general elections. The leading Western newspapers featured front-page articles and editorials.[1] Western optimism was

[1] The following dispatch from the London correspondent of the *Christian Science Monitor* (October 9, 1945) was most characteristic:

"This concrete proof that free elections—as they are understood in the United States and Great Britain—have occurred in at least one Balkan country is heartily strengthened by the Austrian election (November 24, 1945).[2] Although in the Russian Zone of Austria, as in Hungary, assistance of the Red Army was "of no small benefit to the Communist Party," the evidence showed the elections to be free and unfettered, and in both countries the voters expressed their determination not to be bolshevized. In Austria the fact that Communist representation dwindled to four seats in parliament greatly helped the consolidation and effectiveness of constructive forces in domestic policies. But in Hungary, a country under exclusive Soviet occupation, the electoral protests against Communism had an entirely different sequence from that in *felix Austria.* Because the non-Communist parties under the leadership of the majority Smallholder Party were unwilling to cooperate in the wholesale communization of the country, the Communist Party, with the assistance of the Red Army and the Russian-led Allied Control Commission, liquidated the parliamentary system and those vestiges of political freedom which initially had more or less existed under the Russian occupation. This liquidation was a gradual process, in the course of which the whole gamut of Communist technique was applied. At first the Communists sought to use persuasion and pressure, but after their failure to communize the country behind the screen of a coalition the Communist Party turned to drastic measures. These were intensified after a new electoral defeat in August 1947 and culminated in the establishment of the Hungarian People's Republic in August 1949.

In Czechoslovakia the Communists obtained 38 per cent of the

---

welcomed by Anglo-American officials. This election result would indicate that even in areas beyond Anglo-American control—and about which many officials had been privately worrying—the peoples of Europe can be given a chance to choose their own officials honestly and openly. . . . In view of the fact that Hungary is wholly under control of the Red Army and that this quite naturally has been of no small benefit to the Communist Party, some observers had been concerned that it might be difficult to conduct completely free and unhindered elections. The result of the weekend balloting would seem to have disposed of that worry in convincing manner."

Cf. *New York Times,* October 9, 1945; *New York Herald Tribune,* November 6, 1945; *Journal de Genève,* November 9, 1945.

[2] One of the Soviet reasons for allowing free elections in Hungary and in the Russian Zone of Austria might have been to divert attention from Communist seizure of power in Bulgaria and Rumania and Communist domination in Poland and Yugoslavia—countries strategically more important to the Soviet Union than Hungary or Austria. Cf. Isaac A. Stone, "American Support of Free Elections in Eastern Europe," *The State Department Bulletin* (hereafter *Bulletin*), XVII (1947), 311–323, 407–413, 434; also, "Soviet Violations of Treaty Obligations: Document submitted by the Department of State to the Senate Committee on Foreign Relations," *Bulletin,* XVIII (1948), 738–744.

vote in the general elections in May 1946. Communist popularity thereafter declined, and to prevent unpleasant revelations at a forthcoming second election the Communists seized power in February 1948. The coup brought Czechoslovakia into the fold of the Soviet subject nations and put an end to much Western and Czechoslovak wishful thinking that Czechoslovakia could remain a bridge between the Soviet and non-Soviet worlds. These events opened the eyes of those Western statesmen who previously had been inclined to indulge in the comfortable philosophy of "It can't happen here."

After the closing of the Iron Curtain in 1948, and after the forced merger everywhere in East Central Europe of Socialist and Communist parties, there began the final abolition of political freedom throughout satellite Europe. Concomitantly with ruthless communization and sovietization, all actual or potential opposition to the Muscovite brand of Communism was liquidated.

Thus the aftermath of the second World War put an abrupt end to the relations which had existed for roughly one thousand years between the Western and East Central areas of the Continent. Nations living in East Central Europe have come under the military and political control of a foreign tyranny which also exploits the helpless captive nations economically. The Soviet Government exploited even Yugoslavia, as was revealed and documented by the Yugoslav Government in 1949.

Soviet Russia has never accepted the basic concepts and the most universal values of Western democracy—such principles as freedom of thought and expression, civil liberties, freedom of religion, and dignity of the individual. The Communist police states imposed by Muscovite imperialism on East Central Europe are the negation of freedom and democratic principles. While an anticolonial movement has been sweeping Asia and Africa, in the heart of Europe nations with a long record of independent national existence have been subjected to a new and utterly ruthless brand of colonialism. The barbed wire implanted on their western boundaries and reinforced by concrete pillboxes, huge floodlights, and minefields symbolizes this tragedy—their fundamentally changed status in Europe and in world relations. No colonial people was as hermetically separated from the outer world as are the nations living under strict Muscovite Communist political and military control in Russia's Europe.

A plan for the actually existing integration of the Soviet system was announced at the Moscow Conference, November–December 1954, as a retaliation for West Germany's approaching rearmament and participation in NATO. This declaration of intention was followed by the Warsaw Conference in May 1955, which concluded "a treaty of friendship, cooperation and mutual assistance," and established a unified military command for the U.S.S.R., Poland, Czechoslovakia, Eastern Germany, Hungary, Rumania, Bulgaria, and Albania. This treaty was only the formalization of a situation which in reality existed long before 1955.[3]

Passive resistance has remained general. Millions of nameless men and women have been waging a silent struggle against despotism and have held to a faith in a better future. Large-scale Soviet propaganda and incessant Communist indoctrination have not yet proved effective and indeed have often backfired. Slogans contradicted by the realities of daily life could not wipe out the traditions of centuries. Nor could they counterbalance reactions evoked by the brutalities of the Red Army. Popular feelings remain hostile to the promises of Communism. Other well-known Soviet measures have had a similar effect—such as the ruthless police terror, the suppression of freedom, the elaborate system of thought-control with its concomitant insecurity, the worst colonial-style exploitation practiced by the Soviet Union, the neglect of production of consumer goods, and the often so senselessly forced industrialization with its disregard of human costs.

Amidst changing Soviet policies three main forces of passive resistance remain against sovietization, communization, and Russification: the Catholic and Protestant churches with their centuries-old roots in the West, the peasantry with its enduring will and capacity for independence and survival, and the proud nationalism of the captive peoples. The Communist regimes are trying to annihilate these centers of resistance through forceful methods of social engineering and especially by the indoctrination of youth. Despite ruthless Soviet methods, results of bolshevization have so far been limited and superficial. One cannot change the spirit of nations overnight. People still believe that Christianity and the West are able to offer better solutions for contemporary social, political, and economic problems than totalitarian Communist dictatorship imposed on them by a foreign power. But the time factor and the positive attitude and achievements of the free world are all im-

[3] Cf. "The Soviet Alliance System, 1942–1948," *United States Department of State Documents and State Papers,* Vol. I (1948), 219–247.

portant. Disappointments and unfulfilled hopes create adverse reactions. The spirit of resistance cannot be maintained indefinitely.

East Central Europe in World Politics

The enclosure of East Central Europe in the Soviet orbit meant a fundamental change not only to the captive nations but to the whole of Europe. In the past, dividing lines between two worlds have been drawn more than once across this critical area. Today all of East Central Europe belongs to Russia. The Carpathians, the door of Focsani, the Middle Danube Basin, the Polish and North German plains all are in Russian hands. The strategic gates to Western Europe are wide open to the Red Army. The new situation is of momentous significance for Americans, because modern weapons and means of transportation have made the Atlantic Ocean less of a defense line for the United States than the English Channel used to be for Great Britain.

In the light of the events of the past decade the importance of East Central Europe in world politics has at last been generally recognized. This area under Russian control plays a double role. It is a dire threat to the security of the Western world, but it may also prove to be the Achilles heel of the Soviet system. The almost one hundred million people who live in this strategic area belong by history, tradition, and way of life to the Western or Mediterranean culture. Despite popular feelings, the satellites are making an important contribution to Russia in strategic raw materials (coal, oil, bauxite, and uranium), heavy machinery, vehicles, chemicals, and mass-produced consumer goods (textiles, footwear, appliances, etc.). The area receives, on a contractual basis, certain Soviet raw materials—for example, cotton—and returns them to the Soviet Union in the form of finished products. Moscow determines, arbitrarily, the prices of both raw materials and finished products in these relationships. By and large, the diversity of the satellites' industrial output, the skilled manpower available, and the resources of the area represent a decisive addition to Soviet economic power. At present the industrial output of the satellite states equals almost 40 per cent of the industrial output of the U.S.S.R., and the area has greater potentialities.[4] In this crucial mid-twentieth century our concern with the fate of the East Central European nations is thus

[4] For a comparison between certain items of Soviet and satellite output, such as coal and lignite, iron ore, nonferrous ore, and oil, see *Fortune,* XLVII (February 1953), 116–119. Cf. A.Z., "Some Aspects of Soviet-Satellite Economic Relations," *The World Today* (1955), pp. 431–437.

based not merely on sentiment or sympathy; it is inspired as well by general political considerations and has a close connection with the American national interest.

The title given to Part Two of this volume, "Creation of a Soviet Empire in Europe," indicates that the postwar history of these countries has been a gradual integration into the Soviet system. During this period American diplomacy was more active in some countries than in others. A close link existed between the potentialities of American foreign policy and domestic developments in the captive states, the latter, of course, being manipulated by the overwhelming influence of the Soviet Union. After the usual twilight period only political organizations subservient to the Soviet Union and directed by Muscovite agents were tolerated, and from this time American diplomatic moves were even more paralyzed than before.

In Russia's Europe after V-E Day the British and Americans had only poor alternatives—unless they were prepared to use forceful methods. The use of force, however, was hardly possible in the period of the psychological letdown in the postwar years when the Western world was preparing to make peace and the American Army had demobilized. In this psychological climate neither the Western governments nor their peoples were prepared to consider the threat or use of force. When Soviet bad faith and encroachments became only too obvious, Western policy did undergo a certain change. Western protests increased, became stronger in tone, and embraced a large variety of political and economic problems. Despite this change of attitude, it was not difficult for the Russians to see that the Western powers were not prepared to threaten with a "big stick" or even with a twig. The sharpest barbs of American diplomacy were reserved mostly for Russia's attempts to go beyond her political sphere. The aggressive Soviet moves evoked Western determination to resist Communist expansion, which actually was stopped in some areas, such as Berlin and Korea, and prompted the establishment of the North Atlantic Treaty Organization and other defensive agreements. But in East Central Europe itself this stronger Western policy was met by harsh Soviet countermeasures, such as the thickening of the Iron Curtain, the hastening of the process of communization and sovietization of the captive countries, and the tightening of Russian military and political control.

The peace treaties signed in Paris on February 10, 1947 were of little value in Communist-dominated countries. They regained only a nominal sovereignty. The independence of Hungary and Rumania remained entirely fictitious, for the peace treaties authorized the Soviet Union to keep an unlimited number of troops in those countries to maintain the lines of communication with the Red Army in Austria. Simultaneously with the entering into effect of the treaties the Allied Control Commissions were dissolved in Bulgaria, Rumania, and Hungary, and with elimination of these international bodies even nominal Western influence was excluded from the three Danubian states. Incorporation of Czechoslovakia in the Soviet orbit and exclusion of the Western powers from the Danube by the Russian-dictated Danubian convention, signed by the riparian states at Belgrade on August 18, 1948, were only further consequences.

In the face of the obstructive tactics of the Soviet Union and its puppet governments in the captive countries, the system for solution of disputes as contained in the peace treaties did not prove satisfactory. With ratification of the treaties (September 15, 1947), the heads of the diplomatic missions of the Soviet Union, the United Kingdom, and the United States in the satellite capitals, acting in concert, were supposed to give guidance during a period of eighteen months to ensure the rapid and efficient execution of the peace treaties; after this period the interpretation and execution of the treaties, if not resolved by the allied heads of mission within a period of three months, should have been submitted to a commission composed of one representative of each party and a third member selected by mutual agreement from nationals of a third country. Although during the eighteen months the satellite governments committed flagrant violations of the peace treaties, the uncooperative Soviet attitude made impossible any concerted action by the three heads of mission. Subsequently the system provided by the treaty for solution of disputes was defeated by the uncooperative attitude of the Soviet Union and by the refusal of the satellite governments to nominate a representative to the commission.

When Great Britain and the United States repeatedly charged Hungary, Rumania, and Bulgaria with having violated peace treaty obligations requiring them to secure to all persons under their jurisdiction the enjoyment of human rights and fundamental freedoms, Budapest, Bucharest, and Sofia refused to recognize the existence of a dispute. Moreover, the satellite governments denounced the English and American protests as illegitimate interference in their domestic affairs and stated that they had complied fully with the human rights provisions of the peace treaties. Subsequent proceedings before committees and the General Assembly of the United Nations and the International Court of Justice were fruitless. Although the governments of Bulgaria, Hungary, and Rumania refused to cooperate in the efforts of the General Assembly to examine the grave charges made against them with regard to the observance of human rights and fundamental freedoms, and were condemned by the General Assembly because of their behavior, they were admitted to United Nations membership in December 1955.

Whether earlier and better organized Western diplomatic moves in the postwar period would have been more effective is open to speculation. With the advantage of hindsight it is easy to see that the Western powers made a grave diplomatic error in not firmly resisting the first Soviet violations of international obligations. When protests began at last, they were confronted by accomplished facts. Better planned and more energetic Western diplomatic action might have been effective in minor matters, but how far such action could have influenced the general situation in countries under Soviet domination is questionable. Rules of common decency are unknown or meaningless to Soviet leaders, who have few moral inhibitions and restraints. They are not impressed by diplomatic protests unsupported by force. In East Central Europe we have been witnessing in these past few years the emergence of a new world in which normal rules established for orderly international intercourse do not operate.

This development only highlights the fact that the problems existing between the Communist orbit and the countries belonging to the Western state system transcend the usual lines of international relations. The real difficulties lie much deeper and are anchored to the different ways of thinking, different value systems, and different expectations and aspirations of two different worlds. Although the essential objectives of the Soviet Union and the Western democracies are diametrically opposed in many ways, during the perils of the second World War these fundamental differences were often overlooked. The reasons for the Central and Eastern European policy of the Western powers are today well known, having been set forth in published documents, memoirs, and statements. The fact nonetheless remains that the outcome of this policy has been far removed from those wartime pledges which promised to the liberated countries free elections, representative governments, and democratic institutions. An important area has been temporarily lost to the free world.

Vistas for a Better Future

The misfortune of East Central Europe cannot be attributed exclusively to great-power politics. In one man's lifetime the East Central European nations experienced the violent dissolution of several international and domestic orders, and in the course of such overwhelming events almost all nations committed errors and mistakes. If the tragedies of the past are not to be beyond redemption, mutual understanding, reconciliation, and humility must be the presiding spirits over the problems of East Central Europe. Only in this way is there ground for hope, that in a heritage now brought to so low a level of fortune, but which once knew heroism and greatness, misfortune and error, may be found the prospects of a better future. Probably the advantages of a great political and economic unit in East Central Europe, combined with the benefits of democratic equality, with the right of self-determination extended to all nationalities, might lead to a better future. Modern technological developments should make possible large-scale cooperative work—for example, proper utilization of natural resources and especially of water power.

The political difficulties involved are not insurmountable. The feuds and conflicting ambitions of the various nations in the area are well known, but national differences have been greatly exaggerated. There is the obvious fact of geography, which invites intercommunication. There is the fact that for many centuries cooperation in East Central Europe did effectively take place. There is the fact of intermarriage. And there is, above all, for most of the countries similarity of culture, ways of living, and ideals. Cleavages among neighboring nations have often been created by an exaggerated and improper interpretation of their historical traditions and experiences. Emotion has been inflamed by chauvinist propaganda. Ambitious jingo politicians and governments themselves have frequently magnified and exploited differences, having nothing to gain for themselves from unity. But large sections of the population of East Central Europe have no trouble understanding one another across boundaries and would welcome such efforts toward cooperation as have brought results in bygone periods of history.

The common man has everywhere the same basic aspirations which President Roosevelt in his Annual Message to Congress on January 6, 1941 described as the Four Freedoms: freedom of speech and expression, freedom of every person to worship God in his own way, freedom from want, freedom from fear. This presidential message, together with the Atlantic Charter, was like a new Wilsonian proclamation in its effect on the minds of men throughout East Central Europe. Unfortunately for mankind, the practical application of such general principles is a difficult task in most parts of the globe. Moreover, since these lofty ideas were not supported by concrete planning, political determination, and adequate military strength, the aspirations and expectations created by them soon vanished, events turned out differently, and disappointment was great. Yet belief in American good faith and generosity remains, and such gestures as the food shipments of 1954 to Hungary, Czechoslovakia, and East Germany under the President's flood relief program, amounting to about $2.5 million, strengthen these feelings.

We live in a rapidly changing world. Important transformations may yet take place in the international scene through forces working within the Soviet empire and in world relations. The Soviet and non-Soviet worlds necessarily have a constant effect upon each other. There are continuing signs of change in the Soviet empire—for better or worse. The impressive economic progress and increasing military strength of the free world, together with the fact that some major prognostications based on the doctrines of Marx, Lenin, and Stalin have not come true and have indeed been proved false by actual developments, cannot remain secret even in Communist states. The Iron Curtain is not an absolute barrier to ideas, and inclusion within the Soviet system of nations which previously belonged to the Western world may not, in the long run, be an unmixed blessing to the Soviet leaders. Nations cannot long be kept in watertight compartments even by the most ruthless of dictatorships. The barbed wire planted on the western boundaries of the captive states cannot extirpate ideals of human freedom and civil liberties. There are recurring signs of unrest in some regions of the Soviet Union and in the captive countries. The continuing Communist process of elimination and liquidation may foreshadow the historic fate of dictatorships.

The United States at present, then, can help to prepare constructive plans for the democratic reorganization and healthy integration of East Central Europe. Many democratic leaders have escaped from the captive countries and are living today in the free world. It is possible that in this amazingly changing world, full of potentialities and imponderables, the constructive elements in the national *émigré* groups from East Central Europe could fulfill a historic role. With American cooperation they could make serious evaluations of the past and present, and of the permanent and changing factors in East Central Europe, and could work out long-range projects for the future, based on equality and self-determination of the captive nations.

In the course of planning, it would be of utmost importance to study systematically the political, social, and economic changes in the captive countries. The impact of accelerated industrialization, in particular, may cause fundamental economic and social transformations. Certainly the social fabric can never again be the same as it was before the great turnover. If we are not able or willing to evaluate the transformations seriously, the Western nations may not understand the mind of the people and the changed society after the liberation. And the liberated people might understand even less the *émigrés* returning from the West and still thinking in terms of bygone times.

If a serious preparatory work is not done in the fields of politics, economics, history, culture, and education, then liberation might be followed not by constructive cooperation but by the renewal of old quarrels. While East Central Europe organized on a cooperative basis could fulfill a most useful function in an integrated Europe, its compartmentalization would remain the source of future disasters. The neglect of basic research and long-range planning has been one of the greatest omissions in the postwar years. Without earnest preparation and solid foundation a modern structure cannot replace the many ramshackle national homes in East Central Europe.

Since political thinking in East Central Europe is closely related to events of even the distant past, a significant preparation for a better future would be the impartial study of the history of the East Central European nations. The one-sided approach to history in most of these countries and especially the unfavorable characterization of neighboring peoples were largely responsible for creating an atmosphere inimical to healthy international cooperation. The ensuing political conditions not only hindered development of good neighborliness but greatly facilitated in the area the power politics of outside forces. France, Italy, Germany, and the Soviet Union in turn played upon the conflicting national aspirations of the East Central European people for their own interests. Today, history is being interpreted and taught in the light of Soviet-Communist doctrines, and, of course, teaching of history follows the changing party line. The new generations are more confused than ever.

In the free world intercultural committees could be organized among the East Central European nations for a more objective approach to history. Such committees could study in a friendly spirit those biased statements and mutually harmful tendencies which appear in the press, textbooks, and other publications in the various countries. Moreover, these committees could achieve positive constructive work by the collection and propagation of those tenets and facts which would foster a friendly atmosphere among the East Central European nations. Even now cooperative ideas and principles could be popularized beyond the Iron Curtain by radio. Systematic correction of Communist distortions of history would be another important objective. Since nationalism will probably remain one of the most important political factors in East Central Europe, it would be a wise course to direct its forces into constructive and cooperative channels. Recent progress in the fields of science and technology have opened new vistas and potentialities in international relations and should furnish new incentive for cooperative efforts.

The ups and downs of history in the last decades have shown once more that the exaggerations of small-power nationalism do not pay in the long run, and that great-power imperialism can be disastrous not only to the peoples living between the Baltic and Aegean seas but also to all of Europe. In previous generations freedom of thought, inquiry, and communication among European nations made possible a prodigious technical progress and an ever-rising living standard. The borderland of Western civilization fulfilled an important role for the benefit of mankind. Certainly Europe cannot remain divided—half slave, half free—without grave consequences to the free community of nations. The entire world must be concerned with establishing freedom and stability in this danger zone of Europe where the sparks of two world wars were ignited.

Condemnation of some aspects of Stalin's rule and other recent events in the Soviet orbit may open new avenues to change and generate new forces which in the long run could increase the prospects of liberation for the subjugated nations. The withdrawal of Soviet forces and control from Eastern Austria creates a precedent which, if applied to other countries in East Central Europe, may form the beginning of happier developments.

Any optimistic speculations should be grounded in experiences with Soviet Communist tactics over a period of four decades. The self-styled collective leadership of the Soviet Union operates today *fortiter in re et suaviter in modo;* it follows Soviet Russian objectives unremittingly, but skillfully and with studied moderation. Although this policy reflects primarily the more subtle approach of Stalin's successors, the Soviet leaders may be yielding partly to overwhelming pressure. Concessions by Moscow may release forces of a great significance, and changes made for tactical reasons may escape from the control of the Communist operators. It would be a mistake to exclude the possibility of important transformations in the Soviet orbit, but we cannot be optimistic as to the nature or duration of the changes as long as we face in Russia a totalitarian dictatorship which exploits both its own peoples and foreign nations. Statements and tactical concessions are not enough without decisive deeds and, in particular, without the release of the nations of East Central Europe from Soviet captivity.

It is our hope that at this apocalyptic juncture of history the present volume will contribute toward an understanding of facts and ideas in their relation to the United States and East Central Europe, and will stimulate constructive endeavors for the future.

Part One

THE COURSE OF AMERICAN FOREIGN POLICY

Chapter 2

The United States and East Central Europe Before 1941

ROBERT H. FERRELL

TRADITION has it that two of the sailors in Columbus' first voyage to America were Ragusans, natives of that ancient port along the Adriatic coast, and here, perhaps, was the initial contact of America and East Central Europe. A century or so later, during the planting of the first English colony in North America at Jamestown, citizens of Poland were among the settlers. It is recorded that in 1609 when the Indians set an ambush to kill Captain John Smith, the Poles saved his life and captured an Indian chief. Soon afterward, one should add, the Czechs appeared in America. The first Czech immigrant seems to have come to New Amsterdam in 1633 in the employ of the Dutch West India Company, having removed himself to the New World because of the persecutions of the Protestants in Bohemia during the Thirty Years War. It would doubtless not be difficult to find other examples of early migrants to America from the East Central regions of Europe. Yet until the late nineteenth century by far the majority of immigrants to America came from the northern and western areas of the Continent and from England and Scotland. Until well after the American Civil War, contacts between Americans and the peoples of East Central Europe were mostly indirect in nature, and hardly more than incidental to the constant migration and the great commerce in trade and ideas which was rapidly building up an Atlantic community.

Certain events on occasion reminded Americans of the existence of peoples in the Balkans, the middle Danube basin, and the Baltic region of Europe. During the American Revolution two gallant Poles, Casimir Pulaski and Thaddeus Kosciuszko, distinguished themselves in Washington's armies. Pulaski died of wounds in 1779 during the battle for Savannah, shortly after he had written Congress that "I could not submit to stoop before the sovereigns of Europe, so I came to hazard all for the freedom of America." [1] Then during the era of President James Monroe there was much enthusiasm in America for the liberation of the Greeks in Europe, and the term "Greek" came to include virtually all of the Christian peoples of the Balkans. Monroe in the original draft of his famous message of 1823 expressed strong sympathy and ideological support for the liberation of the Greeks, and it was only at the behest of his cautious secretary of state, John Quincy Adams, that the President removed the plea from the text of his message. American opinion also showed keen sympathy for the Poles during the Polish war for liberation in 1830–31.[2] During the latter half of the nineteenth century there was a constant touring of American missionary evangelists and a generous outpouring of American philanthropy in European Turkey and especially Bulgaria. Americans were instrumental in the publication of some of the first Bulgarian textbooks and periodicals and supervised the translation of the Bible into modern Bulgarian. In the twentieth century the American Near East Foundation and the Rockefeller Foundation were active in education and public welfare in Greece, Albania, and Bulgaria. The good works of such "Puritans in the Balkans" [3] are still in partial evidence even today.

In the middle of the nineteenth century, after the failure of the liberal revolutions on the Continent in 1848–49, there arose momentarily in the United States a truly national interest, and a strong feeling of national kinship, toward the defeated revolutionaries of Hungary. The idea was current that America was "young," and that Young America was similar in hopes and aspiration to Young Hungary.[4] The United States was the only gov-

[1] See Miecislaus Haiman, *Poland and the American Revolutionary War* (Chicago, 1932); *Kosciuszko in the American Revolution* (New York, 1943); *Kosciuszko: Leader and Exile* (New York, 1946).

[2] Arthur P. Coleman, *A New England City and the November Uprising: A Study of Editorial Opinion in New Haven, Connecticut, Concerning the Polish Insurrection of 1830–31* (Chicago, 1939).

[3] William W. Hall, *Puritans in the Balkans* (Sofia, 1938). See especially James F. Clarke, "Protestantism and the Bulgarian Church Question," in D. C. McKay, ed., *Essays in the History of Modern Europe* (New York, 1936).

[4] Merle Curti, "Young America," *American Historical Review*, XXXII (1926–27), 34–55. See also Arthur J. May, *Contemporary American Opinion of the Mid-Century Revolutions in Central Europe* (Philadelphia, 1927).

ernment which sought to recognize the Hungarian republic of 1849. When news arrived in the United States that the defeated Hungarian leader, Lajos Kossuth, was languishing in Turkish internment, Congress voted to send the warship *Mississippi* to Constantinople to take the fiery revolutionary to the land of liberty across the Atlantic. Almost with one accord Young America in 1851 and 1852 stretched out a welcoming hand to the great Hungarian. In their admiration Americans agreed with Daniel Webster, who in speaking of Kossuth said that "the world has waited for nearly nineteen hundred years to see his like."

Kossuth found a tumultuous reception in America. It is most interesting to recall that even the American Middle West—the West, as it was then—received Kossuth with open arms. His progress through Ohio in 1852, between Columbus and Cincinnati, marked the largest popular demonstration ever seen in that region. Perhaps 100,000 people lined the railroad tracks, and when Kossuth arrived in Cincinnati the shouts that went up from the mighty throng may have reached the throne of Francis Joseph himself. The exiled Hungarian leader, busily engaged in collecting donations, carefully told the Ohio legislature in a special session that he and the state of Ohio were the same age—that Ohio had been admitted into the Union in 1802, the year of his birth. Thus, he said, his heart had always throbbed with intense excitement at the name "Ohio." "It was like as if something of supreme importance lay hidden in that name for me to which my future was bounded by the very year of my nativity. This day my anticipations are realized." [5]

The era of Young America came to an inglorious and sobering end in the American Civil War, but before it died there were still other examples, in addition to the "Kossuth craze," of America's desire to cleanse East Central Europe of autocracy and illiberalism. Americans, for instance, took a notably keen interest in the Polish revolution of 1863, though their sympathies were diverted by the gestures of Alexander II in sending the Russian fleet to American shores.

The contacts of Americans with East Central Europe remained infrequent until the 1880's, when with the rising industrialization of the United States a demand for cheap labor began to

[5] J. W. Oliver, "Louis Kossuth's Appeal to the Middle West—1852," *Mississippi Valley Historical Review,* XIV (1928), 481–495.

bring immigrants to American shores by the millions. The pattern of immigration itself changed. The "new immigration" was from Central and Eastern Europe; and by the year 1930, after the restrictive legislation of the 1920's had virtually halted the flow of the peoples of East Central Europe to America, there were 1,269,000 Polish-born immigrants in America, 492,000 former inhabitants of Czechoslovakia, 371,000 Austro-Germans, 274,000 Hungarians, 211,000 former inhabitants of Yugoslavia, 194,000 Lithuanians, 146,000 Rumanians, 142,000 Finns, 24,000 Latvians and Estonians.[6] These figures, one should add, are only for foreign-born immigrants in the United States from the regions of East Central Europe in the year 1930, and do not include second-generation Americans; the number of individuals in the United States of East Central European origin by 1930 ran to about eight million.[7] Then there were the innumerable emigrants from East Central Europe who, after a sojourn of several or even many years in the United States, had returned to their homelands.[8]

Seen in retrospect, the new immigration markedly affected both the United States and East Central Europe, and worked to the great advantage of everyone concerned. Yet at the outset it proved a painful experience to the "old-time" Americans who received the newcomers. In religion and customs and standards of living the new immigrants did not fit easily into the traditional frame of life in the United States, and for the first decades of the new immigration many Americans of the old English and Scotch-Irish stock

[6] Warren S. Thompson and P. K. Whelpton, *Population Trends in the United States* (New York, 1933), p. 96.

[7] *Ibid.*, p. 102 offers the following figures for the second-generation Americans of East Central European origin in the year 1930: Poland 2,074,000; Czechoslovakia 890,000; Austria 584,000; Hungary 316,000; Yugoslavia 258,000; Lithuania 246,000; Finland 178,000; Rumania 147,000; Latvia and Estonia 19,000. These figures total 4,712,000. Add to them the 3,133,000 foreign-born individuals from East Central Europe, present in the United States in 1930, and the total of individuals of East Central European origin in the United States in 1930 is 7,845,-000. This compilation does not include emigration from Bulgaria nor Albania, which numerically was small (although in the case of Albania there was a proportionately large emigration); nor does it include emigration from Eastern Germany.

In regard to the above figures one must add that statistics on the national origins of Americans from East Central Europe are frequently confusing because of the territorial changes of the Paris Peace Conference. The census of 1930 was probably fairly accurate, but the above figures are still only approximations.

[8] The importance of the returned emigrant was great. Such individuals carried back to their native villages the disturbing new ideas of American democracy, together with such symbols of American progress as the Singer sewing machine.

exhibited not a little concern. The president of Princeton University in 1902 published a *History of the American People* in which he wrote how

> there came multitudes of men of lowest class from the south of Italy and men of the meaner sort out of Hungary and Poland, men out of the ranks where there was neither skill nor energy nor any initiative of quick intelligence; and they came in numbers which increased from year to year, as if the countries of the south of Europe were disburdening themselves of the more sordid and hapless elements of their population . . .[9]

A few years later Woodrow Wilson would regret this intolerant and ignorant outburst, and in a bid for the Polish-American vote during the presidential campaign of 1912 he attributed his remarks to "my clumsiness in expressing myself."[10] His ill-chosen words were typical of the ideas of many Americans of his day. The memory of Pulaski and Kosciuszko and Kossuth had grown dim.

It is paradoxical but true that by the time of the first World War, after millions of emigrants from East Central Europe had come to the New World, Americans nonetheless had little knowledge of the lands and peoples in that area of the European continent. If most Americans thought of Bohemia, they imagined that the land was inhabited by Gypsies. As late as 1914 many American citizens had heard of Smetana and Dvořák and Paderewski; they knew that the poor countrymen of these estimable musicians were filling up certain quarters of the cities of the American North and East, and working for low wages in steel plants and coal mines and garment industries; they knew little else. Brand Whitlock, the American minister to Belgium in 1914, later confessed that he had never heard of Sarajevo until the name of the capital of Bosnia appeared one day in newspaper headlines.

It was with the World War of 1914–18 that American relations with the peoples of East Central Europe for the first time began to appear important. During the war the new state of Czechoslovakia was in a certain sense "made in America." The rebirth of Poland in 1918, after a century and more of partition, was strongly supported by President Wilson. In the peace settlement after the war

[9] Woodrow Wilson, *History of the American People* (5 vols., New York, 1902), V, 212–213.

[10] Arthur S. Link, *Wilson: The Road to the White House* (Princeton, 1947), p. 386.

the United States helped confirm the new order of Europe in accord with the principle of self-determination.

I

The first World War brought a new order to Europe, especially a change in the East Central European boundaries according to the principle of nationality. The Treaty of Versailles between the Allied Powers and Germany wrought fundamental changes in the life of Europe; but the treaties of St. Germain with Austria and Trianon with Hungary meant nothing less than a European revolution.[11] There was never more than an approximate fitting of territorial boundaries to nationalities in East Central Europe, nor could there be, given the numerous areas where nations for centuries had mingled beyond all hope of disentanglement. The difficulty of fitting the principle of self-determination to the realities of East Central Europe was increased by the preferential treatment given to the new and reborn states which belonged to the victorious camp. In establishing the frontiers of the latter group, historical, geographic, political, economic, and military factors often played a much more significant part than purely ethnic considerations. As a result, the principle of self-determination was often disregarded in the case of the Germans, Hungarians, and Bulgarians. In the hope, however, of making a settlement which would somewhat correspond to the increasing national consciousness of the peoples of East Central Europe—which itself was probably the most important new political fact of twentieth-century Europe—the Paris Peace Conference recognized and established a new European territorial order. There were six new or reborn states: Finland, Latvia, Lithuania, Estonia, Poland, and Czechoslovakia. There were six radically transformed states: Austria, Hungary, Yugoslavia,[12] Rumania, Greece, and Turkey.

The role of the United States in the liberation or transformation of these states was of course both military and diplomatic. It is probably correct to say that only the military contribution of America, in supplies and in troops, enabled the Allies to gain the victory of 1918. The organization of the Continent by the victorious Allies

[11] Harold Butler, *The Lost Peace: A Personal Impression* (London, 1941), p. 134.

[12] Yugoslavia was formed out of the old Serbia and the Southern Slav areas of the former Austro-Hungarian monarchy.

was beyond doubt much different from what would have obtained if the German armies had been victorious. Friedrich Naumann's *Mitteleuropa* would have been established; the Germans by 1918, as was all too evident in the harsh peace of Brest-Litovsk, had gone over to a fully imperialistic policy. A German victory would not have permitted the East Central European settlement, based on the principle of nationality, which in fact prevailed with the success of Allied arms. The United States, then, in its military contribution alone, had a most important effect upon the fortunes of East Central Europe. In its diplomacy, moreover, the liberal, idealistic American nation under its crusading President specially facilitated the new order which after 1918 prevailed in the great regions of Europe between Germany and Russia.

American diplomacy toward the area of East Central Europe was a blend of idealism and realism. It is true that American participation in the war during 1917–18 was an emotional endeavor on the part of broad masses of the American people; President Wilson keyed high the emotions of his people, speaking resoundingly of making the world safe for democracy, of the war to end war. Wilson placed his country's participation in the war on so high a level that the postwar letdown was almost catastrophic in nature; and the defeat of the Treaty of Versailles has sometimes inclined observers to believe that there was nothing more to American participation in the war than sheer emotion. Yet there can be no doubt that during the war the American Government under its dignified "scholar in politics" kept close contact with the so-called "realities" of the war in Europe—the deep rivalries which divided the Central Powers and the Allies, and even the Allies themselves. Nor did Wilson fail to realize the manner in which diplomacy could assist military victory in 1917–18, and he lost few opportunities to use the nationalism of East Central Europe to facilitate an Allied triumph. In after years the citizens of Poland and of Czechoslovakia who came during the war to the United States to urge their national causes sometimes wrote as if they believed that their own realistic endeavors, playing upon American idealism, had changed the policy of the American Government and thus brought the independence of their countries. Thoughtful statesmen such as Thomas G. Masaryk and Eduard Beneš usually made allowance in their memoirs for the fact that American policy toward national independence in East Central Europe became really favorable only in the late spring and summer of 1918 when the military situation dictated a combination of idealism and realism. The pressures of Czech-Americans and Polish-Americans were obviously important in American policy, but the nature of that policy toward East Central Europe during the first World War and at the Paris Peace Conference was not entirely idealistic. The principle of national self-determination, as applied at the peace negotiations, was the outgrowth of wartime policies, as well as the expectations and aspirations fostered during the great struggle.

The manner in which national self-determination became an accepted principle of the Paris Conference is not capable of easy explanation. In 1914 such a principle would have worked against the Russian Empire, and for that reason alone was impossible as an Allied war aim. When Italy in 1915 joined the Allies, after promise in the Treaty of London of certain territories of the Austro-Hungarian Empire, it was expedient to justify some of Italy's proposed acquisitions on the principle of nationality; it was even possible to begin to speak of the rearrangement of the Austro-Hungarian Empire; but Italy feared too much independence for the Southern Slav nationalities, for they might combine in a Greater Serbia which would be far more a menace to Italian Adriatic ambitions than the Habsburgs ever could have been. In the United States, Austria-Hungary was considered—so Masaryk himself later wrote—as a "necessary organization of small peoples and odds and ends of peoples, and as a safeguard against 'Balkanization.' "[13] Palacký's original saying that if Austria had not existed she would have to be invented, represented a widespread view, in America as among the European Allies.

As opinion mounted against German "beastliness," because of the initial invasion of Belgium in 1914 and the subsequent atrocity propaganda and also because of the increasing submarine incidents including the sinking of the *Lusitania,* American dislike of Germany veered ever more toward downright hatred, but a similar feeling never developed against Austria-Hungary. The Habsburg Empire seemed to have been dragooned into war by her German ally. The old Emperor Francis Joseph had in truth entered the war with a heavy heart, and until his death in late 1916 had remained anxious as to

[13] Thomas G. Masaryk, *The Making of a State: Memories and Observations, 1914–1918* (London, 1927), p. 244.

the fate of his empire; at the outbreak of war he had expressed the opinion that he would be very happy if Austria-Hungary got off with a black eye and no bones broken. When the time came in February 1917 for rupturing German-American relations, President Wilson did not include Austria-Hungary; and despite Austria-Hungary's insistence on a break in diplomatic relations in April 1917, he did not ask for a declaration of war against Vienna until December of that year. Even by this late date the belief persisted that in any postwar organization of the Continent Austria-Hungary was a counterpoise to Germany in Central and Southern Europe. It was only with reluctance that the United States finally declared war on Austria-Hungary.[14]

When in the springtime of 1918 there still appeared some possibility of making a separate peace with Austria-Hungary, the American Government allowed an unofficial emissary in Switzerland, Professor George D. Herron, to enter into detailed conversations with a representative of the new young Habsburg Emperor Charles. The interviews between Herron and Professor Heinrich Lammasch, an eminent international lawyer who at one time had been the Emperor's tutor, proved fruitless. Charles was too gingerly in his proposals; and a simultaneous quarrel between the Austrian foreign minister and Clemenceau—over the private Austrian peace approach made to France a year earlier by the Emperor's brother-in-law, Prince Sixtus of Bourbon—resulted in so heated an exchange that the Austrians were forced for the moment to stop all peace *pourparlers*.[15] The Herron-Lammasch conversations perhaps had

[14] Actually the reason for declaring war against Austria-Hungary on Dec. 7, 1917 was a technicality. Creation of the Supreme War Council in Nov. 1917, following the Italian defeat at Caporetto, required American participation in strategy conferences for both the front in France and the front in Italy—and hence membership in the Supreme War Council was impossible without a declaration of war against Austria-Hungary. *War Memoirs of Robert Lansing* (Indianapolis, 1935), pp. 257–258.

[15] The famous Prince Sixtus affair served seriously to discredit the Dual Monarchy. The Austro-Hungarian Government in 1917 had sought a compromise peace, and the Emperor in a confidential letter had even gone so far as to offer to recognize France's right to Alsace-Lorraine. After negotiations broke down, the Austrian foreign minister, Count Ottokar Czernin, avowed publicly that he had rejected French peace offers based upon recognition of French rights to Alsace-Lorraine. This was embarrassing to Clemenceau, who had formed his war ministry under an express promise to carry the war to the bitter end, and he published the compromising Austrian correspondence.

Secretary of State Lansing was outraged by Clemenceau's publication of the Emperor's letter. "As an example of stupid diplomacy," he wrote privily in his diary, "this performance is almost without parallel. It is almost as bad as German diplomacy or as that of the Allies in the Balkans. I was perfectly aghast when I

no chance in any event, for a constant embarrassment in any Allied negotiations with Austria-Hungary was the Treaty of London. The Allies could make peace with Austria on no other terms; and these terms would have become acceptable to the Ballplatz only in the direst of extremities.[16]

A far more important American diplomatic *démarche* toward East Central Europe, coming at the beginning of 1918, was Wilson's speech of January 8 presenting the Fourteen Points. This speech undertook to define American and, by implication, Allied war aims. The President in Point 10 stressed autonomy—the "freest opportunity of autonomous development"—for the subject peoples of the Austro-Hungarian Empire; [17] in Point 11 he asked evacuation of Rumania, Serbia, and Montenegro, with "free and secure access to the sea" for Serbia; and in Point 13 the President declared for an independent Poland, "which should include the territories inhabited by indisputably Polish populations" and have "free and secure access to the sea."

---

read the press account and my amazement increases the more I consider the folly of it all. How any statesman could throw away a strategic advantage without any equivalent other than the personal satisfaction of causing chagrin to an adversary is beyond my comprehension. . . . Hang Clemenceau and his personal pride. He has raised the devil, though we have to pay for his intemperate conduct. Great though he is in many ways he has shown himself an amateur in the field of diplomacy." Lansing diary, Apr. 12, 1918. Lansing MSS deposited in the Library of Congress. For details of this complicated affair, which was not as unfavorable to Clemenceau as Lansing believed, see G. de Manteyer, *Austria's Peace Offer: 1916–1917* (London, 1921), and Mermeix [Gabriel Terrail], *Les Négociations secrètes et les quatre armistices* (Paris, 1919).

[16] Herron had to work under this grave handicap. In addition his personality and credentials were not such as to give promise to his negotiations. A sometime college professor, Herron was an evangelical individual who happened to be residing in Switzerland during the war, and although he was in constant touch with the American Legation in Berne his influence has probably been overrated; his discussions with Lammasch were known to President Wilson, but Herron was only an unofficial intermediary, virtually self-appointed, and his activities were only part of many feelers which went out to East Central Europe from the American Legation in Switzerland. For Herron, see George D. Briggs, *George D. Herron and the European Settlement* (Stanford, 1932); Briggs used the Herron papers in the Hoover Library. The work of the American Legation is detailed in Hugh Wilson, *Diplomat Between Wars* (New York, 1941).

[17] In Point 10 Wilson followed the advice of a memorandum prepared by the Inquiry (see below, p. 40) and dated Dec. 22, 1917, which suggested that American policy must consist "first in a stirring up of nationalist discontent, and then in refusing to accept the extreme logic of this discontent, which would be the dismemberment of Austria-Hungary." *Papers Relating to the Foreign Relations of the United States: 1919, the Paris Peace Conference* (13 vols., Washington, 1942–47), I, 45.

This was a cautious declaration. It did not entirely satisfy the representatives abroad of the Poles, nor did it please the Czechs and Slovaks and Southern Slavs and Rumanians: Wilson had not stipulated for the historic boundaries of Poland; nor had he defined postwar boundaries for Rumania, Serbia,[18] and Montenegro; nor had he asked independence for the Czechs, Slovaks, and other Slav nationalities under the rule of Vienna and Budapest. Wilson indeed had remained consistently cautious in his utterances on East Central Europe. When Lloyd George shortly before Wilson's announcement of the Fourteen Points said that "a breakup of Austria-Hungary is no part of our war aims," he was merely saying bluntly what Wilson himself believed at the time. The American President only the previous month, in asking Congress on December 4, 1917 for war on Austria-Hungary, had said that "we do not wish in any way to impair or to rearrange the Austro-Hungarian Empire. It is no affair of ours what they do with their own life either industrially or politically."

Some individuals later would remember that Wilson, in his important speech of April 2, 1917 asking Congress for war against Germany, had said that America would enter the struggle in Europe for two ideals—democracy, and the rights and liberties of small nations; but when Wilson at any time in 1917 spoke of the rights and liberties of small nations he was not referring to self-determination but to re-establishment of Belgian independence, invaded by Germany, and to the freedom of Serbia from such aggressive attacks as had come from the Habsburg Empire in 1914.

It is true that by January 1918 Wilson was willing to stipulate in his Fourteen Points for the independence of Poland; but this was a special case; by 1918 it required no boldness to advocate national self-determination for Poland: as early as November 5, 1916 Germany and Austria-Hungary had announced creation of an "inde-

[18] The position of Serbia was delicate. The Southern Slavs of Austria-Hungary were represented abroad by M. Trumbić, and he on occasion found himself in conflict with the premier of Serbia, M. Pašić; for Serbia wished to absorb the Southern Slavs of Austria-Hungary. When Trumbić in the autumn of 1918 sought Allied recognition for his Yugoslav committee, Pašić objected. The Southern Slavs, he contended, were not like the Czechoslovaks, because the Southern Slavs already had the Serbian Government to act for them. The American minister to Serbia, H. Percival Dodge, to Lansing, Oct. 8, 1918. Unpublished records of the Department of State, 763.72/11690. (Hereafter all footnoted file numbers refer to Department of State records.)

pendent" Poland, and the Provisional Russian Government which came to power in March 1917 had declared formally, on March 30, the right of the Polish people to an independent state. In January 1918 Wilson was in the mainstream of realistic Continental diplomacy when he asked for Polish independence.[19]

Thus by the beginning of 1918 Wilson and the American Government, because of the war, had become deeply interested in the fate of East Central Europe. This marked a great change from what, prior to 1914, had been a slight American official concern with the area. In the first year of the United States' participation in the war Wilson nonetheless took only a few carefully measured steps toward a new order in East Central Europe. The policy of the United States was cautious and tentative.

In 1918 a new situation emerged, in which the American President found it expedient to change his views toward the preservation of Austria-Hungary. He also committed himself generally to the principle of national self-determination. Yet the changes in American policy during 1918 may easily be overemphasized, for Wilson in that crucial year usually followed events, rather than made them.

II

It was only to be expected that as the war came into its climactic year there would converge upon all the Allied capitals, and especially upon Washington (for Wilson with his speech on the Fourteen Points clearly took over the spiritual leadership of the Allies), the propagandists of the various nations which hoped to profit in some measure at least from the decisions of the eventual peace conference. Czech propaganda in the United States actually had begun

[19] It is illustrative of Wilson's conservatism toward the affairs of East Central Europe that in 1917 he would still speak in terms of autonomy for Poland. When after his re-election in November 1916 he attempted a mediation of the war, he announced in his "peace without victory" speech of Jan. 22, 1917 that "Statesmen everywhere are agreed that there should be a united, independent and autonomous [*sic*] Poland." When the Allies in their famous joint note to Wilson of Jan. 10, 1917 had asked for "liberation of Italians, of Slavs, of Rumanians, and of Czecho-Slovaks from foreign domination," Wilson urged them to abandon this aim, as it stood in the way of his hopes of persuading Austria-Hungary to leave the war. On Feb. 22, 1917 the President offered Vienna limited assurances—"unless continuance of the war causes a change of conditions"—against dismemberment of Austria-Hungary in event of a request for an early peace. *Papers Relating to the Foreign Relations of the United States: 1917, Supplement 1* (Washington, 1932), pp. 57–58.

shortly after the outbreak of the European war, under the spirited direction of the Bohemian National Alliance and one of its leading members, Emanuel Victor Voska. Voska established a courier service between his countrymen in Bohemia and the Allies; and at the behest of Masaryk arranged through the British journalist Henry Wickham Steed, British Government channels, and the Russian ambassador to Britain, that Czechs who deserted across the Eastern battle lines to the Russians would receive a treatment different from other Austrian prisoners of war. It was Voska who in 1915 managed to reveal to the American Government the sabotaging activities of Captains Franz von Papen and Karl Boy-Ed, resulting in the expulsion of these German attachés and also of the Austrian ambassador, Dr. Konstantin Dumba.[20]

When the Czechoslovak National Council was set up in Paris under the supervision of Masaryk, with Eduard Beneš as general secretary, Beneš's brother Vojta undertook to influence the Czechs in Chicago. The latter city, as Masaryk later pointed out in his memoirs, was next to Prague at that time the largest Czech city in the world.[21] Moreover, the Czech-Americans were not only the largest "colony" of emigrant Czechs in the world, but they were comparatively speaking a wealthy group. The bulk of funds for financing the wartime movement for an independent Czechoslovakia came from the United States. Almost a million dollars eventually was raised. Most of this amount was gathered after America became a belligerent. With these American funds the able Czechoslovak leaders abroad carried on their national activity. As Masaryk afterward recalled, they made very good use of what, to a later generation, would be considered a most modest outlay, and by inverting the Czech proverb "Little money, little music" received plenty of music for the money.[22] Czech propaganda in the United States included "a supply of news to the press, personal relationships, memoranda, deputations, public lectures, etc."[23]

Yet it was almost the summer of 1918 before the Czechoslovak National Council in Paris, with its American affiliate, the Bohemian

[20] Emanuel Victor Voska and Will Irwin, *Spy and Counterspy* (New York, 1940), pp. 15–16.

[21] By 1920 Chicago had a Czech population of 100,000. Carl Wittke, *We Who Built America* (New York, 1939), p. 411.

[22] Thomas G. Masaryk, *Making of a State,* pp. 93–94.

[23] Eduard Beneš, *My War Memoirs* (Boston, 1928), p. 117.

National Alliance, was able to observe a change in the American Government's attitude toward the Czechoslovak cause. The autonomy promised in the Fourteen Points was, as we have seen, hardly satisfactory. The Herron-Lammasch conversations—like the Austrian peace approach to France the year before, through Sixtus of Bourbon—worried Masaryk and Beneš greatly, for a negotiated peace between the Allies and Austria-Hungary could probably mean nothing more than autonomy for the subject nationalities. Czech national propagandists bestirred themselves frantically. But their efforts might well have been in vain—and the Austro-Hungarian Empire might have survived—had not certain other events come to the rescue of the Czechoslovak cause. For one, the public quarrel between Clemenceau and the Austrian foreign minister [24] put an end momentarily to all Austrian peace maneuvers, including the Herron-Lammasch conversations. Secondly, in an effort to ingratiate himself with his German ally, the Emperor Charles signed at Spa on May 12, 1918 a new military convention with Germany, for the purpose of strengthening the Austro-German alliance; this agreement actually remained a dead letter, but to the Allies it seemed to indicate a new and very close cooperation between Germany and Austria.[25] Then there was the imminence of an Austrian offensive on the Italian front, and the Allies wished to take any measures of propaganda which might blunt this offensive. All these factors in combination sufficed to force a change in the previously cautious American official attitude toward the Austro-Hungarian Empire.

Secretary of State Robert Lansing took advantage of the meeting of the Congress of Oppressed Races of Austria-Hungary in Rome, held in April 1918, to announce the American Government's "great interest" in its proceedings, and that "the nationalistic aspirations of the Czecho-Slovaks and Jugo-Slavs for freedom have the earnest sympathy of this government." [26] Lansing's announce-

[24] See above, footnote 15.

[25] The agreement depended on an understanding between the two powers over the Polish question, and no understanding was ever reached. Secretary Lansing, however, desired to break up Austria-Hungary, and in a private memorandum dated May 30 he wrote that the reported military agreement should be taken at face value: "I think that we ought to proceed on the assumption that the report is substantially correct and formulate a policy on that hypothesis." *War Memoirs of Robert Lansing,* p. 267.

[26] *Papers Relating to the Foreign Relations of the United States: 1918, Supplement 1* (2 vols., Washington, 1933), I, 809. See also Lansing to Wilson, May 10,

ment came on May 29, more than six weeks after the Congress had adjourned, but it marked a turning of the ways in the policy of the United States toward Austria-Hungary. The Secretary of State acted from a general feeling that there was little use in further cultivating the Austro-Hungarian Empire: "It is my judgment," he wrote privately, "that, primarily as a war-measure, and also because it is just and wise for the future, we should encourage in every possible way the national desires of these peoples." [27] His public statement, which referred only to nationalistic aspirations for freedom, hence not entirely excluding the idea of autonomy within the Habsburg Empire rather than complete independence, was noted with pleasure and seconded on June 3 during a meeting of the Allied Big Three, Clemenceau, Lloyd George, and Sonnino. On this same day the British Foreign Secretary, Arthur Balfour, recognized the Czecho-slovak National Council in Paris as the leader of the Czechoslovak liberation movement. On June 15 came the long-awaited Austrian offensive, which failed, perhaps in part because of revelations by Yugoslav deserters who alerted the Italian command. The new American and Allied policy of favoring the nationalities of East Central Europe seemingly had begun to bring tangible results. The

---

1918, in *Foreign Relations of the United States: The Lansing Papers* (2 vols., Washington, 1939), II, 126–128. To Wilson the Secretary of State cited the example of German policy in Russia, which had successfully disorganized the Russian Empire by appealing to the national jealousies and aspirations of the several peoples under the Tsar's sovereignty.

Professor Victor Mamatey, in "The United States and the Dissolution of Austria-Hungary," *Journal of Central European Affairs,* X (1950–51), 269–270, has studied with admirable thoroughness this declaration of May 29, 1918, and concludes that Czech agitation in the United States had little to do with it, and also that Wilson played virtually no part (Wilson indeed "was little concerned with the Austrian and Slav questions before the Peace Conference"). I would disagree with this latter conclusion. Wilson was intensely ignorant of Czecho-slovak problems, but at every important development of American wartime policy toward Czechoslovakia he acted personally. For example, he typed out on his own portable typewriter—the unmistakable machine with the purple ribbon and small, widely spaced type—the final draft of the recognition of Sept. 3, 1918 and virtually the final draft of the crucial note of Oct. 19 to Austria-Hungary (for these see below, pp. 37–38). 763.72/11136 1/2 and 763.72119/2540. Unfortunately, the Wilson MSS in the Library of Congress seem to have no material of value on Wilson's policy toward Czechoslovakia.

[27] Memorandum of May 30, 1918, printed in *War Memoirs of Robert Lansing,* p. 268. The Secretary of War, Newton D. Baker, strongly encouraged Czecho-slovak recognition. ". . . all proper encouragement," he wrote to Lansing on May 24, 1918, "should be given to this Czecho-Slovak movement. . . . this government will make no mistake in recognizing and aiding such a movement." 763.72/10149.

State Department on June 28 issued a clear-cut statement expressing the American Government's conviction that all Slav peoples living under Austrian or German rule should be completely free.[28]

Allied policy had hardened against Austria-Hungary; and at this juncture Masaryk arrived in the United States. He had come from Siberia where he had been organizing the Czech deserters and prisoners on Russian soil to fight for the Allies and Czechoslovak independence. The famed Anabasis of 50,000 or so of these Czechs had begun in April 1918, and while en route across the reaches of Siberia to Vladivostok this Czech army held numerous Ukrainian and Siberian towns and cities against the Bolsheviks.[29] The latter were seeking to disarm the Czechs. The Anabasis at once became front-page news in the United States, and more than anything else could possibly have done it made the Czechoslovak cause popular with the American people. Masaryk suddenly found himself at the head of a nation. He would have been less than human had he failed to take advantage of his opportunity. Upon arrival in the United States he set to work with great vigor and tact to influence in his nation's favor the leaders of the Wilson Administration.

Secretary Lansing's private secretary was Richard Crane—the son of Charles R. Crane, a wealthy American industrialist who since 1914 had been doing everything possible, including gifts of money, to further the Czechoslovak cause.[30] Then there were many other Americans who aided the kindly, bearded Czech professor upon his arrival from Siberia. There was a Congressional election in 1918, and Congressmen with large numbers of Czechs and Slovaks among their constituents were naturally helpful. Representative Adolph Sabath of Chicago a year earlier, in May 1917, had introduced a resolution in Congress favoring the independence of Bohemia; in

[28] Wilson steadfastly refused to extend this declaration to include the Rumanians. Assistant Secretary of State William Phillips sent a draft of a proposed declaration on the Rumanians to Lansing on Oct. 7, 1918, but the draft soon received the buckslip notation, "The President has turned this down." 763.72/-13461. Some days later there was an official effort by the Rumanian Government: the Rumanian chargé came to the Department "on desire to have Roumanians in Hungary mentioned in a declaration. Declined as time not opportune. He was so persistent that I absolutely refused and he went away sad." Desk diary of Secretary Lansing, Oct. 19, 1918. Lansing MSS.

[29] Not all Czechs joined in the grand exodus. Masaryk modestly wrote that "As I do not know how many Czech and Slovak prisoners there were in Russia, I cannot say what proportion they bore to the total number of our Legionaries. My impression was that a fairly large number did not join us." *Making of a State,* p. 167.

[30] The younger Crane in 1919 became the first American minister to Prague.

June 1918 he interviewed President Wilson on the same subject.[31] Masaryk himself saw Wilson on several occasions, and the two men "understood each other fairly well—after all, we had both been professors." [32]

The full triumph of Masaryk's American visit came in September and October of 1918, when the Austrian Emperor frantically began to seek a basis of agreement with his empire's subject nationalities, upon which he could withdraw from the war and salvage his empire. Charles in October announced that he would transform his Austrian realm—not Hungary—into a federation, but by this time it was too late. It fell to Professor Lammasch, who had conversed earlier in the year with Herron in Switzerland, to preside as prime minister at the dissolution of the Austro-Hungarian monarchy. *"Finis Austriae"*—so Masaryk in jubilant reflection began the chapter of his memoirs which deals with his American activities of this period.

It nonetheless seems safe to say that Wilson actually had made up his mind about Austria-Hungary without much prompting by Czechoslovak leaders. One must assume that in the closing days of the war, occupied with the delicate negotiations for a German armistice, already exhilarated by the prospect of a great victory and a great peace, Wilson gave only slight attention to events in East Central Europe. The sequence of the events in mid-October 1918 which marked complete American acceptance of Czechoslovak independence—Lansing had announced *de facto* recognition on September 3—is admittedly somewhat obscure. But, to use one important example, it is quite erroneous to say with R. W. Seton-Watson that Masaryk had an "absolutely decisive" influence in America.[33] Wilson on October 19 sent an American note which answered the Emperor Charles's peace proposal and stressed the rec-

[31] Guido Kisch, "Woodrow Wilson and the Independence of Small Nations in Central Europe," *Journal of Modern History,* XIX (1947), 235–238. This article probably relies too much on Sabath's influence with Wilson, for Professor Kisch believes that Sabath "converted" Wilson to favoring the destruction of Austria-Hungary.

[32] Karel Capek, *President Masaryk Tells His Story* (New York, 1935), p. 282. Masaryk's understanding of America was further facilitated by his ability to speak English. Moreover, he had married the former Miss Charlotte Garrigue of Brooklyn.

[33] R. W. Seton-Watson, *Masaryk in England* (New York, 1943), pp. 112–113. A further important factor, Seton-Watson believed, was the contacts in Switzerland between Professor Herron and the young Slovak advocate, Stephen Osusky, whom Masaryk and Beneš had sent there as a press attaché. One must say again of Herron that his importance can easily be overemphasized.

ognition of an independent Czechoslovakia and the justice of the national aspirations of the Southern Slavs. Masaryk on October 16 had communicated to Lansing the first draft of a Czechoslovak Declaration of Independence, and the Declaration in final form was published on October 18.[34] Yet the Declaration of Independence does not itself seem to have moved Wilson to demand the breakup of the Austro-Hungarian Empire. In a recently revealed conversation which the head of the British secret service in America, Sir William Wiseman, had with Wilson on October 16, the President said apropos the problem of Austria-Hungary that "We have already recognized Masaryk . . . and we cannot listen to anybody else." [35] There were other contemporaneous statements by Wilson recognizing that the breakup of the Dual Monarchy was necessary.[36] The President's decision was already taken, before he could have read Masaryk's Declaration; and it was hardly a decision at all, but a natural conclusion from the contemporary events in Europe—the Habsburg Empire was obviously falling apart, and Wilson had decided only to accept the inevitable.[37]

[34] These documents are in the records of the Department of State, 861.00/2970 and 3124.

[35] Memorandum by Sir William Wiseman, printed in John L. Snell, "Wilson on Germany and the Fourteen Points," *Journal of Modern History,* XXVI (1954), 367.

[36] On Oct. 7, 1918 Wilson told Sir Eric Geddes, British first lord of the admiralty, that the breakup of Austria-Hungary was absolutely necessary, because of commitments which he had made to the oppressed nationalities. Ray Stannard Baker, *Woodrow Wilson: Life and Letters,* VIII (New York, 1939), 456.

[37] Wilson himself had said to a prominent Czech-American, Charles Pergler, on Sept. 9, 1918, when Pergler was received at the White House: ". . . you have demonstrated that you insist upon complete independence. We have merely recognized an accomplished fact." Charles Pergler, *America in the Struggle for Czechoslovak Independence* (Philadelphia, 1926), p. 56.

The manner in which the Czechoslovak Declaration of Independence received its final form is in itself interesting. Professor Herbert A. Miller, on leave from Oberlin College to assist Masaryk during the latter's American tour, had received from Masaryk on the afternoon of Oct. 16 the first draft of the Declaration, and decided after reading it that the style "would be quite without appeal to the American public which it, in part, sought to influence." As a result Miller and some confreres cut the original draft into a hundred or so parts and put them together in a vastly different manner, "to give a vigor of statement that would appeal to Americans." Meanwhile, of course, the unedited Declaration—a long dissertation—had been given to Lansing and Wilson, the most important Americans it could possibly have influenced. After the Declaration, as finally amended, was released by the Czechoslovak National Council in Paris, it was thought that American opinion might be further influenced by a declaration issued from Independence Hall in Philadelphia. A Declaration of Common Aims was consequently read by Masaryk from the courtyard behind Independence Hall, while a liberty bell tolled, on Oct. 26, 1918. That same day there came a telegram of congratulation from Wilson and a cable from Europe announcing Masaryk's designation as president of the pro-

In the meantime Masaryk during his sojourn in the United States had signed a famous convention with the Slovak-Americans at Pittsburgh, on June 30, 1918. The so-called Pittsburgh Convention was a source of much later difficulty between the Czechs and Slovaks of Czechoslovakia. At the Paris Peace Conference Father Andrej Hlinka on several occasions complained bitterly to Colonel House's assistant, Stephen Bonsal, that the Slovaks had been duped by the Czechs into accepting a joint Czechoslovak state, and that the Czechs were dominating the Slovaks from the new nation's capital in Prague.[38] It is certain that Masaryk in the Pittsburgh Convention agreed to the Slovak demand for an autonomous administration, a diet, and courts of law, with Slovak as the official language. "I signed the Convention unhesitatingly," he later recalled, "as a local understanding between American Czechs and Slovaks upon the policy they were prepared to advocate." [39] In June 1918 Masaryk was not yet head of the Czechoslovak state, and consequently his signature upon the Convention could not carry any force of law. The frequent Slovak criticism of the Prague regime, which by 1938 had turned into an opposition so strong that Hitler could employ it to assist in breaking up the Czechoslovak state, has sometimes been traced back to the Convention at Pittsburgh. With this thorny problem we are not here concerned, except to point out that the very fact that a Czecho-Slovak convention of such importance could be signed in Pittsburgh, U.S.A. is itself an earnest of the importance of the United States in the creation in 1918 of a Czechoslovak state in East Central Europe.[40]

Czechoslovakia, then, was in a certain sense "made in America" —although it is important not to overlook the activities of Beneš and other members of the Czechoslovak National Council in Western Europe, especially in France. For no other state in the east central area of the Continent was the influence of America so important. It is nonetheless true that the United States Government took a considerable interest, at least, in Poland. Perhaps American interest in Poland stemmed from the fact that Polish immigration to

---

visional Czechoslovak state. Herbert A. Miller, "What Woodrow Wilson and America Meant to Czechoslovakia," in Robert J. Kerner, ed., *Czechoslovakia* (Berkeley, Calif., 1940), pp. 71–87.

[38] Stephen Bonsal, *Suitors and Suppliants: The Little Nations at Versailles* (New York, 1946), pp. 145 ff.

[39] Thomas G. Masaryk, *Making of a State,* p. 208.

[40] For the Convention see S. Harrison Thomson, *Czechoslovakia in European History* (2nd ed., Princeton, 1953), pp. 313–315.

the United States had outnumbered that of any other nationality of the East Central European area. The individuals in America of Polish origin by the year 1930 were almost three times as numerous as the Czechoslovaks—3,343,000 compared to 1,382,000—and their very number made them important in American life.[41] They were on the whole not as highly educated or as well-placed in American industry and society as were the Czechs. On the other hand, the Poles in their wartime agitation for a reborn Polish state in Europe enjoyed a certain psychological advantage: the eighteenth-century partitions of Poland had with the passage of time become to many literate Americans a shocking injustice to a gallant nation, an injustice to be righted if possible during the crusade of 1917–18. It is not without importance that Professor Robert H. Lord of Harvard, who had written a doctoral thesis and made his scholarly reputation on the second partition of Poland,[42] became the Polish expert of the Inquiry, the preparatory investigation of problems of European and world peace which Colonel House organized in the summer of 1917. Professor Lord in his recommendations to House and Wilson when they were drawing up the Fourteen Points, and later at the Peace Conference itself, fought long and hard for the rebirth of Poland within its historic frontiers.

The influence within the government of such individuals as Lord was supported and encouraged by Polish representatives in the United States. The pianist Ignacy Jan Paderewski was the best possible person the Poles could have found to present their case to the leaders of the Wilson Administration. The President himself, something of a romantic at heart, could not but have felt moved by the pianist's playing of Chopin at the White House; and Colonel House found Paderewski appealing and attractive. Paderewski was not above exaggeration in his talks with influential Americans, and on one occasion told House that the Colonel was the only man since Napoleon I who understood the importance of a reconstructed Poland to the peace of Europe. Such statements left House "dumb with confusion. If he [Paderewski] were less *naive* and childlike," House recorded in his diary, "I would be suspicious of him." [43] Yet

[41] Figures compiled from Warren S. Thompson and P. K. Whelpton, *Population Trends in the United States*, pp. 96, 102. See above, p. 24 and footnote 7.

[42] Robert H. Lord, *The Second Partition of Poland* (Cambridge, Mass., 1915).

[43] Louis L. Gerson, *Woodrow Wilson and the Rebirth of Poland, 1914–1920: A Study in the Influence on American Policy of Minority Groups of Foreign Origin* (New Haven, 1953), p. 80.

the musician scored a signal triumph. "It was solely through Paderewski," House later wrote, "that I became so deeply interested in the cause of Poland, and repeatedly passed upon the President Paderewski's views which I had made my own. That was the real influence that counted." [44]

The importance of such individuals as Paderewski nonetheless remains something of an enigma. There is no doubt that House was much attracted to Paderewski, and House undeniably wielded great personal influence with Wilson. Probably, however, Wilson's decision to advocate an independent Poland was dictated by less personal means. The Bolshevik seizure of power in Russia required a statement of Allied war aims. The Allies also wished to detach a future Poland from both the Bolsheviks and the Germans. After the decision to support Polish aspirations of independence, the American Government did throw its influence behind Paderewski personally and his political mentor Roman Dmowski. At the Peace Conference the pianist and Dmowski represented Poland. Paderewski in fact served for a time as Polish premier. According to former President Herbert Hoover, who in 1919 was Allied food administrator, the choice of Paderewski as premier was to a certain extent forced upon Jósef Pilsudski, then in *de facto* control of Poland, by the American Government. But there appears to be some doubt of this. It is undoubtedly true that one of Hoover's aides intimated to Pilsudski that Allied assistance to Poland would be futile if Paderewski were not included in the Polish Government; but there were several other cogent reasons—in addition to this unofficial American intervention—for the appointment of Paderewski as premier in 1919.[45]

[44] *Ibid.*, p. 70.

[45] *The Memoirs of Herbert Hoover: Years of Adventure, 1874–1920* (New York, 1951), p. 357. My learned colleague, Professor Piotr Wandycz, informs me that in a book by Wladyslaw Pobóg-Malinowski, *Najnowsza Historia Polityczna Polski* (Paris, 1953), there are excerpts from a letter by Pilsudski to his *homme de confiance* in Paris, Dluski, explaining Pilsudski's reasons for a coalition goverment under Paderewski. These were roughly: lack of credit, food, and arms, and the means of getting them from the Allies; the need of having a united representation at the Peace Conference; the need to avoid internal clashes which might have made the first meeting of the Parliament difficult; no money in the treasury, because the richest province, Poznan, refused to recognize the existing cabinet. According to Professor Wandycz, if we add to these reasons enumerated by Pilsudski a picture of the existing situation in Poland—a *coup d'état* tried by Pilsudski's opponents, the ministry forced to resign by existing conditions, and the triumphant journey of Paderewski from Danzig through Poznan to Warsaw—the part played by the United States Government in "forcing" Paderewski on Pilsudski dwindles to its right proportions.

One can say in conclusion, about the activities of Paderewski in America during the war, that the chief importance of the pianist-statesman was as a popularizer of the new order in East Central Europe as it related to the rebirth of Poland, and that he probably would have been unsuccessful had it not been diplomatically and militarily expedient for Wilson to have taken interest in an independent Poland. Paderewski and Dmowski and their organization of Poles abroad, the Paris Committee, upon consolidation with the Pilsudski regime in Poland was recognized *de jure* by the American Government on January 22, 1919. Great Britain followed suit a month later. The rebirth of Poland had been completed.

The principle of national self-determination has frequently been described as, in essence, an American principle, which in a fit of idealism an unsophisticated American president foisted upon the Paris Conference and the world. There could be nothing farther from the truth. Wilson at Paris did believe that peace could be achieved by allowing each nation in the world to govern itself: obviously (according to the logic of self-determination) any nationality which achieved self-government would also choose to live within its own national territory. Yet the principle of national self-determination of the peoples of East Central Europe in accord with which the Allies redrew the map of the Continent was not the product of Wilsonian logic; it was the culmination of a long movement in European and world history. If anything, the feeling reigned in American government circles at the beginning of the European war, and well into the decisive year 1918, that national self-determination could only bring the "balkanization" of large areas of Europe which for economic and other reasons could best remain together. The Western powers, including the United States, did not call the force of nationality into being in East Central Europe during the first World War, but rather reluctantly recognized it when it appeared and used it, not to win the war, but to hasten its last stages.[46]

III

By the time of the armistice of November 11, 1918 the new order in East Central Europe was largely a fact; new capitals had

46 Alfred Cobban, *National Self-determination* (New York, 1945), p. 15. There is an excellent brief analysis of the breakup of the Austro-Hungarian Empire in Archibald Cary Coolidge, *Ten Years of War and Peace* (Cambridge, Mass., 1927), pp. 241–268.

been established, declarations of independence issued, delegations were beginning to form for the Peace Conference. It remained only for the Conference itself to recognize what already had been established. Czechoslovakia indeed was admitted as a participating nation in the armistice negotiations.

The work of the Conference, so far as it affected East Central Europe, dealt chiefly in terms of controversies such as Upper Silesia and Danzig and Fiume and Transylvania and like concerns. This is not the place to relate the details of the Paris settlement of these matters.[47] The United States, it should be noted, frequently took an independent view toward the boundary problems of East Central Europe. In the Fiume controversy Wilson defended Yugoslavia, one of the smaller nations of East Central Europe, against the ambitious claims of the Italian Government. The United States was reluctant to see Eastern Galicia simply absorbed by Poland without any conditions. Hungary received considerable support from the Americans: in the question of Transylvania the United States delegation urged a more easterly boundary for Hungary than that which finally prevailed; and the American representatives also desired the Hungarian-Czechoslovak and Hungarian-Yugoslav boundaries to be more favorable to Hungary. The Americans urged some sort of economic unity for the Danube basin, to replace the fallen Habsburg Monarchy. The United States favored transfer of Northern Bukovina to a future independent Ukrainian state, and a return of Southern Dobruja to Bulgaria, together with leaving Bulgaria an outlet to the Aegean Sea. But these were American proposals, and in the give-and-take of the Conference they were not achieved. The principle of national self-determination proved intensely difficult to achieve; its application was qualified by many other factors; and the compromises as they finally evolved often pleased no one.

Wilson himself hoped that territorial controversies could in later years be taken to the League of Nations. He constantly kept in mind the beloved Covenant, and after he accepted with great reluctance the idea of a plebiscite in Upper Silesia he told his most trusted adviser that "At least, House, we are saving the Covenant, and that instrument will work wonders, bring the blessing of peace, and then when the war psychosis has abated, it will not be difficult to settle all

[47] For short accounts of the settlement in East Central Europe see Edward M. House and Charles Seymour, eds., *What Really Happened at Paris* (New York, 1921), chs. 3–7. See also President Seymour's *Geography, Justice, and Politics at the Paris Conference of 1919* (New York, 1951).

the disputes that baffle us now." [48] When the United States Senate abruptly disowned the League Covenant, Wilson's hopes were dashed. It was probably naive of him to have imagined that the League could have solved such intense national rivalries as those of the disputed boundaries of East Central Europe. Given the lack of international consciousness among large sections of the citizenry even of the West European nations, only a coalition of great powers, in the traditional manner of European diplomacy, could have ensured the peace. Such a coalition proved impossible because of revisionism in Germany and Italy and the utter unreliability of the regime in Russia. Perhaps Britain and France, even without the United States, could have ensured the Paris settlement if they had been united in their policies after 1919; but, as events turned out, Paris and London only began to act in concert toward East Central Europe, and toward German revisionism in East Central Europe, in the spring of 1939.

In Paris, London, and especially Washington in the interwar years there existed a belief in some quarters that world peace could be preserved through economic arrangements, rather than through armaments, and although this notion was never dignified into a policy it did support a number of intergovernmental loans to the nations of East Central Europe. During the war the United States Government had helped finance the Polish and Czechoslovak national causes, and after the war American intergovernmental loans for a short time assisted the recovery of almost all the East Central European countries. The principal of these "war debts," including the relief loans, totaled $396,700,000.[49] In the 1920's the debts were refunded at low interest rates, with the exception of the Austrian debt, the funding of which was to be held in abeyance until the year 1942.

Refunding arrangements were made with the understanding that the East Central European nations afterward could arrange private loans in the United States, and numerous loans, both on behalf of

[48] Stephen Bonsal, *op. cit.*, p. 129. The entry in Colonel Bonsal's diary is for May 13, 1919.

[49] The sums borrowed by individual nations, as listed in Harold G. Moulton and Leo Pasvolsky, *World War Debt Settlements* (New York, 1926), pp. 79–80, were as follows: Austria, $24 million; Czechoslovakia, 91.8; Esthonia, 14.0; Finland, 8.3; Hungary, 1.7; Latvia, 5.1; Lithuania, 5.0; Poland, 159.7; Rumania, 36.1; Yugoslavia, 51.0. All of these loans were defaulted after the Hoover Moratorium, with the well-known exception of the Finnish debt. Finland had a small debt, and an export surplus which provided her with dollar exchange.

private concerns and the governments of the area, were made. Poland floated a loan of $100,000,000 in the United States, soon after her debt was funded, and Czechoslovakia obtained a loan of $25,000,000. An international loan for the reconstruction of Austria, made in 1923, stipulated for American participation to an extent of $25,000,000; the loan was guaranteed by Great Britain and several other nations, notably not including the United States. In 1924 an international loan of about $50,000,000 was made to Hungary, in which American bankers participated. All public lending by the United States Government, of course, had ceased with the relief loans immediately after the war. The above-mentioned were all private loans, that is, floated in private banking circles in the United States. During the 1920's however there were occasional operations by the Federal Reserve Banks, which were concerned with restoration and maintenance of the gold standard throughout the world.

In cooperation with the central banks of other countries, the Reserve Banks in the summer of 1931 helped effect bill-purchase agreements for the tottering central banks of Austria, Hungary, and Germany. This American action supported the Hoover Moratorium of 1931–32 on intergovernmental debts and reparations. The Moratorium was decided upon chiefly to shore up the German banking structure, which was being buffeted in the Great Depression, but it is worthy of note that the banks of Germany were deeply involved in operations in East Central Europe. The Moratorium, as is well known, lost much of its effect because of the tardy response of the French Government, and proved insufficient to halt the vast liquidation of assets which came after 1929. With the Moratorium, American financial efforts to bolster the economies of East Central Europe came to an end. In the early 1930's there followed frantic efforts in the area to block currencies and raise tariff walls, thereby to obtain some kind of protection from the economic cataclysm. The result, unhappily, was to expose the small nations of East Central Europe to the blocked-mark schemes of Germany's Dr. Hjalmar Schacht.

In view of the difficulties of trade with East Central Europe after 1931–32 it is surprising that American economic interest in the area remained at a fairly high level. American exports to the area in 1937, the last relatively quiet year in Europe, stood at $69,305,000. American investment, as of August 1, 1939, amounted to

$725,100,000. Poland and Czechoslovakia were the largest American customers in 1937, and together with Austria they had attracted, by 1939, the most considerable American investment.[50]

The concern of United States citizens with East Central Europe in the interwar period did not limit itself to economic matters. There was a growing intellectual and scientific exchange. In the interwar years the Rockefeller Foundation carried forward its work of international benevolence, financing medical projects in Zagreb, purchasing books for libraries in Poland, endowing a hygienic institute in Hungary, supporting a statistical bureau in Bulgaria, arranging fellowships for academicians, and sponsoring professorships, journals, conferences, congresses, etc.[51] Through such means, and also through much other private initiative, individual citizens of the United States and of the nations of East Central Europe became better acquainted.

But the American attitude toward East Central Europe, as was true of American policy toward all areas of the world except Latin America, meanwhile had lapsed into almost complete isolation. In the latter 1920's, and during the period 1931–33 when Japan

[50] American exports to East Central Europe averaged, in 1921–25, $35,076,-000; in 1926–30, $48,185,000; in 1931–35, $28,222,000. Imports from the area were, for 1921–25, $37,040,000; 1926–30, $68,464,000; 1931–35, $40,489,000. U.S. Dept. of Commerce, *Statistical Abstract of the United States: 1938* (Washington, 1939), pp. 462–463. American exports to individual countries of the area in 1937 were as follows (figures in thousands): Austria, $3,086; Czechoslovakia, 13,233; Estonia, 1,244; Finland, 12,265; Hungary, 693; Latvia, 1,744; Lithuania, 511; Poland, 26,297; Rumania, 6,938; Yugoslavia, 2,657. Imports by the United States from East Central Europe in 1937 totaled $101,699,000. Total American exports to Europe in 1937 were $1,359,610,000; imports, $843,329,000. Total American exports to all countries in 1937 were $3,349,167,000; imports, $3,083,668,000. *Ibid.*, pp. 460–463.

The U.S. Treasury Dept. in 1943 conducted a census of American-owned assets in foreign countries, and for the first time obtained reliable data on the subject. Property and securities in continental Europe were valued as of Aug. 1, 1939. It appears that perhaps 95 per cent of the value of all property was reported. As for foreign dollar bonds, reporting probably was only between 80 and 85 per cent complete. Because holdings below a certain figure were not reported, it seems reasonable to estimate that about 2 per cent of the total did not appear for that reason. With these qualifications the following figures of American-owned assets would seem to be highly reliable: Albania, $1.3 million; Austria, 138.1; Bulgaria, 11.8; Czechoslovakia, 148.0; Estonia, 1.4; Finland, 10.2; Hungary, 62.3; Latvia, 8.3; Lithuania, 4.9; Poland (including Danzig), 222.4; Rumania, 66.1; Yugoslavia, 50.3. The value of American-owned assets in all of Europe was $4,418,300,000 (including the United Kingdom, valued as of May 31, 1943). The total of American foreign investment in all areas of the world was $13,542,200,000. U.S. Treasury Dept., *Census of American-Owned Assets in Foreign Countries* (Washington, 1947), pp. 67–69.

[51] Raymond B. Fosdick, *The Story of the Rockefeller Foundation* (New York, 1952), pp. 40, 198, 285.

moved into Manchuria, there had seemed to be a growing American appreciation of international affairs; and it is indeed true that the American secretaries of state during these years, Frank B. Kellogg and especially Henry L. Stimson, were deeply concerned with all threats to international peace, knowing that such threats might eventually bring trouble to the United States. Unfortunately the American people themselves did not feel deeply committed to the course of world affairs, and after the harrowing experience of the depression they were quite willing to let Europe and the Far East move in any direction the inhabitants of those distant places desired. Humanitarian considerations, or developments affecting directly the course of American trade, could quickly arouse American interest; but in political matters, which Americans liked to believe were only indirectly connected with humane and commercial questions, there was a general conviction that other peoples should follow their own fancies.

Then too, there had flourished in the United States during much of the interwar period an optimistic hope that the new nations of East Central Europe, having risen in 1918 from the ruins of three great empires, would evolve along democratic ways, and when several of them did not, there often arose uncritical comment that they were not ready for democracy and, perhaps, should therefore not have existed in the first place. When the second World War, as had the first, began in East Central Europe, some Americans were ready to say that because of erroneous policies in the first World War balkanization had spread northward on the Continent to the middle Danube basin and the Baltic region and had brought with it the rivalries which inevitably begat great wars. But, as Oscar Halecki has rightly pointed out, neither of the two world wars really began in East Central Europe; they arose out of the rivalries and implacable hatreds of the great powers; had the spark not flamed up in some region of East Central Europe, it would have done so elsewhere.[52] This view was not widely held in America in the 1930's, and Americans then as in 1914 tended to blame at least in part the irresponsible excesses of small-power nationalism. They looked upon the congeries of small nations in East Central Europe as a weak, troublesome area, a sort of fault in the political structure of the world, an unformed, improperly developed part of the Con-

[52] Oscar Halecki, *Borderlands of Western Civilization: A History of East Central Europe* (New York, 1952), pp. 352–355.

tinent lying loosely and insecurely between its great neighbors, Germany and Russia.

Because of such reasoning it was difficult for Americans to become concerned over political developments in East Central Europe. The wish became father to the thought, and they believed that the area had no connection with the problems of the United States. Hence the Austrian crisis, the Munich crisis, and in early 1939 the German occupation of Prague and complete absorption of what had been Czechoslovakia failed to bring any drastic reordering of American policy toward East Central Europe. It did wipe out the vague feeling among many Americans that Germany after 1918 had been badly treated; it strengthened the willingness of a considerable part of the American people to support Britain and France; but the policy of political unconcern continued until 1940, by which time the entire area had been virtually partitioned by Germany, Russia, and Italy.

In February 1938 George Messersmith, then Assistant Secretary of State, sent a prophetic memorandum to Secretary of State Cordell Hull, which in turn was sent to President Franklin D. Roosevelt. In this Messersmith set down with vivid realism the importance to the United States of the regions of East Central Europe. He contended that if Germany received

> economic or political control, or both, of Southeastern Europe she will be in a position to put England and France into a secondary place in Europe and practically immobilize them. This can only mean the gradual disintegration of the British Empire . . . With England and France in a purely secondary position and with the Empire disintegrated, we in this country would stand practically alone, and that our troubles would come a little later does not give me any comfort.

The failure of American public opinion to understand the implications of this situation, Messersmith believed, was "the most difficult problem with which we now have to deal." [53] But the American peo-

[53] Memorandum of Feb. 18, 1938. *Papers Relating to the Foreign Relations of the United States: 1938,* I (Washington, 1955), 17–24. See also a similar memorandum in the same volume, pp. 68–69, dated Aug. 20.

At the time of the Munich crisis Messersmith wrote in a memorandum to the Secretary of State that "A wise man asked me yesterday what the difference was between Hitler taking something which didn't belong to him and had never belonged to his country and between Chamberlain and Daladier giving away something which wasn't theirs and had never been theirs. I am fearful that in the arrangements about to be made, and which may be made in the near future growing out of the Munich meeting, someone other than ourselves is going to give away something precious that belongs to us." Memorandum of Sept. 29, 1938, transmitted to President Roosevelt on Oct. 1. *Ibid.,* pp. 706–707.

ple continued to lack understanding of the importance of East Central Europe, and the American Government, despite the prescience of such individuals as Messersmith, continued to employ toward Germany and Italy such hopeless tactics as exhortation and protest. In the United States there was unreality in the highest governmental quarters. Messersmith in approaching his chief, Secretary Hull, felt compelled to couch at least part of his argument in terms of the effect of Hitler upon the Secretary's program of reciprocal trade agreements.[54]

In September 1938 during the Munich crisis President Roosevelt sent personal messages to Hitler urging a general policy of peace; the German leader scorned such appeals.[55] In early 1939, after German absorption of Bohemia and Moravia, Roosevelt proposed to Hitler a long list of nations, including all the little countries of East Central Europe, which he asked the German dictator to promise not to attack. Hitler redoubled his demands for Danzig and the Polish Corridor. There followed the Nazi-Soviet pact, the German invasion of Poland, the beginning of the second World War.

In such catastrophic events, of course, there was enormous American interest. The German attack on Poland seemed to Americans utterly inexcusable, and the consequent partition of Poland violated in a most flagrant manner the right of national self-determination. From the attack of Russia upon Finland in 1939–40 there emerged a feeling of outrage that a large nation should attack a small one. After the fall of France in June 1940 there came the long overdue reordering of American opinion toward all the problems of Europe and the world. With the collapse of France and the rapid appearance of governments-in-exile in 1940–41 American opinion grew ever more sympathetic toward the Allies and the occupied European countries. By 1941 there was certainly a well-defined feeling in the United States that the conquered peoples of East Central Europe had an absolute right to national independence as a result of the war.

It is perhaps fair to conclude that the history of relations between the United States and East Central Europe until the time of the second World War was not marked on the American side by a continuing wisdom and discernment. During the first World War developments in American policy toward that area of the Continent were quite closely related to America's participation in the war, and

[54] *Ibid.*, pp. 21–22.
[55] *Ibid.*, pp. 657–707.

the new order of 1918–19 evolved more out of the requirements and ultimate fact of Allied victory than from any carefully laid plans, either in Washington or elsewhere. There can be no doubt that the great emigration from East Central Europe to the United States which began about the year 1880 and lasted unbroken down to the first World War has had a deep effect upon American life, and has changed the nation in countless ways. But in diplomacy that emigration has not had a marked influence. The United States by 1941, upon entrance into the second World War, was only beginning to understand the importance to the American national interest of the peoples and nations of East Central Europe.

Chapter 3

Hopes and Failures: American Policy Toward East Central Europe, 1941–1947

PHILIP E. MOSELY

When the attack on Pearl Harbor plunged the United States into its second world war, the immediate concern of political leaders and public opinion alike was to train its manpower and to mobilize its industrial resources as the first step in the long uphill climb from initial defeat to decisive victory, first against Germany, then against Japan. Its prime political aim was to forge and maintain an effective working alliance with its major allies, Britain and the Soviet Union. If either faltered or failed in the joint effort, the road to victory and postwar security would stretch out beyond the horizon. After almost two decades of self-imposed isolation, American power was now to be concerned intimately with decisions, taken or not taken, which would in turn affect all parts of the world.

Of sympathy for the peoples of East Central Europe there was no lack, at least among the informed minority which took an active interest in what was happening abroad. There was no acceptance of the Nazi *Grossraum* theories, with their specious parallel to the Monroe Doctrine. Whatever division of opinion there had been over the absorption of Austria disappeared with Hitler's march into Prague. American critics had been prompt to condemn the British and French "appeasers" of Munich, but very few even of the critics assumed that the United States had any power to exert in Europe or any responsibilities to shoulder. During the events which completely shattered the prewar structure of East Central Europe, the United States, prior to December, 1941, had alternately exhorted and condemned. It had not acted. It had no policy, in any effective sense of the word.

After the United States had entered the war, the Roosevelt administration adopted the basic position that the nation's first aim was to win the war as quickly as possible and to do so without making specific commitments on "local" questions of postwar settlement. All particular questions, especially territorial claims, were to be held open for decision in the peace conference. This decision, it was hoped, would avoid a repetition of some of the mistakes which had been made during World War I. Makers and students of American policy had heard over and again of the bad effects of the secret treaties of 1914–1918 on the peace settlement which followed. Temporary strategic necessities had led the European powers to give and receive promissory notes which prejudiced many important issues, particularly through the promises made to Japan, Italy and Rumania. They were also hopeful that even the defeated nations might receive a fairer hearing than in 1919, in order to lay a firm basis for a genuine pacification of Europe.

After the fighting was over, exile governments, serving as trustees for the interests of their nations, could be replaced by freely elected and genuinely representative regimes, qualified to approve territorial adjustments and to enter into long-range commitments in support of general and regional security arrangements. Meanwhile, it was doubtful whether they could, constitutionally or conscientiously, make basic decisions affecting their nations' postwar futures. While exile governments were happy to claim additional advantages through wartime negotiations, they were prompt to retreat behind constitutional barriers when they were called on to pay part of the cost.[1] It also seemed impossible to satisfy, during the war, any one set of national claims without settling all of them, and since many of the claims, even among allies, were incompatible, there was a real danger that the main purpose of the war would be lost sight of. From the point of view of American constitutional procedure, the executive could not commit the government as a whole on the terms of peace, and therefore, even if the United States Government had been willing to hold a whole series of detailed peace-aims negotiations during the war, it was doubtful just how effective that effort, if made, would have been.

For long anxious months there was a genuine uncertainty about

[1] For example, the Arciszewski Government in London, formed in late November 1944, declared itself incompetent to agree to the detachment of any part of Poland's pre-1939 territory until the Polish state had been restored within its prewar boundaries and the people could be consulted under constitutional processes.

the outcome of the war. If the Soviet Union collapsed, and if Hitler were then free both to intensify the sea and air blockade of Great Britain and to resume his drive through the Middle East and India to link up with the advancing Japanese forces, of what use would be detailed and specific commitments on the peace terms of victory unfulfilled? While Stalin and Molotov argued vehemently for a postwar guarantee of the Soviet boundaries of 1941—a guarantee which the British leaders were willing to give—Roosevelt and Hull held out against it. Even during the critical German advance of 1942 into Russia, the United States clung firmly to the principle of "no-predetermination," and, under American insistence, the territorial guarantee was omitted from the Anglo-Soviet twenty-year treaty of May, 1942. The American logic was that, if one set of territorial claims received such powerful confirmation during the war, then all territorial claims could be pushed with equal right and soon the allies would be squabbling over a division of the spoils instead of pushing on to victory. Since the United States had no territorial claims, except perhaps for the Japanese mandated islands, its Government was naturally reluctant to allow its energies and those of its allies to be dissipated in this way.

The reluctance of the American Government, during hostilities, to discuss the "details" was reinforced by an awareness of its unfavorable military posture. By the time of Pearl Harbor the United States had mobilized only a modest part of its resources in preparation for war, and after Pearl Harbor it had to train and equip tremendous forces, on land, on sea, and in the air, as well as to provide a large part of the needs of its allies. All this took time and tremendous exertions. While the Soviet Union, fighting on its own territory and suffering tremendous losses, was carrying, as Churchill said, "the main burden" of the war, the United States was not in a good position, it seemed, to bargain hard with it over the "details" of a postwar settlement. Would the Soviet leaders, if threatened with the only bargaining-counter available—a cutting back of lend-lease—feel any compunction later about repudiating promises wrung from them in time of mortal danger? Or would they not satisfy their own claims and then make a separate peace with Hitler, thus enabling him to thwart the cross-Channel liberation of Western Europe? On the other hand, the successful invasion of Western Europe would greatly raise the power and the prestige of Britain and America, which, on Germany's defeat, would be at the peak of their power. This military prospect, which promised a far stronger voice at the end of the war for American purposes, reinforced the political arguments, both international and domestic, for avoiding wartime commitments which would prejudge and preshape the postwar settlement. That the principle of "no-predetermination" was partially abandoned later, during 1944 and 1945, did not make it any less attractive during 1942 and 1943 to hard-pressed war leaders. Once the Soviet Union, after Stalingrad, had begun to display an increasingly clear policy of subjugating the peoples of East Central Europe, it was difficult to meet its pressures with a deliberate policy of "no-policy."

Finally, there was strong doubt as to the extent to which, after the war, American opinion would be willing for its government to remain involved in the problems of Europe or to commit its power to the enforcement of specific settlements. President Roosevelt was ever mindful of the way in which American sentiment had turned against the Versailles peace, and, if anything, he leaned over backward to avoid committing his country to continued participation in the postwar problems of Europe. Roosevelt had continually on his mind the necessity for bringing the armies home just as rapidly as possible after the defeat of Germany, and the prospect that a weakened Britain would stand alone, facing the huge Soviet forces, caused great anxiety to Churchill.[2]

On the assumption of a weakened, overcommitted Britain and an America which had withdrawn from military commitments in Europe, the dangers of all continental Europe coming under Soviet domination were great. As Admiral Leahy wrote Secretary Hull on May 16, 1944:

> . . . It is apparent that any future world conflict in the foreseeable future will find Britain and Russia in opposite camps. . . . In a conflict between these two powers the disparity in the military strengths

[2] On November 18, 1944, Roosevelt to Churchill: "You know, of course, that after Germany's collapse I must bring American troops home as rapidly as transportation problems will permit. . . ." November 19, 1944, Churchill to Roosevelt: "Para two of your 649 causes me alarm. If after Germany's collapse you 'must bring the American troops home as rapidly as transportation problems will permit' and if the French are to have no equipped post-war army or time to make one, or to give it battle experience, how will it be possible to hold down western Germany beyond the present Russian occupied line? We certainly could not undertake the task without your aid and that of the French. All would therefore rapidly disintegrate as it did last time. I hope, however, that my fears are groundless. I put my faith in you." *The Conferences at Malta and Yalta, 1945* (Washington, 1955); Department of State Publication 6199, pp. 286–287.

> that they could dispose upon that continent would, under present conditions, be far too great to be overcome by our intervention on the side of Britain. Having due regard to the military factors involved—resources, manpower, geography and particularly our ability to project our strength across the ocean and exert it decisively upon the continent—we might be able to successfully defend Britain, but we could not, under existing conditions, defeat Russia. In other words, we would find ourselves engaged in a war which we could not win even though the United States would be in no danger of defeat and occupation.[3]

If the ablest military leaders were so pessimistic about the postwar capability of Britain and the United States to defend the highly industrial and strategic area of Western Europe, they were even more sceptical of American ability to influence effectively postwar developments in East Central Europe, which lay in the path of the Soviet advance against the Nazi citadel.

The logical conclusion from these premises, and from the assumption that Soviet-American interests were less in conflict than Anglo-Soviet ones, was that the United States should exploit its middleman position to bind the three major powers together, so as to hold postwar conflicts within manageable bounds. And this was the conclusion which Admiral Leahy drew.

> It is apparent that the United States should, now and in the future, exert its utmost efforts and utilize all its influence to prevent such a situation arising and to promote a spirit of mutual cooperation between Britain, Russia and ourselves. So long as Britain and Russia cooperate and collaborate in the interests of peace, there can be no great war in the foreseeable future. . . . From the broader view of national and world-wide security, . . . the United States should not support any such British proposals [concerning disposition of Italian overseas possessions] prior to ascertaining Russian views, lest post-war disunity of the three great powers be thereby fostered with all the possibility of ultimate impact upon the military position of the United States which such a disaster would entail.[4]

From these assumptions it logically followed, during hostilities against Germany, that British views concerning what could or could not be achieved on behalf of the peoples of East Central Europe carried a special weight, often counterbalancing traditional American aspirations, because the responsibility for maintaining whatever postwar adjustment could be reached in Europe between British and Soviet power would have to be enforced by Britain,

[3] *Ibid.*, pp. 107–108.
[4] *Ibid.*, p. 108, and n. 4, pp. 106–107.

feebly seconded by an absent America and a weakened France.

Despite its definite commitment against undertaking specific political and military obligations in postwar Europe, the United States Government could and did take the lead in stating in universal terms the war aims of the coalition. There is no need to review the specific words of the Atlantic Charter or the Declaration of the United Nations, both of which received the adherence of the Soviet Government, or of the Moscow Declaration of November 1, 1943, the first statement of purposes which was actually negotiated among the three great powers. In addition, particular declarations and appeals, addressed jointly by the "Big Three" to the occupied nations and to members of the Axis, were also supposedly expressions of Soviet as well as American and British intentions.

The "futility" of these and similar general declarations has often been denounced in later years, and the United States has often been condemned for its "failure" to enforce the fulfillment of these promises. Two factors are often forgotten. First, the United States did not promise and could not have promised to use its military forces, which, incidentally, it no longer possessed shortly after V-J Day, to compel the execution of these promises by a hostile major power. Second, the fact that the United States strove conscientiously to fulfill the aspirations to which it had given expression does not make it responsible for the contrary conduct of the Soviet Government, over which it had no power of control or compulsion.

One possible way to protect the future of Europe against overweening power from the East was to build up regional organs by which continental Europe could cope with its immediate problems of reconstruction. Through promoting the establishment and work of the Emergency Economic Commission for Europe, the Emergency Inland Transport Organization, the Emergency Coal Organization, and the United Nations Relief and Rehabilitation Administration, as well as the more broadly based Bretton Woods agreements and the Interim Commission on Food and Agriculture, the United States hoped to foster the ability of all Europe to revive its shattered economy and thus to avoid a prolonged period of economic and social disorder, such as had followed World War I.[5] Soviet policy-makers, on the other hand, were deeply suspicious of

[5] E. F. Penrose, *Post-War Economic Planning* (Princeton, N. J., 1953).

all "European" projects and effectively cut off Soviet-dominated Europe from participation in all except UNRRA. The administrative arrangements of UNRRA, which placed Soviet representatives at the head of several of its missions in East Central Europe, unwisely recognized, at least symbolically, the pre-eminent role of the Soviet Union in that region.

One further duty of the United States Government during hostilities was to define its postwar aims in clear and detailed terms, even if their implementation was to be held in suspense during hostilities. Between January, 1942, and July, 1943, a series of advisory committees, including high officials of the Department of State, carried through a detailed review of the problems which would confront the United States in making peace.[6] The deliberations of the committees laid the foundation for the Charter of the United Nations. In considering the specific problems of peace settlements the Advisory Committees were uncertain, in that period, as to the degree of power which the Soviet Union would exert and were inclined to visualize a grand and concentrated process of peacemaking, on the pattern of the Paris peace conference of 1919. By mid-1943, however, a more realistic picture of Soviet intentions began to emerge. As the actual documents of the period become available, it will become clear that, whatever attitudes the urgencies of coalition warfare imposed upon the top leadership, there was, among the experts and diplomats, who had more time for reflection and prognostication in a period of "technological unemployment" imposed on them in time of war, no wish to escape into rosy dreams of a conflictless world. The studies prepared by the Country and Area Committees within the Department of State during 1943 and 1944 will show, when published, that there was a keen awareness of the menace of Soviet domination over East Central Europe and an equally keen desire to ward off this menace. And both this awareness and this desire were fully shared by the Department's Committee on Post-war Programs.

Just because Roosevelt and Truman realized that allied unity, maintained precariously during a war for survival, would be gravely jeopardized after the defeat of the common enemy, they pressed on, even under the stress of war, to establish the United Nations before the close of hostilities. For the United States, certain of its

[6] Harley A. Notter, *Postwar Foreign Policy Preparation, 1939–1945* (Washington, 1949); Department of State Publication 3580.

need and hope for worldwide peace and doubtful of its ability or willingness to undertake specific commitments as, for example, in East Central Europe, "universal" obligations—shared in words with its major allies—were easier to contemplate than particular and local responsibilities. One of its hopes was to prevent the division of the globe into spheres of influence.

In November, 1943, in his address to Congress reporting on the Moscow Conference, Secretary Hull proclaimed as its greatest achievement the abandonment of "spheres of influence."

> As the provisions of the Four-Nation Declaration are carried into effect, there will no longer be need for spheres of influence, for alliances, for balance of power, or any other of the special arrangements through which, in the unhappy past, the nations strove to safeguard their security or to promote their interests.[7]

Hull's optimism found some outward support in the discussions of the three foreign ministers at Moscow, for, when prodded by Hull, both Molotov and Eden had hastened to disclaim any interest in "separate zones or spheres of influence." Molotov could even "guarantee that there was no disposition on the part of his government to divide Europe into such separate zones." [8] Fourteen months later, the briefing papers prepared by the State Department for the Yalta Conference gave a fairly clear analysis of the growing tendency for zones of wartime military responsibility to harden into postwar spheres of influence, as well as a prescient forecast of the dangers which this presented to the peoples of East Central Europe and to their ability to shape their postwar futures.[9] Meanwhile, military events and actions had been giving shape to the very spheres of influence which Secretary Hull and his department strove to avert. In any spheres-of-influence arrangement East Central Europe would fare badly. While American military leaders concentrated all effort on winning the war as quickly and as painlessly as possible, the Soviet leaders were not likely, after "the ball game was over," "to shake hands and go home."

Even as Hull spoke, military necessities had already created "spheres of responsibility," precursors of the postwar "spheres of influence." Of course, the eastern front was the primary "sphere" of Soviet action, which gradually expanded westward from Stalin-

[7] *The Memoirs of Cordell Hull* (New York, 1948), II, 1314–1315.
[8] *Ibid.*, II, 1298.
[9] *The Conferences at Malta and Yalta, 1945,* pp. 103–106.

grad to the Elbe as the Soviet armies fought on to victory. The Soviet sphere, by the agreement of 1941 with the British, included northern Iran. At Yalta, Manchuria and the Kuriles were assigned to the Soviet sphere, and, by a last-minute decision in August, 1945, Korea north of the 38th parallel.

While the other fronts were, in concept, Anglo-American in direction, the spheres-of-responsibility principle was also applied to them. On March 8, 1942, Roosevelt proposed that ". . . the British alone should assume the responsibility for the Middle East, the Americans the responsibility for the Pacific, while both nations jointly should operate in the critical Atlantic theater." [10] In general, by the end of 1943 the Mediterranean area, including Italy, Greece and Turkey, was regarded primarily as a British, not an American, responsibility. When Greek leaders, worried at the prospect that only British troops would take part in the liberation of their country, requested the sending of some American troops, the request was turned down.[11] According to Admiral Leahy, at Casablanca Roosevelt had accepted Churchill's view that Turkey was within the British sphere.[12] The same source also notes, almost casually, that ". . . we recognized Italy as being primarily in the British sphere of influence . . ." [13] As Churchill cabled Halifax in December, 1944, after the British veto on the nomination of Count Sforza as Foreign Minister of Italy, ". . . we have been accorded command in the Mediterranean, as the Americans have command in France, and therefore we have a certain special position and responsibility." [14]

Similarly, the war in the Pacific was conducted primarily by the American Joint Chiefs of Staff, with only a limited coordination with the Anglo-American Combined Chiefs of Staff. This special responsibility, it was assumed by Secretary of the Navy Forrestal, was to continue into an indefinite future.

> I take it as a premise about all discussions of world peace that the United States is to have the major responsibility for the Pacific Ocean security, and if this premise is accepted there flows from it the ac-

[10] Henry L. Stimson and McGeorge Bundy, *On Active Service in Peace and War* (New York, 1948), p. 416.

[11] William D. Leahy, *I Was There* (New York, 1950), p. 181 (early September 1943).

[12] *Ibid.*, p. 173.

[13] *Ibid.*, p. 264.

[14] *The Conferences at Malta and Yalta, 1945,* p. 267.

ceptance of the fact that the United States must have the means with which to implement its responsibility . . .[15]

The "special responsibility" of the military commander covered the entire range of political and economic activity in "his" theater: from public order, justice, punishment of war criminals, labor regulation, supply of food, fuel and raw materials, and use of property, up to the appointment or removal of high officials. American commanders might be fully, and British commands largely, committed to exercise their proconsular powers primarily to meet immediate military needs, and might be prepared to give them up as soon as possible, but this abnegation could hardly be expected of Soviet representatives in the countries overrun by the Red Army. Nor could even the most "unpolitical" commander remain aloof from civil strife; during the autumn of 1944 the Anglo-American SHAEF gave frequent and anxious thought to what the role of their forces should be in case the widespread turbulence within France boiled over into civil war.

While both the British and Soviet commanders in various theaters received their political instructions from a well-coordinated political-cum-military leadership and therefore operated under unified policy direction, there was no similar degree of unity within American policy-making because of the serious cleavages among the President's various military and political advisers. In a belated effort to overcome the separation between diplomatic and military policy-making, the SWNCC (State-War-Navy Coordinating Committee) was established at the end of 1944. One reason for the gap in policy-making was that the President, as Commander-in-Chief, could make many decisions in wartime which would not have been feasible for a civilian authority. Another was the widespread and generally unwarranted fear of the War Department, from the landing in North Africa in 1942, that control of civil affairs might be transferred from it to the State Department.[16]

One result of the lack of systematic coordination was that many important decisions were taken on an *ad hoc* basis, without adequate consideration of their implications. For example, the terms of the Italian armistice were negotiated between London, Washington and SACMED (Supreme Allied Commander, Mediter-

[15] *The Forrestal Diaries,* edited by Walter Millis (New York, 1951), entry for April 17, 1945; dots as in original.

[16] Stimson and Bundy, *op. cit.,* p. 559.

ranean) without consideration of the Russian claim to participate. For some days there was no thought even of inviting a Soviet signature to the armistice or of providing for Soviet representation in any part of the allied control machinery, on the ground that Italy was not a "Soviet theater." State Department officers, learning accidentally of the proposed arrangements, protested strongly, pointing out that this precedent would allow the Soviet Government in its turn to exclude the United States and Britain from any participation in the armistices with Hungary, Rumania, Bulgaria and Finland. Only then was provision made for token participation by Soviet representatives in the Italian surrender and later in a powerless Advisory Council. As a matter of fact, the Western Allies took a far more active part in negotiating the armistice terms for the ex-Axis satellites and in the operations of the Allied Control Commissions. The difference in the outcome within the two areas was due, not to the negotiated arrangements, but to the Soviet ability to operate at all levels, through the political police, the Communist Party and the Communist-dominated trade unions in each country, and also through massive terror against the local population. The experience of World War II suggests that the only way in which the United States could have exercised a determining influence on the postwar status of East Central Europe was to appear there with large military forces.

In recent years it has often been argued that, if the American leadership had accepted the Churchill-sponsored project for an invasion of the Balkans in 1943, the later fate of East Central Europe might have been a very different one, for the need and opportunity for Soviet-style "liberation" would have been averted. The plans for a Balkan approach have remained obscure, as to forces proposed and limits of advance and schedule, but there has been no indication that they called for more than an advance northward to the Danube-Sava line. If carried out, this plan would presumably have brought Bulgaria within the British safety-zone for the Mediterranean, but it is probable that Yugoslavia would have remained under the control of Tito's forces. In any case, Poland and Czechoslovakia, Hungary and Rumania would have remained within the Soviet military theater, with all the consequences deriving therefrom. In addition, the SHAEF invasion of Western Europe could not have been carried out during 1944. It is possible that not only all of Germany, but also Denmark, the

Netherlands, Belgium and perhaps France would have experienced Soviet-style "liberation."

There was much more to be said in favor of Churchill's proposals, in the summer of 1944, that the Anglo-American forces should advance through the Ljubljana Gap into Austria and perhaps into western Hungary, but the American Joint Chiefs of Staff also overruled this proposal in favor of the invasion of southern France. By that time Hitler could no longer afford to withdraw forces from Western Europe to reinforce his hold on the Danube area, and Soviet forces were at the outskirts of Warsaw and on the eastern frontier of Hungary. An alternative campaign, discussed to some extent at the time, called for the use of Allied forces in Bulgaria and Albania, but this diversion of forces was also opposed by the American Chiefs. It is easy, in retrospect, to say that the landing in southern France in August, 1944, was unnecessary and that this force should have been directed against the Balkan or Danubian area. But who can blame a commander for making assurance doubly sure at a time when the decisive campaign in Normandy hung in the balance?

Churchill's persistent advocacy of a Balkan campaign had one unfortunate repercussion on American planning for the postwar status of East Central Europe. After the great debates of 1943 over strategy and the postponement of the Normandy invasion to May, 1944, the American Joint Chiefs of Staff ruled, in the autumn of 1943, that the United States should take no responsibilities "in the area of the Balkans including Austria." It was many months before this veto against American participation in Austrian affairs was lifted. In May, 1944, Ambassador John G. Winant, United States representative on the European Advisory Commission, took occasion to explain in person to President Roosevelt how serious it would be for the United States to refuse to participate in the re-establishment of an independent Austria. American abstention would leave Russia and Britain face-to-face as occupying or liberating powers and would result in the partitioning of Austria into two zones, thus nullifying the assurances which the three powers had given in their Declaration on Austria, of November 1, 1943. As a result, the Joint Chiefs of Staff agreed in June, 1944, that the United States could participate in the central control machinery for Austria, but maintained their refusal to consider accepting an American zone of occupation.

At the end of December, 1944, as the time for negotiating concrete arrangements for Austria was drawing near, Winant reopened directly with Roosevelt the question of policy toward Austria. In a series of strong messages Winant explained that, if the United States was to have an effective voice in Austrian affairs, it must also have a zone to administer. At the end of December, 1944, the Joint Chiefs of Staff reluctantly agreed that the United States would administer a zone in Austria; since the United States had agreed, in September, 1944, to occupy the southern zone in Germany, bordering on its proposed zone in Austria, there was no longer any logistical reason for refusing to participate in the reestablishment of the Austrian state.

However, if Austria seemed to the military leadership to be a part of the "Balkans," and was thereby excluded for so long from political as well as military planning, how much prospect was there that any of the countries of East Central Europe would fall within the sphere of effective American action? Echoes of this persistent military position were heard at the crucial White House conference of April 23, 1945, called by President Truman to discuss the American attitude toward the flagrant Soviet violations of the Yalta agreements. At this conference Secretary Stimson argued that "the Balkans and their troubles were beyond the sphere of proper United States action"; he urged caution in opposing the Soviet flouting of the Yalta agreement on Poland and the Yugoslav seizure of Trieste.[17]

The opposition of the military to the American acceptance of responsibilities in spheres lying outside their own theaters of command was reflected in political planning and action. Because of the reluctance of the President and the military to make political commitments regarding areas outside American direct control, the State Department was left adrift, to "make do" the best it could by means of notes and exhortations. One result was that, just as the Mediterranean was regarded as a wartime and postwar British sphere, East Central Europe, until Yalta and Potsdam, was also treated, between the British and Americans, as primarily a British concern. The location of the governments-in-exile in London, and their partial financial dependence on the British Government, made it plausible for many people in Washington to regard both the governments and their countries' problems as peculiarly a

[17] Stimson and Bundy, *op. cit.*, p. 609 and n. 6.

British concern. Suggestions that they would like to move to Washington were firmly rebuffed.

At both the Moscow and Teheran conferences, in late 1943, the American assumption was that the first and most important step was to secure Soviet support for certain basic policies, such as an agreed policy toward Germany and the establishment of the United Nations. Once the central problems of security were resolved to the mutual satisfaction of the "Big Three," "minor" problems, such as the future boundaries of Poland or the postwar regime of Yugoslavia, would, it was hoped, lose much of their urgency in Soviet eyes and could then be resolved in some way compatible with the internal independence of the East Central European nations.

At the Moscow conference of October, 1943, the British raised the questions of restoring Soviet relations with the Polish government in London, of resolving the Tito Mihailovich clash in Yugoslavia, and of promoting the creation of a Danubian confederation which might help the peoples of the area to defend themselves against a resurgent Germany.[18] Molotov promptly accused Eden of wanting to rebuild a *cordon sanitaire* against Russia, and, after long discussion, the British agreed to drop this item from the agenda. Obviously, any idea of federation or confederation in East Central Europe was anathema to the Soviet leaders.

The more real issue of the Soviet-Czechoslovak twenty-year treaty of mutual defense, whose signature had been held up for many months by British objections, also caused sharp discussions at the Moscow Conference. After urging that this and similar postwar commitments should be deferred until the exile governments had returned to their homelands and had been confirmed as representing their people and until the question of the compatibility of separate alliances with the future United Nations could be studied, the British again gave in, and it was agreed that the Beneš government would sign the alliance, as it did in December, 1943.

When the character of the postwar Polish and Yugoslav regimes came up for discussion, the British again bore the brunt of the argument. Mr. Hull, pressed for his opinion, said that he hoped his British and Soviet colleagues would talk it over and come to a meeting of minds. Molotov, quick as a rapier, then pressed to know if the United States would accept whatever the British and Soviet

[18] An incomplete account in Hull, *op. cit.,* II, 1298–1299.

delegations agreed on. Hull, of course, evaded this invitation to "bow out" from the entire complex of East Central European problems, but he made it equally clear that the United States Government was not really concerned about this area of Europe, at least in comparison with the "big" issues. Certainly, this must have been the Soviet impression of the American position.

A similar tactic of playing down the American concern about the postwar prospects of East Central Europe was followed by President Roosevelt at the Teheran Conference, although he did not follow Churchill in endorsing the claim of the Soviet Government to recover the boundary of June 22, 1941. Again, he left it to the British representatives, despite their acceptance of the Curzon line as Poland's eastern boundary, to uphold the interests of the West in the postwar status of the peoples of East Central Europe.

If the most influential American leader was uncertain whether his country would be willing to guarantee any specific postwar settlements even in Western Europe, the pressure on Britain to accept Soviet-imposed decisions in the area of the Red Army's advance and thereby to gain some bargaining advantage for British interests elsewhere became almost irresistible. If no outside force could deter or dissuade the Soviet leaders from having their way in areas under their military control, then it was important for the British to accept the inevitable as early and as gracefully as possible and thereby to gain some counterpart, for example, through Soviet recognition of Britain's paramount interests in the countries bordering on the Mediterranean. If the Soviet Government was determined on building its own sphere in East Central Europe, then London must secure in advance a Soviet promise to respect the British lifeline to the East.

This question became especially acute with the Soviet entry into Rumanian territory, in April, 1944, and in May the British Government proposed, first to Moscow and then to Washington, that Russia have a controlling influence in Rumania and Britain in Greece. Shortly after, Churchill also proposed assigning Bulgaria to Russian control and Yugoslavia to British. Following strong protests by Secretary Hull, Roosevelt cabled Churchill that he preferred to see consultative machinery for the Balkans set up to resolve misunderstandings and to prevent the development of exclusive zones of influence. However, two days later Roosevelt yielded to Churchill's pressure and agreed that the proposed division of responsibility would receive a three-months' trial, after which it would be reviewed by the three governments.[19]

Four months later, in October, 1944, an even more elaborate Anglo-Soviet agreement was negotiated by Churchill and Eden at Moscow. According to one version, it assigned to Russia 75/25 or 80/20 preponderance in Bulgaria, Rumania and Hungary, while in Yugoslavia Russia was to share influence with Britain 50/50.[20] When, at Yalta, American influence began to be exerted more positively in favor of the national independence of the peoples of East Central Europe, this shift occurred against a long record of general declarations seasoned with inaction and with a weather-eye cocked to detect Soviet reactions. The question always asked was whether it was worthwhile to risk a Soviet separate peace with Germany, later, a Soviet abstention from entering the war against Japan, in order to protest against Soviet actions which the United States was powerless to prevent. Perhaps the final outcome would have been the same, but those who were charged with negotiating were never given any valuable counters to use; they were left with the frustrating invitation to win over the Soviet Government to American views by means of words alone. When at Yalta the United States began shifting from passivity to active interest, its British partner was too far committed to a division-of-spheres policy to render strong support.

For East Central Europe the crucial year was 1944, which saw the conclusion of several armistices and the installation of massive Soviet power, backed by Communist Parties and the Soviet secret police, in most of the area. Unlike the Soviet role in determining surrender terms for Italy, the Western powers negotiated actively, if ineffectively, on the terms of the armistices. In the long negotiations on the Bulgarian armistice, for example, the author proposed that the Allied Control Commission operate under the "general direction" of the Soviet commander only during the period of hostilities against Germany. Several weeks of close negotiation in London, in the European Advisory Commission, ended when, dur-

[19] Hull, *op. cit.*, II, 1451–1459.

[20] *Ibid.*, II, 1458. According to an unpublished official record, the ratio was stated to be 60/40 or 70/30 with respect to 'predominance' in Hungary. In Churchill's version (Winston S. Churchill, *Triumph and Tragedy*, Boston, 1953, p. 227), the ratios he proposed were: Rumania 90/10 and Bulgaria 75/25 in favor of Russia, Greece 90/10 in favor of Britain, Yugoslavia 50/50 and Hungary 50/50. The discrepancies in the various percentages reported cannot be fully clarified on the basis of present evidence.

ing the Churchill-Eden visit in Moscow in October, 1944, the British representatives agreed to abandon the provision for tripartite and equal control in the post-hostilities period. As a result, both the Bulgarian armistice of October 28, 1944, and, after it, the Hungarian armistice of January 20, 1945, provided that

> During the period between the coming into force of the armistice and the conclusion of hostilities against Germany the Allied Control Commission will be under the general direction of the Allied (Soviet) High Command.

But they made no corresponding provision for the period between the surrender of Germany and the coming into force of the peace treaties.[21]

During the period between the armistices of 1944 and the Yalta Conference of February, 1945, it had become clear that the wartime policy of postponing to a peace conference the settlement of the specific issues of East Central Europe was no longer tenable. Reflecting both hope and alarm, the State Department staff, in preparation for Yalta, prepared detailed studies and recommendations in support of a positive United States policy designed to safeguard the internal independence of the one hundred million people of this area. In addition to specific recommendations for strengthening the American role in each of the countries, the State Department also prepared a draft Declaration on Liberated Europe and a detailed plan for creating a four-power Emergency High Commission for Liberated Europe, empowered to carry out the lofty intentions of the Declaration.[22]

At Yalta Roosevelt put forward the draft Declaration, which, after a relatively brief discussion, was approved with minor changes. He decided not to present the proposal for establishing an Emergency High Commission. Why? On this the record is obscure. Perhaps he was fearful of jeopardizing Soviet participation in the war against Japan.[23] Perhaps he disliked the inclusion of the French Provisional Government in the proposed four-power commission.

[21] For terms of armistice with Bulgaria, see Executive Agreement Series 437 (Washington, 1945); with Hungary, Executive Agreement Series 456 (Washington, 1945); with Rumania, same series, 490 (Washington, 1946).

[22] *The Conferences at Malta and Yalta, 1945,* pp. 97–103; concerning the attitude of President Roosevelt to the proposed Commission, see Edward R. Stettinius, Jr., *Roosevelt and the Russians; the Yalta Conference* (Garden City, N.Y., 1949), pp. 36–37, 85, 88–89.

[23] For the basic Joint Chiefs of Staff recommendation on the necessity of Soviet cooperation in the defeat of Japan, January 23, 1945, see *The Conferences at Malta and Yalta, 1945,* pp. 396–400.

In any event, the opportunity, perhaps the last during the war, to assure a more active and perhaps more effective participation by the United States in the wartime and postwar reshaping of East Central Europe was lost. The signing of the Declaration on Liberated Europe was, in itself, not enough to convince the Soviet leaders of the new and serious interest which the United States was now prepared to assert in the affairs of that region. Nor did the Yalta agreements on the affairs of Poland and Yugoslavia resolve the basic contradictions between the Soviet and American aims.

Between Yalta and Potsdam the cleavage between Soviet and Western aims in East Central Europe grew ever wider. In violation of the Yalta Agreement on Poland, in April the Soviet Government recognized unilaterally the unreconstructed Lublin regime. In violation of the Agreement on Zones of Occupation in Germany, in June it transferred a major part of the Soviet Zone to Polish possession. The United States withstood the Soviet pressure to admit the Lublin government to the San Francisco Conference, but by the June, 1945, compromise, itself a compromise within the Yalta compromise, the Soviet leaders secured the substance of power within Poland for their puppet regime by giving only token representation to the parties and leaders which represented the great majority of the Polish people. Within Yugoslavia Soviet encouragement to the Tito regime blithely ignored both the substance of the Yalta agreement and the Anglo-Soviet agreement for a 50/50 sharing of influence, as the Yugoslav Communists zealously consolidated their undivided control. At the end of February, in disregard of the Yalta Declaration and of strong American protests, Vyshinsky dismissed the Radescu government in Rumania and imposed the Communist-dominated Groza regime. Roosevelt's pleas and protests over Soviet actions in Poland and Rumania were dismissed abruptly by Stalin. By the time of Roosevelt's death the cleavage between Soviet actions and American hopes was complete.

Molotov's visit to Washington, on his way to the San Francisco Conference, gave occasion for the new President to review the Yalta agreements on East Central Europe and to consider what could be done to secure their fulfillment. At an important White House meeting on April 23, 1945, Truman received contradictory advice. Stettinius, Harriman and Forrestal urged a strong stand, meeting the issue head-on. Leahy urged accommodation and Stimson argued that "the Balkans and their troubles were beyond the sphere of proper United States action," while Marshall warned that a break with Moscow might destroy the hope "for Soviet participation in the war against Japan at a time when it would be useful to us." President Truman felt that "our agreements with the Soviet Union so far had been a one-way street and that he could not continue." [24] His firmer stand succeeded in some details but was to fail in its broader purpose. By June, through the Hopkins mission to Moscow the outward form of agreement on the new Polish Government was all that could be salvaged.[25]

By the time of the Potsdam Conference the Truman administration was no longer shackled by the gnawing fear that through a "strong" policy on East Central Europe it might forfeit Soviet participation in the war against Japan, but the urgency of reaching agreement on post-hostilities policy toward Germany and a multitude of other pressing issues limited severely the pressure which could be exerted on behalf of the freedom and independence of the peoples of East Central Europe. Despite strong misgivings over placing so much German territory under Polish administration, the best that could be done was to leave open the final decision on the new western boundary. Even this agreement was promptly repudiated a few days later by the Soviet Government, which, in August, 1945, guaranteed to Poland the annexation of the German territories which had been placed under its "provisional administration."

Despite State Department hopes that the Allied Control Commissions in Hungary, Rumania and Bulgaria would henceforth be placed under three-power direction, the best that could be achieved was an agreement that directives would now be issued by the Soviet chairmen only after "coordination" with their British and American colleagues. Even this concession was promptly vitiated by Soviet action; sidestepping the Commissions, henceforth the Soviet commanders issued their orders, as military commanders, directly to the Communist members of the puppet regimes. Stalin also agreed to freedom of movement and reporting for Western correspondents, but he firmly rejected plans for "internationalizing" the Danube and Rhine rivers.

The basic Soviet demand at Potsdam was for the immediate

[24] An incomplete account of the April 23, 1945 conference, Forrestal, *op. cit.*, pp. 48–51; also, Stimson and Bundy, *op. cit.*, p. 609 and n. 6. Cf. *Memoirs by Harry S. Truman*, Vol. I, *Year of Decision* (Garden City, N.Y., 1955), pp. 77–78.

[25] Robert E. Sherwood, *Roosevelt and Hopkins, an Intimate History* (New York, 1948), pp. 883–917.

and unconditional recognition of the Soviet-dominated regimes in Hungary, Rumania and Bulgaria. Obviously, if accepted, this meant abandoning all the Yalta promises of free elections and representative governments, and Truman and Byrnes insisted again and again that they would not recognize governments in these countries until they had a "free government established by themselves without pressure from beyond their borders."[26] Stalin made the Soviet position clear when he stated that "any freely elected government would be anti-Soviet and that we cannot permit."

After the vigorous assertion of the American policy of promoting free and representative governments in East Central Europe, Stalin and Molotov must have been somewhat confused by Secretary Byrnes' sudden suggestion that "the United States would approve of any arrangement that was accepted by the United Kingdom and the Soviet Government" concerning the recognition of the three satellite regimes.[27] This was a last echo of the wartime assumption that East Central Europe was more a British than an American area of concern. After Potsdam it was clear that whatever pressure Britain and America could muster in support of the Yalta Declaration would be determined primarily by American determination and political skill.

The new and stubborn American stand at Potsdam had some significant repercussions within East Central Europe. In Rumania King Michael refused to sign the decrees of the illegal Groza government. In Bulgaria the elections, which were being "prepared" by the Communists with great ruthlessness, were postponed at the last moment. In Hungary the non-Communist parties rejected the Soviet demand for a single-list election, though they agreed to continue the coalition with the Communists regardless of the outcome of the election. Thus, Potsdam encouraged a courageous posture by the non-Communist political forces, while the postponement of the evacuation of American forces from western Czechoslovakia enabled the coalition government to negotiate the simultaneous withdrawal of the Soviet forces. Potsdam also ratified a major reshuffling of ethnic distributions, through its approval for removing the German populations not only from Poland, Czecho-

[26] Leahy, *op. cit.*, pp. 405–406; James F. Byrnes, *Speaking Frankly* (New York, 1947), pp. 73–76, 79–81.

[27] Leahy, *op. cit.*, p. 421.

slovakia and Hungary, but also from the "Polish-administered" areas east of the Oder-Neisse line.

The first meeting of the Council of Foreign Ministers, held at London in September, 1945, made clear the deadlock which had developed between Soviet and American aims in East Central Europe. Molotov made it plain that his government insisted on having its way in the settlements with Hungary, Rumania and Bulgaria, and in support of Yugoslav claims against Italy. He insisted over and over on immediate and unconditional recognition of the Soviet-dominated regimes in the satellites. As at Potsdam, he denounced Secretary Byrnes' insistence on free elections as a desire to establish "anti-Soviet regimes" in these countries and to re-create the *cordon sanitaire* against the Soviet Union. To illustrate the absence of hostile intention on the American side and to make clear the American definition of free elections, Byrnes offered then and there to extend recognition to the Hungarian Government, provided it assured a relatively free and unimpeded vote. Following a complete deadlock between the two positions, on September 22 Molotov injected the Soviet demand for equal participation in the control of Japan, and when the American representatives were unwilling even to discuss this Soviet incursion into an American "sphere of responsibility," Molotov broke up the conference.

The strong American stand at Potsdam and London in favor of free elections in East Central Europe threw a few handfuls of grit into the grinding wheels of the Soviet power-machine, but it could not stop their turning. Meanwhile, a similar tug-of-war, this time in favor of the American position, was taking place between Moscow and Washington over the postwar control of Japan. At the Moscow Conference of Foreign Ministers, in December, 1945, the United States received Soviet acquiescence in the substance of its claims to sole control over occupied Japan, and the Soviet Government gained the substance of American acquiescence in the policies which it was following in East Central Europe, making only a few concessions of form by allowing Western-nominated ministers to sit in the Rumanian cabinet. A similar Soviet promise to "suggest" to the Bulgarian Government the inclusion of Western-recommended ministers was promptly vitiated in Sofia by Vyshinsky's "suggesting" the opposite. The defeat of the American effort to assure to the nations of East Central Europe the enjoyment, in some degree, of the right of self-determination—an effort begun belatedly at Yalta—was sealed within the same year at Moscow.

What could American policy do henceforth to help the peoples of East Central Europe to escape the yoke which was being pressed down upon their shoulders? One hope was to use the offer of American economic aid to strengthen their ties with the West. Through the sale of surplus supplies and the timing of the restitution of stolen property and shipping, some efforts were made in this direction, but there was no consistent plan and no popular understanding of the need for one. Another, and somewhat contradictory, line of action was to press for the protection of American property rights. This was a feeble and two-edged sword, for it fed the Communist propaganda against the "imperialists" at the same time that the United States was committed in principle to accepting the nationalization of foreign-owned properties provided the principles of non-discrimination and compensation were observed.

A more substantial hope was that the speedy conclusion of the peace treaties and the withdrawal of Soviet troops would allow the non-Communist forces to recover control of their national destinies. To hasten the conclusion of the treaties the American Government accepted many unfavorable provisions, including those for establishing the Free Territory of Trieste and for submitting the future status of the Danube to decision by a Soviet-packed conference. The Soviet negotiators made haste slowly. Agreed to in December, 1946, the treaties were signed in February and entered into force in September, 1947. In Hungary complete Communist domination had been established in May, 1947, the Communist grip on Bulgaria and Rumania was unshakable, and the Polish "elections" of January, 1947, set the seal on Communist control. In all these countries, except Albania, Soviet-dominated regimes had received American recognition, despite flagrant violations of the Yalta agreements. Soviet forces also remained stationed in Hungary, Rumania and Poland.

March, 1947, saw a major extension of American responsibilities. Greece and Turkey, which had been within the British sphere since 1942, were transferred to American protection by the adoption of the Truman Doctrine. By the Marshall Plan, proposed in June, 1947, the United States abandoned its previous assumption that Europe could see to its own economic reconstruction and promised large-scale and continuing American assistance. In June, 1948, it took on an added responsibility for assuring the rebuilding of Western Germany.

Just how far the Marshall Plan was predicated upon cooperation with the Soviet Union and the Soviet-dominated countries of East Central Europe remains obscure. In any case, Moscow chose to attack the plan as an "imperialist plot" to destroy its domination in East Central Europe, and in July, 1947, it ordered the Czechoslovak coalition government to withdraw its tentative agreement to attend the Marshall Plan conference. With the founding of the Cominform, in September–October, 1947, the Soviet leaders openly proclaimed their determination to exert a monopoly of decision-making in East Central Europe, while continuing their probing of the vulnerabilities of Greece and Turkey. Soviet domination of East Central Europe, tentatively outlined as early as 1942, pursued relentlessly from 1944, and aquiesced in reluctantly by the West in 1946, was an accomplished fact, except where, as in Yugoslavia, strong local forces later proved able to defend their own, Communist-oriented independence.

During the war of 1941–1945 the United States moved from a parochially continental concept of its responsibilities to the exercise of leadership over the more productive half of Europe and over Japan, and to the development of new policies toward the British Commonwealth and the Middle East. The two areas where its new concept of responsibilities failed were China and East Central Europe. The expansion of American interests and responsibilities had been unforeseen and unplanned. As late as 1946 American policy-making assumed that, having defeated the aggressors, the United States would be free, once again, to limit drastically its commitments in other continents, leaving the United Nations to take care of what minor troubles and conflicts might arise.

Between 1941 and 1947 American hopes for a democratic and liberal future for the one hundred million people of East Central Europe rose and fell. Hopes were high so long as American opinion failed to realize that in East Central Europe Soviet aims and American aspirations ran directly counter to each other. Here two separate wars were being waged, but Washington failed during the war to assure power positions from which it could achieve its hopes after the war. The location of forces at the close of hostilities was to be, more than was realized at the time, the decisive factor in the divergent fates of East Central and Western Europe. Wartime strategy, in the event, determined the shape of postwar diplomacy. The strategy of coalition called for the assignment of military "spheres of responsibility," and these, as the Cassandras of the State Department warned over and over, were likely to harden into postwar "spheres of influence" and into competition and conflict between them.

Despite gnawing doubts as to how far the administration in power could commit the United States to the enforcement of specific postwar settlements anywhere in Europe, Roosevelt and Truman found strong support at home for the hopes which were expressed in the Yalta Declaration on Liberated Europe. But the new and active course was begun with a whole necklace of incubuses hung around its neck. Not least of these was the continuing failure to coordinate the use of political, military and economic power within American policy-making. By the end of 1946, against unyielding Soviet insistence on transforming East Central Europe into a closed preserve, the American Government had a heap of broken Soviet promises to point to as a reminder that hope, divorced from power, is not a policy.

Chapter 4

Containment? Liberation? Coexistence? American Policy Toward East Central Europe, 1947–1955

ROBERT F. BYRNES

AMERICAN policy toward East Central Europe since 1947, indeed since the last years of World War II, has operated within limitations and constrictions which have in effect defined American goals and seriously restricted the means available to attain those goals. To begin with, by early 1948 Soviet control over East Central Europe was complete, with all opposition crushed or obliterated. On the other hand, the United States after the war had rapidly dismantled its military forces and had neither the strength nor the will to challenge the Soviet position in East Central Europe.

Finally, in 1947 the economic, political, and spiritual position of Western Europe was desperate, far more critical than was realized at the time. The governments of our principal friends and allies in Western Europe were overwhelmed by serious domestic and colonial problems, which delayed their realizing the dread significance of the disappearance of East Central Europe behind the Iron Curtain, prevented their devoting time and resources to the affairs of their neighbor states, now controlled by Communists, and made them generally ineffectual supporters where questions concerning East Central Europe were concerned. The timidity demonstrated by the governments of Western Europe toward the Soviet Union and their indifference toward East Central Europe have had a clear effect upon American policy, which has been hampered to a considerable degree by the weakness and irresolution of its allies.

During World War II, the United States and the principal Western states allied with the Soviet Union against Nazi Germany had been friendly, cooperative, and even generous toward the Soviet Union. However, the vacuum created in Central Europe by the defeat of Germany, the economic, social, and political crisis which prevailed throughout most of Europe, the presence of Soviet forces in the very heart of Europe, and the stimulus provided by victory over such a mighty enemy as Nazi Germany all helped to ripen in the minds of the Soviet rulers the idea inherent in the basic concepts of Stalinism—that of extending Communist power as part of the drive to conquer the world. Achievement of these goals in East Central Europe, which had been carefully planned in Moscow during the last years of the war, was facilitated by rapid American disarmament.

The war dreams of cooperation with the Soviet Union were destroyed by the Russians themselves as they liquidated non-Communist political parties and leaders in East Central Europe; supported Yugoslavia, Albania, and Bulgaria in violating the Greek frontiers; adopted an intransigent policy with regard to reparations from Germany; used the veto freely in the UN; blocked the American atomic energy control plan; refused to participate in world economic reconstruction; maintained huge armed forces; and sought through pressure, propaganda, and Communist parties to bring other nations under their control.

By 1947, most Americans, and most American policymakers in particular, had recovered from their wartime admiration for the Soviet Union and were beginning to realize that "patience and firmness" were not sufficient to restrain the Soviet leaders or to resolve the serious political and economic crises which faced Western Europe and other parts of the world.

Containment

Gradually, to meet the new challenge posed by the Soviet Union, the policy which came to be known as "containment" was hammered out. This policy, which placed a great strain on the American citizen and taxpayer and on the resourcefulness and flexibility of American diplomacy, represents one of the major turning points in the history of the twentieth century. It meant fundamentally that the United States had decided clearly and finally to resist Soviet aggression, to assist those states threatened by Communist pressure, and to strengthen forces within the Soviet system which would help to bring about a change in Soviet conduct.

The policy of containment, which since 1947 has dominated the American approach to the problems posed by the Soviet Union, has rested mainly upon the following foundations:

(1) The United States and its allies must increase their military strength and determination so that they may contain Soviet expansive tendencies "with unalterable counter-force at every point where they (the Russians) show signs of encroaching upon the interests of a peaceful and stable world." The skillful and resolute use of this growing strength would serve "to increase enormously the strains under which Soviet policy must operate, to force upon the Kremlin a far greater degree of moderation and circumspection than it has had to observe in recent years, and in this way to promote tendencies which must eventually find their outlet in either the breakup or the gradual mellowing of Soviet power." [1]

(2) The United States must hasten to ensure the economic recovery of the states of Western Europe so that they may resume their role in world affairs, so that the weaknesses and ills upon which Communism thrives would be reduced or even eliminated, and so that the freedom, strength, and prosperity of Western Europe would reduce the power of the Communists within Western Europe itself and would influence the Soviet empire in a way favorable to Western interests. (This policy was later extended in some degree to other areas of the world, particularly through the Point Four program, which was established to help increase productivity and to raise living standards in the less advanced areas.)

(3) The non-Communist states, especially those in the North Atlantic and Mediterranean areas, must coordinate their policies and unite their forces.

(4) Western Europe must work toward economic and political unity in order to end the conflicts which have plagued Europe, to heighten resistance to the Communists, to erect a political system and a concept which would attract the peoples of East Central Europe, and to exert a disintegrating influence upon the Soviet empire.

(5) The conduct of the United States in particular and of the non-Communist states in general should be such as to reaffirm the basic spiritual values of civilized society, to restore the con-

[1] X, "The Sources of Soviet Conduct," *Foreign Affairs,* XXV (July 1947), 581, 582. Mr. George Kennan has since acknowledged that he was the author of this article and has included it in his volume, *American Diplomacy, 1900–1950* (Chicago, 1951).

fidence of all peoples in democratic government, to expose the myths behind which Communism skulks, and to exert a magnetic attraction upon the Communist system, "which bears within itself the seeds of its own decay."

We tend now to assume that the achievements of the past decade were an inevitable development and to forget both the problems involved and the opposition to the Truman Doctrine, the Marshall Plan, and other elements of the "containment" program as they unfolded. It is difficult now to comprehend the enormity and the gravity of the crisis facing Western Europe, Greece, and Turkey in 1947 and 1948, and we do not reflect upon the magnitude of the disaster which would have overwhelmed the non-Communist world if the United States had reverted to isolationism in 1947–1948 or if the United States had reached some kind of compromise with the Soviet Union which allowed continued Soviet expansion. Such developments might have had even greater significance than the Communist victory in mainland China has had. Among other things, they would have opened Western European states to Communist rule, swung the world balance of power very sharply to the advantage of the Soviet Union, and destroyed both the foundations for an effective American policy toward East Central Europe and any hope of ultimate liberation there, except through nuclear war.

The "Great Debate"

The American people made this series of crucial decisions only after a long and thorough "Great Debate." There were some Americans who were more concerned with British colonialism than with Soviet imperialism. There were some who believed that gentleness and toleration toward all Soviet actions would persuade the Soviet Union to abandon its ambitions and to moderate its program; there were others who thought that resistance to Communist expansion was responsible for the crisis. Still others, while aware of the threat posed by the Communists, were convinced that Western Europe was beyond recovery and that the United States should concentrate upon defending the Americas. Some Americans believed that the United States could not be—or at least would not be—attacked.

Many Americans declared that the Marshall Plan would lead to the re-establishment of wartime controls over the economy, that the tax burden would destroy the initiative and enterprise which were the foundations of American economic growth, that aid would soften the resolution of the Europeans, and that the program would intensify American shortages and credit problems and create inflationary pressures. Others criticized the whole policy of containment because it was based on three false assumptions: that Soviet expansion was based solely upon force; that the United States had the patience, skill and resolution to direct a world-wide campaign against Soviet pressures for an extended period; and that the United States could build a group of "disorganized, discontented, and divided" states into an "unassailable barrier." Some condemned it as a defensive policy which allowed the Soviet Union to retain the initiative and to consolidate its empire in preparation for another, later drive for world domination. Still others lost faith as the crisis wore on, particularly late in 1950, when the armies under General MacArthur in Korea were in desperate retreat. Some Americans then advocated our withdrawal from Korea, Western Europe, and the United Nations. Thus, ex-President Hoover in December 1950 urged that the United States retain control over the Atlantic and the Pacific, preserve the Atlantic hemisphere, build its sea and air strength, and give no more aid to Western Europe until it had regained its strength (and no longer needed aid).

The Truman Doctrine in particular was attacked because it bypassed the UN, because it represented the first step toward an international WPA, and because it might lead to "Soviet reaction and then a third World War." Indeed, some American liberals condemned Truman for "saving British chestnuts" and for allying the U.S. "with a notoriously rotten and reactionary government to gain a tactical success." Some conservative isolationists denounced the plan as a gross and futile waste of American resources.[2]

However, all of these arguments were overwhelmed by the general recognition that vital American interests were involved in the defense and restoration of Western Europe. Beginning in March 1947, a series of decisions were made under the general heading

[2] This position was defended best and represented most accurately by Senator Robert A. Taft, "who voiced the doubts and prejudices, the hopes and fears, the frustrations, the hesitations, and the dissatisfactions that the American people felt as they slowly and ponderously went about the business of adjusting to their changed role in the world." See John P. Armstrong, "The Enigma of Senator Taft and American Foreign Policy," *Review of Politics,* XVII (1955), 206–231, especially 214–228.

of the containment policy which helped to stem the spread of Communism, to revivify and unite the non-Communist world, and to lend encouragement to those behind the Iron Curtain.

The Achievements of Containment

American policy after 1947 was marked by a series of significant achievements which should clearly be labelled triumphs. The first of these was the victory in Greece, where the Communist guerrillas supported by Yugoslavia, Albania, and Bulgaria were finally defeated in 1949, after more than three years of civil war, by Greek determination and sacrifice and by American economic and military assistance. This defense of "the public order and the territorial integrity of Greece" and the provision of military and economic assistance to Turkey enabled these states to defend their democratic institutions and provided an area from which the United States and its allies were later able to exert pressure upon the Soviet empire in behalf of the people of East Central Europe.

The Truman Doctrine served not only to contain Soviet expansion toward the Mediterranean, but also helped to make possible the defection of Tito from the Soviet empire after 1948. American policy toward Tito has always had to be managed with particular care, because Yugoslavia has remained Communist, because of American domestic attitudes toward Tito's Communism, and because of the problems caused by uncertainty within the West concerning Tito's ultimate domestic and international policies. In general, American policy toward Tito has been managed with considerable skill, and Tito and the Western states have both moved cautiously and gradually toward the present position, which finds Yugoslavia independent and "neutral," but allied with Greece and Turkey, which are both members of NATO. The principal steps through which American policy, and the policies of Britain and France, have moved are: the relaxation of export controls and the unfreezing of credit in late 1948 and early 1949; support of Yugoslavia for a Security Council seat in 1949; a warning to the Soviet Union concerning aggression against Yugoslavia late in 1949; massive economic assistance to Yugoslavia, beginning after the 1950 drought; and military assistance since 1951. The United States during the past five years has given to Communist Yugoslavia about one billion dollars worth of economic and military aid. This aid and indications that an attack upon Yugoslavia might lead to general war have helped Yugoslavia to retain its independence.

While Titoism was snuffed out in the satellite Communist parties, the Yugoslav incident did expose the Soviet system as it had not been exposed before. It probably reduced Soviet eagerness to gain Communist control in areas which the Red Army had not conquered, and it has created a precedent for other Communist leaders who may be able to break free from Soviet controls. Above all, the recent reversal of the Soviet attitude toward Tito and toward "questions of internal organization or differences in social systems and of different forms of socialist development," as defined in the Belgrade Declaration of June 2, 1955, constitutes an extraordinary Communist Canossa. This may ultimately have immense import for the peoples of East Central Europe.

Tito's defection from the Soviet empire also made possible the slow resolution of the complicated Trieste issue, and contributed heavily to the general easing of tension in the eastern Mediterranean. This led finally to the mutual aid treaty of August 1954 between Yugoslavia, Greece, and Turkey, which buttressed the Western position in the eastern Mediterranean and which may lead ultimately to a Balkan assembly, which would prove a particularly attractive magnet for the Balkan peoples now under Soviet control.

In 1947, the United States "faced the choice of quitting Europe altogether or of completing the task of European recovery." The United Kingdom's economy was in a critical position, and a food and dollar crisis affected every Western European state which had fought in World War II. Communists were members of coalition governments in France and Italy, and Communist power over the trade unions in those countries was almost sufficient to enable them to obtain control of the State.

American acceptance of leadership in this crisis, and massive American injections of economic and technical assistance, helped Western Europe to defeat the efforts of the domestic Communists, to resolve the economic crisis, and to lay the foundations for the extraordinary economic growth of the past few years. This inspired effort toward economic reconstruction on a regional basis constituted an important step toward European integration and gave body to a new concept of Europe, which has been one of the most vitalizing ideas to affect Europe since World War II. United States support has been an important factor in the establishment and maintenance of the organizations of a federal character which thrive today in Western Europe and which provide some hope that conflicts within the European community can be eliminated—the Brussels Pact, the Council of Europe, the Office of European Economic Co-operation, the European Payments Union, the Coal and Steel Community, and the Western European Union.

These tremendous achievements have smothered Communist hopes of seizing the states of Western Europe and reduced the strength of extreme nationalist forces. Continued progress will increase pressure on the Soviet Union to seek similar results in the satellite states, thus constituting a great strain for the Soviet system.

The European Recovery Program was soon accompanied and ultimately overshadowed by the program to rebuild American and general Western military strength, which began to receive heavy emphasis in 1949 and 1950, especially after the invasion of South Korea. The growth of American military strength, the spread of American bases, particularly to the UK, France, Morocco, and Turkey, the stationing of American forces in Western Europe, the extension of military assistance to many of the states of Western Europe, and the creation of NATO in 1949 began the development of the shield behind which the West has been able to rebuild in confidence. By 1955, the balance of power had been restored and the damage done by World War II and by rapid American disarmament after the war had been overcome. The United States and its allies now have the military strength—though not yet the resolution and determination—to balance the Soviet Union and to hold out some hope to the captive peoples for the gradual relaxation of the Soviet bonds through a Western diplomacy reflecting power and conviction.

The rebuilding of Western European economic and military strength was the greatest and most significant achievement of the years following 1947, but the Western triumph over the Soviet blockade of Berlin in 1948 and 1949 was the most spectacular. In demonstrating the technical ability and the courage to supply 2,500,000 people in West Berlin by air for eleven months, the United States and its allies revealed to the Russians, to the captive people of East Central Europe, and to the world at large that Soviet pressure could be resisted, that the West would defend its practical positions and its principles, and that hope therefore remained for the peoples behind the Iron Curtain. Allied success in the Berlin blockade also ensured the triumph of Allied policy with regard to reparations and the level of West German economic production, the establishment of a federal, democratic government in West Germany, and the allegiance of the vast majority of West Germans to the Allied cause. West Germany was admitted to the Council of Europe in November 1949, achieved extraordinary political and economic progress, attained full sovereignity in 1954, and became a member of WEU and of NATO in 1954 as a rehabilitated democratic state.

All of these successes failed, however, to demonstrate to the Soviet Union that the United States in particular was determined to prevent Soviet expansion, even if this involved armed conflict and a sharp increase in the likelihood of general war. The crucial test for the policy of containment appeared when North Korea invaded the Republic of South Korea in June 1950 in what Hanson Baldwin described as "war by proxy." The decision of the United Nations to resist this invasion and, above all, the courageous decision of President Truman to use American armed forces to help defend South Korea, showed the Communist leaders that the United States and other non-Communist states had the will and the strength to fight to contain Soviet expansive tendencies. The UN "police action" in South Korea, in which the United States suffered the heaviest losses in lives and in treasure, was almost certainly a decisive turning point in the relations between the Soviet Union and the United States. Its significance has been blurred by stresses within the United Nations camp concerning the conduct of the war, by the indecisive armistice, and by the failure of the United States to adopt as clear a policy in 1954 in Indo-China. Nevertheless, the war in Korea served as an effective demonstration to the Soviet Union that the will to resist Soviet expansion was powerful and active in the West and that the United States was determined to fight, if necessary, to attain its defensive goals.

Political Warfare

The means for more direct action to assist the peoples of East Central Europe and to harass their Soviet rulers were restricted generally to so-called political warfare and to trade policy. Since

Americans only slowly began to comprehend the nature of Communism and of the battle for men's minds and souls which the Communists had launched, and since political warfare capabilities generally reflect military capabilities, American effectiveness in struggling on this kind of battlefield has not been notably great. Even in 1956, the United States on occasion displayed extraordinary ineptness in this field.

Political warfare today incorporates every facet of the activities of the American Government and of the American people. Selecting the favorable aspects of American society and the unfavorable aspects of Soviet society and spreading the comparison throughout the world to some degree resemble advertising, in which Americans have demonstrated great proficiency. However, this also falls into the category of political propaganda, toward which Americans during the past three decades in particular have developed a strong aversion. This genuine reluctance to have the United States Government engage in the propaganda side of political warfare has helped to weaken our entire political warfare effort. Indeed, in 1947 the United Kingdom was spending three times as much as the United States on its international information program. Congress adjourned in July 1947 without authorizing an information program and after reducing the total appropriations for information activities to $12,400,000. This was repaired on January 1948 by the Smith-Mundt Act, which provided permanent legislative authorization for information and exchange operations and which helped lead to the reorganization of the Voice of America.

The Voice of America and Radio Free Europe of the Free Europe Committee have been very effective instruments for spreading the American point of view throughout the world, but their influence behind the Iron Curtain has been seriously reduced by Soviet jamming. Both the Voice of America and Radio Free Europe have countered Soviet jamming with some success, have helped keep hope alive, and have aided the captive peoples to understand their role in the struggle against Communism. They have on occasion influenced Soviet and satellite policy by their revelations and by their careful instructions to the captive peoples concerning techniques and programs for use against their Communist rulers. However, both lack full access to the captive peoples. They have also been hampered by their American advertising approach, by

American inexperience in psychological warfare, and by general lack of knowledge concerning the peoples behind the Iron Curtain.

Trade Policy

American trade policy has been hampered not so much by the Soviet Union as by our allies, for whom trade with East Central Europe has been an important and traditional resource. The Soviet policy of reducing or eliminating trade with the West, except for strategic goods in short supply throughout the Soviet empire, and of binding all of the channels of trade to Moscow has simplified American policy, which has generally sought to restrict all trade with, and to eliminate the export of strategic materials and goods to, the Soviet empire. This policy has enabled us to hamper Soviet growth, it applied some small pressure against the Soviet Union, and it has served as a safety-valve for wounded feelings and the general sense of helplessness, especially during periods such as those during which William Oatis, an American newspaper correspondent, was in a Czech prison. However, the machinery created to control this trade was cumbersome and often ineffective. Moreover, the frequent conflicts with our allies over lists of embargoed goods and the disadvantages deriving from our adopting such a restrictive policy reduced the benefits from this trade policy considerably. The "balance of advantage," which the Battle Act of 1951 tried to attain, probably accrued to the United States, but the net advantage was not great.

In summary, the United States during the critical years after 1947 helped to defend Western Europe and to advance its recovery, to create a foundation from which to exert pressure upon the Soviet system, to demonstrate to the Soviet Union that expansion would be resisted by force, to keep alive hope and determination in East Central Europe, and to attract to the West hundreds of thousands of refugees, who proved the falsity of Communist claims concerning these states and who joined those seeking from the outside to weaken and eliminate the Soviet system. While the Soviet rulers and their Communist puppets were able easily to maintain control and to eliminate even potential sources of opposition, they were made to realize that Western Europe was recovering in such a way as to become a potential rival magnetic core of attraction for the captive peoples.

Consolidation of Soviet Control

As Western Europe began its long recovery, Americans and Western Europeans both began to appreciate more clearly the dreadful significance of the Soviet hold over East Central Europe, which served both to threaten and to neutralize Western Europe. The Soviet Union, determined to make no concessions to the West on an area it considered its own, moved to eliminate all opposition in East Central Europe and to consolidate its hold there, even before the program for containment had been launched. Thus, by early 1948 the Communists had full control of every government, and those politicians who had led the opposition had either fled to the West, been imprisoned, or been killed. East Central European States were forbidden to participate in the Marshall Plan in July 1947, and the Cominform (Communist Information Bureau) was established in September of that year. The defection of Tito served to "justify" purges of all so-called "national Communists" from the Communist parties in 1948 and 1949, and all of the instruments of control, especially the police and the army, were put under disciplined Moscow Communists. By the end of 1949, each satellite government had passed through the coalition stage into that of the "People's Democracy." Treaties of friendship, cooperation, and mutual aid bound the satellites to each other and to Moscow, and Soviet control was so absolute that Western analysts often wondered when the Soviet Union would incorporate these states as Soviet Socialist Republics.

The consolidation of Soviet control meant the elimination of all direct Western influence from East Central Europe. In this campaign, the Communists struck at religious groups which had ties with the West. They harassed Western diplomatic missions, flouted Western treaty rights, tortured employees of Western missions, closed Western information agencies, restricted and then eliminated Western news services, and nationalized Western properties. This campaign led to several spectacular cases involving individual Americans, notably Robert Vogeler, an American businessman who was imprisoned in Hungary as a spy from February 21, 1950 until April 1951, and William Oatis, the American newspaper correspondent who was sentenced to jail as a spy in Czechoslovakia from April 26, 1951 until May 16, 1953. These two cases dramatized Communist control over East Central Europe and Western inability even to defend and protect Western citizens in the area. These cases, and similar incidents, led the United States to reduce the size of satellite diplomatic missions and to restrict travel rights and trade, but none of these actions had any effect upon the Soviet Union or its puppets. Indeed, they all served as an impressive demonstration to the world of American helplessness.

Protests by the United States and Britain against violation of the 1947 peace treaties by the Bulgarian, Rumanian, and Hungarian governments had almost no effect. These treaties, which restricted the size of the armed forces of these states and which bound them to guarantee basic human rights and civil liberties, were openly and deliberately violated by the satellite states. The West did succeed in putting these treaty violations into the record, notably in November 1950, when the General Assembly of the United Nations voted 40–5 to condemn the three satellite states for their treaty violations. However, this had no effect on Soviet policy and served as just another demonstration of American weakness in this area.

Liberation: Background

Even so, it was not the failures of the containment policy with regard to East Central Europe which led in the United States to the growing wave of criticism of containment and to a flirtation with the language and the idea of liberation. The victory of the Chinese Communists over the Nationalists in 1949 was an event of such magnitude and had such strong repercussions upon the American domestic political scene that it led to vigorous criticism of the foundations of American foreign policy, its conduct, and the American Foreign Service as well. These critiques became especially acute and the popularity of liberation became particularly great as the Korean war dragged into its third year, with no satisfactory solution in sight and with America's allies increasingly irresolute. As the Korean war was prolonged, its costs, those of the rearmament program, and those of the European Recovery Program were felt more painfully by the American taxpayers, who now looked back upon more than a decade of sacrifice and forward to apparently endless conflict.

This sense of frustration and failure led to caustic analyses of the extensive American alliance system, which in the eyes of hostile critics constituted a series of American commitments to areas which did not contribute to our strength or military posture, but which absorbed American assistance, diluted American military power, and slumbered under American guarantees of protection. Many Americans, watching the Communists consolidate their hold over East Central Europe and over the mainland of China and surveying the Communist threat to many areas of the world, began to wonder whether the new "trench warfare" and the continued state of "paralyzed tension" were not sapping the balance of power inevitably in favor of the Soviet system, and leading to a situation in which the Communist states would ultimately encircle the non-Communist part of the world.

This bafflement, disappointment, and impatience were stimulated by new weapons developments and portents of still more revolutionary designs. Published data on atomic and hydrogen bombs and advances in chemical and biological warfare, high-speed and long-range aircraft, and guided missiles in particular raised doubts among many Americans concerning American strategy and concerning the need for large ground forces, overseas bases, and apparently weak and unreliable allies. These doubts naturally nourished hopes for a substitute for containment, which would be simpler, cheaper, more effective, and less dependent upon other states and peoples.

Out of this background blossomed the flirtation with liberation in 1952 and 1953. In the election campaign of 1948—the year of the Communist coup in Czechoslovakia—the principal issues, as far as foreign relations were concerned, were the civil war in China and America's China policy, the Italian colonies, and the general conduct of our relations with the Soviet Union. In 1952, America's policy with regard to China was a burning issue, but even this was overshadowed by the attack on containment and by the popularity of the notion of quickly freeing the captive people in East Central Europe.

The period during which the concept of liberation was both an official and a popular doctrine was brief, but nevertheless of great significance. The containment policy had been criticized from its first appearance, but the idea of liberation became a national phenomenon only in the summer of 1952, when the Republican Party began to prepare for the national elections of November of that year. With the election of President Eisenhower and a Republican Congress, liberation became an official concept for the American Government. It remained so for somewhat more than a year, when it was gradually allowed to fade away.

However, there was never a clear definition of the meaning of liberation or, above all, a precise program for achieving it.[3] Indeed, there was little actual disagreement between most advocates of containment and most proponents of liberation. Both groups, and the great majority of all Americans, agreed that the expansion of the Soviet Union and of Communist China must be resisted and prevented. Both agreed on the vital need for freeing the peoples of East Central Europe from Soviet control, and both were determined to avoid war and to prevent war. Except for the few extremists, the differences were of small degree. One group believed that a policy which checked Soviet expansion and which furthered peace and prosperity in the rest of the world would release natural forces within the Soviet system which would cause its modification, moderation, or even collapse. The other group emphasized somewhat more the application of external pressures upon the Soviet system to hasten its collapse and thereby the emancipation of the captive peoples. As Mr. George Kennan has pointed out, one group adopted the approach of a gardener and the other that of a mechanic. In short, the goals of American policy were not revised between 1951 and 1953, but there was considerable confusion concerning the means by which these goals should be attained.

American campaign documents are generally full of pious platitudes, and the platforms for 1952 were no exception. The following planks from the Republican platform were typical of the entire liberation drive in the vigor of the attack on containment and in the enthusiastic ambiguity as to the new means to be used:

> We shall again make liberty into a beacon light of hope that will penetrate the dark places. That program . . . will mark the end of the negative, futile, and immoral policy of 'containment' which abandons countless human beings to a despotism and godless terrorism, which in turn enables the rulers to forge the captives into a weapon for our destruction.
>
> The policies we espouse will revive the contagious liberating influences which are inherent in freedom. They will inevitably set up strains and stresses within the captive world which will make the rulers im-

[3] This vagueness can be seen in Senator Robert A. Taft's proposals for "substantially building up a love for freedom in Soviet-dominated territory" and for supporting an active underground "which would give the Soviet Government something to worry about behind the iron curtain itself." Senator Robert A. Taft, *A Foreign Policy for Americans* (New York, 1951), pp. 118–120. Senator Taft's ideas on infiltration and subversion were not only carelessly developed, but were also in conflict with the substance of his principal ideas on American interests.

> potent to continue in their monstrous ways and mark the beginning of their end.

President Eisenhower in his State of the Union speech on February 2, 1953 declared that "the free world cannot indefinitely remain in a posture of paralyzed tension" and that the new administration had begun the definition of a "new, positive foreign policy" including "all peaceful methods and devices." This speech was not notably different from Truman's address less than a month earlier, except for the announcement of three decisions apparently designed to launch a new program. These decisions withdrew President Truman's order to the American Seventh Fleet to prevent Chinese Nationalist action against the Chinese mainland (the so-called "unleashing" of Chiang Kai-Shek); urged an increase in aid to South Korea for rearmament; and implied repudiation of the Yalta agreement, by indicating that the President would "ask the Congress at a later date to join in an appropriate resolution making clear that this government recognize no kind of commitment contained in secret understandings of the past with foreign governments which permit this kind of enslavement." Shortly after this speech, General Omar Bradley was replaced as chairman of the Joint Chiefs of Staff by Admiral Radford. General Bradley was known as a supporter of containment, as an opponent of expansion of the Korean war, and as a cooperative Allied leader, while Admiral Radford was considered an advocate of more aggressive action in the Far East and the favorite of politicians who were prepared to ignore our allies in that area.

Liberation: Effects

This new emphasis in policy almost certainly contributed to the final achievement in 1953 of an armistice in Korea, and the Communist rulers may have been impressed for some time by the apparent vigor and assertiveness of the new administration. The liberation period in our policy may also have persuaded the Russian and Chinese Communist leaders that they had reached the danger point in their relations with the United States. However, at least so far as we can see, the talk about a rollback and about liberation had no influence upon the Soviet grip upon the peoples of East Central Europe.

On the other hand, the apparent American infatuation with the belief that East Central Europe could quickly be emancipated frightened our allies in Western Europe, increased the strain upon American relations with Britain and France in particular, stimulated the wave of anti-Americanism in the anti-Communist, the neutral, and the neutralist countries, and contributed substantially to the Soviet Union's remarkable achievement in portraying the United States as an aggressor state and the Soviet Union as the leader of those seeking peace. Finally, it helped to weaken the movement for European integration. For example, the French Parliament would have accepted the European Defense Community only with the most grudging reluctance in the best of circumstances. However, an apparently "reckless American policy" contributed to the defeat of EDC by helping persuade many Frenchmen that the United States was an aggressive state which in EDC sought an organization under German control to help drive the Russians from East Central Europe. The French Chamber of Deputies would probably have accepted EDC in the atmosphere of August, 1955; it could not accept it in the atmosphere of August, 1954.

The leaders and peoples of Western Europe were more alarmed concerning American policy than the facts warranted. However, their alarm was an accurate reflection of their extreme anxiety. They were jittery because of their continued dependence upon American aid and upon American strength and leadership; their fear of the return of isolationism in the United States; their uncertainty concerning the Republicans, after twenty years of dealing with the Democrats; the apparent power of Senator McCarthy and the extreme right-wing Republicans in the new administration; and the growing comprehension of and fear of nuclear war. Liberation to Western Europeans implied that the American Government sought the violent overthrow of Communist rule in East Central Europe; it meant the resurgence of a Big Stick, go-it-alone movement in the United States; it increased the likelihood of expansion of the Korean war or of the Formosa conflict into a general war. Thus, the speech of Secretary Dulles (January 12, 1954) in which he said the United States would henceforth "depend primarily upon a great capacity to retaliate, instantly by means and at places of our choosing," to many Europeans meant almost the end of the world.[4] In short, while we did not significantly influence our enemies, we terrified our friends with our new enthusiasm.

[4] The phrase, "No annihilation without representation," attributed to Mr. Arnold Toynbee, became popular in England after Mr. Dulles' speech.

Gradually, even the most worried West Europeans began to comprehend that the new doctrine of liberation was largely political and verbal. The new administration spoke belligerently, but reduced expenditures for American armed forces. It accepted an armistice in Korea for which the previous administration would have been furiously attacked. In spite of the new political warfare organizations and of the talk concerning psychological warfare gimmicks and "seizing the initiative," it allowed the June 1953 riots in Eastern Germany and Czechoslovakia to pass without Western interference. Indeed, the American Government waited two weeks before it announced any policy. It then revealed that it did not intend to intervene, although it emphasized the significance of the unrest and the warmth of American friendship for the peoples of East Germany and Czechoslovakia. Three and a half weeks after the uprisings had begun, the United States offered food to the Soviet Union for the German and Czechoslovak people. Ultimately, 4,000,000 food parcels served as a substitute for assistance in breaking Communist control.

Even American failure to act upon the June revolts did not eliminate West European fear concerning American ambitions for liberation, because American speeches and occasional American actions in the Far East kept the suspicion alive. The United States decision not to intervene in Indo-China, especially during the long agony of Dien Bien Phu; the gradual "leashing" of both Syngman Rhee and Chiang Kai-Shek; American assistance to the Chinese Nationalists in evacuating the coastal islands; the new approach toward the atomic peril, especially President Eisenhower's December 8, 1953 proposal for an atomic pool under the UN and for cooperation in developing peacetime uses of the atom; the gradual disappearance of references to liberation and rollback; the obvious unwillingness of the United States to use force or even pressure to bring about the reunification of Germany and Korea; and the new emphasis upon peace and prosperity have finally convinced both our friends and our enemies that the American Government does not seriously consider a policy of pressure or force to free the peoples of East Central Europe from Soviet control.

Containment Revisited

American policy during the past two or three years has apparently swung dizzily from the mean of containment to the extremes of intervention and appeasement, as one crisis followed another and as one or another school of thought seemed to gain ascendancy. There has been serious conflict within the administration concerning policy with regard to these extraordinarily difficult problems, and there has often been public disagreement among the President, his Secretary of State, and the Republican leaders in the houses of Congress, especially the Senate. There has also been wide discrepancy between policy speeches and policy itself. Consequently, it is difficult to define and describe American policy toward East Central Europe over the past two years, particularly when that program has been largely a reflection of policies for other areas of the world or of some general strategy with no immediate implications with regard to this area.

The word and the concept of liberation began to lose currency early in 1954, and disappeared even before the fall elections of that year. The opposition to the abandonment of the liberation theme has often been noisy, but it has never been effective. Indeed, criticism of the Geneva "summit" conference in August 1955 was almost negligible, although the American Government had within a few months completely reversed its position toward such a meeting.

There has thus far been no substitute for liberation, although the currently popular Communist phrase, "peaceful coexistence," has been adopted by some anti-Communists, even, on occasion, by President Eisenhower and Sir Winston Churchill. In any case, there has been little change, if any, with regard to general American goals. However, there have been important tactical changes and, even more important, the strategic basis of American policy concerning the conflict with Communism may have been considerably revised.

The new policy rests upon a new global strategy and above all, upon a revised military policy. As President Eisenhower remarked in February, 1955, the world is in a situation in which "neither side is getting what it desires in this whole world struggle," but in which both "at least have enough sense to agree that they must not pursue it deliberately and through force of arms." Both the Soviet Union and the United States apparently realize that there is now no alternative to peace.

American policy is now based on the view that there is no predictable date of maximum danger and that the strength and determination of the Communists confront the United States with a long struggle, such as that over the Eastern Question or that involved in the defense of the frontiers of the Roman Empire against the barbarians. It has been heavily influenced by the attitude of most Americans toward the huge costs and the delicate complications involved in our program. It was spurred by reflection concerning new weapons, nuclear weapons and guided missiles in particular, and their impact on costs, planning, and policy. It has been affected, but only slightly, by the apparent shift in Soviet tactics, notably the trip of several leaders to Belgrade, where Khrushchev apologized for previous Soviet actions and sought to improve Soviet-Yugoslav relations; the sudden Soviet decision to accept a treaty with Austria; the generally affable and relaxed attitude recently displayed by the Soviet leaders; the visit of Khrushchev and Bulganin to India, Burma, and Afghanistan; and the new Soviet emphases upon the Middle East and upon economic assistance to "underdeveloped countries."

Fundamentally, American policy since about the summer of 1954 has created a new version of containment. The United States seeks to prevent war, to prevent the expansion of Communist power, to strengthen the areas of the world most susceptible to Communist manoeuvres, to persuade the Communist rulers that this country will resist expansion but that it will not attack the Communist states, and to direct the energies of all of the peoples and governments of the world away from war and toward the constructive endeavors of peace. This last goal, which is assuming ever greater significance as the stalemate between the Communist powers and the West becomes more firm, may be the most important of all. In effect, the American Government is seeking to create a kind of peaceful competition, in which the principles upon which democracy is based would compete with those of Communism in a contest for the minds and souls of the world. In the words of President Eisenhower as he spoke to the American Bar Association in Philadelphia on August 24, 1955: "The system or group of systems which most effectively musters its strength in support of peace and demonstrates its ability to advance the well-being, the happiness, of the individual will win the support and the loyal friendship of the majority of the peoples of the world.

The new containment, like the old containment, rests basically on faith in Western civilization and on faith that the Soviet system bears the seeds of its own decay. It has abandoned the search for a sudden "violent upthrust of liberty," and instead relies upon sustained Western firmness and progress to contribute to the slow erosion or modification of the Soviet system.

This new approach involves certain shadings or emphases which were ignored or neglected during the brief period during which the hope for immediate or early liberation burned so high. It places renewed stress upon a close and genuine partnership with other free nations in a joint effort. It recognizes that most of the problems facing this country and the world are infinitely complicated and that solutions can be attained only by slow, laborious, joint effort. It places a heavy accent upon diplomacy and upon trying to break up the present tight political relationship between the Soviet Government and the governments of the other Communist states. Conversely, it places somewhat less emphasis upon promoting revolution or upon turning peoples against their Communist governments. In other words, it assumes the continued survival of Communism and of Communist governments, and it clearly indicates that the United States will not attempt the violent overthrow of the Soviet Government or the forceful ejection of Soviet authority from East Central Europe.

Above all, the American Government seeks to turn the thoughts and energies of the world away from war and toward peace and the peaceful, constructive use of the world's resources. This approach, which has been most clear and most significant in the Eisenhower program for peaceful development of atomic energy, aims to reduce fear, to demote military power, to channel competition into peaceful currents, and to create a new concentration upon economic growth, assistance to underdeveloped territories, and peaceful competition, where the hazards are least and where the free world can compete most successfully with the Communist system.

The new policy or program does not ignore the maintenance or development of Western military strength and unity. Indeed, it recognizes that the maintenance of the American capability to destroy the bases of Soviet strength constitutes the principal deterrent to aggression. It also places a high priority upon continental air defenses as a deterrent to aggression and a factor in an effective containment policy.

However, the military program has new emphases or accents, due both to new weapons developments and to the progress made during the past eight years in rebuilding the military strength of the United States and of Western Europe. Thus, the budget for this fiscal year made the Air Force the preponderant military arm of the nation, both in terms of money investment and in terms of manpower. Under this budget, the Air Force was granted almost as much money as the Army and Navy together, and the number of men in the Air Force was fixed at almost the same level as that in the Army.

The United States seeks to reduce its expenditures for military purposes to something like a plateau, high enough to prevent war and to make containment an effective policy and yet not so high as to be unbearable or crushing in the long strain ahead. The new program emphasizes the continued production and refinement of nuclear weapons, the development of air power and air defense, the reduction of air and sea forces to a stable level, and the attainment of greater mobility, so that forces may be moved quickly from the United States to areas of conflict or to points where the Soviet threat is great. For example, the United States Army on June 30, 1956 will have a strength lower by 700,000 men than it had when the Eisenhower administration took office. To some degree, this new program threatens the effectiveness of containment, because it relies so extensively upon nuclear and air power and because it reduces the capability of the United States to prevent or to fight the most likely kind of war—the local, "limited" action, such as that in Korea or Indo-China.

American strategic policy continues to emphasize the maintenance and extension of the Western alliance system. NATO has vastly greater military resources at hand now than it did in 1949, and it has been enlarged to include Greece, Turkey, and Western Germany. Moreover, the years of joint effort have laid solid foundations for new common military customs and traditions, and experience in cooperation and coordination in the military field will almost certainly have political and economic effects far beyond the military sphere. Finally, the American system of alliances has been extended throughout the world by an administration which many Western Europeans feared as isolationist.

In addition, the United States seeks controlled world disarmament. There has probably been more misunderstanding, confusion, and plain boredom—largely Soviet inspired—concerning disarmament and programs for dealing with nuclear weapons than concerning any other issue of the past ten years. The United States has always been willing to submit to genuine international armament control, providing an effective system of inspection and supervision were devised and accepted. The Soviet Union has blocked all efforts to achieve an effective system, but the recent spectacular effort of President Eisenhower may so reduce Soviet suspicion that a new approach which works gradually toward lower armament levels may ultimately be accepted by the Soviet Union. Controlled disarmament would help free East Central Europe from Soviet control by creating a new international atmosphere and by reducing the military means now at the heart of the system for enforcing Soviet rule.

The gradual death and disappearance of the concept of liberation and the slow development of a new pattern in American policy have led to some worry lest East Central Europe be forgotten or abandoned. This fear has been particularly strong among refugees from Soviet control and among the millions of Americans whose parents or grandparents came from East Central Europe. It has grown considerably since the Geneva "summit" conference, which can be interpreted as the first attempt of the powers to seek "coexistence."

This is a natural, indeed, an inevitable and healthy reaction, but there is little evidence to support the view that the United States has modified its basic goals. It is true that President Eisenhower at the Geneva conference did not press hard to place the plight of East Central Europe on the conference agenda, and Marshal Bulganin was not challenged when he declared that the "popular and democratic republics were established in those countries by the peoples themselves and on the basis of their own free will." However, the speeches of President Eisenhower and of Vice-President Nixon to the American Bar Association effectively refuted the charge and re-emphasized the key position which East Central Europe plays in the American program. As President Eisenhower declared: "We asserted then [at Geneva] and we shall always hold—that there can be no true peace which involves acceptance of a *status quo* in which we find injustice to many nations, repressions of human beings on a gigantic scale, and with constructive effort paralyzed in many areas by fear."

Conclusions

In spite of all the efforts the United States and its allies have made in behalf of the captive peoples of East Central Europe, their plight in 1955 was even worse than it was in 1947. In fact, Soviet control is more firm, and the reshaping of this area along Communist lines is proceeding at a rapid pace.

However, the Soviet position in East Central Europe is by no means as secure as it appears. The American people and the American Government have freely and knowingly accepted the responsibilities of world leadership, and they have learned that American security will remain in peril so long as other peoples are oppressed and so long as the Soviet Union remains astride Central Europe. This progress is clear not only from positive American actions, but also from "negative" developments, such as the collapse of the Progressive Party, the conversion of most of those who advocated submission to the Soviet Union at the Soviet price, and the gradual fading away of those who believed the United States should adopt a belligerent attitude, even if it cost the friendship of our allies. Finally, while the United States recognizes that the entire world is now locked in a military stalemate with no real alternative to peace, it has clearly rejected the Soviet theme of "peaceful coexistence." Secretary Dulles in a speech at Williamsburg in the spring of 1954 asserted most effectively that there could be "no agreed partition between freedom and despotism" and that the conflict could not be settled so long as Communist objectives remain unchanged. This remains at the heart of American policy.

Nevertheless, the United States has not only failed in its efforts to free East Central Europe—which it was not within its power to accomplish—but it has not yet succeeded in helping Western Europe to regain its old power and confidence. Western Europe is still dependent on the United States for its security, and it will be many years, if ever, before Western Europe will become an effective counterweight to Soviet power. Moreover, with the failure of EDC as an effort to include Western Germany into an *integrated* Western Europe, the entire German problem remains one which could destroy the entire edifice so laboriously constructed over the past few years. The American program to unify Europe and the entire effort to contain Soviet power may yet founder in Germany.

It is easy to criticize American policy toward East Central Europe, but one should realize that American statesmen have had numerous handicaps or disadvantages. The United States, which seeks to preserve important values and institutions, cannot use the same methods as the Communists, who are uninhibited in their strategy and in their tactics. American leaders are not only responsible to the American people but are also sensitive to the wishes of the peoples of allied states, while the Soviet leaders have no political limitations upon their powers. Moreover, the American leaders are governing a nation just a few years removed from isolation at a time when every corner of the world seeks American advice, assistance, and leadership. The United States is also at the head of an alliance system for the first time in its history. Managing an alliance is a difficult endeavor for even the most experienced state, and the present system is subject to strains and conflicts such as no other alliance has endured. The United States still lacks a system for co-ordinating all the agencies and institutions involved in American and allied policy. Above all, the United States and its allies have not yet created a positive philosophy or "applicable body of theory" upon which to base the broad outlines of their policy in this time of great crisis.

In summary, American policy toward East Central Europe since 1947 has been courageous, generous, principled, generally consistent, and as effective as American power and the world situation allowed. The United States has refused to adopt an aggressive attitude toward the Soviet Union, and at the same time it has refused to abandon East Central Europe to its present fate. It has based its policies on the brutal fact that in an atomic age there is no alternative to peace. It has rejected solutions to the present crisis which would have provided temporary advantage, but which would have denied justice and equity, increased the peril to Western Europe, and promoted world fear and insecurity. It has also decided not to flirt with intervention or with insurrection, which are dangerous and contrary to Western principles, although for a brief period it succumbed to the thesis that the captive peoples could somehow easily be liberated. Instead, the United States rests its program on defensive strength and on faith in "the vast possibility for peaceful change." As the author of the containment thesis wrote, United States policy is based on "long-term, patient but firm and vigilant containment of Russian expansive tendencies" and on the belief that strength and union, the exposure of the Soviet system, and steady adherence to the basic principles upon which Western civilization is based will sooner or later pull the captive peoples free from the Soviet embrace.

Part Two

CREATION OF A SOVIET EMPIRE IN EUROPE

Chapter 5

Baltic States

ARVID SCHWABE

Twenty Years of Coexistence

THE BALTIC nations were the first to try to coexist peacefully with the Soviet Union. In the peace treaties of 1920 with Estonia, Latvia, and Lithuania, the Soviet Union recognized "forever" the sovereignty and independence of the Baltic Republics, with all legal consequences emanating from such recognition. But, at the same time, Bolshevik propaganda did not conceal the Kremlin's belief that treaties concluded with capitalist countries are only temporary devices, giving Communism respite for preparing the road to world revolution.

Taking advantage of a decree on the right of self-determination of nations, enacted by the Council of People's Commissars on November 15, 1917, eleven minority nations of the Russian Empire proclaimed their independence. At that time the number of Great Russians amounted to 75 million, out of a total population of 140 million in the Russian Empire. But only the Finns, Estonians, Latvians, Lithuanians and Poles succeeded in defending their independence against Soviet Russian aggression. The main driving power in subduing the nations which had tried to break away from Russian Bolshevism was Joseph Stalin, who was then Commissar for the Affairs of Nationalities in the Soviet Empire. After having inherited Lenin's mantle, Stalin renewed efforts to gain control of the Baltic Republics. But after he had failed in an attempted Communist revolt in Estonia, in December 1924, further Soviet efforts to reconquer the Baltic States were abandoned for the time being.

The year 1933 inaugurated a series of fateful international

developments which ultimately led to the second World War. Japan had marched into Manchuria. Hitler came into power in Germany. In September of 1934, the Soviet Union joined the League of Nations. The question of organizing an Eastern Locarno to curb Hitler's aggressive designs became a subject of discussion between the great European powers. But before anything came of it, Hitler started to change the map of Europe. On March 13, 1938, he invaded Austria. On September 29, Great Britain and France signed the Munich Agreement with Nazi Germany. On March 15, 1939, mutilated Czechoslovakia ceased to exist as an independent state, and on March 22, Lithuania was forced to cede Germany the Klaipeda district. Immediately thereafter Hitler came forth with territorial demands against Poland, to which Great Britain replied with the conclusion of a British-Polish defense pact.

In April of 1939 negotiations between the Soviet Union, Great Britain and France to create a united front against the Axis powers, were opened in Moscow. They failed, because the Kremlin engaged in parallel negotiations with Hitlerite Germany, which offered Moscow more favorable terms. The objections of Chamberlain to granting the Soviet Union unilateral power to occupy the Baltic States precipitated the replacement of Litvinov by Molotov as Foreign Commissar. On August 23, 1939, Molotov and Ribbentrop signed the Soviet-Nazi pact of friendship and nonaggression. In addition they signed a secret protocol, according to which Germany agreed to the inclusion of Finland, Estonia, Latvia and Bessarabia in Soviet Russia's sphere of influence. In a subsequent agreement Lithuania was also included in the Soviet sphere.

Treaties of Mutual Assistance

On September 1, 1939, the German *blitzkrieg* invasion of Poland began, and in four weeks Poland was conquered. On September 17, the Red Army crossed Poland's eastern border, allegedly to liberate Western Ukraine and Byelorussia from the yoke of the Polish lords. The Baltic States had declared their neutrality. Polish refugees swarmed into Latvia and Lithuania. A Polish submarine found refuge in the harbor of Tallin. On September 29, the two aggressors signed an agreement to divide Poland between them. *Izvestia* defined the Kremlin's attitude in an article of October 9 as follows: "One may respect or hate Hitlerism just as any other system of political views. This is a matter of taste. But to undertake war for the annihilation of Hitlerism is to commit criminal folly in politics."

The next victim of Soviet intrigue was Estonia. Using as a pretext the escape of the Polish submarine, mentioned above, from internment in Tallin, Molotov informed the Estonian Envoy in Moscow, on September 20, that the Red Navy had been ordered to steam into Estonian territorial waters, since Estonia obviously was not in a position to defend them herself. Molotov invited the Estonian Foreign Minister to come to Moscow, allegedly to talk about trade relations. But there he was faced with an ultimatum to sign "a mutual assistance pact." Estonia was to lease land on Estonian territory to the Soviet Union for naval and air bases, and to admit Russian garrisons up to 25,000 men.

Well aware that huge Soviet armed forces had been concentrated at the Estonian border, the Estonian Government had no choice but to bow to Moscow's dictate. Estonia signed on September 28. Latvia's turn came next, and on October 5, a Soviet-Latvian treaty of "mutual assistance" was signed in Moscow. Lithuania followed suit on October 10. All three agreements were identical, with exceptions in some details. The military occupation of the Baltic States became an accomplished fact, even though on paper the Baltic Republics had ceded the Soviet Union bases on their territories in a leasehold agreement for a limited period only. The chain of Red naval bases extended from Paldiski over the Estonian islands to Liepaja, permitting the Soviets to block all approaches to the Baltic ports.

The Soviet-Baltic pacts, identical in form and contents, were masterpieces of cunning. The real aims of the Kremlin became apparent soon thereafter. Article 5 of the pact with Latvia reads: "The carrying into effect of the present pact must in no way affect the sovereign rights of the contracting parties, their economic and social system, and their military measures." It has later been established that as soon as these agreements had come into effect, the General Staff of the Red Army issued operative maps of the Baltic territories, dated "First Edition, 1939" and carrying a title in large letters: "Lithuanian and Latvian Socialist Soviet Republics."

Thus it appears that even in 1939 the Kremlin was bent on the annexation of the Baltic Republics. The formal completion of the annexation was, however, delayed because of Finland's resistance against signing on similar terms. Having renounced the Russo-

Finnish nonaggression pact, Russia invaded Finnish territory on November 30. On December 14, the League of Nations branded the Soviet Union as an aggressor and expelled her from the League. After one hundred days of heroic resistance, Finland was forced to capitulate, and to grant to the Soviet Union important territorial concessions.

On March 29, 1940, in an address to the All-Union Supreme Soviet Molotov said of Soviet-Baltic relations: "In rebuttal of the opinion held in imperialistic circles inimical to the Soviet Union, the independence and political freedom of Estonia, Latvia and Lithuania have not suffered . . . The pacts with these States are being carried out in a satisfactory manner, and this creates promises for a further improvement in relations." The real meaning behind these words of Molotov became apparent ten weeks later, when the Kremlin cast away its mask posing as a protector of Baltic independence. Having never had any illusions with regard to the Soviet aims in the Baltics, Hitler had, in October 1939, already invited the Baltic Germans (*Volksdeutsche*) to resettle in the newly conquered western provinces of Poland. For this purpose, he had concluded special repatriation agreements with the Governments of the Baltic States, which were later complemented by a similar agreement with the Soviet Union.

As long as the Soviets were engaged in the Finnish War, their occupation forces in the Baltic bases behaved with restraint. However, the import of Soviet propaganda materials, such as pamphlets and films, was being greatly stepped up, and hundreds of trained Soviet agents were smuggled into the Baltic States as "technicians," needed for the construction of fortifications in the Soviet bases. In April and May of 1940, proclamations were distributed, inviting the workers to overthrow their "fascist" governments. But when nothing came of it, the Soviet Legations in the Baltic capitals denounced such "provocations by irresponsible elements" as harmful for friendly relations between the Soviet Union and the Baltic States. On May 17, 1940, the Latvian Government, having been alerted by the duplicity of the Soviet attitude and foreseeing no good for the future, granted special emergency powers to Charles Zarine, the Latvian Envoy in London. By virtue of these powers, Minister Zarine was granted the right to transfer, dismiss and appoint diplomatic and consular representatives of Latvia in foreign countries.

On May 25, Molotov suddenly presented the Lithuanian Government with a note accusing Lithuania of kidnapping two Soviet soldiers. A Lithuanian proposal to bring the case before a mixed Soviet-Lithuanian commission of investigation was rejected by Moscow, which was bent on creating a pretext for the annexation of the Baltic Republics. On June 8, Molotov came forth with accusations against all the Baltic States, charging them with having formed an aggressive military alliance against the Soviet Union, even though Molotov's charges were completely unsubstantiated. On June 14, he presented the Lithuanian Government with an ultimatum, demanding free admission of unlimited Soviet armed forces. He also demanded the establishment of a new Government "friendly" to the Soviet Union and ready to assure the "honest" execution of the mutual assistance pact. The Red Army invaded Lithuania in force on June 15. President Smetona, unwilling to endorse this act of violence, fled to Germany the same day.

On June 16, Moscow presented similar ultimata to Latvia and Estonia. Molotov notified the Envoys of these countries orally that the Red forces deployed at the frontiers would start marching on June 17. The same day, *Pravda* repeated Molotov's accusations with added comments that the Baltic "fascist" Governments had been preparing an attack on the Soviet Union. If there had been an ounce of truth in these charges, the Soviet authorities, after having seized the Baltic archives, had ample opportunity to publish the text of any such aggressive treaty of alliance, but there was none.

According to the testimony of Professor V. Kreve-Mickevicius, who was Deputy Prime Minister of the Lithuanian puppet Government in 1940, Molotov had, in a personal conversation which took place in Moscow on July 2, 1940, spoken as follows about Soviet aspirations in the Baltics:

> . . . You must take a good look at reality and understand that in the future small nations will have to disappear. Your Lithuania along with the other Baltic nations, including Finland, will have to join the glorious family of the Soviet Union.
>
> . . . .
>
> We are more firmly convinced now than ever that our brilliant comrade, Lenin, was not mistaken when he assured us that the Second World War will help us to gain power throughout all Europe as the First helped us to gain power in Russia.
>
> . . . .
>
> Lithuania cannot remain an exception . . . You would be doing the most intelligent thing if you would accept without any hesitation the

leadership of the Communist Party which is determined to effect the unification of all Europe and the application of the new order.[1]

Soviet Absorption of Baltic States

The events which took place in the Baltic countries during the summer of 1940, after military occupation had been completed, were scenes from a puppet-show, made in Moscow. The new "people's governments," destined to prepare their countries for the forthcoming incorporation into the Soviet realm, were handpicked and directed by three emissaries of the Kremlin, who had installed themselves in the Baltic capitals. They were V. Dekanozov, Deputy Foreign Commissar, in charge of Lithuania; A. Vyshinsky, Deputy Chairman of the Council of People's Commissars, in charge of Latvia; and A. Zhdanov, Politbureau member and Party Secretary for the Leningrad District, in charge of Estonia. In order to cover Soviet violence by a veil of legality, President Päts of Estonia and President Ulmanis of Latvia were temporarily retained in office, though they were in actual fact prisoners of the occupation regime, even previous to their deportation in July.

The head of the new Soviet-approved Government of Estonia was J. Vares, a writer with leftist inclinations; A. Kirchensteins, a professor of veterinary medicine, was installed as Prime Minister of Latvia, and the journalist J. Paleckis emerged as head of the Lithuanian puppet Government. For the transitional period, preceding actual annexation, the Moscow wire-pullers had deemed it wise to appoint preferably fellow travelers and befuddled leftists to cabinet posts, rather than Communists. Only the Ministries of the Interior and the political police were directed by genuine Communists. All the decrees and declarations of the puppet Governments emanated from the respective Soviet Legations, to be released to the public by the "sovereign" Baltic Governments. Press, radio, and telegraph were under Soviet Russian control.

On July 14 and 15 "elections of people's parliaments" were held in all three Baltic Republics. The Communists had corrupted the franchise laws, providing for universal and secret ballot, by depriving the courts of the right to check on the legality of the procedure. Only one list of candidates—the Communist-sponsored "Union of the Working People"—was approved by the Communist

[1] Third Interim Report of the Select Committee on Communist Aggression, 83rd Congress, 2nd Session (Washington, 1954), pp. 341–344.

Electoral Committee, and all dissenting lists were rejected. In Estonia and in Latvia, a group of patriotic citizens had attempted to present to the voters a list of independent candidates. According to the law, this was perfectly legal. But such action was immediately suppressed by the government, and the initiators were arrested. In spite of all-out propaganda for participation in the ballot, and unmistakable threats against absentees, a great many citizens, particularly in rural districts, abstained from voting for the single pro-Communist list of candidates. But passive resistance on the part of the people was of no avail. The results of the elections had been calculated by Moscow well in advance, with no one being in a position to contest the count. The day after the elections it was announced that 92.8% of the voters had cast their ballot for the single pro-Communist slate in Estonia, 97.6% in Latvia, and 99.19% in Lithuania. By mistake the London representative of Tass reported the results as early as July 15, while the elections were still in progress.

All three Baltic puppet parliaments convened on July 21. While the question of joining the Soviet Union had been deliberately banned from discussion during the election campaign, it now became the first order of the day. The buildings where the deliberations took place were surrounded by Red troops and tanks, and agents of the NKVD in civilian clothes supervised the behavior of the delegates. On the very first day the Lithuanian and Latvian diets voted "unanimously" for joining the Soviet Union. But the Estonian Communists, having requested to be granted the semi-independent status of Outer Mongolia, yielded only on July 22, after their request had been declined by Moscow. The voting procedure was illegal in any case, because the Baltic constitutions provide that fundamental changes in the form of government or of sovereignty must be confirmed by a referendum, in order to become legal. No such referendum or plebiscite has ever been held, nor could be legally held under foreign occupation. Nevertheless the All-Union Supreme Soviet, assembled in Moscow, "accepted" the Baltic Republics into the Soviet Union. Lithuania was annexed on August 3; Latvia on August 5; and Estonia on August 6, 1940. The diplomatic representatives of the Baltic States, accredited in the United States and other free foreign countries, immediately protested against this illegal incorporation.

The absorption of the Baltic Republics into the U.S.S.R. was recognized by the Axis powers and a few neutral countries, including Sweden. However, most of the free Western democracies followed the example of the United States in declining recognition. On July 23, Mr. Sumner Welles, Acting Secretary of State, had come forth with a declaration (allegedly drafted by President Roosevelt personally), condemning the "devious processes" by which "the political independence and territorial integrity of the three small Baltic republics were to be deliberately annihilated by their more powerful neighbor," that is, the Soviet Union. After due tribute to "the admirable progress in self-government" of the Baltic nations, the Acting Secretary emphatically declared that "the people of the United States are opposed to predatory activities no matter whether they are carried on by the use of force or by the threat of force." The United States has, up to the present day, steadfastly adhered to the principles expressed in this declaration, and the diplomatic representatives of the Baltic States continue to enjoy official recognition and freedom of action in the fulfillment of their duties, even though their countries are subjected to Soviet occupation.

First Mass Deportations

The predatory designs of the Kremlin towards the Baltics, even before the start of the war, are well illustrated by the infamous Serov order No. 0001223, issued on October 11, 1939, the same day that Molotov gave a banquet in honor of the Lithuanian Foreign Minister who had just affixed his signature to the text of the Soviet-Lithuanian "mutual assistance" pact. The order of General Serov, Deputy Commissar of State Security of the U.S.S.R., devoted to "the Procedure for Carrying out the Deportation of Anti-Soviet Elements from Lithuania, Latvia and Estonia," consists of a series of most inhuman instructions to the agents of the NKVD, who were organizing mass deportations of Baltic citizens, to be carried out after the incorporation of the Baltic States into the Soviet Union. The first preparatory step for this crime of genocide was the compilation of lists of "socially dangerous elements" in the Baltic Republics, by agents of the secret police, while the pacts of "mutual assistance" were still in force. A schedule of seizures was planned so that prospective victims would move in several waves to slave labor camps, for work in the various construction programs of the NKVD, such as building roads, digging canals, lumbering, mining, etc.

Owing to its magnitude, the "Serov plan" required much time and effort for preparation and execution. Due to the outbreak of the German-Russian war in the summer of 1941, only the first phase of the deportation plan could be put into operation, because of the swift advance of the German armed forces. In the early hours of June 14, 1941, tens of thousands of innocent and unsuspecting Baltic citizens, men, women and children, were dragged from their homes, to be loaded for transportation to far away concentration camps. At the railroad stations of departure, the heads of families were separated from their wives and children, never to see them again. These unfortunates had not been charged with any crimes, but were simply carried away on the basis of Serov's administrative order, as a preventive measure against "undesirables."

Arrests and convictions of "counterrevolutionaries" had already started in 1940, as soon as the NKVD had assumed full control. They were tried in accordance with the Soviet Criminal Code for "crimes" committed during the years of Baltic independence, even though the Soviet code was not in force at that time. In less than a year, 7,161 persons were arrested in Latvia alone, among them 404 women. In the summer of 1941, after the Soviet agents had hastily left under pressure of the German armed forces, 979 bodies of Soviet victims were uncovered in mass graves in Latvia, 1,950 in Estonia, and 1,114 in Lithuania. Some of the inmates of prisons had been carried away to Soviet Russia before the Germans arrived, but others were shot without trial. Arrests and deportations continued even after June 14, up to the last days of Soviet rule in the Baltics. The number of deportees from Estonia during this period approximated 60,000; from Latvia, 35,000; and from Lithuania, 34,000. Among the deportees were the Presidents of Estonia and Latvia, many former cabinet ministers, members of parliament, army officers, judges, priests, educators, and other representatives of the national intelligentsia. But the majority of the deportees were employees and laborers—53% in Latvia, and 59% in Estonia.

Nationalization and Sovietization

On July 22–23, 1940, the Baltic puppet parliaments had adopted decrees of nationalization of land, banking, and large industrial and commercial enterprises. Individual farming was not abolished at that time, but it was stipulated that no farming units should exceed 30 hectares (74 acres). All land in excess of this norm was expropriated and turned over to a State land fund, for allocation to peasants who had little or no land. The maximum grant for new farmers was 12 hectares (approximately 30 acres) in Estonia, and 10 hectares in Latvia. This reform had purely political aims.

There were at that time about 660,000 farms in the three Baltic countries. In Latvia the reform led to the expropriation of 21.4% of all privately owned farmland, yielding the State land fund 961,394 hectares. Out of this land fund 51,762 new farms were created, and 23,321 small holders received an additional plot of 3 hectares or less. Besides, 30 State farms, or *sovkhozy,* were created, averaging 670 hectares.[2]

The new farms were to be financed with State loans, and to be equipped with farm inventory and livestock expropriated from the more prosperous peasants. But actually very few loans were granted, and there were not enough farm implements and livestock available for all to start with. According to official Soviet data, only 6% of the new farmers in Latvia owned a horse, and only 8% had a roof over their heads in the spring of 1941. Similar conditions prevailed in the other Baltic Republics. It did not take the new farmers long to realize that the "land reform" was a hoax, devised by Moscow for justifying the "social revolution" which they had imported to the Baltic countries, and for paving the road to collectivization. The majority of the landless farmers ignored the opportunity to receive land on Bolshevik terms. In Latvia, only 62% of the expropriated land was actually allocated to new tenants. In Estonia, 354,000 hectares, out of a land fund comprising 758,258 hectares, remained uncultivated. In order to pauperize the more prosperous farmers, excessive and progressively increasing taxes were levied on them, exceeding by ten times the taxes they had been paying during the period of independence.

While the Bolshevik agrarian reform of 1940–41 spelled disaster for agriculture, the nationalization and socialization of industry and commerce proceeded in a more orderly manner. The Baltic constitutions of 1940 provided for either State property or cooperative property, while small private enterprises had not yet been

[2] A. Drizul, *Ustanovlenie Sovetskoi vlasti v Latvii,* Akademia Nauk SSSR, Istoricheskie Zapiski, Vol. 45 (Moscow, 1954), pp. 70–74.

abolished at that time. Previous to the Soviet occupation, Latvia had 6,067 industrial enterprises. By December of 1940, the Soviet regime had nationalized 1,477 of the larger factories, which altogether employed 65% of all industrial workers and were responsible for 84.4% of the total production. Only 15.6% of the total industrial production remained in private hands. By the same time 1,147 commercial firms, responsible for 71% of all turnover, had been nationalized, leaving only 29% of the turnover to private management.[3] The largest and most modern factories were taken over by the Moscow Government and were managed by Russian specialists. The nationalization of banks, apartment houses, and the real property of organizations and churches had taken place already in October of 1940. All bank deposits in excess of 1,000 lats, litai, or kroons, were confiscated. All gold funds and foreign securities were transferred to Moscow. Baltic assets in foreign countries were claimed by the Soviets as Government property. But, since the Roosevelt administration had, on July 13, 1940, frozen all Baltic assets in the United States, Soviet efforts to get hold of them failed. Great Britain acted in a similar way. Later, in 1950, after total sovietization and collectivization of the Baltic countries had been completed, even the smallest private enterprises and shops were prohibited, and corresponding changes in the constitutions were made.

Members of the Soviet armed forces and of the occupation regime were amazed by the high standard of living which they found in the Baltic countries in 1940. They marvelled at the abundance of consumers' goods and their availability on the free market for comparatively low prices. This contrasted grossly with conditions with which they were familiar at home. They eagerly supplied themselves and their families with much wanted goods, and shipped them in great quantities to Russia. In order to crush "the economic power of the bourgeoisie" in the Baltic countries, and to bring their standard of living down to the Soviet level, Moscow introduced on November 25, 1940, a new rate of exchange for the Baltic currencies, the purchasing power of which had been about ten times above the ruble. The Estonian kroon was declared equal to 1.25 rubles, the Latvian lat to 1 ruble, and the Lithuanian litas to 0.90 rubles. In order to make the devaluation of the Baltic currencies less painful for the workers and other wage-earners, wages

[3] *Ibid.*, pp. 64–66.

and salaries were raised to the allegedly "higher" Soviet level. But while the nominal increase of wages amounted to about 150 per cent, prices in rubles rose from 100 to 400 per cent, so that the cost of living on the average was increased by about one third. Four months later, the Baltic currencies were suddenly and without warning withdrawn from circulation, thus depriving many persons of their savings, which they had failed to convert into Russian rubles.

Parallel to the destruction of the economic and social foundations of the Baltic nations, the Bolshevik occupiers waged a ruthless war against the ideological and moral resistance of the people to Communism. Their efforts were in particular directed towards winning over the souls of the youth. Many thousands of books, dealing with questions of history, political ideology, religion, and philosophy, were taken out of the libraries and book stores and were destroyed. Even statistical publications were included, because in the Soviet realm statistics are secrets of the State. Though the Soviet Constitution grants all citizens freedom of the press and assembly, as well as to form organizations, it was declared on the authority of Mr. Vyshinsky that these freedoms are only for the working people, the vanguard of which is the Communist Party, and are denied to "class enemies." Accordingly, all political, cultural and religious organizations which did not conform with Communism were prohibited.

The universities and other higher institutions of learning were being sovietized. The schools for theology, history and philosophy at the Baltic universities were liquidated. Instead, the study of the Soviet Constitution and the "Short Course of the History of the Communist Party" were introduced as obligatory subjects. The school system was radically reorganized, with a trend towards Bolshevization and Russianization. Study of the Russian language became obligatory for all school children and students. Communist Youth organizations were established in all high schools, and pioneer groups in all elementary schools. Many school teachers and college professors, suspected of nationalistic leanings, were dismissed. In June of 1941, some 372 teachers and 2,057 students and school children were deported from Latvia alone.

Even though the Soviet Constitution provides that "the freedom to follow religious faiths, as well as the freedom of anti-religious propaganda, is recognized for all citizens," the churches in the Baltic countries were subjected to severe persecutions. Bibles, hymn books and other religious literature were partly confiscated and destroyed, and it was prohibited to print new editions. Church holidays were abolished, and Sundays were replaced by workless days. Church buildings were nationalized and some were devoted to profane usage. Where churches continued to be used for religious worship, rent was charged at a rate ten times higher than that charged for housing space. During the first year of Soviet occupation, thirty-five members of the clergy were deported from Estonia, forty-one from Latvia, and forty-two from Lithuania.

Nazi Occupation

The unnatural friendship between Hitler and Stalin ended on June 21, 1941, when the German Ambassador, Schulenburg, presented a note to Mr. Molotov announcing the opening of hostilities against Russia on the part of the Nazi Reich. Concerning the Baltic countries, the note declared: "It has become obvious that the USSR, contrary to her declaration made at the conclusion of the treaties of 1939 that she does not intend to Bolshevize and annex the countries falling within her sphere of influence, was intent on pushing her military might westward . . . into Europe. The actions of the USSR against the Baltic States, Finland, and Rumania show this clearly."

Hitler availed himself of the opportunity to pose as a liberator, and there were some who believed in his sincerity, or at least that he would annul the nationalization decrees, which the Soviet Union had enacted in the Baltic States. They were sadly mistaken. It is recorded in the so-called Borman Protocols that on July 16, 1941, when most of the territory of the Baltic States was already in German hands, Hitler explained to his henchmen that "the entire Baltic area must be incorporated into the Reich." On June 24, the Wehrmacht had already occupied Kaunas and Minsk. On June 25 Liepaja fell; on June 29, Lvov, and on July 1, Riga. On July 5 the German army forced the "Stalin Line" at Ostrow. On July 8 Pskov was taken and on July 10, Vitebsk. The swift German advance into the Baltic area was greatly facilitated by the actions of Baltic partisans, many of whom were former members of the national armed forces, who had saved themselves from deportation by going into hiding.

The Red occupation forces there only made a stand in northern Estonia, where they held out for two months. Narva fell to the Germans only on August 17 and Tallin on August 28. This gave the Russians time for a general conscription in the northern part of Estonia. When they withdrew, they carried away about 33,000 Estonian conscripts, most of whom were put to forced labor in northern Russia. Many perished there, but the survivors were pressed into an Estonian rifle corps which was formed in the Ural region in the spring of 1942, while a Latvian rifle corps had already been formed in the fall of 1941. Its core consisted of conscripted Soviet citizens of Latvian nationality. Later, however, Latvian men who had been evacuated or deported to Russia were also enlisted in the Red Latvian rifle corps.

On the other hand, after the Germans had occupied the Baltic countries, many young people volunteered for the so-called eastern battalions, bent on taking revenge against the Bolsheviks for the deportation or murder of their relatives and friends. Even though these battalions were allegedly formed only for police service behind the lines, they were soon distributed among German formations on the eastern front and, though poorly armed, were thrown into battle.

In the fall of 1942, when it became apparent to the Baltic peoples that the Bolsheviks and Nazis were birds of the same feather, the flow of volunteers stopped completely. Germany's police chief, Himmler, counteracted this lack of enthusiasm by mobilizing the local police forces and national guardsmen for military service. At the end of 1942, and in the spring of 1943, all able-bodied men in Estonia and Latvia were drafted. In order to circumvent the Hague Convention of 1907, which prohibits conscriptions in occupied countries, the conscripts were officially labelled as "volunteers." In flagrant violation of the said convention, the Nazis extended the draft to 28 conscription years. Even high school students were mobilized for service in air-defense units. In this way, 146,000 Latvian men and youths were drafted up to July of 1944. Of these, 30,000 men were formed into two divisions of the so-called Latvian Legion. In Estonia, men were conscripted in similar manner. Greatest resistance against compulsory military service under German auspices was offered in Lithuania. Consequently most of the Lithuanian conscripts were sent to do defense labor in Germany, and only a few thousand Lithuanians served in military and paramilitary capacity.

When in the summer of 1941, the Red Army started to retreat under German pressure, revolts against the Soviet occupiers broke out in all three Baltic countries, and provisional national governments were formed. On June 23, Lithuanian patriots seized the radio station and government buildings in Kaunas. Similar events took place in Riga on July 1. Hostilities in Estonia ended only on August 28, when the Germans entered Tallin. However, on July 17, Hitler had already appointed a commissar of the Reich for the administration of the so-called *Ostland,* comprising Estonia, Latvia, Lithuania and Byelorussia. The policy for *Ostland* was shaped by the German *Ostministerium,* headed by Alfred Rosenberg, who was a German of Baltic descent. At the Nuremberg trials Rosenberg admitted that the Nazis had planned to deport most of the Estonians, Latvians and Lithuanians to Byelorussia and the Pskov District, and to replace them with German settlers.

With such ultimate designs in mind, the Nazi occupiers did not care to repeal the Soviet nationalization decrees in the Baltic Republics. They claimed, instead, all nationalized property for the Reich, arguing that Germany had recovered it from the Soviet State. The Soviet *Gosbank* was replaced by the German *Notenbank Ostland,* which during the German occupation period issued two billion ostmarks. In the beginning the rate of exchange of the ostmark was fixed at ten Soviet rubles. At the end of the German occupation the purchasing power of the ostmark had declined eighty-fold. Except that the nationalized enterprises were now managed by the German *Treuhandverwaltung,* the Soviet-introduced economic system was otherwise essentially retained.

Workers were not permitted to change employment at will, and many thousands were shipped to forced labor in Germany. Nationalized agricultural land was placed under the management of the fiduciary *Landwirtschaftsgesellschaft Ostland*. The farmers were merely usufructuaries of the land which once had been their own. Soviet established State farms were managed as before. Only in 1943, after Germany had suffered irreparable defeats on the eastern front, some landed property was gradually restored to the owners. But the process was so slow that most of the former owners never actually benefited from this act of "Hitler's generosity." While taxation in kind was moderate at the beginning of the German occupation, it gradually increased, until the farmers were no longer able to meet the norms which were imposed upon them, and in consequence their cattle were confiscated without mercy. All important concerns of social and economic life in the Baltic countries, such as rationing, taxation, labor service, wages, conscriptions, etc., were determined and administered by the German civil administration. Organs of local self-administration and courts were left to function, but their competence was extremely restricted, and officers, judges and even priests were appointed and dismissed by the German General Commissioner.

The Nazi *Gestapo* and *Sicherheitsdienst,* which had superseded the Soviet NKVD, attended not only to the rooting out of Communists and other enemies of Nazism, but aspired also to supervise all means of information and cultural concerns, such as radio, press, publishing business, movies and theaters. In the political field, Himmler's Gestapo distinguished itself by its genocidal extermination of Jews, Gypsies and Russian prisoners of war. Prisons were once again overcrowded with political captives, among whom were many Baltic patriots. This was because since 1942 underground resistance movements against the Nazis had come into being. They were led by a council, composed of active members of the principal political parties. They were persecuted mainly because of their leanings towards the Western democracies, on whom they relied for ultimate liberation. Apart from the concentration camps, which the Hitlerites had established on Baltic territory, about 40,000 citizens of the Baltic States were held in the Stutthof camp near Danzig, in Dachau, Flossburg, and other camps in Germany. Thousands of Baltic internees in these camps met death through execution or maltreatment.

Second Soviet Invasion

After a successful offensive in the winter 1943–44, the Soviet armed forces once again invaded the Baltic countries. This new westward turn of the Russian tide was to a great extent facilitated by American lend-lease supplies, which began to pour into Russia in vast quantities during the second half of 1942. On June 26, 1944, the Reds reached Vitebsk; on July 3, Minsk was taken, and on July 13, Vilnyus. From then on, the center of attack was shifted to the western Baltic front. On July 21 Ostrov was taken, bringing about the collapse of the German "Panther Line." On July 27, a second Red army group occupied Daugavpils and Rezekne, in Latvia, and Siauliai in Lithuania. On July 31 the Reds captured Jelgava by a sudden northward thrust, and on August 1, Tukums, near the Gulf of Riga. With this strategic move, the Soviet forces had entrapped two German armies which were still offering resistance in Estonia and Latvian Vidzeme, to the northeast. On August 25 Tartu surrendered, and on September 22 Estonia's capital, Tallin, was in Russian hands. From there the Red forces proceeded swiftly south to occupy Riga, Latvia's capital, on October 13.

One of the two divisions of the Latvian Legion, which had managed to retreat westward to Schwerin, surrendered to the Americans in January of 1945. After the Soviet forces had occupied Eastern Prussia in October of 1944, 31 German divisions and one division of the Latvian Legion found themselves entrapped in the westernmost Latvian province, Kurzeme. For seven months this so-called Kurzeme fortress held out against savage Russian assaults. When Germany capitulated on May 9, 1945, about 190,000 men were taken prisoners, among them 14,000 Latvian legionnaires. They were sent to forced labor in Russia and Siberia. Some of the Latvian legionnaires preferred to hide in the woods, rather than to surrender. Together with Lithuanian and Estonian partisans, they engaged the Soviet occupation regime in guerrilla warfare, which lasted for years.

With Estonia's doom approaching, about 24,000 Estonian citizens fled to Sweden in fishing boats and other small craft. Several thousand Latvians followed their example. But when the flood of Red invasion came full, endless streams of refugees from all the three Baltic countries poured westward into crumbling Germany, driven from their homes and countries by war devastation and fear of Bolshevik terror and revenge. Thousands were recaptured during the flight by the advancing Soviet steamroller. However, about 199,000 Balts, of whom 120,000 were Latvians, escaped from the long arm of the Soviet political police and into the American and British zones of Western Germany. Most of them have since emigrated to overseas countries, chiefly to America.

Collectivization and Deportations

The Soviets established in the reoccupied Baltic countries a network of screening camps. At these all men of military age and other persons suspected of collaboration with the Germans were held and scrutinized as to their past activities. Many thousands were subsequently imprisoned and deported. The number of persons who fell victim of the Soviet purges during 1944–46 cannot be established with certainty, although it is known that the total by far exceeded the number of deportees during the first year of Soviet occupation. The Polish writer, K. M. Smogorzewski, estimates that some 371,000 Balts were deported in the first three years of the postwar period.[4] A third wave of mass deportation took place between March 24 and 27, 1949. This time the victims were chiefly farmers who resisted compulsory collectivization. According to Smogorzewski, the number of Baltic deportees in the spring period of 1949, when collectivization was ruthlessly enforced, amounted to approximately 170,000. This estimate, of course, being based on unconfirmed data and circumstantial evidence, cannot pretend to be absolutely correct, but may be accepted as an approximation.

After the return of the Red regime, a second "agrarian reform" was introduced. It resulted in further deterioration of agriculture. The purpose of this reform was plainly defined by J. Kalnberzins, First Secretary of the Latvian Communist Party, who admitted that since 1944 "the Party and the Government passed from the policy of restricting and eliminating the kulaks to the liquidation of the kulak as a class. The measures taken against them helped to accelerate the process of collectivization." [5] Although the Soviet law provides no definition of what a "kulak" is supposed to be, in practice it means a farmer who uses hired help, or is politically unreliable. There were over 100,000 farmers in the Baltic countries who fell within this category, and they and their families were marked for liquidation, in the wake of compulsory collectivization.

Attempts to induce the farmers by propaganda, threats and exorbitant taxation, to enter collective farms voluntarily, had only met with failure. By the end of 1948, only 9.4% of agriculture in Latvia had been collectivized. Resistance was finally broken by means of brutal mass deportations inaugurated in March 1949, and thereafter collective farms sprang up in all Baltic Republics like mushrooms after a rain. By September there were 2,975 kolkhozes in Estonia, 3,879 in Latvia, and 6,549 in Lithuania, encompassing in all some 75 to 80 per cent of all arable land. With relentless terror continuing, the number of collective farms increased steadily, and in 1954 only two per cent of the land was still being tilled individually. Having been driven into kolkhozes

[4] K. M. Smogorzewski, "The Russification of the Baltic States," *World Affairs*, IV, New Series (1950), 468–481.

[5] J. Kalnberzins, *Ten Years of Soviet Latvia* (Moscow, 1951), p. 173.

by force, the Baltic farmers were deprived of all incentive to work on the kolkhoz fields. In consequence, the farmers' earnings from work in the kolkhozes are pitiful—about one third of the average during Baltic independence, or one eighth of the average income of American farmers. In order to keep their families alive, the Baltic collectivized farmers devote most of their energy to tending their tiny kitchen plots, which the Government permits them to keep for private use. The size of these plots is 0.25 to 0.6 hectares (0.6 to 1.5 acres), and there the farmers may keep one or two cows, two calves, one hog, ten sheep and an undefined number of fowl. They are, however, not permitted to own a horse.

Since the introduction of collectivization, the Baltic Republics are no longer able to produce grain, sugar and meat in sufficient quantities to feed the population. But, up to 1953, when Khrushchev for the first time revealed the catastrophic lag of agricultural production in the Soviet Union, the Baltic puppet Governments were prohibited from publishing information about agriculture in absolute figures. Then, in April of 1953, the Latvian Minister for Agriculture revealed that the area of grain cultivation in Latvia had decreased by 400,000 hectares, or 18.2%, and that the number of cows had decreased by 510,000 heads, or 57%. In August of 1953, Vilis Lacis, Prime Minister of the Latvian puppet Government, informed the Latvian Supreme Soviet that in some districts there were only 12.5 heads of cattle for each 100 hectares of arable land, as compared with an average of 32.5 heads of cattle for 100 hectares in independent Latvia. According to Lacis, the average yearly milk output per cow in the district of Dagda was only 714 kilograms in 1952, as compared with an average of 1,912 kilograms for Latvia in 1938.

While collectivization inevitably led to a critical decline of agricultural production, heavy industry was artificially boosted with subsidies by the Moscow Central Government, which is in direct charge of all large industrial enterprises in the Baltic Republics. Nevertheless, the average productivity of the industrial workers in the Baltics has fallen 30% below the productivity of workers during the period of independence. The main reason for this is the excessive increase of the administrative personnel, and, also, the low working capacity of the Russian workers, who have been imported to the Baltic countries in great numbers.

The Soviet regime has expanded the heavy industry of the

Baltic countries by 30 to 35%, as compared with 1939. Estonia ranks first in this respect, and Lithuania last. The Soviet Five Year Plan for 1946–50 granted seven billion rubles of capital investment for the expansion of industry in the Baltic States. Half of this amount was diverted to Estonia's oil-shale production, 75% of which is reserved for supplying the Baltic fleet with fuel oil and Leningrad with gas.

Baltic Communists and Russification

Whereas in 1940 the Latvian Communist Party consisted of only 1,600 members, including those Communists who had infiltrated from the U.S.S.R., by 1949 the number of party members, who composed the most privileged class, had grown to 31,000. The Latvian Party Congress of December 1951 was attended by 480 voting delegates, of whom 50% were Latvians, 40% Russians, and 10% of other nationalities. According to professions 49% were employees, 43% laborers, and 8% farmers. In 1952 the Latvian Communist Party had 50,000 members, comprising 2.3% of the population. The figures for Lithuania were: 36,000 members, or 1.2%; for Estonia, 31,000 members, or 2.5%.

Each of the Communist parties in the Baltic Republics is headed by a Central Committee consisting of approximately seventy members. The Committee, in turn, is controlled by a Presidium of eleven, and has four secretaries. The hierarchy of the Baltic Communist parties, as well as the Governments, is composed of persons selected and directed by Moscow, and they are subject to periodical purges.

In theory the Supreme Soviets of the Baltic Republics, elected every four years, at the rate of one deputy for every 10,000 inhabitants, are sovereign law-making bodies. In fact, however, they are but a window-dressing for the decrees of the Kremlin, which they invariably approve "unanimously." Membership in the Supreme Soviet is a sort of honorary degree for deserving bureaucrats. In the Latvian Supreme Soviet, elected on February 27, 1955, only 8% of the delegates are representatives of labor, and 5% representatives of kolkhoz workers.

The 1953 edition of the *Great Soviet Encyclopaedia* estimates the population of the Baltic countries in 1940 at 6,017,000. The figures for the individual states are: Estonia, 1,117,000; Latvia, 2,000,000; Lithuania, 2,900,000. Soviet sources do not reveal, however, how many of the original inhabitants are at present still residing in their home countries and how many Soviet Russians have settled there since 1944. Smogorzewski estimates that in the period between 1940 and 1950, the number of Estonians living in Estonia has fallen from 998,000 to 684,000, the number of Latvians from 1,472,000 to 1,222,000, and the number of Lithuanians from 2,084,000 to 1,645,000. According to this estimate, the Baltic peoples are still in the majority in their native lands by at least 60 per cent. Nevertheless, all their cultural, social and economic affairs are completely dominated by Moscow, and must conform in spirit and contents with the ideology of the Russian Communist dictatorship.

Teaching of the Russian language is compulsory in all schools of the Baltic Republics. Apart from that, the Soviet regime tries to precipitate the Russification of the young people by gradually increasing the number of Russian high schools, that is, such schools in which the language of instruction for all educational subjects is Russian. Thus, in 1950, of the 15 high schools in Riga, nine were entirely Russian, two were partly Russian and partly Latvian, and only four schools were Latvian. In the Baltic institutions of higher learning instruction in the Russian language is steadily gaining ground, particularly in the field of technical education. The present educational level of the academic teachers is very low, measured by the standards of prewar times, because most of the Baltic university professors fled to the West in 1944–45. For example, in 1950–51 the University of Latvia had five hundred teachers and instructors, but only thirty of these had a doctor's degree and only 44 were full professors, while 66 were candidates of sciences. The remainder, 358 persons, or 71%, had no academic degree at all.[6]

United States Policy toward the Baltic States

At the first Inter-Allied Conference, held in London in September 1941, the Soviet Government gave its endorsement to the principles of the Atlantic Charter. "The Soviet Union," said Ambassador Maisky, "defends the right of every nation to the independence and territorial integrity of its country, and its right to establish such social order and to choose such form of government as it deems opportune and necessary for the promotion of its economic and cultural prosperity." Dr. F. W. Pick, commenting on

[6] *Ibid.*, pp. 230–231.

Maisky's statement, says: "These were proud words, almost identical with the words used by the peace treaties with the Baltic States in 1920, wholly in keeping with the ideals the western world stands for." [7] However, coming from a Soviet spokesman, they were deliberately deceptive. Litvinov was singing the same tune on January 1, 1942, when signing the Declaration of the United Nations, on behalf of his Government.

The interpretation of what was really in Stalin's mind with regard to the self-determination of nations, was given to Eden when at the end of 1941 he went to Moscow, to confer about mutual aid in the war. At his first conference in the Kremlin, Stalin explained to Eden, in some detail, what he expected the postwar frontiers of the Soviet Union to be in Europe. They were to encompass all the territories which the Soviets had gained in connivance with Hitler, including the Baltic States. Winston Churchill reveals in his memoirs that Stalin, on meeting Eden for the second time on December 17, "pressed for the immediate recognition by His Majesty's Government of the future frontiers of the U.S.S.R., more particularly in regard to the inclusion within the U.S.S.R. of the Baltic States . . . He made the conclusion of any Anglo-Soviet Agreement dependent upon agreement on this point." [8]

Churchill presented Eden's report to the British Cabinet for discussion. The Cabinet rejected Stalin's demands as being incompatible with the principles of the Atlantic Charter, to which the Soviet Union had also subscribed. In his wire to Eden on December 20, Churchill cautioned his Foreign Minister with regard to Stalin's claims for possession of the Baltic countries: "To approach President Roosevelt with these proposals would be to court a blank refusal, and might cause lasting trouble on both sides." In his dispatch to Eden on January 8, 1942, the Prime Minister expressed himself even more bluntly: "We have never recognized the 1941 frontiers of Russia except *de facto*. They were acquired by acts of aggression in shameful collusion with Hitler. The transfer of the peoples of the Baltic States to Soviet Russia against their will would be contrary to all the principles for which we are fighting this war. . . ." [9]

Even though these words of the British Prime Minister record

[7] F. W. Pick, *The Baltic Nations* (London, 1945), p. 145.

[8] Winston S. Churchill, *The Grand Alliance,* Vol. III of *The Second World War* (Boston, 1950), p. 629.

[9] *Ibid.,* pp. 630, 695.

a high sense of morality in international affairs, he reversed himself completely two months later, under the pressure of the unfavorable development of the war. On March 7 he wrote to President Roosevelt: "The increasing gravity of the war has led me to feel that the principles of the Atlantic Charter ought not to be construed so as to deny Russia the frontiers she occupied when Germany attacked her . . . I hope therefore that you will be able to give us a free hand to sign the treaty which Stalin desires as soon as possible."[10] Churchill tried to justify his sudden change of heart by Britain's inability at that time to bear the heavy load which the defense of Baltic independence in accordance with the principles of the Atlantic Charter would have imposed on her.

In the subsequent diplomatic skirmish on the Baltic question between the capitals of the Big Three, Washington prevailed in the end. Secretary of State Cordell Hull categorically objected to any territorial concessions to Stalin in conflict with the Atlantic Charter, while the war was still on. Great Britain was forced to keep in line with America, and on May 26, 1942, Molotov signed a twenty-year Anglo-Soviet treaty of alliance in which the definition of the postwar Soviet frontiers was left open. Molotov, having no choice, even agreed that "both powers will act in accordance with the two principles of not seeking territorial aggrandizement for themselves and of non-interference in the internal affairs of other States."

For the Soviet Union the underwriting of these principles was merely an empty gesture, with the silent understanding that the Baltic Republics, allegedly being inherent territories of the Soviet Union, were in no way affected by the principles of the Atlantic Charter. On May 1, 1942, only a few weeks previous to the conclusion of the Anglo-Soviet pact of alliance, Stalin had come forth with a declaration that it was the aim of the Soviet war effort "to liberate the Soviet homeland and the peoples of Ukraine, Byelorussia, Lithuania, Latvia, Estonia and Karelia." He thus excluded these territories from any agreement with the Western democracies. Professor Arnolds Spekke comments in this connection in his booklet *Latvia and the Baltic Problem:* "The whole battle took place in the complete silence of the great chancelleries, which means that it was feared to touch these things openly . . . The sure indica-

[10] Winston S. Churchill, *The Hinge of Fate,* Vol. IV of *The Second World War* (Boston, 1950), p. 327.

tion that the Baltic cause was taking a bad turn is that in Washington a radical solution was mooted, namely the evacuation from their homelands of all the Balts who did not want to remain under Russian domination."

The Kremlin rejected even this indirect recognition of its dominion, insisting upon undisputed mastery, without interference from Washington. On the occasion of the Moscow Conference in 1943, President Roosevelt instructed Secretary of State Cordell Hull to approach Stalin with the suggestion of holding a plebiscite in the Baltic Republics after the war, in order to raise Soviet Russia's respectability among democratic countries. At the Teheran Conference President Roosevelt renewed his efforts to clarify Stalin's intentions with regard to the Baltic States. But Stalin reacted either evasively or impatiently, until he finally declared that the Baltic nations had expressed their wish to belong to the Soviet Union, and that the issue was closed.

In anticipation of the forthcoming creation of the United Nations organization, Stalin came out with a clever trick in granting on February 1, 1944 "the right of handling their relations with foreign nations directly" to all sixteen Federative Soviet Republics, sealing his "generosity" with adequate changes in the Soviet Constitution. Subsequently the Kremlin came forth with the demand that all 16 Soviet Republics shall be represented in the Assembly of the envisaged United Nations. Apart from trying to gain a disproportionate influence for the Soviet Union in the affairs of the United Nations, this Soviet maneuver aspired to obtain in a roundabout way Western recognition for the absorption of the Baltic nations into the Soviet realm.

Faced with indignant rebukes from the free world against such unwarranted pretensions, the Kremlin beat a swift strategical retreat at the Yalta Conference. During the plenary session of February 7, 1945, Molotov modified the previous stand of the Soviet Union, declaring that Moscow would be satisfied with the inclusion of Ukraine, Byelorussia and Lithuania among the initial members of the United Nations. President Roosevelt proposed to postpone a decision on Molotov's proposals, arguing that the question demanded serious study. In that he was backed up by Churchill. In the final result Molotov agreed to drop Lithuania from his list of "sovereign" Soviet representatives to the United Nations, in exchange for the admission of Ukraine and Byelorussia. Thus the

Baltic nations were saved from an international sell-out to Soviet Russia by a narrow margin.

At the close of the Yalta Conference on February 11, 1945, the three principals issued a joint communiqué, Section V of which envisages "the restoration of sovereign rights and self-government to those peoples who have been forcibly deprived of them by aggressor nations." By an irony of fate, this lofty document carries the signature of Stalin next to Roosevelt's and Churchill's. Moreover, Stalin unhesitatingly underwrote a solemn promise to contribute to "a secure and lasting peace which will, in the words of the Atlantic Charter, afford assurance that all the men in all the lands may live out their lives in freedom from fear and want."

At the time when Stalin affixed his signature to this joint communiqué, the Red Army had far advanced beyond the Soviet frontiers, and thus he already held the key to Eastern and Central Europe. Today no less than one hundred million people on 264,200 square miles of Soviet "liberated" Europe still live in constant fear and want behind the Iron Curtain. Among them are the three Baltic nations, Estonia, Latvia and Lithuania. Their hope for ultimate liberation rests upon America's nonrecognition of the Soviet seizure of their countries, first proclaimed by the Roosevelt Administration on July 23, 1940, and subsequently re-stated by President Truman and President Eisenhower.

With most of the Western democracies conforming with the attitude of Washington, the continuity of Baltic independence with regard to international law and justice is thus being upheld.

The United States policy of repudiating Soviet claims of sovereignty over the Baltic nations was exemplified by Secretary of State George Marshall, when on April 20, 1949, he confirmed Jules Feldmans as Latvian diplomatic representative to the United States, to replace Alfred Bilmanis who had died in August 1948. After the death of J. Feldmans, in 1953, Secretary of State John Foster Dulles accepted Dr. Arnolds Spekke as his successor, exchanging notes of accreditation on May 24, 1954. In both cases the appointment emanated from Charles Zarine, Latvian Minister to Great Britain, on the basis of Special Emergency Powers vested in him on May 18, 1940 by the last legal Latvian Government, shortly before the first Soviet invasion of Latvia.

The necessity to counteract Communist aggression after the war led the United States to re-emphasize its Baltic policy in unmistakeable terms. In 1951 the Voice of America extended its program with broadcasts to the Soviet enslaved Baltic peoples in their native languages. At the same time Committees for a Free Estonia, Latvia and Lithuania came into being, under the sponsorship of the National Committee for a Free Europe.

A most important recent development for the Baltic nations was the creation of a Select Congressional Committee on Communist Aggression in the summer of 1953. This Committee started its activities with an extensive investigation of Soviet aggression against the Baltic States and of the circumstances which led to their incorporation into the U.S.S.R. A great amount of documentary and eyewitness evidence about Soviet atrocities in Estonia, Latvia and Lithuania was compiled and published by this Congressional Committee during 1953–54.

At the opening of the Committee's public hearings which took place in Washington, D.C., on November 30, 1953, Secretary of State John Foster Dulles appeared in person, presenting a statement on the United States policy towards the Baltic Republics. Among other things, he said:

> The United States, for its part, maintains the diplomatic recognition which it extended in 1922 to the Baltic nations. We continue to deal with those diplomatic and consular representatives of the Baltic countries who served the last independent governments of these States . . . The captive peoples should know that they are not forgotten, that we are not reconciled to their fate and, above all, that we are not prepared to seek illusory safety for ourselves by a bargain with their masters which would confirm their captivity.

Chapter 6

Poland

OSCAR HALECKI

Defeat in Victory

IN ALL countries of East Central Europe Soviet Russia used and is still using similar methods of enslavement. There are, however, important distinctive features in each individual case, and these differences necessarily affected American foreign policy. There was, in particular, a basic difference between the legal position and the expectations of those countries which in World War II had been allies of the Western powers, including the United States, and of those which had been fighting, were it even unwillingly and temporarily, on the side of the defeated enemy. Dealing with Central European nations of the first group, Moscow had to use much subtler methods in order to create appearances of "liberation" by the Red Army and to replace the constitutional allied governments by Communist controlled regimes. This proved particularly difficult in the Polish case. For Poland not only was an allied power, but the struggle against Hitler had started in Poland and for Poland's independence and territorial integrity, so that the Polish people were convinced that in agreement with the Atlantic Charter this independence and integrity would be fully restored to them after a complete victory to which they had contributed throughout the war both by their underground resistance at home and by the participation of the armed forces of the exiled Polish Government in the allied war effort on various fronts.

Of this the United States was, of course, fully aware, but what was quite insufficiently realized was the fact that the enslavement of Poland was one of the most important war aims of Soviet Russia, and this not only in the period of Nazi-Soviet cooperation, but also when the Soviet Union had become, unwillingly and temporarily, an ally of the Western democracies. And even less realized in America was the historical continuity of Russia's anti-Polish design, which must be traced back to the foreign policy of the Czars and to the initial program of the Bolshevik revolution.

The Background of Poland's Partition in 1939

The founder of Moscow's power, Ivan III (1462–1505), having united all Great Russian lands, claimed the Ruthenian provinces (Byelorussia and Ukraine) of the Polish-Lithuanian Confederation which he found in the way of Muscovy's western expansion and therefore tried to encircle. Plans of advancing as far as the Vistula and partitioning the Commonwealth appeared already under Ivan the Terrible. Peter the Great, without changing the frontier of 1667 which for more than a century divided the Ukraine between Poland and Russia, tried to make the whole of Poland a satellite of his Empire. Such was also the original aim of Catherine II who, however, had to accept the Prussian plan of partitioning Poland, and established the frontier between Russia and the German powers at the line which in our times was misleadingly called the Curzon line. To Russia's share in the three partitions Alexander I, at the Congress of Vienna, after claiming practically all of Poland, added her central part as an autonomous "kingdom" which in spite of its struggles for liberation was gradually incorporated into the Russian Empire.

The Czarist war aim of 1914 was again the unification of all parts of Poland under Russian rule. After seizing power, the Bolsheviks denounced Czarist imperialism and annulled the partition treaties, but only to reclaim Poland on other grounds. Two days after the armistice in the West they revealed their plan to include Poland in the union of Soviet republics under Russian leadership. Hardly liberated from German occupation, Poland was threatened at once by the Red Army, which in the summer of 1920 tried again to conquer Poland as a gateway to Western Europe. The Soviet Government seemed inclined to grant Poland an eastern frontier more favorable than the Curzon line, but had already prepared a Communist puppet regime for the whole country when the battle of Warsaw, on August 15, reversed the military situation. Even so, the Treaty of Riga of March 18, 1921, left to the Soviets almost all that Czarist Russia had gained in the first two partitions of Poland.

In spite of the nonaggression treaties of 1929 and 1932, the

Soviet Union was waiting for an opportunity to destroy "the ugly offspring of the Versailles Treaty." In the secret protocol of the German-Soviet Treaty of August 23, 1939, it was decided that "in the event of a territorial and political rearrangement of the areas belonging to the Polish state the spheres of influence of Germany and the U.S.S.R. shall be bounded approximately by the line of the rivers Narew, Vistula and San." The question of "whether the interests of both parties make desirable the maintenance of an independent Polish state" in reduced boundaries, was then left open. But soon after September 17, when Russian forces had invaded Poland, already all but overwhelmed by the Nazi invaders, Stalin and Molotov decided against the existence of a "residual Polish rump state" and in favor of a partition which, as finally agreed on in the treaty of September 28, extended the German border to the Bug River. Already in October, after fake elections held under the strongest pressure, the eastern half of prewar Poland, including areas west of the Curzon line and also Eastern Galicia which never belonged to Czarist Russia, was incorporated with the Byelorussian and the Ukrainian Soviet Republics. There started immediately a violent process of Sovietization and at least one million and a half of the population, most of them Poles, were deported to the Asiatic parts of the Soviet Union.

The Failure of Polish-Russian Cooperation, 1941–1943

The return to the conception of a German-Russian partition of Poland lasted as long as Nazi-Soviet cooperation. On July 30, 1941, five weeks after Hitler's invasion of the U.S.S.R., the Soviet Government, signing the London Treaty with the Polish Government in exile, admitted that the arrangements made with Germany in 1939 had "lost their validity" and granted an "amnesty" to the deported Poles. This was not, however, as Poland hoped, a recognition of the frontier of 1921 nor even a sincere decision to cooperate with the constitutional Polish Government whose head, General W. Sikorski, came to Moscow to sign on December 4 a declaration of friendship. On the contrary, not only did the Soviets question the Polish citizenship of the deported peoples, but at the very time of Sikorski's visit a "Union of Polish Patriots" was created in Moscow as a nucleus of a Communist regime to be forced upon the Poles after their "liberation."

It soon became obvious that the U.S.S.R. was determined to

reclaim most of the area which she had gained through the partition of 1939, pretending that the peoples themselves had "voted" for inclusion in the two Soviet republics and misinterpreting the Allied suggestions of 1919 and 1920. The Allies of 1941 were not aware that the so-called Curzon line was never supposed to be the final eastern boundary of Poland and had been extended into Galicia only through an error. Furthermore, they wrongly believed that if only Russia's territorial claims were satisfied, she would respect the independence of the remaining part of Poland under her legitimate, allied Government.

What was, unfortunately, completely misunderstood was Russia's additional claim that the Polish Government must be "friendly" to her, a claim which was considered justified from the point of view of allied unity. In the Russian interpretation such a "friendly" government was supposed not only to sign away half of Poland's territory, but also to be subservient to Soviet Russia, a tool in helping her to sovietize the other half of Poland also and to make it a Russian satellite. Therefore, though the Sikorski Government was certainly friendly to Russia in the usual sense of that word, frictions were soon to develop in connection with the liberation of the deported Poles and with the formation, out of these people, of a Polish army which was expected to fight on the Russian front.

Finally, that army, under General W. Anders, had to be evacuated through the Near East and joined the forces of the Western Allies, distinguishing itself particularly in the Italian campaign. However, most of the Polish officers who had been made prisoners of war during the Russian invasion of 1939 were missing, and the Polish Government tried in vain to get any information about their fate. Suddenly, in April 1943, the Germans discovered the mass-graves of about 4,300 officers who had been executed and buried in a forest near Katyn, in the Smolensk region. Without admitting in advance the German charge that these Polish P.W. officers had been murdered by the Russians, the Polish Government asked for an investigation by the International Red Cross.[1] Soviet Russia, whose guilt was later proven beyond any doubt, used this Polish request as a welcome pretext to break off, on April 26, diplomatic relations with "the London émigré regime" and openly

1 Recent investigations revealed that about 14,000 regular and reserve officers who were placed in three camps perished in Russian captivity.

to oppose to it the Communist puppets who were trained in Moscow for taking over all power in Poland.

"Liberation" by the Red Army

While the Red Army continued its victorious advance toward Poland's prewar frontier, the Western Allies tried in vain to heal the break between the Soviet and the Polish Governments, which after General Sikorski's death in an airplane crash, on July 4, had as Prime Minister the peasant leader Stanislaw Mikolajczyk. No progress, however, was achieved at the Moscow Conference of October 1943, and, a few weeks later in Teheran, President Roosevelt and Winston Churchill tried in vain to appease Stalin by tacitly admitting his claim that the Curzon line be recognized as the eastern boundary of Poland.

It was in vain, too, that the Polish Government instructed the Home Army to cooperate with the Russians when at the beginning of 1944 they entered Poland's territory. On the contrary, these Polish resistance forces, though they contributed on various occasions to the German defeat, were promptly liquidated, and when six months later, after again occupying Eastern Poland the Red Army crossed the Curzon line, it was accompanied by the Communist agents who were now proclaimed a "Polish Committee of National Liberation." Even before settling in the city of Lublin, that Committee, on July 22, 1944, issued from Chelm, the first town west of the Curzon line which was taken by the Russians, a manifesto to the Polish people. The date is now celebrated as the national holiday. The manifesto was, in fact, the proclamation of Poland's enslavement by Soviet Russia. For it declared the "émigré government in London and its agency in Poland [the underground state which had functioned throughout the German occupation] . . . an illegal and self-styled authority." And pretending to act on behalf of the "National Council of the Homeland" (a small Communist controlled group presided over by Boleslaw Bierut) and on the basis of the Constitution of 1921, it implicitly surrendered the eastern part of the country which was claimed by the Soviet Union, and, furthermore, it announced a radical agrarian reform which expropriated all owners of more than 50 hectares, anticipating that part of the land would be "set aside for collective farms."

At the same time the Russian radio called upon the people

of Warsaw to rise against the Germans, but when this was done on August 1, the Red Army stopped at the gates of the capital, left the insurrection under General T. Bór-Komorowski without any support and made it practically impossible for the American and British air forces to bring any effective assistance to the city. While desperate street fighting continued for sixty-three days, the negotiations which Prime Minister Mikolajczyk conducted in Moscow remained fruitless. Wherever the Germans had been expelled, the Communist regime proceeded to its land reform according to the decree of September 6, and on September 13, Bierut was elected President of the Liberation Committee, that is, provisional head of state.

After another unsuccessful trip of Mikolajczyk to Moscow in October, at the time when the Germans were systematically destroying Warsaw, and after his replacement as Prime Minister by the Socialist leader Tomasz Arciszewski who refused to surrender to Russia, the Lublin Committee was proclaimed a "Provisional Government" of Poland, on December 31, at once recognized as such by the Soviet Union, and when Warsaw was taken from the Germans on January 17, 1945, transferred to the capital on February 1. Almost all of prewar Poland was indeed liberated from the Germans, but only to be occupied in turn by the Russians and controlled by their agents. Such was the situation when President Roosevelt and Winston Churchill were preparing to meet Stalin at Yalta in the Crimea.

From Yalta to Potsdam

No question received more attention at the Yalta Conference than the Polish problem. In no other matter was the success of Soviet Russia more complete. Under the impression of the last German offensive and of reports which overrated Japan's power of resistance, the United States and Britain were extremely anxious to secure full Russian cooperation in ending the war. They were equally anxious to continue that cooperation after victory in the framework of the United Nations Organization. They therefore surrendered on both of the controversial issues regarding Poland in which Russia was primarily interested. The territorial conflict between Poland and the Soviet Union was now openly decided in favor of the latter: President Roosevelt's last minute effort to save for Poland at least Lwów and the Galician oilfields failed, and for the first time in history the Curzon line, extended to the Carpathians, was sanctioned as Poland's eastern frontier. The allied Polish Government, though still recognized by all powers except the U.S.S.R., was not even mentioned, and contrary to the American desire to see an entirely new Government formed, the Communist-controlled Lublin Committee was accepted as the nucleus of the "Provisional Government of National Unity." How the Soviet sponsored group would be enlarged by the addition of an undetermined number of "democratic leaders" was not specified, but the United States and Britain promised in advance that such a government would receive their recognition even before the holding of "free and unfettered" elections. Neither in the frontier question nor in that of the government were any Polish representatives heard, and the composition of the government was to be determined in Moscow by a committee composed of Mr. Molotov and the American and British Ambassadors to the Soviet Union.

America and Britain were soon to realize that the Yalta Declaration of February 11, 1945, meant not only a new partition of Poland but the end of her independence. The best evidence of that was the kidnapping of the sixteen most prominent underground leaders who, under the pretext of being invited to participate in the formation of the Polish Government, were brought to Moscow for trial as war criminals. The Western powers protested against that act of violence at San Francisco, where the Polish chair was left empty, but nevertheless Harry Hopkins was sent to Moscow at the end of May and accepted the Russian list of those Poles who would be permitted to discuss the composition of their government. He succeeded only in having included in the list Stanislaw Mikolajczyk who, however, was no longer a member of the legitimate Polish Government which had unanimously rejected the Yalta decisions. While the sixteen underground leaders were sentenced, most of them to long prison terms, the "government" of sixteen Communists was "enlarged" in Moscow, on June 29, by the inclusion of two minor peasant leaders from inside Poland and two Poles from London (a third refused), namely, Mikolajczyk, who became second Vice-Premier and Minister of Agriculture, and a Socialist who became Minister of Labor. It was in favor of that regime that on July 5 the United States and Britain, soon followed by most of the other powers, withdrew recognition from the Polish Government in exile which had been their faithful ally and had directed the Polish war effort.

On August 1, at the Potsdam Conference, it was formally declared that this constitutional Government, still followed by all free Poles, had ceased to "exist." At the same time the Poles were supposed to receive the "substantial compensation in the West and in the North" which had been promised to them at Yalta for their losses in the East. While, however, the attribution to Soviet Russia of part of East Prussia with Königsberg was made final, the former German territories east of the Oder-Neisse line were merely placed under Polish administration, the "final determination" of the frontier being left to the future peace conference. Yet the Potsdam Conference authorized the transfer of the German population from that area to the West, and all Poles considered that territorial settlement permanent, realizing that even so their country would be left twenty per cent smaller than before the war.

The apparent support received in that vital matter from the Soviet Government, with which the Warsaw regime had signed a treaty of alliance and friendship as early as April 21, 1945, was a powerful asset for Russian propaganda. On the other hand, the reluctance of Britain and the United States to recognize Poland's western frontier as definite, as later expressed in the Stuttgart speech of Secretary of State James Byrnes on September 6, 1946, was resented by the Poles and contributed to the difficulties of the mission of United States Ambassador Arthur Bliss Lane who had arrived in Warsaw on July 31, 1945. He "saw Poland betrayed" and did his best to convince the Polish people of the sympathy of the Americans in general in spite of the growing tension between the United States Government and the Soviet controlled regime. That regime was indeed illegal from the outset, but since it had received international recognition and since Poland was occupied by strong Russian forces and encircled by Soviet Republics in the east and by the Russian zone of occupation in Germany in the west, the gradual sovietization of the country and the elimination of all resistance could proceed without any spectacular coup.

There was, therefore, a striking difference between the methods of enslavement in Poland and those used in other Central European countries: in Poland the Communists, supported by the Red Army, had seized power even before the war was over; there had been no democratic interlude between the German occupation and full control by Soviet Russia; and the Polish people never had any opportunity of free elections which would have revealed the extreme weakness of the native Communist elements. The elections promised at Yalta and Potsdam were simply postponed long enough to wear out and terrorize the forces of opposition, and the ambassadors of the Western powers who tried in vain to support these forces could only report on a situation which was the natural consequence of the Yalta agreement.

Referendum and Elections

The long delayed elections were preceded and prepared by the "referendum" of June 30, 1946, in which the Polish people had to answer three questions. The last one was uncontroversial, since the regime had taken advantage of the unanimity of the whole nation in the matter of the western frontier as "fixed on the Baltic and on the Oder and Neisse," and merely asked for an approval of that settlement. It was equally certain that a large majority would vote in favor of making permanent the land reform which was already practically accomplished, and "the nationalization of the basic industries with maintenance of the rights of private enterprise," as the question was carefully worded. The real test was to be the answer to the first question: "Are you in favor of the abolition of the Senate?" since this implied an arbitrary change of the democratic constitution of 1921, which the regime still pretended to observe.

In spite of Communist terror, an overwhelming majority voted against, as evidenced by the ballot boxes from no less than 2,805 districts, which were saved by non-Communist members of the voting commissions and contained 83.54 per cent of negative answers. Nevertheless, it was officially announced ten days later that 68 per cent of the voters had answered "yes" to the first question. The impression was thus created that there was no notable opposition against the Provisional Government. Both the American and the British governments were fully aware "that grave irregularities occurred in connection with the referendum," and protested against "oppressive acts which prevent normal democratic activity." They therefore asked for guarantees that the elections themselves, which at last they insisted should take place, would really be "free and unfettered," as promised at Yalta. Since, however, the Yalta agreement had not provided for any such guarantees, it was easy to foresee that those elections, finally fixed for January 19, 1947, would be an even greater fraud and mockery.

The new campaign of terror which preceded the voting was carefully watched by the American Ambassador, Arthur Bliss Lane. But the notes of August 19 and November 22, 1946, in which he outlined the prerequisite conditions for fair elections, remained unanswered, and in spite of his last minute appeals of January 5 and 9, 1947, in which he reminded the Provisional Government of its international obligations, the acts of violence directed especially against the Polish Peasant Party (which on October 7, 1946, had refused to join the governmental "bloc") made any free ballot completely impossible. The result was that in the new Parliament of 444 members the Government "bloc" received 394 seats, three split parties which still were tolerated by the regime won 22 seats, and the Polish Peasant Party, which in the elections had been supported by all opposition elements, won 28 seats. There followed immediately protests of the United States and British governments that the provisions of the Yalta and Potsdam agreements had not been fulfilled, and that "these elections were not a true reflection of the will of the Polish people." But no action was taken, the regime which thus had strengthened its position continued to be recognized by the Western powers, and on February 4, 1947, President Truman, receiving the new ambassador of Communist controlled Poland, Mr. Jozef Winiewicz (who replaced Professor Oskar Lange, a former American citizen largely responsible for misleading American public opinion in the whole matter), merely expressed his own and America's "deep concern" with the recent elections.

On that same day the new Sejm (Parliament) met in Warsaw, elected Boleslaw Bierut President of the Republic on the following day by a vote of 408 to 25, and constituted on February 7 a new government in which the opposition was no longer represented. Even before, on January 23, Mr. Lane resigned from his post as United States Ambassador. He was replaced on March 31 by Mr. Stanton Griffis, who soon arrived at the conclusion that "the rising tide of anti-Americanism" fostered by the regime made normal "diplomatic chores" impossible and that he "was wasting the public's money in remaining as ambassador to Poland." In October of the same year, Mr. Mikolajczyk, now convinced that there was no chance whatever to oppose the sovietization of his country, escaped with American help and came to the United States.

Toward the One-Party System

Before adjourning, the Sejm adopted on February 19 a "little" (provisional) Constitution which seemed to postpone full sovietization and on February 22 a Declaration of Rights which still paid lip service to democratic principles; but already in May, the Vice-Premier and Secretary General of the Communist Party's Central Committee, Wladyslaw Gomulka, announced that the Polish Socialist Party, the only strong element in the Government "bloc" besides the (Communist) Polish Workers' Party, would have to merge with the latter. It is surprising and typical of the careful methods which were applied in the enslavement of Poland, that such a merger through the creation of a "United Polish Workers' Party" was not achieved before December 15, 1948. The reason for that delay was not so much the initial resistance of the Socialists led by Prime Minister Jozef Cyrankiewicz but rather a "deviation" among the Communists which had to be suppressed first. In a speech made in June 1948 before the Central Committee of the Party, Gomulka himself suggested that Polish Communism should take an independent course, disassociate itself from the condemnation of Tito, and, without becoming anti-Russian or pro-West, safeguard Poland's national sovereignty. In connection with another statement by Gomulka that the specifically Polish form of people's democracy did not need the dictatorship of a single party, he was accused of both "rightist and nationalist deviation," severely censured at the meeting of the Central Committee (August 31–September 3, 1948), and removed at once from his post of Secretary General; a few months later, in January 1949, he also lost his vice-premiership and in November 1949 even his membership in the Central Committee. Finally in July 1951, soon after the arrest of General Marian Spychalski, who had been used to incriminate Gomulka, the latter himself was put in jail. The expected spectacular trial did not take place, but Bierut's leadership in the party remained unchallenged after the bloodless "purge" at the end of 1948.

The merger of the Communist and Socialist parties was, therefore, accomplished to the exclusive advantage of the former, and strictly following the Russian pattern. And since the other small parties, the so-called Democrats, the Christian Labor Party and a new "United Peasant Party" which had disassociated itself from Mikolajczyk's opposition, had practically no influence, the one-party system triumphed. Thanks to the strict control exercised by the secret police under a special Minister of Public Security, Stanislaw Radkiewicz, and thanks to a series of political trials in which alleged "American spies" were sentenced to death or long prison terms, the last elements of underground resistance were liquidated or disappeared in forced labor camps, and the time seemed ripe for putting the Polish Army openly under Russian control. This was achieved when on November 7, 1949, the former Soviet Marshal Constantine Rokossovsky, apparently of Polish descent, was made Minister of Defense and Commander-in-Chief of the Polish armed forces, in which all higher positions were occupied by Russian officers. The continued presence in Poland of strong Russian forces, under the pretext of safeguarding the communication lines with the Russian occupation army in Eastern Germany, made the domination of Poland by the U.S.S.R. even more complete.

Russian Control of Poland's Foreign Relations

Under these conditions Poland could not have any independent foreign policy. Instead of the legitimate Polish Government which continued in exile, first under the wartime President Wladyslaw Rackiewicz and after his death on June 6, 1947, under August Zaleski, it was the Warsaw regime which was invited to sign the Charter of the United Nations Organization where Communist delegates, first Oskar Lange, then J. Katz-Suchy, pretending to represent the Polish people actually followed the instructions of the U.S.S.R. How fully dependent the "new" Poland was on Soviet foreign policy, was evidenced in the summer of 1947, when Poland was forbidden to participate in the Marshall Plan and when the new international organ of Russian-controlled Communism, the so-called Cominform, was created at a congress held in Poland. A year later, after Tito's formal break with Stalin, Poland had to follow the U.S.S.R. and other Cominform countries in their policy hostile to Yugoslavia.

Poland also had to follow Russia's policy in her relations with Russian-occupied East Germany. It so happened, however, that as far as these relations were concerned, the attitude which was dictated by Moscow seemed really to correspond to the vital interests and desires of the Polish people. For the Communist regimes in both Warsaw and Berlin had to come to an agreement which recognized the new boundary on the Oder-Neisse line as a permanent "frontier of peace." This was proclaimed by the two regimes, after a gradual improvement in their relations, on June 7, 1950, sanctioned in an agreement at Zgorzelec on July 6, 1950, and confirmed at Frankfurt on the Oder on January 27 of the following year. Visits of the respective leaders in the capitals of the neighbor countries were supposed to evidence that the problem of German-Polish relations, including the big territorial issue which was involved, had been definitely settled under the sponsorship of Soviet Russia. This was and is the strongest single factor which consolidated the Communist regime and the Russian influence in Poland. And it is significant that only a little later, on May 22, 1951, a minor exchange of border areas along Poland's new eastern border was to indicate that this frontier, too, had to be considered final.

Reconstruction and Economic Control

This same impression was forced upon the Polish people by the transfer to the territories recovered in the west of almost all Poles who, after the earlier deportations to the U.S.S.R., still remained east of the Curzon line. The reconstruction and rehabilitation of those valuable but completely devastated territories, including the ports of Szczecin (Stettin) and Gdańsk (Danzig), and their integration with the rest of the country, was certainly a remarkable achievement, especially as the devastation of all Poland, particularly the city of Warsaw, also required an effort of reconstruction much greater than after World War I. However, the amazingly rapid results of this twofold effort must be attributed mainly to the Polish people themselves and to the fact that in that field—and in that field only—the people really and willingly cooperated with the otherwise abhorred regime. That the hold of the regime on the whole country was thus strengthened, is, of course, equally obvious.

The same is true of the unquestionable progress in Poland's industrialization, which was the main feature of a planned economy on the Soviet pattern, and which by 1953 increased the share of industry in the national income to 52 per cent. As early as 1947 an ambitious Three Year Plan was started. This was followed in 1950 by a Six Year Plan which was based on even closer relations with the Soviet Union. Official propaganda certainly exaggerated in stressing that the goals of these plans were in general reached and even surpassed in some cases; but production, especially in the heavy industries, was growing so quickly that in many fields (coal, coke, iron, steel) it soon went beyond the prewar level. Therefore, the man who from the outset directed that program and held the most important positions in the economic administration, Hilary Minc, was one of the few individuals who remained in power throughout the whole decade of Communist rule.

There were, however, two painful consequences of that economic policy. First, it served the interests of the U.S.S.R. more than those of Poland, where the standard of living remained extremely low. For the immediate purpose of the accelerated industrialization was the building up of war potential for the possible use of the Russian controlled Soviet bloc. Furthermore, in spite of efforts to develop trade relations with the other satellites and even with the Western countries also, a whole series of trade agreements with the Soviet Union oriented Poland's exports and imports in a way so favorable to the eastern neighbor that it led to a ruthless exploitation of Poland's economic resources by Russia. This started immediately after the war under the pretext of compensation for the 15 per cent share in the reparations from Germany, promised to Poland by the U.S.S.R. The coal deliveries to the Soviet Union at a "special" greatly reduced price, which were explained as a compensation for Russia's waiving of her "rights" to former German mines, were the most typical example.

Furthermore, the progress in the field of industry was, to a large extent, achieved at the expense of agriculture. The radical and hasty land reform could not satisfy the needs of the peasants, who were alarmed by the prospects of soon losing their private ownership to the Government through the introduction of kolkhozes on the Russian model, a system that was totally alien and unacceptable to the traditionally individualistic Polish farmer. The regime was careful enough not to start the collectivization of agriculture immediately and to create appearances that this was to be a purely spontaneous and gradual process. Nevertheless, as soon as the pressure in that direction increased, especially after Stalin's break with Tito, and the number of collective farms reached a greater proportion (about 8,000 in 1954), it became evident that owing to the reluctance of the peasants the production in those farms would be particularly low and that, in general, the resistance of the peasant masses, although necessarily passive, was one of the two strongest forces against Communist rule.

The Struggle on the Religious and Cultural Front

The other, a force of resistance from the very beginning, was the Catholic Church. After the loss of the eastern, partly Greek Orthodox borderlands, the extermination of most of the Jews during the German occupation, and the transfer of most of the Lutherans to Germany, the remaining population was almost completely Catholic (96 per cent against 75 per cent before the war), and not only belonged formally to the Roman Church, but proved more attached to its religious tradition than ever before in consequence of the ordeals of the war and postwar years. In this case, too, the Communist administration wisely avoided any early and open persecution and preferred to act through subtler methods.

One of the methods which was applied at once was a systematic propaganda campaign against the Vatican. Under the pretext that the Holy See had violated the Concordat of 1925 during the German occupation and also because the Vatican was one of the few powers, almost all Catholic, that continued to recognize the legitimate Polish Government in Exile, the Communist regime denounced the Concordat as early as 1946. Furthermore, in addition to the general slogan that the Pope was a "warmonger" serving the interests of American imperialism, the impression was created that the Vatican favored German revisionism directed against the new western frontier of Poland.

The Catholic hierarchy of Poland tried to explain the reason why the ecclesiastical organization of the western provinces encountered initial difficulties, declaring at the same time its full solidarity with the nation's determination to consider the transfer of these territories final. In view of the immense authority and popularity both of Cardinal Hlond, Archbishop of Gniezno (now also Warsaw) and Primate of Poland, and of the Archbishop of Cracow, Sapieha, who was also made a Cardinal in 1946, the regime carefully postponed any action directed against the Catholic Church. Cardinal Hlond died, however, in October 1948, and, at a time when Cardinal Sapieha happened to be absent in Rome, the Communist administration, after taking over the organization of Catholic charities, forced upon the hierarchy the Church-State agreement of April 14, 1950.

That ambiguous agreement was difficult to reject, since it did not contain anything contrary to Catholic principles, recognized the Pope's supreme authority in matters of faith and morals, and seemed to guarantee what still remained of freedom of worship and religious education. But that same text implied a recognition of the regime and a condemnation of any resistance against it, and opened the door to arbitrary interference of the administration with practically all aspects of religious life. A pledge of the hierarchy to support the movement in favor of international peace was immediately used as a pretext for repressions against those members of the clergy who did not want to sign the Communist-sponsored Stockholm appeal, and the trials of priests who seemed suspect to those in power continued on an even larger scale.

Cardinal Sapieha, who had anticipated all these dangers, died on July 23, 1951, but the Catholic Church of Poland had already found a no less courageous defender in the person of Cardinal Hlond's successor, the new Primate Archbishop Stefan Wyszyński. Soon after his elevation to the cardinalate, the decree of February 9, 1953, made all appointments to ecclesiastical offices subject to government approval, and three months later the Primate felt obliged to address to President Bierut a memorandum which protested against all measures taken against the Church in violation of the 1950 agreement, including a most dangerous diversionist action through a certain number of so-called "patriotic" priests. After the particularly shocking trial of one of the bishops, there came on September 26 of the same year the arrest of Cardinal Wyszyński, who was thus prevented from exercising his authority and of protecting the clergy against a growing wave of discrimination and persecution.

The struggle against Poland's Catholic tradition and unity with Rome was part of an equally systematic distortion of the very foundations of Polish culture and of an interference with the whole spiritual life of the nation, whose age long ties with the West were to be replaced by a one-sided intellectual penetration of Russian and Communist influence. This process, too, was carried out gradually, after a short period of apparent relief which followed the ruthless cultural policy of the German invaders. In addition to a growing trend towards Russification, education on all levels was distorted by the compulsory teaching of Marxist materialism, admission to the numerous institutions of higher education became dependent on political orthodoxy, and Communist elements were put in control of the faculties.

There was indeed an increase in the number of schools and

publications, but with a strong emphasis on technical education and on Communist propaganda which resulted in the enforced liquidation of the leading learned societies. On April 10, 1952, they were replaced by a new Academy of Science on the Soviet pattern and under Communist leadership. Intellectual leaders who did not conform were reduced to silence, and the whole country, after a few years of strictly controlled participation in UNESCO, was cut off from intellectual cooperation with the outside world, until in 1954 the time was ripe for permitting the return of a Polish Communist delegation to UNESCO, which at last was joined by the U.S.S.R. itself. The "palace of culture" which the Soviet Union, in the spring of 1952, decided to erect in the very center of Warsaw, is to be a symbol of Russia's domination even in the intellectual field.

Under the 1952 Constitution

The year 1952 proved even more decisive in the constitutional development of Poland. The new Constitution adopted by the Diet on July 22 gave clear evidence that the enslavement of the country, which had started eight years before, was now considered complete. It is true that the system of controlling all political life by a hierarchy of "people's councils" similar to the Russian "soviets" was already fully developed on March 20, 1950, and can be traced back to the creation of such councils on September 11, 1944. And the equally Soviet Russian conception of a "Presidium" exercising supreme power in the interval between the sessions of the Diet already appeared in the "little" Constitution of February 19, 1947. But it was the Constitution of 1952, drafted, with misleading appearances of free public discussions, by a Commission appointed on May 26 of the preceding year, which coordinated these preparatory initiatives and abolished all that still remained of Poland's traditional, democratic form of government, including even the office of the President of the Republic. It was the chairman of the new "Council of State," corresponding to the "Presidium" in the U.S.S.R., and supervising the activities of the "people's councils" of all levels, who now became the head of the State, a position entrusted to the Communist leader Alexander Zawadzki, while Bierut was named Prime Minister. Even that constitution was interpreted as an intermediary solution on the way from "people's democracy" to complete "socialism" (i.e., Communism), because "rural capitalism" was not yet liquidated. But the electoral law of July 31 of the same year was another step in that direction and made the elections held on October 26 even more fictitious than those of 1947. The single list of the so-called "National Front" was reported to have won an overwhelming victory, with more than 95 per cent of the voters casting their ballots.

Thanks to his new position, the dictatorial power of Bierut was still enforced, because the number of ministries placed under his control continued to grow on the Russian model. The total reached thirty-five in 1954. But even more significant was another change in his position, when in March 1954 he once more abandoned the premiership to the former Socialist Cyrankiewicz and preferred to limit himself to the post of Secretary General of the Central Committee of the United Workers Party. Exactly as happened in Russia after Stalin's death, the accumulation of offices in the hands of one individual was avoided, but the leadership of the Party and the primary importance of its organization now became as obvious as in the U.S.S.R. On the same occasion a leading position, that of Vice-Premier, was for the first time given to Jakob Berman, who from the earliest days of the Communist regime had exercised a decisive power behind the scene. There was no longer any reason to conceal the composition of the small group of men who really ruled Poland. Only annexation by the U.S.S.R. and formal transformation of Poland into a Soviet republic could be a further phase in the absorption of the "liberated" country by its big neighbor in the East.

Poland's Present International Position

Such a step would, however, quite unnecessarily shock the outside world, and the present situation is indeed more advantageous for Russia's foreign policy. For under the appearances of national sovereignty, her chief European satellite is perforce obliged to conform completely to that foreign policy and to support it through an apparently independent vote in the United Nations and at any other international conferences.

In order for Poland to fulfill this role, a prerequisite condition is a continuous deterioration of her official relations with the chief opponent of the U.S.S.R.: the United States. The closing of the United States Information Service in Warsaw, on August 9, 1951, was symbolic in that respect and was followed, of course, by similar measures taken by the American Government. But even more eloquent is the long series of protests which the Warsaw regime had to send to Washington usually complaining against alleged American espionage in connection with trials against so-called foreign agents and diversionists. How the Polish people really feel in that matter is best evidenced by an equally long series of frequently spectacular escapes from the enslaved country and by the revelations of all those who thus decided to "choose freedom." Only in one respect the official protests addressed to the Western powers express the genuine concern of the nation: the rearmament of Germany could not but create among the Poles serious apprehensions which the regime was only too glad to use as one of its most efficient propaganda weapons.

The apparent solidarity of Communist controlled Poland and the whole Soviet bloc in the Far East has one particular aspect which deserves attention. Official Polish participation in the armistice discussions and commissions dealing with both Korea and Indo-China had led to a *rapprochement* between Warsaw and Peiping, which after the Geneva Conference in the summer of 1954 found expression in an exchange of visits between the Polish and Chinese Communist leaders in their respective capitals. It remains to be seen whether the cooperation of the Warsaw regime with Red China, which is more independent from Moscow than the European satellites, might contribute to increased independence for Poland as well. But in any case this would mean merely a stronger position within the Communist bloc and not any real progress on the way towards liberation.

How distant that goal still is today, and how much firmer Moscow's hold on Poland and the other enslaved countries than ever before, clearly appeared during 1954. A Polish delegation headed by Prime Minister Cyrankiewicz had to attend the Moscow Conference from November 29 to December 3, a conference which was invited to discuss the general problem of European security without waiting for any solution of the German question. Since only the Communist controlled satellites were represented, the result was merely a consolidation of the Soviet bloc under Moscow's unquestioned leadership. The decision to develop an even closer military cooperation was carried out on May 14, 1955, at another conference held in Warsaw where a treaty was signed which is supposed to be a counterpart to NATO. All this could only confirm the misleading impression that Poland, the strongest among the satellites and more than the others alarmed by the renascence of German military power, was occupying a key position in the defense system of the whole Russian orbit and was definitely integrated with that political system. Furthermore, in the case of Poland more than in any other it soon became evident that, in spite of an apparent easing of the tension between West and East during and after the Geneva Conference, the Soviet Union was not willing even to discuss any changes in the conditions of the captive nations of East Central Europe under the pretext that this would be an interference with their sovereignty.

The Russian reinterpretation of Poland's place in Europe, which makes her an outpost not of Western Christendom but of the East in its struggle against the West, is contrary not only to Poland's whole tradition but to the intimate aspirations of the Polish people. Their present enslavement, for which the West is not without responsibility, has not altered their desire freely to join an integrated Europe, nor their conviction that Poland's liberation can only be achieved through the support of the United States. This is, of course, equally true for all enslaved nations of East Central Europe, but here again some specific features of the Polish case must be stressed.

In no other case are the traditional ties of friendship with the United States older and stronger. No other nation of East Central Europe has had such a numerous emigration to America which can be traced back to the colonial period. The memory of Woodrow Wilson's part in the rebirth of Poland still thrives there, as does that of Herbert Hoover's relief action after World War I, and the Polish people realize that the leading role of the United States in the final peace settlement after World War II is far from being closed or determined by the mistakes made in 1945. And a free Poland would obviously be America's most reliable ally in Central and Eastern Europe where she would occupy again a real key position.

But it is equally clear that the American foreign policy with regard to Poland is part of the larger, general problem of dealing with the whole area which ten years ago came under the control of Soviet Russia. The last illusions that Poland's total enslavement could be prevented by "free" elections under the Communist controlled regime disappeared in 1947, and since that date the American Embassy in Warsaw is merely a symbol, without any possibility of contact with the Polish people, while the Polish Embassy in Washington was from 1945 nothing but a center of Communist propaganda. Occasional American contacts with diplomatic representatives of the Warsaw regime who pretend to represent the Polish people create only appearances of American-Polish relations, or rather of American-Polish hostility. Relations with the emigration which rightfully represents free Poland are at present the only possibility of preparing a better future.

Chapter 7

Eastern Germany

KARL C. THALHEIM

Structure and Importance of the Soviet Zone

THE GERMAN territories held by the Red Army at the time of the "unconditional surrender" (May 8, 1945) in the main constituted the eastern part of prewar Germany. The highly developed industrial areas of central Germany, namely, the *Länder* (states) Saxony, Thuringia, and Anhalt as well as the Prussian province of Saxony, were, on the other hand, occupied completely or for the most part by American or British troops, the former having slowed their advance, especially in Saxony, in view of the boundary lines of the occupation zones. These boundaries had already been drawn and agreed upon. The territories in the hands of the Soviet troops were predominantly agrarian, excepting Silesia, the city of Berlin, and parts of the Prussian province of Brandenburg, and for that reason were far less attractive to the Soviet Union, in view of its intense interest in restoring Soviet industrial potential.

The agreements regarding the boundary lines of the occupation zones (approved at Yalta, but drawn up by the European Advisory Commission some months earlier) were carried into effect on July 1, 1945. Consequently, the English and American troops who had advanced beyond the new demarcation line moved back

[*Editor's Note:* This essay examines mainly developments of the internal East German scene which were affected by U.S. policy for Germany and the impact of events in West Germany. These aspects, as well as East Germany's international status and her actions in the realm of foreign policy, could not be explored in more detail because of limitations in space. The author has made the following statement of his objective: "This presentation deals only with developments in the Soviet Occupation Zone of Germany, the present 'German Democratic Republic,' to the exclusion of the territories east of the Oder-Neisse Line now under Polish administration." The chapter was translated by Karl Jorda.]

to positions farther west, relinquishing to the Red Army all of central Germany. On the other hand, approximately two thirds of Berlin, the former capital of the *Reich,* was taken over by American, British, and, later, French troops. Thus, Berlin became an island in the midst of the Soviet Occupation Zone. The Soviet Union, for its part, made over to Poland all the territories east of the Oder-Neisse Line—as delineated at Potsdam—with the exception of the northern half of East Prussia, which the U.S.S.R. appropriated for itself.

The economic potential to which the Soviet Union became heir in its zone of Germany was considerable. The states of Saxony and Thuringia possessed a highly developed manufacturing industry: its productive capacity for machine tools and appliances, precision tools and optical instruments, automobiles and some electro-technical items proved particularly appealing to the Soviets, to say nothing of huge lignite and potassium deposits, notably in the Prussian province of Saxony, which formed the basis of a gigantic chemical industry. Even before the Nazi era there were in the region very large chemical plants belonging for the most part to *I. G. Farbenindustrie,* for example, the Leuna factories near Merseburg, the largest industrial plant of the Soviet Zone and one of the biggest in Germany. In this area also, the Nazis had pushed forward the development of synthetic fuel and rubber production. Thus, since 1935 the largest plants for the extraction of synthetic fuel and buna (synthetic rubber) had been constructed here. Furthermore, the Soviet Union was well aware that this industrial aggregate of central Germany in its gradual growth had developed a highly qualified labor force—the lack of which in the Soviet Union is still one of the most serious obstacles to efficient production.

Psychologically, the retreat of the Western Allies had a negative effect on the population of these territories. There was, it is true, in the industrial region of central Germany a traditionally strong Socialist movement of a rather radical tinge. But the percentage of actual Communist Party members was negligible, and unfavorable reports from the Soviet-occupied region concerning Red Army conduct and existing conditions did not arouse popular sympathies for the Soviets. During the weeks of military collapse the great majority of the people had desperately hoped that the Western powers would be the first to enter and occupy their area, and naturally considered the change in occupying powers as disastrous. From a psychological point of view it was particularly inopportune that to the very last moment the people were left in the dark about the forthcoming change in occupation. Only a small circle of extremely important persons, such as scientists, were given a chance to move to the West with the withdrawing American and British troops.

Beginnings of Soviet Occupation Policies

After delimitation of the occupation zones, the Soviets held in Germany an area of 107,173 square kilometers (41,379 square miles) with a population of 17,330,000, not including Soviet-occupied Berlin with its 1,100,000 inhabitants. The Soviet Zone consisted of five *Länder:* Saxony (mostly the former *Land* Saxony), Saxony-Anhalt (the former *Land* Anhalt and about two thirds of the former Prussian province of Saxony), Thuringia (the former *Land* Thuringia plus the southern part of the former Prussian province of Saxony), Mecklenburg (the former *Land* Mecklenburg plus the western part of the former province of Pomerania), and Brandenburg (that part of the former *Land* Brandenburg west of the Oder-Neisse Line).

Very soon it became obvious that the differences in occupation policies consisted not only in the dissimilarity in uniforms of the occupation troops but also in completely discrepant political and economic principles. Two of the decisions of the Potsdam Conference (July 17 to August 2, 1945) read in part:

> II. A. 2: So far as is practicable, there shall be uniformity of treatment of the German population throughout Germany.
>
> II. B. 14: During the period of occupation Germany shall be treated as a single economic unit . . .

Neither of the directives was heeded. The objectives pursued by the Soviet Union regarding reorganization of Germany differed entirely from those of the three Western occupation powers. All four powers had agreed to the principle, enunciated at the Potsdam meeting, that the final reorganization of Germany's political life was to be sought on a "democratic basis." However, the respective interpretations of "democratic" varied greatly: "democracy" for the Soviet Union was synonymous with the political, economic, and social system that had evolved in the U.S.S.R.

The first Soviet measures did not fully reveal Soviet intentions.

The immediate suspension of operations of all private banks and insurance companies pursuant to order No. 1 of the SMAD (Soviet Military Administration of Germany) of July 23–25, 1945 did not exclude the possibility of their later reinstatement. But in fact the order meant the end of the banks, except for an insignificant number of unimportant private banks in Saxony and Thuringia. Likewise, decrees issued by the administrative bodies of the five *Länder* between September 3 and 12, 1945 on land reform, dispossessing all farmers who owned land in excess of one hundred hectares (247.1 acres), could not be regarded as specifically Soviet, because similar steps toward a reorganization of the agrarian structure had been taken in other countries not in the Soviet orbit. Yet the absence of compensation for the expropriated owners and the compulsory changing of residence to a different county were, of course, irreconcilable with legal conceptions of the Western world. The purpose behind the measure did not at first appear to be a Soviet-style collectivization but, on the contrary, a strengthening of, and an increase in, small individual farms, for another decree ordered that farms of dispossessed proprietors were to be parceled into small holdings and distributed primarily to refugees and agricultural laborers. Nevertheless, a considerable part of such farmland was not distributed but managed as state property. There are now over five hundred of these state farms, which approximately correspond to the Soviet *sovkhozy* and which in East Germany are called *Volkseigene Güter* (VEG)—"people's farms." But distribution of the rest was sufficient to change substantially the social structure of agriculture in regions where large estates constituted a large percentage of farm area, as in the *Land* of Mecklenburg and parts of Brandenburg. Thus, 210,000 new farms were created.

Expropriation measures in industry had extremely incisive effects. In this connection the Soviets availed themselves very cleverly of the possibilities created by the Allied Control Council's directive No. 38 for the elimination of "war criminals, National Socialists, and militarists." SMAD orders Nos. 124 and 126 of October 30–31, 1945 listed a number of categories of property to be confiscated and put under trust-administration. These categories were so broad that private enterprise was eliminated entirely from heavy industry and to a great extent also from medium-sized industries. In addition, two hundred of the biggest and most important industrial plants that had not been dismantled were immediately transferred into Soviet ownership as so-called SAG (Soviet stock company) enterprises. Among these were all of the *I. G. Farben* mammoth chemical plants. Only a few insignificant factories were returned into private hands. In Saxony, the fate of the other industrial enterprises, that is, elimination of private ownership by expropriation, was decided by a "plebiscite on dispossession of war criminals and Nazi activists" on June 30, 1946, while the other four *Länder* ejected private owners by means of administrative orders on the *Land* level. Needless to say, there was no compensation for such dispossession. Since East Berlin was dealt with in a like manner, the polarity of the economic principles applied by the occupation powers in the three western sectors, on the one hand, and in the eastern part of Berlin, on the other, became especially conspicuous.

Legally enacted expropriation, substantially identical in all five *Länder,* was achieved only for one Soviet Zone industry, mining. It is characteristic of the regional differences still possible then that the bourgeois parties in the *Land* of Saxony-Anhalt succeeded in achieving a proper and just compensation for owners not incriminated politically. This, however, remained without practical significance. The effectiveness of extralegal expropriation methods is evidenced by the fact that already in the spring of 1948 socialized enterprises produced 40 per cent of the entire industrial output of the Soviet Zone. With another 25 to 30 per cent coming from SAG enterprises, a mere one third of the entire production was left for private industry. Numerically, however, socialized enterprises accounted only for approximately 8 per cent of all the industries, while nine tenths were still private. A comparison of these two figures shows clearly that only small plants and a few medium-sized enterprises, especially in the manufacturing of consumption goods, like textiles, had escaped socialization. It is, then, remarkable that the Soviets successfully converted all of the important industrial potential of the Soviet Occupation Zone into state property (or Soviet property) without the need of a socialization law—apart from the one above-named exception.

In their effect upon industry, the expropriation measures of these first years of occupation left no doubt that the Soviet Union was intent on assimilating the economic system of its occupation zone to that established in Russia. Yet at first, in economic matters as well as in general and cultural politics, the Soviets cautiously camouflaged this intention to bring about sovietization, by utilizing watchwords associated with eradication of militarism and Nazism and democratization of Germany. For instance, the manifesto of the revived Communist Party of Germany (KPD), published on June 11, 1945, states:

> We believe that a policy of forcible sovietization of Germany would be wrong, because such a step does not take into consideration the present conditions in Germany. Rather we are of the view that the decisive interests of Germany under present circumstances dictate other measures, namely, building up an antifascist, democratic regime, a parliamentary republic guaranteeing the people all democratic rights and liberties.

Political development soon revealed that this proclamation was not at all expressive of the real intentions of the Communist Party leadership, which, headed by Wilhelm Pieck and Walter Ulbricht, consisted predominantly of persons who as emigrants had lived in the Soviet Union during the National Socialist era. The proclamation was solely designed to lull into security not only the non-Communist population, which far outnumbered the Communists, but the Western powers as well.

The Struggle of Communism for Political Hegemony

As early as June 10, 1945—considerably sooner than in the Western occupation zones—Marshall Zhukov, then chief of the SMAD, permitted the formation and activities of "antifascist parties and trade unions" in the Soviet Zone pursuant to SMAD order No. 2. These parties sprang up in rapid succession: Social Democratic Party (June 15), Christian Democratic Party (June 26), and Liberal Democratic Party (July 5). From the very first the Communist Party was, of course, in special favor. SMAD order No. 17, of July 25, created eleven "German Central Administrations" for the Soviet Zone, all of which had economic functions, with the exception of the "Central Administrations" for justice, health, and education. The majority of these administrative agencies were headed by non-Communists, but characteristically enough, Communists were appointed to preside over three of the most vital "Central Administrations," namely, those of education, industry, and agriculture.

Toleration of non-Communist parties and appointment of non-Communists to responsible posts were intended to signify that the Soviet Zone was devoted to principles of democracy not unlike those of the West. In truth, the efforts of the Communist bosses, masters in political manipulations, centered first and foremost around the capture of vital policy-making positions in the political and economic life of the Soviet Zone. In this they were greatly aided by the occupation power. To further intensify Communist influence, the Soviets resorted to so-called "people's front" tactics in the form of "bloc politics." On July 14, 1945 the four authorized parties, for instance, formed the "Antifascist-Democratic Bloc" in Berlin. The main objectives of cooperation among the four parties, as enunciated in the resolution adopted then, were: purging from Germany of all vestiges of Nazism, joint efforts for a speedy reconstruction of the German economy, re-establishment of law and order on the basis of a democratic constitutional state, granting of religious freedom, and regaining of the trust and confidence of other nations. In the framework of this cooperation the non-Communist parties seemed assured for the time being of an ample measure of self-determination and an opportunity to formulate policies. Yet, in less than half a year, a serious conflict marked the beginning of the events that led only a few years later to a complete emasculation of the non-Communist parties. When the two chairmen of the Christian Democratic Union (CDU), Dr. Hermes and Dr. Schreiber, attempted to test this presumed independence by remonstrating against the expropriation of large estates without compensation, an issue considered vitally important by the SMAD, the latter immediately seized upon the chance to silence CDU opposition: it invoked a clause of its order No. 2, of June 10, 1945 (referred to above), to the effect that the licensed parties were expressly subject to control by the SMAD. Then, under Soviet pressure the executive council of the CDU prevailed upon the two attacked chairmen to resign from their positions. They were succeeded by Jacob Kaiser, a leader in the Christian labor union movement, and Ernst Lemmer, a Berlin journalist, both of whom suffered a similar fate after only one year.

Among the three non-Communist parties, the Social Democratic Party (SPD) must have appeared to the Communists as a possible source of the most dangerous competition. The SPD could depend upon an age-old tradition of Social Democratic predominance throughout the industrial areas of central Germany, a source of support and membership whose nucleus survived the Nazi interlude unshaken. Moreover, the SPD was above all a workers' party, and among its members were a number of leading personalities who clearly were not at all willing to submit to Soviet power politics without opposition; and it boasted relations with sister parties in Western Germany that were now growing stronger. To undermine this position of the SPD in order eventually to seize absolute power through "bloc politics" was naturally the immediate goal of the Communist Party. The KPD, therefore, very early launched a propaganda campaign advocating a merger of the two workers' parties. Their strongest argument was that Hitler's bid for power in Germany had been successful primarily because of the political split within the German labor movement, and that the battle against a recrudescent "fascism" could be fought only by a united labor front. But these captious phrases did not beguile one segment of the Social Democratic leadership that was aware of the danger of being engulfed by the Communists. Gradually, however, partly by threats and partly by lures, the Communists succeeded in preparing the ground for a subsequent merger. They prudently refrained from polling members of the SPD on their attitude regarding union with the KPD. Finally, the last two separate party conventions of the SPD and KPD, on April 19, 1946, resolved to merge and create the Socialistic Union Party of Germany (SED). Two days later a convention of the newly unified party was held. Communist Wilhelm Pieck and Social Democrat Otto Grotewohl were elected chairmen with equal rights. Thus, Grotewohl, an extremely ambitious politician, was requited for giving up his initial opposition to a merger. His later reward was to be even greater. After the creation of the "German Democratic Republic" ("DDR") in October 1949, he became prime minister. He has remained in office to the present time.

Developments in Berlin, however, indicated clearly that the merger was not at all to the liking of the SPD members. The four-power administration of that city made it impossible for the Communists to thrive and capitalize on the same pressure methods used in the Soviet Zone. They met with staunch opposition from local SPD leaders, who demanded that their followers in Berlin be polled on the question. Such a polling was undertaken on March 31, 1946; its outcome was a high 82 per cent opposed to union with the KPD. This failure of Communist effort in Berlin was to become exceedingly momentous for the city's subsequent political fate. It is a fair assumption that secret balloting of the SPD in the

Soviet Zone would not have yielded a substantially different result.

Municipal and *Länder* elections held in the Soviet Zone in September and October 1946 furnish further evidence to refute the contention that the SPD had endorsed the merger. Those elections, the last reasonably free elections in the Soviet Zone, may be taken as actually free expressions of opinion, in spite of many restrictions and even in spite of open favoritism in the propaganda possibilities available to the SED. For example, in the municipal elections of September 15, votes cast for the SED totaled 48 per cent, while the CDU and LDP obtained approximately 20 per cent each. Almost 10 per cent of the votes were classified as "invalid." In the parliamentary elections of October 21 the SED obtained 47.4 per cent of the ballots, while 24.8 per cent of those who exercised their right of suffrage voted for the LDP, 24.6 per cent for the CDU, and 3 per cent for the Union of Farmers' Mutual Assistance (VdgB), a group largely dependent on the SED. In Mecklenburg, the SED was given almost an even half of the votes; in none of the other four *Länder* did it obtain majority status. These election returns show, then, with absolute clarity, that a great many former SPD members cast their votes not for the newly unified party but rather for one of the bourgeois parties. In this connection it is particularly noteworthy that in the city of Leipzig, a big industrial center with a strong labor population and a traditionally Socialist majority, the non-Communist parties garnered more votes than the SED, although Leipzig's former middle-class population had already been greatly reduced. The five *Länder* governments, set up by the SMAD, were composed of representatives of all three bloc parties, with the SED typically ensconcing itself in key positions. To illustrate: four prime ministers (except in Saxony-Anhalt), four ministers of the interior (except in Brandenburg), all ministers of education, three ministers of economy (except in Saxony-Anhalt and Mecklenburg) were SED men.

This whole development was colored by attempts of the Soviet occupation power to simulate adherence to democratic ways. It was behind the scenes, therefore, that the battle for expansion and solidification of the Communist power position was unceasingly and obstinately waged. This above all is the explanation for the fact that none of the Western powers offered to take a firm stand against the dangers, becoming ever more obvious, to a really democratic reorganization of the Soviet Zone. Early conflicts were engendered mostly because of Russian methods of exploiting industrial resources in their zone. These methods were glaringly inconsistent with the Yalta and Potsdam agreements, and the conflicts gained considerable momentum in the general framework of the "cold war" then developing.

Exploitation of the Soviet Zone's Industrial Potential

Reconstruction of the Soviet Union, severely hit in many parts by wartime destruction, and fulfillment of the first Soviet postwar Five Year Plan were immensely aided by the fact that the Soviet Union could in substantial measure draw on the production of its wartime enemies, especially on that of the Soviet-occupied part of Germany. There the Soviets found the largest industrial potential of any of the countries under their domination and there they encountered the least resistance. Under these circumstances, it is easy to understand the Russian eagerness to take advantage of the possibilities of radical exploitation without regard to the material situation of the people.

The claims of the Soviet Union for restitution of war damages had already played an important role at Yalta. In implementing the Yalta Protocol on German Reparations that "Germany must pay in kind for the losses caused by her to the Allied Nations in the course of the war," the Potsdam Conference reached the following agreements:

1. Reparation claims of the U.S.S.R. shall be met by removals from the zone of Germany occupied by the U.S.S.R., and from appropriate German external assets.
2. The U.S.S.R. undertakes to settle the reparation claims of Poland from its own share of reparations.

In addition to these reparations, the Soviet Union was to have a share, in a certain percentage, in industrial machinery and equipment from the Western occupation zones "which was not necessary for the German peacetime economy and was, therefore, earmarked for dismantlement."

In another clause the Potsdam agreement had set forth general principles controlling Germany's payment of reparations:

> Payment of Reparations should leave enough resources to enable the German people to subsist without external assistance. . . . The proceeds of exports from current production and stocks shall be available in the first place for payment for such imports.

To carry out these directives the Potsdam agreement stipulated:

> The determination of the amount and character of the industrial capital equipment unnecessary for the German peace economy and therefore available for reparation shall be made by the Control Council under policies fixed by the Allied Commission on Reparations, with the participation of France, subject to the final approval of the Zone Commander in the Zone from which the equipment is to be removed.

The principles determining reparations were rather clear: German reparation payments were to be borne in the first place by that part of German industry's capital equipment considered by the Control Council as "unnecessary for the German peace economy." (To this must be added German capital and investments in foreign countries—although details need not be discussed here. The "German foreign assets in Bulgaria, Finland, Hungary, Rumania, and Eastern Austria" were transferred to the Soviet Union pursuant to the Potsdam agreement (III. 9.). Obviously, the Allies intended to limit Germany's industrial resources uniformly in all four occupation zones. But there is no mention whatsoever in the Potsdam agreement of reparations out of current production.

The "Plan for Reparations and Postwar Status of German Industry," promulgated by the Control Council on March 31, 1946, contains similar principles. Its essence was the postulate "that Germany be regarded as a single economic unit," and its main purpose was the determination of the limits of the industrial potential to be left Germany in its categories and total capacity as well as in its annual production, which was not to be exceeded without special authorization. For instance, production of crude steel ingots was limited to 5.8 million tons yearly. This plan aimed at reducing German industry to 50–55 per cent of its prewar standard (1938), exclusive of the construction industry and its auxiliary branches. On some industries there was a complete prohibition.

Prior to these decisions, the Soviet Union had already started large-scale dismantling of factories and plants in its zone of occupation, particularly in Berlin. Thus, while the Soviets were the sole masters of the city for only two months, they dismantled and shipped out an estimated 75 per cent of the capital equipment of Berlin's industry.[1] The Red Army had hardly entered the Eastern

[1] See the detailed presentation on the scope of dismantling in Berlin and the Soviet Zone, published by the Commission for Industrial Research of Bremen under the title, *Am Abend der Demontage—Sechs Jahre Reparations politik* [*At the Close of Dismantling—Six Years of Reparations Politics*] (Bremen, 1951), pp. 59–113.

Zone when they set out to dismantle and remove about half of its industrial equipment. This also illustrated the extraordinary economic importance of the Saxonian and Thuringian territories which the Western Allies had ceded to the Soviet Union. The most comprehensive but still incomplete list of plants either wholly or partly dismantled includes 1,923 industrial enterprises. The following is a breakdown of this total by *Länder* (Berlin is excluded):

Saxony	1,052
Saxony-Anhalt	262
Thuringia	406
Brandenburg	167
Mecklenburg	36

The increase in industrial capacity which the Soviet Union secured from German plants in the Soviet Zone came in the first place from those richly industrial areas originally occupied by the Western powers but then relinquished to the Soviets. In this connection it is significant to point out that the extent to which dismantling was carried was not governed by principles set out in the "reparations plan." For instance, as late as 1946–1947 the Soviets still proceeded to remove machines and equipment from lignite mines and briquette factories, expressly exempted by the "reparations plan."

Besides, the Soviet Union very soon advanced claims for reparations from current production, and beginning with 1946 such reparations were to affect the Soviet Zone's economy most severely for several years to come. At Yalta the extent of these reparations had been a disputed and not definitely settled problem. James F. Byrnes reported [2] that the Soviets demanded for themselves reparations of $10 billion, half of the proposed total to be paid by Germany. Churchill as well as President Roosevelt objected on the ground that after the first World War payments of reparations by Germany created great difficulties and were finally made possible by American loans to Germany. Stalin countered by arguing that those difficulties were due to the provision that reparations were to be paid in specie. Finally, it was agreed that a reparations commission should fix the total of the German reparations.[3] Byrnes also

[2] James F. Byrnes, *Speaking Frankly* (New York, 1947), pp. 26 ff.

[3] According to Byrnes (*ibid.*, pp. 28–29), President Roosevelt explained at Yalta that "the Reparations Commission 'should take, in its initial studies, as a basis of discussion the suggestion of the Soviet government, that the total sum of reparations should be twenty billions and that 50 per cent of it should go to the Soviet Union.' " This statement by Roosevelt was in all subsequent negotiations interpreted as consent to the Russian demands.

expresses regret that without discussion at the Conference a statement was entered in the record that "the Reparations Commission could consider 'the use of labor' as a possible source of reparations." This statement proved of great importance for the attitude the Russians subsequently took. The main argument from the American side against Soviet demands for deliveries of goods out of current production was that the latter must be used primarily to defray the costs of vital imports into Germany. Byrnes is quite explicit about the fact "that nowhere in the Potsdam Protocol is there any provision for the payment of reparations from current production."

The controversy between the former Allies over Russian reparation demands undoubtedly contributed to the dissolution of the wartime coalition. But American protests against the extent of Russian claims could not prevent a substantial decline of current production in the Eastern Zone as a consequence of shipments to the Soviet Union. In spite of extreme Soviet secrecy as to pertinent facts, an investigation of this exploitation has brought to light that shipments to Russia of officially designated "reparations" constituted only a small fraction of the total industrial equipment, stripped from the Soviet Zone. In addition to dismantled industrial machinery, other forms of payments and services were exacted from the Soviet Zone, such as occupation costs (provisioning of Soviet armed forces in the Soviet Zone, except for weapons, was done almost completely from its production); purchases of the Soviet Military Administration, which likewise constituted deliveries to the Russians for no return because they were paid for in old reichsmark currency; transfer of two hundred of the biggest industrial enterprises, which had been left intact, into Soviet ownership as so-called SAG plants; and lastly, requisition of the labor force of the Russian Zone for Soviet purposes. As to this last point, it was particularly in the uranium mines, chiefly in the Saxon Erzgebirge, that the Soviets put to work directly or indirectly almost a quarter million people at the peak of the development. In the summer of 1955 approximately 150,000 workers were probably still there.

On August 22, 1953 the government of the U.S.S.R. and a delegation of the "German Democratic Republic" signed in Moscow a "protocol on the cancellation of German reparation payments and on other relief measures for the financial and economic obligation of the DDR which were incurred as a consequence of the war." This protocol provided for the cessation of reparations payments of the Soviet Zone as of January 1, 1954, and further announced a limitation of occupation costs to 5 per cent of the revenue in the budget of the "DDR" (1.6 billion East German marks) and the restitution of the last thirty-three industrial enterprises that had been Soviet property since 1945. Already in 1950 the Soviet Union had reduced its original claim for $10 billion to $6.829 billion. Reparation payments to the end of 1951 amounted to $3.658 billion. This sum includes the value of dismantled factories and other industrial installations, as well as payments from the current production over a span of approximately five years. The real value of all deliveries to Russia from the Soviet Zone was undoubtedly much higher.

Reparations and all other deliveries and services of the Soviet Zone to the occupying power have become a primary political problem, not only in the relationship of the former Allies with one another, but also in the relationship between the people of the Soviet Zone and the Soviet Union. Above all, these reparations caused the living standard of the people during the first postwar years to plunge to an intolerably low level, and this in turn was responsible for a dreadfully high mortality rate.

The Berlin Blockade

To differentiate between the situation of the Soviet-occupied territory in Germany and that of the Soviet satellites, reference must be made to the essential fact that the existence of the three Western sectors in Berlin made quite impossible an equally definite disruption of relations with the Western world. Berlin was still a unit from an administrative point of view when separate administration of the other occupation zones had already become a reality, and the Control Council no longer had practical significance as the organ of a unified government for Germany. The possibility which the people of the Soviet Zone took liberal advantage of, to keep alive direct connections with the Western world by visiting the Western sectors of Berlin, was significant not only as a considerable limitation on the almost absolute monopoly of the promulgation of news, as exemplified in all other Communist-dominated parts of the globe, but also as a means to strengthen incalculably the internal resistance to the Communist system by an overwhelming majority of the people of Eastern Germany. The existence of this "island of the free world," led by a statesman of historical stature, Ernst Reuter, presented for the Soviet occupation power a highly discomforting reality, counterbalanced only by the material gains from the central German industrial area, originally held by the Western powers but then exchanged for Berlin.

The positive opportunities afforded the Western powers in the possession of the Western sectors of Berlin, with a population of over two million, proved the more momentous as the "cold war" more and more replaced the "strange alliance" of the second World War. Every attempt to extend the Soviet orbit farther westward must have appeared to the men in the Kremlin, who undoubtedly contemplated such expansion in a very real and concrete sense, as a highly questionable possibility as long as Berlin, a bastion of the West, stood steadfast and unshaken. Its elimination, therefore, was to be achieved by a blockade. This was a unique attempt in the history of mankind to starve a city with more than two million residents in a period of peace. Unhampered by humane considerations, the Soviets took ruthless advantage of the fact that all connecting links between West Germany and Berlin led through Soviet-held territory and that the Western powers, in their unbelievably blind confidence, had not insisted during the negotiations in 1945 on a written guarantee to safeguard the right to use the main roads to Berlin.[4] Only agreements concerning the use of air lanes by the Western Allies had been drawn up in writing.

The attempt to starve West Berlin met with determined and courageous resistance by the city. The attitude of the population during the eleven months the blockade lasted—from June 24, 1948 to May 12, 1949—unmistakably manifested to the world and to the Soviets that the Berliners were firmly determined to maintain their freedom. General Lucius Clay makes this comment in his memoirs:

> The determination of the people did not falter. They were proud to carry their burden as the price of their freedom, and though the price was high it had brought them something in return that had become dear. They had earned their right to freedom; they had atoned for their failure to repudiate Hitler when such repudiation on their part might have stopped his rise to power.[5]

[4] [*Editor's Note:* For an authoritative explanation the reader might want to consult Philip E. Mosley, "The Occupation of Germany: New Light on How the Zones Were Drawn," *Foreign Affairs,* XXVIII (1950), 580–604. Cf. the note of the U.S. Government to Ambassador Alexander S. Panyushkin of July 6, 1948 concerning the Soviet Blockade of Berlin. *Bulletin,* XIX (1948), 85–86.]

[5] Lucius D. Clay, *Decision in Germany* (Garden City, N.Y., 1950), p. 388.

This determination to preserve the freedom of Berlin, a city wholly encircled, would have availed little had it not been for the political decision on the part of the Western powers, especially the United States, to use air transport as only modern technology made possible. In the beginning, responsible men were by no means unanimous in the belief that the Western powers should stay in Berlin in spite of the Soviet blockade. But General Clay, then American military governor in Germany, contended vigorously that Berlin would have to be held by all means, lest West Germany in a matter of time fall prey to Soviet expansionism. The organization of the airlift created the technical basis: it was thus possible to supply not only food for Berlin's population but also a certain minimum of coal to keep West Berlin's industries in operation, even though this was practicable only to a limited extent.

The Soviets were confronted with a situation they had in no way anticipated. At the beginning of the blockade they must have expected to force Berlin to surrender within a few weeks. When the winter had passed and the besieged city had successfully endured its hardest time of trial, the Soviet leaders had to recognize that their hopes were shattered and that their open and ruthless drive for expansion had intensely strengthened the resistance of the free world. At the same time, the economy of the Soviet Zone suffered more and more tangibly from the effects of the "counterblockade" carried out by the Western powers, because the Soviet Zone could not then do without West German goods exchanged in interzone commerce. The growing shortage in materials appreciably retarded production in the Russian Zone, while the West German economy, propped by a secure and stable currency and freed from the fetters of rigid state control, took rapid strides forward. The difference in living standards between West and East Germany, relatively negligible before the currency reform in Western Germany, increased perceptibly.

These facts soon impelled the Russians to take up secret negotiations. On May 4, 1949 the public was informed that the occupation powers had come to terms on raising the blockade, and during the night of May 11–12 normal traffic and transit between Western Germany and West Berlin were resumed. The fiasco of the Berlin blockade was the first big setback to the Soviet Union's drive for further expansion of its European bloc, although as recently as February 1948 Czechoslovakia had been engulfed in the Soviet orbit. Soviet expansion in Europe has remained checked to this moment.

The importance of the decisions made by the American Government in June and July 1948, and of the means used to break the blockade, cannot be stressed enough. The victory of the West in the struggle for Berlin immensely influenced the psychological attitude of the city's people. Surrender of that outpost would have deprived its population of the last hope that resistance against the Communist system could ever be successful. It is also obvious that surrender of Berlin would have fatally affected the attitude of the people of West Germany.

The Founding of the "German Democratic Republic" and Its Road Toward a "People's Democracy"

The failure of the Berlin blockade and the opposition to further expansion which the Soviets encountered, and which could no longer be overcome without a war, clearly shattered the Soviet Union's hope of swallowing all of Germany in a fairly short time. Since then, the object of Soviet politics in East Germany has been to incorporate it firmly into the Eastern bloc. The first step in such a plan necessitated a complete sovietization of all facets of life, a goal that had so far been pursued with considerable restraint and with an eye on its possible psychological effect in West Germany. There could be no more talk of German economic unity, it is true, but then the separate currency reform of June 1948 also removed the monetary basis for such an economic unity. Moreover, the economic systems of the two Germanies became increasingly different. In West Germany an essentially free enterprise system had replaced the state-controlled economy in effect before the currency reform, whereas in the Soviet Zone the system of a centrally planned state economy patterned after its Soviet model was more and more solidified.

Finally in 1949 the fiction of a unitary Germany represented by the agency of the Allied Control Council was completely discarded. The concept of a German central administration for the Soviet Occupation Zone had already originated in the SMAD order No. 138 (June 27, 1947) in the form of a "German Economic Commission," which was divided into a number of "German Central Administrations." Vested at first with relatively little power and authority, it had functioned as a coordinating agency in relation to the governments of the five *Länder*. However, on February 12, 1948 the powers and functions of the "German Economic Commission" were substantially enlarged. It was virtually endowed with the character of a German central government without a parliamentary basis but was completely controlled by the SMAD and clearly dominated by the SED.

Shortly after the establishment of the enlarged "German Economic Commission," the Allied Control Council was dissolved when the Soviet delegates walked out of a meeting on March 20, 1948. The centralized administration of Berlin alone still subsisted in the institution of the "Allied *Kommandatura,*" formed by the four occupation powers. But the ideological antithesis between the Soviet Union and the three Western occupation powers paralyzed it almost completely, and on June 16, 1948 the Soviet commandant of Berlin participated for the last time in a *Kommandatura* session. Specious arguments were advanced to explain the refusal to cooperate in the Allied Control Council, as well as in the Berlin *Kommandatura*. Even after the dissolution of the Allied *Kommandatura,* German administrative agencies of the former capital of the *Reich* continued to function for the whole city. But difficulties multiplied after the Soviets had launched the blockade, and it became evident that the SED was aiming to split Berlin as well. The rift took place on November 30, 1948, when the city council elected a new "Magistracy of Greater Berlin" in an illegal assembly called by the vice-chairman of the city council, a Communist. This new municipal council could act only in behalf of the Soviet sector, but even there it was supported only by a minority of the people. In the elections of 1946, when the SPD acted as an independent party, many more votes were cast for it than for the SED (341,000 to 233,000). There was no reason whatsoever to assume that the number of SED members had increased; the contrary might well be true. The composition of the new East Berlin city council, thoroughly influenced by Communism, did not reflect the actual political will of the people.

The new elections for city councillors for West Berlin, held on December 5, 1948 in the Western sectors, truly revealed the attitude of the people of Berlin, who were extremely provoked by the Soviet blockade and by the absolutely undemocratic way in which the split of the city had been manipulated. The SED preferred to keep out of these elections—in due recognition of its weakness and lack of appeal. It asked its members to abstain from voting and attempted to put the people of West Berlin under pressure by various propaganda methods, especially in announcing the early departure of the Western Allies. But in spite of this, and in spite of the severe privations and trials of the blockade, an amazingly high percentage of the people—83.6 per cent—went to the polls. The Social Democratic Party obtained 64.5 per cent of the ballots cast, the Christian Democratic Union 19.4 per cent, and the Free Democratic Party 16.1 per cent.

The Soviet occupation power prohibited these elections in the Eastern sector of Berlin. Had they been held there, a Communist defeat would have been no less a foregone conclusion. That the people of West Berlin had the opportunity of democratic elections, to demonstrate and manifest their political determination to reject Communism in the face of pressure and propaganda, was undoubtedly an important victory for the firm stand of the Western powers against the Soviet blockade.

Both the population of the Soviet Zone and that of East Berlin, on the other hand, were deprived of any opportunity to express their actual political feelings. Under strong Soviet and SED pressure their territories were, after 1948, more and more turned into a "People's Democracy." So far, an absolute one-party system modeled after its Soviet precedent has not been effected, but non-Communist parties have lost the last semblance of real influence, and the pseudo-democratic forms of the system are simply façades. All essential political decisions are made by a small clique of SED leaders in close cooperation with the Soviet occupation power.

Decisive for the fate of the non-Communist parties in the Soviet Zone was the outcome of the struggle for leadership within the CDU, the largest of these parties. Its two chairmen, Jacob Kaiser, at present federal minister for all-German problems in the Bonn government, and Ernst Lemmer, had exploited all given possibilities to defend the independence of the CDU against SED encroachments and to oppose the ever growing totalitarian practices of the latter. They also refused to participate in the "Congress of the German People for Unity and a Just Peace," staged in East Berlin in December 1947. This convention was essentially an attempt of the SED to establish a kind of pseudo-parliament without any genuine democratic legitimacy. The LDP, weak in its leadership, took part in this convention and thus facilitated the suppression of the last vestige of opposition against the Communists, all the easier since the non-Communist parties did not even present a unified front.

On December 20, 1947 the political advisor to the head of the SMAD, Colonel Tulpanov, announced that the SMAD refused further to associate with Kaiser and Lemmer as chairmen of the CDU and declared their election invalid. With the appointment of a new executive, most of whose members were overly compliant to the will of the Soviets and the SED, the decisive resistance of the CDU was broken. The chairman of the LDP, Dr. Wilhelm Külz, an honorable man and former minister in the Weimar Republic, who more than anyone else in that party was able to resist the drift toward Communist totalitarianism, died a few months later (October 4, 1948). Insofar as resistance against the absolute claim to leadership of the SED was offered by the bourgeois parties on the local and regional level, the occupation power in conjunction with the SED employed all available means to crush it: some of the leaders of the two parties (among them a considerable number of ministers and other high officials of the government) were, upon refusing to give up their opposition, imprisoned or compelled to flee to Western Germany. Thus the SED was soon in a position where it did not have to be mindful of opposition from the two bourgeois parties to essential points of the SED program.

The soil had thus already been prepared for a Communist state when in October 1949, after the Federal Republic of Germany composed of the three Western zones had come into existence, the Soviet occupation power presented its creation: the "German Democratic Republic." The West German federal republic was legitimately based on democratic elections, while the Soviets and the SED never dared to test the real political feelings of the people by allowing free elections. On May 30, 1949 the "Third German People's Congress," which was formed without a true democratic basis, elected a "German People's Council" and ratified the draft of a constitution for the "German Democratic Republic." In October 1949 the people's council proclaimed itself the "Provisional Parliament" (*Provisorische Volkskammer*) and approved four basic laws, one of which was the "DDR" constitution. For reasons of propaganda, the former Social Democrat Otto Grotewohl became prime minister of the provisional government. Real power, however, was put into the hands of Walter Ulbricht, a Communist of long standing trusted by the Soviet leaders. Wilhelm Pieck, who had also been a Communist for many years, was elected president of the "DDR" on October 11, 1949. All decisive key positions in the government of the "DDR" were given to reliable Communists.

On October 15, 1950 the new state attempted to acquire a pseudo-parliamentarian legitimacy by means of so-called "elections." These elections, however, cannot claim to have been a true expression of the voters' opinion—to say nothing of the questionable way in which they were conducted—because already on July 7, 1950 the so-called "Antifascist-Democratic Bloc" of parties and mass organizations of the Soviet Zone had agreed on and announced a single list with a predetermined distribution of mandates. Besides the three "old" parties, two newly licensed parties belonged to this bloc: the "National Democratic Party of Germany" and the "Democratic Farmers' Party of Germany." These two parties were satellite creatures of the SED from their inception, and had no possibility of independent political decision. The "Antifascist-Democratic Bloc" also comprised "democratic mass organizations," like the "Free German Federation of Labor Unions," the "Free German Youth," the "Cultural League for a Democratic Reconstruction of Germany," the "Union of the Persecuted of the Nazi Regime," the "Democratic Women's League of Germany," the "Union of Farmers' Mutual Assistance." These "mass organizations" were controlled by Communists. The SED, as such, officially obtained only 25 per cent of the mandates of the single list, but it virtually controlled 55 per cent upon adding those of the "mass organizations," or even 70 per cent if those of the two satellite parties are also added. An "election" on the basis of such a single list was in its very conception a political farce, and, of course, the composition of the parliament that resulted from such elections in no way represented the real political will of the people. All objective observers of the conditions in the Soviet Zone agree that the number of those who really support the Communist system and would vote for the SED in free elections is even today hardly more than 15 per cent of the people. Among the youth, however, the Communist influence is persistently growing under the impact of Communist education and propaganda. The political situation in the Soviet Zone is significantly revealed in the fact that of four hundred representatives "elected" to the parliament (*Volkskammer*) in 1950, forty-four lost their seats, nine were imprisoned, and fifteen had to take refuge in West Germany in the course of the first legislative term.

Likewise, the second "elections," held on October 17, 1954 and manipulated by means of the same principle of predetermined single lists, are not conclusive. Furthermore, not even the *Volkskammer* can boast any real importance in terms of formulating policies, because it is, as is true of all parliaments in Communist countries—and also descriptive of the *Reichstag* in the National Socialist state—a typical pseudo-parliamentarian institution, designed to conceal from the world the existence of a small oligarchical clique of party bosses. The actual power is concentrated in this small group, essentially coextensive with the politburo of the SED. The members of the SED have as little influence in setting up and selecting this elite as have the lower and intermediate functionaries. On the other hand, there exist, of course, very close and intimate relations with the Communist Party of the U.S.S.R. These relations guarantee that the policies of the "DDR" will remain consonant with those of the Soviet Union. The Western concept of sovereignty is, from what has been said, equally as inapplicable to the status of the "DDR" as to the status of other European satellite states.

Sovietization of the Economic, Social, and Cultural Life

The process of assimilation of the political structure of the "DDR" to the political system of the Soviet Union went hand in hand with a progressive assimilation of economic and social life to the Soviet economic and social order and a progressive economic integration of the "DDR" into the Soviet bloc. Neither has been carried to its fullest possible extent, but the "DDR" has already gone a long way on the road to total sovietization, and will complete this process of assimilation and integration if its present political system continues to be closely tied to that of the Soviet Union.

The process of socialization in the industrial sphere, the beginnings of which were described earlier in this chapter, has been so intensively advanced by legal and illegal means that there remain at present only negligible remnants of private enterprise in, and private ownership of, the means of production. In industry the method of so-called "cold socialization" was chiefly employed. Moreover, new investments are almost exclusively made in the socialized *"volkseigenen"* (owned by the people) part of industry. Consequently, by the spring of 1955 only 14.5 per cent of the total production was yielded by private industry, which with rare exceptions is composed only of small manufacturing plants that produce goods for consumption. Basic industries are entirely state owned and state controlled, as is also true to a great extent of the manufacture of the means of production. Conforming to the pattern existing in the Soviet Union, the larger socialized enterprises are immediately subject to "centralized direction" from the competent ministry. Smaller socialized plants of only local importance are as "local industry" subordinated to local or regional authorities. Even the structure and organization of the socialized industries are copied from the Soviet model.

While the basis of the present economic order of the Soviet Zone, as regards industry as well as the totally socialized bank and insurance business, was laid immediately after the war, the process of eliminating private enterprise in trade and commerce did not begin until considerably later, notably after 1948–1949. In the wholesale trade, of vital importance for the proper functioning of any modern system of economy, socialization then became very rapid. This was all the easier because, within the framework of a system of centralized planning, dispossession of private wholesalers was not necessary; their functions were simply transferred to newly established state agencies for the wholesale trade. It is particularly in the field of wholesale trade that suppression of private initiative has wrought fateful consequences. No other branch of the economic state administration has performed so poorly as the wholesale trade, which has been, therefore, in the course of the past years the subject of constant reorganizations. But the sources of the continually recurring difficulties have not yet been rooted out. With respect to the retail trade, the Soviets and the SED contented themselves during the first postwar years with vigorously promoting cooperatives at the expense of private retail trade. Sales of cooperatives steadily increased. A system of state retail trade was not set into operation until the end of 1948. This also progressed very rapidly in the desired direction, because the considerable difference between producers' prices and retail prices of numerous types of merchandise represented a coveted revenue source for the state. Retail stores and restaurants taken over by the state mercantile organization are called HO (*Handels-Organisation*), that is, state-owned retail stores. These stores and restaurants (together with other, less important types of HO establishments) have captured 40 per cent of the total sale of retail goods, while the cooperatives and the private retail trade each share 30 per cent of the turnover. The latter is constantly diminishing.

The structure of the crafts has been least affected by the process of sovietization. As a direct socialization of shops would meet with great difficulties, the attempt was made to coordinate individual artisans in an artisans' cooperative association and thus to destroy their independent status. This process is still in its beginnings, but efforts to carry it through have been recently intensified.

As in all other satellite countries, the process of sovietization in the "DDR" encounters very great difficulties when it reaches the small farmers. The distribution of an overwhelming number of large estates led to a considerable multiplication of small farms. Later, an intensive propaganda campaign was launched against the big farmers, who as a group of the farm population correspond to the kulaks in the Soviet Union. Imitating Soviet methods, the SED tried hard to propagate the idea of "class struggle in the village," a concept which had been alien to German conditions. Every farmer who owned more than twenty hectares (approximately fifty acres) of farmland was branded as a landed property owner. Through massive economic pressure, particularly imposition of high obligatory deliveries of produce for low prices, the Soviets succeeded in reducing by more than half the number of larger farms existing at the end of the war. More specifically, this was accomplished when a great many of these big farmers were in arrears in delivering their produce and were therefore imprisoned or forced to flee to West Germany. The elimination of these farms had very deleterious effects on the total agricultural production, because they had been highly efficient and productive.

Small and middle-sized farms were as yet left unmolested. It was only at the Second Party Conference of the SED (July 9–12, 1952), which demanded more intensified "building up of socialism," that Ulbricht announced the establishment of "Cooperatives of Agricultural Production," or in other words, the introduction of the same means and methods which the Soviet Union has employed to collectivize the greatest part of its farms. Of course, it was thought advisable not to proceed too fast. Therefore, three different types of farmers' cooperatives were provided for, none of which is completely identical with the Soviet kolkhozes. But the third type, which envisages even common management of the livestock on all the farms incorporated in the cooperative, already resembles the Soviet prototype very closely.

The material advantages that accrue to the farmers' cooperatives as against the individual farmers are appreciable. Moreover, the Soviets had also paved the way for later collectivization by handing out to new settlers only very small farm lots on which subsistence was in the long run impossible. But farmer opposition to collectivization is very resolute, and since the SED prudently forbears—it has been especially wary about running risks since the people's revolt of June 1953—to use outright force to coerce farmers into kolkhozes, the process of collectivization made little headway. Only recently has collectivization been proceeding at a fairly rapid pace, especially in the conversion of existing cooperatives into the third type. The extent of farm collectivization, as a matter of fact, would have been even smaller had not a great number of East German farmers been compelled by political and economic pressures and hardships to seek refuge in West Germany, leaving behind their farms, which were then, wherever possible, annexed to cooperatives. At the beginning of 1955 there were 5,264 cooperatives cultivating a total area of over one million hectares (approximately 2.5 million acres). In the spring of 1954 the total arable area of the Soviet Zone fell into these categories (given in per cent):

State-owned farms	4	
Cooperatives	12	
Farms deserted—managed by the state	14	
"Socialized" farm area		30
Small farms (0.5–5 hectares)	14	
Medium-sized farms (5–20 hectares)	46	
Large farms (20–100 hectares)	10	
Private farm area		70

It is a reasonable assumption that by the summer of 1955 the socialized farm area had increased to 35 per cent of the total arable land; but two thirds of the agricultural area is still in the hands of independent farmers, who seem determined to assert their individual existence as long as they possibly can.

In accordance with the Soviet pattern, the majority of tractors and agricultural machinery are concentrated in state-owned stations for machines and tractors. These are important footholds of the Communist system in the countryside, because beyond their economic utility they constitute centers for political propaganda and control over the farm population.

On the basis of such an extensive socialization, which rendered the state the sole employer in many spheres, subjecting the lot of the individual more and more to the omnipotent will of the state, a system of centralized planning has been built up. In doing that, not only have the basic lines been meticulously copied from the Soviet Union, but so have the structural organization and the procedural methods of establishment, execution, and control of a centralized economy.

With respect to the objectives of this system of methodical planning, the Soviet background and interests are also very clearly revealed, particularly since the initiation of the first Five Year Plan of the "DDR" (January 1, 1951). These objectives indicate the trend toward a basic change in the economic structure of East Germany to make it a highly valuable partner in the Moscow-dominated economic bloc of Eastern states. For this reason, the buildup of heavy industry, with special, one-sided emphasis on processing of raw materials and manufacture of the means of production, takes the lead. On the other hand, agriculture, the construction industry, and manufacture of consumption goods, that is, branches of the economy that supply the immediate needs of the consumer, are assigned a secondary position. Between 1951 and 1955 those industries were primarily built up that would enable the Soviet Zone to sustain itself without imports from the West and even without imports from Western Germany (e.g., iron and steel, heavy machinery) or to export quality products to the countries of the Soviet orbit (e.g., various kinds of machines, electro-technical and chemical products, precision tools, optical apparatus, and ships).

In effect, the Soviet Zone in its former economic relations has been severed from the Western world and incorporated into the Soviet bloc. Some 70 to 80 per cent of the exports of the Soviet Zone are shipped to countries of the Soviet sphere, inclusive of Red China; before the second World War it was less than 20 per cent.

An equally intimate bond between the Soviet Zone and the system of the Soviet Union can be discovered in the cultural sphere. The extensive cultural isolation from Western Germany and the rest of the free world is one of the most painful effects of sovietization for the people of the Soviet Zone. The attempt of the dominant party to establish dialectical materialism as the sole official ideology has repeatedly brought about conflicts with the churches. The structure of today's universities and schools in Eastern Germany, as well as applied educational methods, is also in complete conformity with Soviet standards. Likewise, policies of the Soviet Zone in the field of the press, radio, and creative arts are typically and clearly adapted to their Soviet counterparts.

Developments Since the Policy of the "New Course" and the People's Revolt of June 17, 1953

The process of sovietization was only temporarily interrupted or slackened by the so-called "New Course." The policy of the "New Course" was initiated with resolutions of the SED's politburo on June 9, 1953. These resolutions were promises to show more regard for the interests of the consumer, to spare or promote the remainder of private enterprise and industry and notably individual farms, to guarantee greater security of law, and so on. This surprising step was the first in a series of similar measures taken during the subsequent months in almost all satellite states and ultimately even in the Soviet Union. Analysis of the causes and background of this new outlook is beyond the scope of this presentation; its explanation lies in the fact that after Stalin's death the political situation within the Soviet bloc changed. Beyond this, it was the extraordinary increase of mass escapes to West Berlin and West Germany that contributed to this new course in the Soviet Zone.

At the height of this escape movement (spring 1953), unique in all history, as many as fifty thousand refugees passed over the border from the Soviet Zone in a single month. This furnishes the best evidence of the political and economic pressure exerted upon a large section of the population and manifests clearly the internal rejection of the process of sovietization. Even more demonstrative of the rejection of the arbitrary system and the dominant party was the uprising of the people, June 16–17, 1953. To it there is no parallel in the annals of the Soviet Union and the Soviet orbit.

The immediate occasion for its outbreak was a decree of the government of the "DDR," raising the work norms by 10 per cent. This exasperated the labor force. This decree was a policy move of the government in its struggle, waged over years, to increase production. Since it had so far been rather unsuccessful, it staked its only hope on such a drastic measure, little realizing what potentially dangerous forces would thereby be unleashed.

The uprising began on June 16 when construction workers started a strike at a big building site on East Berlin's Stalin Avenue and marched to the government building to protest against the raising of work norms. As they marched, the number of demonstrators multiplied constantly. News of this occurrence spread rapidly in East Berlin and soon the whole Soviet Zone as well. Ever larger masses were seized by the agitation in reverse proportion to the helplessness of a dumfounded government which showed clear signs of weakness. On June 17 almost the whole labor force of East Berlin and a large segment of that of the Soviet Zone were engaged in a general strike. In East Berlin and in a considerable number of Soviet Zone cities this movement approached revolutionary proportions as the hatred of the regime by the oppressed burst forth. State-owned retail stores (HO) and party offices of the SED were broken into and often destroyed, police troops disarmed, and political prisoners freed. At first the motivations behind this revolt were purely economic or social, but soon the insurgents formulated political aims and clamored for free elections and release of political prisoners.

The SED attempted to brand this popular uprising, supported preponderantly by workers, against the ruling system as a "fascist *Putsch*," engineered by Western agents. But the facts bespeak clearly a different situation; if there has ever been a truly spontaneous people's revolt, it was that of June 16–17, 1953 in Eastern Germany. The utter lack of systematic organization and unified leadership cogently refutes the propaganda line about Western instigation.

Nevertheless, on the evening of June 17 the Communist regime would have been crumbling throughout the Soviet Zone had it not been buttressed by the use of Soviet troops. Already toward noon on the 17th the military commandant of the Berlin Soviet sector proclaimed martial law, and Soviet troops and tanks were employed against the uprising. The same action was taken in the Soviet Zone. The failure, therefore, of a revolt of unarmed masses had become inevitable.

Chancellor Adenauer dispatched telegrams to the chiefs of government of the three Western powers on June 21, appealing urgently in view of the events that they might "do everything in their powers to put an end to this situation, to reinstate the violated human rights, and to return unity and freedom to the whole German nation, which alone would guarantee an enduring and peaceful evolution in

Europe." President Dwight D. Eisenhower replied to the Chancellor with this statement on June 26:

> With great interest and deep compassion I received your message of June 21. The recent events in East Berlin and East Germany have aroused the hearts and hopes of men the world over. This enthusiastic evidence of courage strengthens our belief that years of suppression and attempted ideological indoctrination have not extinguished the spirit of liberty behind the Iron Curtain. It is obvious that repercussions of these events will be felt in the whole Soviet orbit. . . . Even though the Communists could be forced by these powerful demonstrations in Eastern Germany to moderate their present policies, it seems clear that future security of the people of Eastern Germany would be guaranteed only by a unification with West Germany based on free elections which we urgently requested the Soviets to permit. This request was conveyed to the Soviets in form of notes by the American, British, and French governments on September 23, 1952. We have always been convinced that this is the only viable method to achieve unification of Germany and I assure you that my government will continue to strive toward that goal. I am convinced that the people of East Germany know in these hours of trials and privations that their cry for freedom is heard in the whole world.

The daring courage with which the people of the Soviet Zone rose against a regime that has powerful means at its disposal was acclaimed everywhere. But the West was unable to do more than make this profession of solidarity. The people of the Soviet Zone then were naturally overcome by a deep resignation when the uprising, which many held impossible in a totalitarian state, broke down in the face of the power marshalled by the Soviets.

The "New Course" brought the people a few alleviations for some time. But since the beginning of 1955, signs have increased that the government of the "DDR" has returned to its previous course. The only hope of those in the Soviet Zone who reject Communism—still an overwhelming majority—is a reunification of Germany on the basis of free elections and a reinstitution of basic democratic rights. The stand of the Western powers, especially the United States, toward the problem of German reunification, and their corresponding actions, will be of decisive moment for the future political attitude of the people of the Soviet Occupation Zone.

Chapter 8

Czechoslovakia

IVO DUCHACEK

IN THE LAST eighteen months of the second World War Czechoslovakia's chances of emerging from the Nazi occupation as a democratic, reasonably prosperous nation friendly to both East and West seemed better than those of most East Central European countries.

Unlike the Axis satellite states, Czechoslovakia was considered an Allied nation. Diplomatically it had a status similar to that of Poland. Czechoslovakia's territory was considered as temporarily occupied by the Nazis on March 15, 1939. The exiled political representatives of Czechoslovakia had formed in London a provisional government, recognized by the British on July 21, 1940.

The Allied status was granted to Czechoslovakia notwithstanding German incorporation of the western provinces of Czechoslovakia into the *Reich,* under the name of the German Protectorate of Bohemia and Moravia. A pro-Nazi Czech local government was established in Prague, a pattern not followed by the Nazis in Poland. The central part of the country, Slovakia, became an "independent" state under German protection. The puppet government of Slovakia sent some of its divisions to fight alongside the Nazis against the Red Army on the Eastern Front (a fact which may appear meritorious to some in 1956) and declared war on the United States. With the *Reich*'s permission, Hungary proceeded to occupy Subcarpathian Ruthenia, the easternmost part of Czechoslovakia. By March 1939 Czechoslovakia, a creation of Versailles, had disappeared from the map of Europe after being carved to pieces by the notoriously anti-Versailles Axis powers.

Thus, Czechoslovakia became a very dramatic illustration of the folly of appeasement, as well as of the great injustice done in its name. A good deal of bad conscience on the part of Great Britain and France made the Czechoslovak cause more popular during the second World War than it might otherwise have been. The Czechoslovak Government-in-exile was able to attract a great deal of sympathy to its cause through a skillful propaganda effort in the West. The Nazis had razed to the ground many villages in Yugoslavia, Poland, and France, but the Czech mining village of Lidice became for the West the most impressive symbol of Nazi brutality.[1]

Czechoslovakia's right to be restored as an independent country within her pre-Munich boundaries was not seriously questioned. The Munich agreement, which in 1938 had detached Sudetenland from Czechoslovakia, as well as its ramifications concerning Poland and Hungary,[2] was formally repudiated by Foreign Secretary Anthony Eden on behalf of the British Government on August 5, 1942. General De Gaulle chose the fourth anniversary of Munich, September 29, 1942, to make a similar declaration on behalf of Free France. As the United States had not been a party to Munich, it did not need to make any formal repudiation. However, President Roosevelt's appeal on the eve of Munich (September 26, 1938) seemed to associate United States policy with Chamberlain's and Daladier's emphasis on peace, rather than with Czechoslovakia's defense of her security and territorial integrity.

The Soviet Government condemned Munich in 1938 as a settlement from which the Soviet Union had been excluded by the Western agreement with Hitler. Six months later the Soviet Government openly denounced the Nazi occupation of Bohemia-Moravia and destruction of the Czechoslovak Republic as a logical consequence of the Western policy of appeasement. The Czechoslovak Legation in Moscow was allowed to function as a symbol of pre-Munich, free Czechoslovakia.

Following the conclusion of the Nazi-Soviet Pact, however, previous Soviet condemnations of the Munich agreement were contradicted by several Soviet deeds. In the fall of 1939 the Soviet Government complied with a Nazi suggestion and ordered the Czechoslovak Legation in Moscow closed. The Czechoslovak Minister, Zdeněk Fierlinger, was obliged to leave Moscow and live in

[1] The Nazis destroyed Lidice in retaliation for the assassination of the Nazi protector of Bohemia and Moravia, Reinhard Heydrich, on May 27, 1942 in Prague. The assailants were Czechoslovak parachutists trained in England.

[2] The prewar authoritarian regimes of Poland and Hungary joined the Nazi pressure against Czechoslovakia by claiming and obtaining the area of Těšín for Poland and Southern Slovakia for Hungary.

England until 1941. The Soviet Government established diplomatic relations with the Slovak State; thus, in the framework of Nazi-Soviet cooperation, it formally confirmed the disappearance of the Czechoslovak Republic and its replacement by a new Nazi order in East Central Europe. In the fall of 1939, exactly one year after Munich, the Soviet Union, previously a violent critic of the Western agreement with Hitler at Munich, committed in agreement with Hitler a series of acts which, with respect to Poland and Czechoslovakia, well deserve a cumulative label: "super-Munich."

In 1941, following the Nazi attack on Soviet Russia, Moscow resumed its previous anti-Munich attitude: the Czechoslovak Legation in Moscow was reopened, its status was raised to that of an Embassy, former envoy Z. Fierlinger returned from London to his post in Moscow, and Czechoslovakia was promised Soviet help in her efforts to restore her pre-Munich unity and boundaries.

Nevertheless, in spite of its renewed verbal condemnations of Munich, the Soviet Union was to become the only power that violated the pre-Munich boundaries of Czechoslovakia, by annexing Subcarpathian Ruthenia *de facto* in February 1945. This annexation was confirmed by a treaty imposed on Czechoslovakia on June 29, 1945.

Although the Soviet annexation of Subcarpathian Ruthenia had considerably toned down general optimism concerning Czechoslovakia's future, in comparison with Poland Czechoslovakia seemed to present a lesser problem for the Western powers and their relations with the Soviet Union. In 1941, following the Nazi attack upon Russia, the Czechoslovak Government-in-exile and the Soviet Government renewed diplomatic relations. There were no major territorial disputes. Although his views were not shared by all Czechoslovak non-Communist leaders in exile, President Beneš considered the problem of Subcarpathian Ruthenia a marginal one and consequently subject to possible amicable solution. In Czechoslovakia there was no legacy of anti-Russian feelings as in Poland. On the contrary, since the nineteenth century the Czechs and Slovaks had often looked toward the Russians as their potential protectors or allies in the fight against German and Hungarian pressures. In December 1943 the Czechoslovak Government-in-exile signed a treaty of alliance with the Soviet Union. This was the second Czechoslovak-Soviet alliance, the first one having been signed in 1935, in agreement with France. The new treaty contained not only a pledge of mutual assistance in the event of renewal of German aggression but also a promise of mutual nonintervention in the domestic affairs of the signatory powers.

The British and American governments did not finally object to the treaty, although originally they had seriously questioned the wisdom of bilateral treaties, if concluded before the end of the war and prior to the establishment of a new collective security system. However, the British objections did not sound very convincing, as the Czechoslovak-Soviet Treaty closely followed the spirit and even the text of the British-Soviet Treaty, also concluded before the end of the war and prior to the establishment of the United Nations Organization.

The promising outlook for the Czechoslovak future also seemed justified in view of Czechoslovakia's own record in democratic government and social progress. Czechoslovakia's respect for the rights of its ethnic and religious minorities, although not spotlessly clean, was certainly better than that of any other Central European country. There was also hope that the Czech-Slovak antagonism, partly motivated by the previous centralist tendencies of the government and its direction of the economic life favoring Bohemia, could be overcome in an atmosphere of democracy, especially as the Slovaks were expected to try to wipe off the pro-Nazi record of the Slovak State by their reunion with the Czech people, symbol of an oppressed nation. In addition, a relative absence of potentially explosive social cleavages supported the conclusion that Czechoslovakia might prove the least fertile ground for Communist exploitation of social discontent and economic backwardness.

Inferior Power and Tactics

When in the spring of 1945 the Red Army liberated a major part of Czechoslovakia, political aspects of the liberation and reports on the actual behavior of the Red Army raised new questions concerning Czechoslovakia's future. Nevertheless, its picture appeared much brighter than that of neighboring Poland or Hungary. The Czechoslovak leaders in exile, after negotiating a treaty of friendship with the Soviet Union in 1943, managed in addition to reach a friendly agreement with the Czech and Slovak Communist leaders who had spent their wartime exile in Moscow. It seemed that Czechoslovakia, having avoided the danger of two rival governments—one sponsored by the distant West, and the other by

Moscow—would be able to hold her own politically, despite the presence of the Red Army. Contrary to the case of Poland, the London Czechoslovaks and the Moscow Czechoslovaks agreed on a coalition government for liberated Czechoslovakia at the time when the Red Army had liberated half of it. This was on March 27, 1945. Although formed in Moscow, this government had been officially proclaimed in the capital city of liberated eastern Slovakia, Košice, and was subsequently referred to as the "Košice Government."

For the first time in Czechoslovak political history, the Communist Party had entered a coalition government. However, in Czechoslovakia this seemed to be a less sensational development than elsewhere in East Central Europe. Unlike other Communist Parties of that area, the Czechoslovak Communist Party had not been outlawed or driven underground between 1920 and 1938, but, until the Munich dismemberment of Czechoslovakia, was allowed to operate openly and legally within the parliamentarian framework. An average Czechoslovak citizen was accustomed to view the Communists as competitors at the elections (in the 1935 elections, the last before the second World War, the Communist Party polled 10.3 per cent of the votes); the Communist Party had often appeared the most radical and troublesome, but had neither the stigma nor the aura of a revolutionary, illegal organization.

Coupled with the performance of individual Communists as resistance leaders or victims of Nazi persecution, this prewar reputation of an almost parliamentary respectability played well into the hands of the Party in the postliberation period. It also induced some non-Communist leaders, including perhaps President Beneš himself, to forget that Lenin had labeled all parliaments as Communist schools for extraparliamentary methods of political struggle. Generally, an optimistic assumption was made by many non-Communist political leaders that democracy would not only prove immune to Communism but even contaminate and soften it. With this expectation, non-Communist leaders finally consented to the distribution of ministerial posts in the postliberation government, a distribution extremely favorable to the Communists. The key ministries of Interior, Agriculture, Information and Education went to the Communists. The Prime Minister, Zdeněk Fierlinger, was a Social Democrat and had been wartime Ambassador in Moscow. However, President Beneš, well known in the West, retained his office. It was assumed by most Western observers that President Beneš's orientation had remained liberal and pro-Western in spite of his almost pathological obsession with the wrong which in Munich England and France had inflicted on him personally, on Czechoslovakia especially, and on the cause of democracy generally. Jan Masaryk, son of President and Liberator Thomas Masaryk and his American wife, remained Minister of Foreign Affairs. While the program of the Košice Government laid very heavy emphasis on socialist principles of economy and the alliance with the Soviet Union, mention of civil liberties and friendship for the West was not totally absent. Under the circumstances, it was an arrangement in which the non-Communist forces had yielded more than they should have but it seemed to be a compromise rather than a Communist victory.

The "Košice compromise" seemed to reflect the general situation in which Czechoslovakia had found itself on the eve of victory: Czechoslovakia, unlike the other Allied countries, was liberated by both the American and the Soviet armies. But the Americans liberated only about one sixth of the territory.

Non-Communist political leaders in Czechoslovakia based their politics on the assumption that Czechoslovakia, although incapable of resisting the overwhelming impact of the Soviet power, would at least be able to escape complete engulfment into the Soviet orbit. Foreign Minister Masaryk, expressing this wishful thinking, labeled liberated Czechoslovakia a bridge between East and West. The slogan expressed the hope, shared at the time by the United States, that Czechoslovakia would remain such a bridge without becoming an exclusive bridgehead of either side. This tendency to neutralism must have received new impetus in the Czechoslovaks' hopeful interpretation of the "Geneva spirit" in 1955–1956, for the concept of Czechoslovakia as a neutral bridge, after an interval of almost ten years, was again attacked by the Communist press in December of 1955.

In politics the success of one group is only partly the reflection of its superior power and planning. To a considerable extent its success is often a reflection of its opponents' lack of courage, foresight, or appropriate tactics.

Czechoslovakia's final enslavement should be explained primarily by the superior power of the Soviet Union, displayed or exercised in the crucial area at the crucial moment. The impact of this power was certainly further enhanced by either the faintheartedness or the errors of Czechoslovak non-Communist leaders and Western powers. Generally speaking, the strength of pro-Western and democratic trends in Czechoslovakia was overestimated, the hypnotic effects of the Soviet power and the Communist techniques of infiltration underestimated. To this sin of wishful thinking one could perhaps add the error of an orthodox or old-fashioned diplomatic treatment of an unorthodox and novel situation.

Tradition of Democracy Weakened

While in some parts of Europe the nation-states created or reshaped after the first World War had more often emphasized narrow-minded nationalism than civil liberties, Czechoslovakia gained the reputation of being the only country in East Central Europe capable of establishing democracy in the Western sense of the word. When in the 1930's many East European countries turned to fascism or royal dictatorship to cure their economic and social ills, Czechoslovakia remained an island of freedom and enlightenment in their midst.

This vision of Czechoslovakia certainly lingered on in the lounges of the United States Congress and in the offices of the East-European Division of the Department of State on the eve of V-E Day. But was this vision still essentially correct on May 9, 1945?

Between the image of truly democratic Czechoslovakia of 1935 and the reality of liberated Czechoslovakia of 1945 lay ten years, marked by a disappointing experience with France and England during the Munich crisis of 1938, and by Nazi oppression in Bohemia-Moravia and the Nazi-supported authoritarian regime in Slovakia. For six years the Nazi system (and its imitators in Slovakia) shaped the institutions and developments of formerly democratic and unified Czechoslovakia. The trade unions were unified and reorganized to fit the Nazi pattern (*Arbeitsfront*). Similar methods were applied to the youth movement and peasant organizations. The Nazi anti-Semitic laws, as well as the Nazi judicial system, were introduced in Bohemia-Moravia and in somewhat different form in Slovakia. The one-party system was extolled, and the parliamentarian and multiparty system of prewar Czechoslovakia was denigrated.

While in Bohemia-Moravia the Czech universities were closed and the lower educational institutions refashioned according to the Nazi system, in Slovakia, where the life under domestic totalitarianism was easier, Slovak institutions of higher learning remained open.

However, in Bohemia-Moravia as well as in Slovakia all educational institutions were antidemocratic and authoritarian in their emphasis.

The Nazis had well prepared the ground for the Communist one-party system. Later it became evident that the Communist Party had been able to take over the Nazi-shaped framework with minor alterations, often merely replacing the swastika by a hammer-and-sickle sign on the front door. "Hitler, in fact, has been to an even greater extent the midwife to the new birth of Bolshevism than was Ludendorff to the first." [3]

Under such circumstances democratic values could hardly be fully appreciated and understood by the younger generation. This is perhaps why the Communist Party insisted on, and obtained, the lowering of the voting age in Czechoslovakia to eighteen years. They calculated that a boy or girl who on March 15, 1939 (when the Nazi troops marched into Czechoslovakia) was eleven years old and for seven formative years had been exposed solely to totalitarian indoctrination would tend in May 1946 to be a Communist voter. This at least was their hope.

The imprint of the Nazi system on Czechoslovak institutions was not the only useful ally of the Communist Party. The character of the anti-Nazi national resistance proved equally useful. During the war the Nazis were opposed by the Czechs on a national rather than ideological basis, that is, as Germans. The struggle was pictured as a clash between a unified Czech people irrespective of ideological or party differences on one side, and a unified German nation on the other. Party differences were banned as harmful to the national fight for freedom. The Communists adroitly carried over the slogan of national unity from the wartime emergency into the period of peace, when a maximum emphasis was put on a unified national effort to rehabilitate and reconstruct the country. In the name of national unity, necessary for postwar reconstruction tasks, the Communists were able to obstruct the development of a diversified party system, healthy criticism, and formation of a real opposition. All six parties [4] participated in the National Front Gov-

[3] "Reserves for the Kremlin," *The Economist*, London, December 1949, pp. 1454–5.

[4] After the war, only four political parties were authorized in Bohemia and two (later four) in Slovakia. This was a drastic change, in view of the fact that before the war often as many as twenty-seven political parties presented their candidates at the Czechoslovak parliamentary elections. This ban concerned the two strongest parties of prewar Czechoslovakia: the Agrarian Party and the Slovak Catholic People's Party. Their leaders were accused of the crime of col-

ernment. This coalition government remained without parliamentary opposition until the Communist coup.

The slogan of national unity, combined with the traditional trade unionist program of a unified labor organization, proved a great assistance to the Communists whenever their monopolistic position in the unified Central Labor Union (*Ú.R.O.*) was challenged by the non-Communists and a return to the prewar multiunion pattern advocated.

Before the Nazi occupation there were almost as many trade unions as there were parties. The Czech and Slovak trade unions reflected different ideologies of political parties (Social Democratic, Communist, National Socialist, Catholic, etc.) and were controlled by them. When the war ended, the Communists were able to take over a highly centralized and fully unified labor organization into which the Nazi government had forced all Czechoslovak trade unions in 1939.

The importance of the Communist control over the mass of wage-earners was further enhanced by the nationalization of all heavy industry and most other industry. President Beneš decreed this fundamental transformation of the Czechoslovak economic structure on October 25, 1945, using his emergency powers a few days before the first postwar Czechoslovak Parliament, the Provisional National Assembly, composed of nominated members, was to meet.

Since most of the key positions in the government were in the hands of the Communists or their fellow travelers (the minister of industry was left wing Social Democrat Bohumil Laušman) and the labor movement under the control of the Communist Party, nationalization of industry under such conditions was bound to have political consequences different from similar collectivist although less extensive measures which had been carried out in Great Britain, France, or Italy.

The Central Labor Union became a Communist agency with overwhelming economic power: it was able to manipulate the work-

laboration with the enemy (this charge was only partly justified); it was not only revengeful patriotism but also perhaps the hope of the coalition parties to divide the spoils which finally extended the charge of collaboration with the enemy to the whole membership of both parties. While in Slovakia the former voters for the Catholic People's Party had transferred their loyalty to the new Slovak Democratic Party in spite of its Protestant leadership, the former voters for the Agrarian Party in Bohemia-Moravia divided their loyalties more or less evenly among all four contending parties, including the Communists.

ing masses and, with the help of the old revolutionary slogan of "workers' control," to interfere with the management of the nationalized industries as well as the remaining privately owned factories and establishments. Thus, already in 1945, the Central Labor Union had in fact become a state within a state, that is, an alternative government under full Communist control, while full control of the cabinet and parliament was still to be gained.

The question may be raised: why did the non-Communist leaders keep their soft policy toward the Communists for such a long time? Aware of their international isolation, as well as a low civic spirit among the population, they dreaded a premature clash with the power of the Communists. They tended to temporize, and thus to gain a breathing spell until an ideal set of circumstances (e.g., victory at the polls) would allow them to act with a reasonable chance of success. By cooperation with the Communists within the coalition government they hoped to be able to keep them within the parliamentarian framework and thus prevent the Communist Party from choosing extraparliamentary means of political struggle. This strange method of "fighting the Communists by cooperation" tended to confuse the rank and file of non-Communist political parties. When the non-Communist leaders finally decided to act (February 1948), the very power to act had already slipped through their fingers.

The administrative chaos in Czechoslovakia after the war was another factor fully exploited by the Communist Party. Experience shows that the slogan of democracy when used prematurely by political demagogues may be turned into a very effective weapon with which to kill democracy before it can take real roots. In a country like Czechoslovakia, in 1945 just half-awakened from foreign oppression and not fully conditioned for a really democratic process (elections and representative government), a well organized minority could win applause from a crowd hurriedly gathered on the main square, proclaim such applause to be a true expression of the people's will, and then proceed to organize a local government on its basis. This actually happened in many parts of Czechoslovakia during the spring and summer of 1945.

The presence of the Red Army contributed to the confusion as well as to the loss of civic spirit. The confusion was partly due to a genuine feeling of gratitude toward the Red Army for liberating Czechoslovakia from the Nazis. The loss of civic spirit was often the result of the brutal behavior of the Red Army, as well as local alliances and cooperation between commanders of the Red Army and Communist leaders. To oppose such an alliance could be interpreted not only as ingratitude but also as an indication of regret that things had changed and the Nazis had gone.

In addition, many people, especially in Bohemia and Moravia, had developed a certain tendency toward submissiveness, the result of six years of Nazi oppression during which the aim of sheer physical survival was often pursued, regardless of the cost in moral and political values. In view of the new postliberation oppression, resulting from the combination of the Red Army and local Communist leaders, economic as well as physical survival remained the highest value. Thus the behavior of the Red Army frightened a great many Czechs into the Communist Party, especially those who had reasons to fear prosecution by the Communist Ministry of Interior for their conduct under the Nazi occupation. Others opportunistically decided to howl with the wolves while they were around, hoping sincerely that they might be able to sing with the angels when the Red Army would be gone.

Unlike the more emotional Slovaks, the practical Czechs seem inclined to rationalize, with a considerable degree of political sophistication, many an adverse situation rather than to deal with it boldly. It is true that life for some nine million Czechs, in proximity to mighty Germany, has never been too comfortable. This is why many Czechs consider their national survival in such adverse geographical location primarily the result of their flexible politics or of favorable shifts in the balance of power between their foreign friends and enemies, shifts they feel uncontrollable in any case. Czechoslovakia was twice (in 1918 and again in 1945) freed from *foreign* enemy occupation by *friendly* foreign troops.[5] The last large-scale fighting on Czech territory waged by domestic forces occurred in the seventeenth century. It was the famous Battle of the White Mountain, which led to the transformation of the independent Kingdom of Bohemia into a province of Austria. In both world wars legendary Czechoslovak legions, composed of political exiles, fought bravely alongside the Allied armies on different fronts. Within an appro-

[5] Cf. "If it were possible for the people to be well governed in spite of themselves, their good government would last *no longer than the freedom of a people usually lasts who have been liberated by foreign arms without their own cooperation.*" (Italics mine.) John Stuart Mill, *Considerations on Representative Government* (New York, 1875), Ch. III.

priate framework, these legions proved the Czech and Slovak capacity for achievement on battlefields, but their example did not quite counterbalance the somewhat excessive Czech reliance on outside help.

With some groups of the population, which certainly did not constitute a majority, the Nazi system left another kind of pathological imprint: they learned not only to respect authority and brute force, as symbolized by the Nazi high boots, but also to desire to wear them when and if the opportunity might arise. The Communist Party and the Red Army guiding the organization of local governments gave them this opportunity. The reversal of the former master-slave relationship in favor of the latter had been desired by some more than a return to a democratic normalcy. During the transfer of the Sudeten-German minority from Czechoslovakia (1946–1947), which involved 2.5 to 3 million Czechoslovak citizens of German origin, it was this type of SS-contaminated Communist who added pathological brutality to the transfer of population.

It was in this period of administrative chaos, political confusion, anxiety, and opportunistic struggle for better positions—in the summer and fall of 1945—that the Communist basis of local government in Czechoslovakia was established. In the 1920's and 1930's in some American cities, under the shadow of gangsters' rule, and in Czechoslovakia in 1945, under the shadow of the Red Army, the hypnotic impact of brute force and lawlessness made many people reluctant to take the witness stand against violators of the law. While democracy seemed to be somewhat preserved in the central government in Prague, there was an anemia of democracy in the rest of the body and its extremities.

In May of 1946, one year after the departure of the Nazi Army and five months after the departure of the Red Army, the first post-war elections in Czechoslovakia were held. Communist seizure of the local government in the previous year may be considered one of the most important factors in explaining the high percentage of votes obtained by the Communists (38 per cent).

Yet in spite of all the above factors, democratic traditions and spirit could still have been revived. After all, the spine of the Czechoslovak people was not broken, only bent, by Munich, by six years of occupation and privations, and finally by the overwhelming presence of the Soviet and Communist power and the absence of a visible Western counterweight.

The non-Communist press and members of Parliament agitated against the Communist misuses of power with great courage and skill. A curious situation developed: they often engaged in vigorous polemics with the Communists and the Soviets, while the top leaders of the non-Communist parties, anxious to avoid a premature open clash with the Communists, tried to work out political compromises in the coalition cabinet. As the Western powers either kept on believing in the possibility of agreement with the Soviet Union or limited themselves to diplomatic paper protests, the courage of those journalists, members of parliament, intellectuals, and students who between 1945 and 1948 kept on opposing the Communists was both praiseworthy and tragically ineffectual.

The Czechoslovak democratic leaders also hoped that in time, following the departure of the Red Army and assuming that the Soviet-American balance of power would prevent a direct Soviet intervention, the Czechoslovak voters would regain both the spirit and sense of political discrimination. The correctness of this analysis was confirmed only too well by the Communist February coup, which prevented the Czechoslovak population from expressing its will through the free and unfettered elections scheduled for May 1948. When the elections finally took place, the victorious Communist Party significantly introduced single-list elections.

Slovakia—a Special Case

In the previous paragraphs Czechoslovakia has been treated as one single administrative and political unit, as it had been before the second World War and as it is now. However, it must be borne in mind that the psychological, cultural, and political differences which separate the Slovaks from the Czechs have always been greater than the similarity of their languages and their life in one common state suggest. These differences were sharpened during the second World War. In his policy of "divide and rule" Hitler applied a stick to Bohemia-Moravia while reserving the carrot for Slovakia. The Slovak State, created by Hitler on March 13, 1939, appeared to the Czechs of Prague as a symbol of Czechoslovakian dismemberment, greatly facilitated by the Nazis' ability to exploit the open and hidden anti-Czech tendencies among the rightist Slovak political leaders. But to many Slovaks, their state, although a Nazi puppet, symbolized their capacity to run their affairs more or less on their own, without the irritating patronage of the Czechs. The errors which the Czechs had committed in their treatment of Slovakia between 1918 and 1938 did not consist in really oppressive and colonial attitudes. Rather, they were psychological. The Czechs, trying to bring Slovakia to a higher level of administrative or economic order, tended to treat the Slovaks not as a different ethnic group but as a backward part of one nation. The Slovaks, however, did not consider themselves either "lesser Czechs" or backward.

In addition, there were clashes between Slovak emotionalism, deeper religious feeling (the influence of the Catholic Church on the Slovak masses was greater than in Bohemia), and tendency to political bravura on one side and the Czech businesslike pragmatism and political sophistication on the other.

For the young Slovak generation the Slovak State of 1939 offered new administrative and commercial careers for which, at last, there was no more need to compete with the more skillful and experienced Czech elite. Under wartime conditions, the Slovak State was relatively prosperous—in any event, more prosperous and easygoing than its exploited and oppressed Czech neighbors. Many Slovak firms were able to participate, via Switzerland, in the international black market which during any war has always proved profitable for neutrals or semineutrals. The Slovak masses were favorably impressed by their nationalist fulfillment as symbolized by the usual paraphernalia of an independent nation. (There was a Slovak president, a prime minister and a whole cabinet, a diplomatic and a civil service, and a Slovak Army and Air Force, as well as Slovak postage stamps.) It mattered little that Slovak independence, received from Hitler, and the wartime prosperity were artificial—after all, what was not artificial in East Central Europe while the fronts were moving rapidly back and forth?

When in the spring of 1944 the Red Army had reached the Carpathians on a broad front, the Nazi Government decided to occupy Slovakia. In order to prevent the German occupation, scheduled for the summer, the underground resistance groups, composed of the Communists and right-wing opponents of the Germans and their system, organized the Slovak National Uprising. After its liquidation, the Slovaks experienced direct Nazi occupation and oppression (for about six months) while for the preceding four and a half years they had lived under a somewhat milder form of domestic authoritarianism. As a result, there was less fatigue and less concern with sheer physical survival in Slovakia when the war ended than in neighboring Bohemia-Moravia, exhausted both morally and physically. There was also perhaps less tendency to translate automatically—as many Czechs had done—anti-Nazism into pro-Sovietism.

The first and last free elections in postwar Czechoslovakia, held on May 26, 1946, significantly mirrored the difference in outlook, fatigue, and wartime fate between the Czechs and Slovaks. While the Communist Party polled 43.26 per cent of the votes in Bohemia and 34.46 per cent in Moravia, in Slovakia the percentage of the Communist votes was the lowest of all Czechoslovakia: 30.37.

The Soviet Union Replaces the West

The pro-Western orientation of the Czechoslovak political leaders and people before the first World War was beyond any doubt. In their fight against the Austro-Hungarian Monarchy, both before and during the first World War, the majority of Czechs and Slovaks had always looked hopefully toward the West for inspiration and help. The revolutionary idea of democracy—the right of the people to make and unmake governments—was interpreted by the Czech intelligentsia as obviously meaning also the right of the people to unmake multinational empires and create nation-states. In post-Versailles Czechoslovakia the political institutions, educational system, culture, and even the army were frankly copied on the French or, to a lesser extent, on the British pattern.

The absolute majority of the country—since the recatholicization in the seventeenth and eighteenth centuries, following the Protestant chapter in Czech history—was Roman Catholic and thus was, in addition to the political links, often in spiritual communion via Rome with the Catholic West. The Protestant minority had had traditional links with England, the United States, and the Scandinavian countries. The Russian Orthodox Church was practically nonexistent in Czechoslovakia. In Eastern Slovakia and Ruthenia the Greek Catholic Church, which once had an important number of followers, was forcibly separated from Rome after the second World War and subjected to the jurisdiction of the Russian Orthodox Church.

From the geographic point of view it was, of course, Germany which had always been the most immediate West for the Czechs—either a bridge to France or England, or a barrier. Many good things but also a number of most despicable ideas came to Czechoslovakia from that direction. For centuries Germany had been the main political and military preoccupation of the Czech princes and kings as well as Czechoslovak presidents.

The anxiety of the small Slavic nation about its powerful German neighbor had always underlined Czech political attitudes, and still does. (The Slovaks were more concerned with Hungary than with Germany.) Before the second World War Czechoslovak foreign policy may be characterized as a continuous effort to obtain protection against Czechoslovakia's immediate western neighbor from the Western powers, geographically located beyond Germany. It was in this connection that a link of formal alliances and sincere friendship had developed between Czechoslovakia and France before the second World War. In view of the similarity of interests with respect to her German neighbor, France appeared as the best possible protector of Czechoslovakia's security and territorial integrity after Versailles.

Czechoslovakia's feelings toward Great Britain and the United States were somewhat more mixed. While England with her parliamentarian democracy was admired and copied, her reluctance to make any commitment in Eastern Europe was known and regretted. As to the United States, its democratic form of government and its wealth were widely known, as was also the prosperity in the United States of Czech and Slovak immigrants who had left the social and political misery of the Austro-Hungarian Empire at the turn of the century. In addition, during the first World War the principle of Czechoslovak national independence was proclaimed on American soil. President Wilson, thanks to his defense of the right of national self-determination, had become one of the most popular Allied leaders of the first World War. To the great amazement of the Czechs and Slovaks, their admiration for Wilson was not shared by many of Wilson's own compatriots in the U.S. Senate.

The admiration for France, coupled with an implicit reliance on her military strength and the continuity of her involvement in Central Europe, mounted in direct proportion to the postwar decline of British interests in Eastern Europe in particular and American interests in Europe in general.

When in 1938 France, the admired protector of the Czechoslovak territorial integrity, sided with Hitler and Mussolini in Munich in the mutilation of the Czechoslovak state, the Czechoslovak sense of betrayal was directed against Daladier's France, an ally, more than against Chamberlain's Britain, the real initiator of Munich but not a formal ally of Czechoslovakia. Thus, between 1918 and 1938 Czechoslovak feelings toward France ran the whole gamut from uncritical love and admiration to a frank expression of anger. The number of Czech officers or civilians who, after Munich, had returned French decorations and medals to the French embassy in Prague was significant. These acts were obviously dictated by a love tragically betrayed.

The French collapse of June 1940 somewhat softened these feelings of anger. Many Czechs and Slovaks then realized that the West —which to Czech and Slovak opinion was France—did not let them down in Munich because it was treacherous, but because it was weak. Politically, however, the stature of France suffered in this way even more: it became clear that, while politicians who lack foresight or are traitors might quickly be replaced, the physical weakness of France could not be repaired so rapidly.

In the fall of 1940, while the United States and the Soviet Union were still not fully active participants in war, the hopes of the Czechoslovak people obviously turned to England, dominated by the colorful personality of Winston Churchill. The sudden popularity of Great Britain, now assuming the symbolic role of the potential savior of Central Europe from its German neighbor, was enhanced by establishment of the Czechoslovak Government-in-exile in London. In addition, the excellent quality of the B.B.C. broadcasts beamed to Czechoslovakia, the creation of the refugee Czechoslovak Army on British soil, the performance of the Czechoslovak Air Force (an autonomous part of the R.A.F.), and above all the heroic stand of Great Britain as a lone fighter against a Nazified European continent led the Czechs and Slovaks not only to forget Chamberlain and Munich but actually to transfer during the period of the Blitz (1940–1941) their admirations and hopes from France to Churchillian England.

In 1941, when the United States and the Soviet Union were added to the anti-Axis front, the situation changed considerably. Although in the first year of war the actual military performance of the Soviet Union was disappointing, after Stalingrad in 1943 the Soviet Union emerged as a potential candidate for the role of protector of Slavic Eastern Europe. The victories of the Red Army were not only impressive but had occurred in places familiar to Czechoslovak ears. A British victory at Benghazi or El Alamein did not appear to the Czechs half so meaningful as the Russian liberation of cities with familiar Slavic names like Kharkov or Kiev. The All-Slav Congress, created by the Soviet Government in Moscow, started to manipulate with considerable skill the old Slavic and anti-German slogans. The latter had been in cold storage during the Nazi-Communist honeymoon of 1939–1941. The Pan-Slavic ones had not been used for an even longer time (since 1917). Now, not only the Communist and Socialist groups having ideological sympathies for the Soviet Union but even right-wing groups in Czechoslovakia started to view the second World War as a clash between the Germanic and Slavic worlds which might end in the reversal of the traditional roles and establishment of Slavic supremacy over the Germans.

The admiration of the military might and skill of the Russians was further enhanced by complimentary statements made at that time by Allied war leaders President Roosevelt, General Eisenhower, Prime Minister Churchill, and General de Gaulle. They were in tune with the pro-Russian enthusiasm in occupied Czechoslovakia. It was in this period of general extolling of Russian qualities, and also in the framework of anti-German and Slavic emotionalism, that the concept of Czechoslovakia as a purely Slavic state became an object of diplomatic negotiations. In 1941 the Czechoslovak Government-in-exile approached the Big Three with the proposition of a forcible transfer of the non-Slavic minorities from Czechoslovakia. This proposition concerned 3.5 million Sudeten-Germans, mostly in Bohemia and Moravia, and 750,000 Hungarians living mostly in Slovakia. The Big Three approved the proposition concerning Sudeten-Germans at Potsdam in 1945. It was implemented in 1946–1947; the U.S. Zone in Germany accepted two thirds and the Soviet Zone one third of the total number of expellees. The plan to expel also the Hungarian minority, although raised at the Paris Peace Conference of 1946, was not carried out.[6] Consequently, the Hungarians in Czechoslovakia constitute at present the strongest single non-Slavic minority.

While the Western powers expressed their approval of the transfer of the Sudeten-German minority in somewhat halting terms, the Soviet Union—which at the beginning of the war had liquidated the German Volga Republic in its territory—supported the Czechoslovak proposition with great gusto. Obviously, it was in the interest

[6] For the details, see the chapter on Hungary, pp. 242–243.

of Communism and Soviet power to create as deep an abyss as possible between the Czechs and their defeated German neighbor. An increase of Czechoslovak-German enmity—resulting from a forcible transfer of the German minority—as well as the Czechoslovak apprehensions that a new Germany might press in the future for a restoration of the right of the Sudeten-Germans to return to Czechoslovakia, made the need for protection of Czechoslovakia against Germany by an outside Great Power appear even more imperative than that following the first World War. The Soviet Union was more than ready to fill this role of protector and ally of East Central Europe, especially as it seemed that the West in general and France in particular had almost voluntarily removed themselves from that area.

Geography and the impressive victories of the Red Army in the immediate neighborhood of Czechoslovakia, the lack of any active policy of the Western powers, and above all the memory of the Munich default to Hitler, which lingered on as a symbol of Western withdrawal from Central Europe, combined in creating an impression among many Czechoslovak leaders that Russia's pre-eminent role in Eastern Europe was not only inevitable but actually desirable in view of the assumed German enmity.

The United States and Czechoslovakia *

When the United States and Czechoslovakia became wartime allies (the United States established diplomatic relations with the Czechoslovak Government-in-exile in 1942), the concept of the United States in the minds of the Czechoslovak non-Communist political leaders and of the majority of the population as well was certainly not uniform. It was a composite picture containing some very positive features as well as some negative ones.

The positive aspects may be listed as follows:

1. The United States, under President Wilson, was known to be the political birthplace of Czechoslovak national independence.

2. The United States Government had no direct part in the Munich Conference, which, in view of the Czechs' complex about Munich, was an important factor in itself.

3. The political, economic, and technological achievements of

* This section is based on research material gathered for a study on "The Red Decade (Czechoslovakia, 1945–1955)," undertaken by the author and supported by a grant from the American Philosophical Society.

the American people were frankly admired by the majority of Czechs and Slovaks.

4. The generosity of the American people (e.g., the Herbert Hoover Relief Program) was still fresh in the memories of the leaders and people alike.

The less positive or frankly negative features of the image of America were:

1. Isolationism—as demonstrated by the defeat of Woodrow Wilson and the failure of the United States to participate in its own creation, the League of Nations.

2. The military potential of the United States was not really known. There was a general belief that the first World War was won by the French while the United States' participation was only limited to the last-minute fighting.

3. The reluctance of the United States to commit itself in Europe, and in particular in Central Europe, was regretfully accepted as a matter of fact.

When in July of 1947 the Czechoslovak democratic leaders were weighing the pros and cons of the Soviet ultimatum requesting the Czechoslovak Government to cancel its acceptance of an invitation to the Paris conference on the Marshall Plan, one Czech politician raised the following question: "Is it worthwhile to risk the certainty of the Soviet-Czechoslovak alliance, which we need against Germany, for such an uncertainty as is a proposition by Mr. Marshall, made at some American university [Harvard], which—similar to Wilson's League—may not even be approved by the U.S. Senate?" [7]

The impressive demonstration of American military might in Europe in the last two years of the second World War completely changed one feature of the concept of the United States, but it did not alter the doubt concerning the permanence of its active participation in European affairs.

In short, the United States appeared to most Czechoslovak democratic leaders as a mighty friend who at times might interrupt its isolation from Europe, be helpful and even generous, but could not be counted on to be permanently active in European politics. The actual implementation of American foreign policy in Central Europe between 1942 and 1948 seemed to confirm this view.

The first indication of American aloofness came in April 1944, one year before the end of the second World War. By the eighth of

[7] This statement was made by Norbert Pexa, a member of the parliamentary group of the Catholic People's Party, at a meeting on July 9, 1947.

April the Red Army had reached the Carpathians, the boundary between Czechoslovakia and the Soviet Ukraine. The Czechoslovak Government then proposed to the Soviet Union, Great Britain, and the United States conclusion of a treaty concerning the administration of the liberated territory. Similar treaties were concluded between the Western Great Powers and exiled representatives of Belgium, Netherlands, and Norway. The American and British governments, pointing to the physical impossibility of the Anglo-American Forces reaching the Central European area at any time —this was still almost two months before the establishment of the Second Front in Normandy—refused to negotiate any such treaty. The Soviet Union accepted the proposition. The Soviet-Czechoslovak Treaty on the Administration of Liberated Territories was signed on May 8, 1944.

This was perhaps the first official indication of Anglo-American acceptance of the fact that Czechoslovakia was to be exclusively within the zone of operations of the Red Army. The implications were certainly not lost on the Czechoslovak leaders: the Soviet power, *in agreement with the Western powers,* was to be preeminent in Czechoslovakia.

In August 1944, under joint political guidance of the Communist and non-Communist resistance leaders, partisan groups as well as a part of the Slovak Army succeeded in holding a part of Central Slovakia against the advancing elements of the Nazi occupying forces. Like the Warsaw uprising, the Slovak Uprising required some outside help against the German forces. The nearest possible source of help was the Red Army on the Carpathians. It never came. The Slovak Uprising was liquidated by the Nazi forces at the end of November 1944.

The Soviet Government, which was unable to send any substantial military help—with the exception of a Czech parachutist brigade serving with the Red Army—nevertheless proved able to send some Communist leaders from Moscow to assume the political leadership of the uprising. During the Nazi liquidation of the Slovak partisan pockets, one of the most talented Czech Communist leaders, Jan Šverma, froze to death in the high mountains to which he had fled.[8]

The liquidation of the Slovak Uprising does not seem to confirm

[8] In 1952, during the anti-Zionist and anti-Titoist trial in Prague, Rudolf Slánský, former Secretary General of the Communist Party of Czechoslovakia, confessed his responsibility for the death of Jan Šverma. *Rudé Právo,* Prague, November 27, 1952, p. 2.

the widely accepted theory that the failure of the Red Army to assist in uprisings was due to a Machiavellian plan which, by permitting the Nazis to liquidate the non-Communist resistance leadership, would thus rid the Communists of potential competition in the future. Rather, in view of the presence of the most important Communist leaders at the helm of the uprising, it would seem that the lack of flexibility of the Red Army Command was primarily responsible for the tragic outcome of the Slovak National Uprising.

On the other hand, the history of the Slovak Uprising of 1944 seems to confirm, beyond any doubt, that the Soviet Union preferred an uprising liquidated by the Nazis to one helped by the West. Moscow certainly did all in its power to prevent any Western political influence from developing in East Central Europe. The emotional and political association of the United States with the glory of a successful uprising would have remained an unnecessary challenge to Soviet prestige and claims of exclusive influence in the area.

The Soviet High Command, following the request of the Czechoslovak Government-in-exile and of the United States authorities, finally allowed a single flight of three Flying Fortresses from Bari to the airstrip of Tri Duby in the partisan-held part of central Slovakia. Their mission was to pick up American airmen who had previously bailed out over Slovakia and found refuge with the Slovak patriots, and to deliver medical supplies to the insurgents. Sending of weapons was not cleared by the Soviet High Command; the O.S.S., however, managed to smuggle a few bazookas and some ammunition into the partisan camps. That the United States Government found it necessary to smuggle weapons into the area, so that anti-Nazi forces might fight against the common enemy of the Soviet Union and the United States, was but another indication of the respective statures of the Soviet Union and the United States in East Central Europe.

In the same year the United States agreed to have a Soviet citizen as head of the UNRRA mission to Czechoslovakia, and thereby responsible for the distribution of relief to which the United States contributed more than two thirds of the total.

When in the winter and spring of 1945 the Red Army finally crossed the Carpathians and entered Slovakia on a broad front, the Czechoslovak Government-in-exile—according to the Soviet-Czechoslovak Treaty on the Administration of Liberated Territories —was ready to assume its political and administrative role in the rear zones of liberated parts of Czechoslovakia. While President Beneš and the majority of political leaders traveled to the liberated territories by air via Moscow, a British ship sailing from Glasgow, Scotland was supposed to bring to liberated Czechoslovakia, via the Mediterranean and the Rumanian Black Sea port of Constantza, the first contingent of Czechoslovak administrators and health personnel, as well as a nucleus of the diplomatic corps. This corps, composed of twenty-two British, fifteen American, four French, one Belgian, and one Dutch diplomat, was to be stationed in Košice, the provisional seat of President Beneš and the Czechoslovak Government. On March 28, 1945, the day of the departure, after the luggage of the Western diplomats had been loaded on the ship and their apartments in London given up, the Soviet chargé d'affaires with the Czechoslovak Government in London, Mr. N. Chichaev, informed his colleagues of the diplomatic corps that the Soviet Government did not consider the situation in the rear of the Red Army, then still fighting in Czechoslovakia, propitious for the establishment of the diplomatic corps in Košice, especially in view of the housing and food difficulties. The British and American diplomats had no option but to comply. The unloading of the luggage of the diplomatic representatives of the Western powers from the ship in Glasgow seemed a portent of things to come, and was thus interpreted by a great many Czechoslovak politicians.

This series of Soviet steps clearly indicated that the position of the Soviets in Czechoslovakia had become dominant, while this situation was being accepted (although reluctantly) by the Americans and British.

On April 18, 1945, thanks to an extraordinary sweep of General Patton's armies through southern Germany, the American forces (90th Infantry Division) quite unexpectedly entered western Bohemia. Suddenly, irrespective of the views expressed three weeks before by Mr. Chichaev in London, the Czechoslovak territory was open not only to fifteen American Foreign Service officers but to thousands of G.I.'s.

In addition, on May 5, 1945 an uprising took place in Prague. When the Revolutionary Committee, following the refusal of the German garrison in Prague to surrender to the Czech revolutionary forces, was faced with the vastly superior armor and firepower of the Nazi troops, it appealed to all Allied armies for help. This was technically possible, as one of the Prague broadcasting stations was seized by the insurgents. The advanced elements of the American forces were at that time from thirty to sixty miles from Prague. The nearest Soviet troops inside Czechoslovakia were at least double that distance from Prague.

Following an exchange of dispatches between General Eisenhower and the Soviet Commander, General Antonov, the United States Army advance toward Prague was halted at the line Karlovy Vary-Plzeň-Budějovice (Karlsbad-Pilsen-Budweiss). While the Soviet Command justified its refusal to permit the American Army to advance toward Prague because of the risk of potential confusion (did this mean that the Soviet armies, having established a bombing line west of Prague, might mistakenly bomb the American troops?), General Eisenhower showed his concern for Fighting Prague by expressing a hope as to "the ability of the Soviet forces to advance rapidly" toward Prague.[9]

Since in European countries the capital city is indeed the nerve center and heart of a nation's politics, education, culture, and history, a tremendous psychological advantage was given to the Soviets and their claim to supremacy in Czechoslovakia when the American advance in western Bohemia was halted. While the American Army, possibly without any fighting whatsoever, could have accepted the German surrender in Prague on May 7, 1945 (forward detachments of the O.S.S. mission were able to enter Prague without disguise on that day), Fighting Prague was to wait another two days before she could be liberated by the Russian Army.

Later, the circumstances of the liberation of Prague became, ironically enough, a continuous Communist argument against the United States and its Army. The Czechoslovak Communist Party,

[9] General Antonov's letter, transmitted by the U.S. military mission to SHAEF on May 5, 1945, reads as follows:

". . . Your letter indicating General Eisenhower's intention to advance the line Karlsbad-Pilsen-Budweiss, following the capture of these three points, for the purpose of clearing the west banks of the Elbe and Vltava rivers, if the situation dictates, was received yesterday. The Soviet Command requests General Eisenhower to refrain from advancing the Allied forces in Czechoslovakia beyond the formerly designated line, that is Karlsbad-Pilsen-Budweiss, so that a possible confusion of forces can be avoided. . . . It is hoped that with respect to the advance of the Allied forces in Czechoslovakia, General Eisenhower will accede to our desires."

General Eisenhower's answer, sent on May 6, 1945, reads as follows:

". . . The Allied Forces are under instructions to remain at the line Karlsbad-Pilsen-Budweiss. The ability of the Soviet forces to advance rapidly for the purpose of clearing up the situation in the center of the country is presumed." The State Department release issued on May 9, 1949, fourth anniversary of the liberation of Prague, *New York Times,* May 10, 1949.

while extolling the Soviet merit in saving Prague, accused the United States Army of having remained a cowardly or cynical onlooker while Prague was struggling for life.

An article published by the central organ of the Communist Party of Czechoslovakia, *Rudé Právo,* one month before the coup of 1948, concentrated on refuting the argument that the United States Army could not have helped Prague because of the Soviet-American agreement concerning the demarcation line Karlsbad-Pilsen-Budweiss. After enumerating the composition of the U.S. force in Czechoslovak territory (i.e., V-Corps, the 16th and 4th Tank Divisions, and the 1st, 2nd, 90th, and 97th Infantry Divisions), the article said:

> The Prague revolutionaries were of unusual courage but they needed help. During the fight they broadcasted appeals in English, Russian, and French, saying, "The uprising is drowning in blood. Please, help. Brothers from the Red Army. American and English friends. We trust that by tomorrow you will defend the sky above Prague with your planes."
>
> These signals were heard all over the world. Stalin's soldiers, in spite of human exhaustion after the battle of Berlin, hurried to help Prague. It was a difficult and significant march of Soviet troops.
>
> Where were the American troops at that time?
>
> It is fully known that the American troops were not very far. The Third Army of General Patton, which without heavy casualties [!] made its way through central Germany, stood in Czechoslovakia . . . armed to the teeth though it had not seen a shadow of the battles the Soviet troops had to fight in Berlin, it was standing on Czechoslovak territory . . . while the uprising was drowned in blood. . . .
>
> All Prague saw the Soviet tanks but there was no one who had seen American and English tanks near Prague.
>
> Why? Those [i.e., anti-Communists] who consider it their duty to rehabilitate their overseas protectors explain it by the existence of a "demarcation line." . . .
>
> To help people in danger "demarcation lines" do not exist.[10]

This Communist accusation remained unanswered at that time. For some inexplicable reason the United States Government did not decide to publish the contents of the letters exchanged between Antonov and Eisenhower until more than one year after the Communist seizure of power.

In 1956 it is probably quite irrelevant to speculate about the results had the U.S. High Command ordered General Patton to pro-

[10] *Rudé Právo,* January 18, 1948.

ceed to Prague. The possible effects of an American liberation of Prague certainly should not be overrated, since the basic distribution of power in Eastern Europe would have remained essentially the same. But of one different aspect of the situation we may be reasonably certain today. No Czech would have been able to excuse his lack of opposition to local Communists by such a remark as the following, heard by the author in the summer of 1945: "If the U.S. Army, with its armor, did not dare to displease the Russians, why should I? Besides, I have my family to think of."

Following the Soviet liberation of Prague, the demarcation line between the Soviet and American armies was maintained until December of 1945, when both armies left Czechoslovakia. The wise decision to keep the American Army in Czechoslovakia after V-E Day probably forced the Red Army to an earlier evacuation of Czechoslovakia. The Western diplomats whose luggage was unloaded from the ship in Glasgow in March still had to make their entry into Prague, an entry dependent on travel permission issued by the Soviet Army commanders in Bohemia. Some of them, in order to avoid the lengthy Soviet procedure, made use of the administrative chaos prevailing in the Soviet-held areas after the end of the war and entered Prague illegally, via the Soviet Zone. The author of this chapter, at that time a liaison officer with the G-5 of the U.S. Army, had the opportunity to bring to Prague the first advance party of British diplomats. Their task was to open up their Embassy. This experience, however thrilling personally (because of the necessity of using a forged pass to allow the party to proceed through the Soviet Zone), was on the whole a sobering one. That it was necessary for the representatives of victorious Churchillian England to be smuggled into Prague could hardly mean that the Western powers had the physical means of playing a powerful role in Czechoslovakia.

The U.S. Embassy in Prague

Despite its intimate knowledge of the local political scene, a diplomatic mission usually reflects the policies—and wishful thinking—of its central office. So did the American Embassy in Prague. Often in contrast with the reality of Czechoslovak political developments, the Embassy mirrored Washington's optimistic assumptions concerning Czechoslovakia.

The lack of knowledge of the Czech and Slovak languages only partly hampered the political task of the Embassy personnel and their endeavors to encourage the anti-Communist forces. A much greater handicap in the political work of the Embassy seemed to be its rather rigid adherence to the principle of nonintervention in the domestic affairs of Czechoslovakia.[11]

In the summer of 1947 the author suggested to a high-ranking U.S. diplomat in Prague that the Czechoslovak People's Catholic Party could be assisted in transferring one million crowns to the United States for the purchase of an additional printing press there —this in view of the coming elections in Czechoslovakia. The suggestion was turned down, not only because of the U.S. budgetary aspects of such operation, but also because "an assistance in such matter would have constituted an American intervention in the domestic affairs of Czechoslovakia." A few months earlier, the Communist Party of Czechoslovakia had been able, with the help of the Soviets, to purchase a modern printing press, originally ordered in Switzerland by a newspaper in Nazi-occupied France.

During the Communist coup in 1948, the Soviet Embassy was transformed into a residence for the Soviet Deputy Foreign Minister Valerian A. Zorin, who did not bother to conceal, but actually publicized, the daily visits of the Czechoslovak Communist leaders to his temporary headquarters. On the other hand, during the coup the U.S. Embassy carefully avoided any open contact with the anti-Communist leaders. This was in line with the principle of nonintervention and probably also with the hope that American self-restraint might induce the Soviet Government to maintain the same aloofness with regard to the crucial developments on the Czechoslovak political scene.

The situation was unorthodox, and called perhaps for a greater use of the second level of political operation in a foreign country. The first level is the traditional diplomatic one, which keeps the foreign representatives in open contact with a government, whatever political color it may have. This includes the formal as well as social contacts. The second level, less open and often frankly conspiratorial, keeps the foreign representatives in contact with the opposition to the very government to which the official embassy is accredited. For example, the Soviet Embassy in Paris, while on the first level toasting the members of the French Cabinet with

[11] This American attitude was manifest not only in Czechoslovakia. Cf. below, pp. 245–246. (Ed.)

vodka, on the second level plots with the French Communist Party the overthrow of the same Cabinet. In the last thirty-five years the Soviet embassies, representing both the Soviet nation and the world base of Communism in democratic countries, have developed this bilevel diplomacy into a fine art.

The conservative concept of diplomacy, as well as probable lack of experienced and trained personnel necessary for such "second-level" operation, induced the U.S. Embassy to handle the prerevolutionary situation in Czechoslovakia with a rather traditional approach. The question may be raised whether in 1945 the U.S. Embassy could have or should have adopted a bilevel diplomacy in Prague, with emphasis on the second, unofficial and conspiratorial level.

Here lies, of course, the agonizing dilemma of all democracies and their leaders: what is the amount of foul play which a democracy is permitted to employ in its fight against the foul play of its opponents, without running the risk of losing its reputation and its claim to be a symbol of fair play in human and political relations?

Communist Infiltration and Seizure of Power

The Czechoslovak Communists seized power on February 25, 1948. The timing of the coup was significant. It occurred roughly six months after the foundation of the Cominform and three months before Tito was ousted from the Cominform. However, the most important factor in the Communist timing was the date of the Czech elections, scheduled for May of 1948. The pre-election polls seemed to indicate a definite decline, although not a sharp one, in the Communists' popularity and simultaneously an awakening of civic spirit in Czechoslovakia.

Several months before the actual crisis developed, the Communist Party of Czechoslovakia and the Communist-led labor unions made every effort to charge the atmosphere with a high-voltage tension. Time bombs were sent to three most prominent anti-Communist leaders (Vice-Premier Petr Zenkl, Foreign Minister Jan Masaryk, and Minister of Justice Prokop Drtina). The Slovak Democratic Party, which in May 1946 succeeded in winning the elections against the Communists in Slovakia, was accused by the Communists of high treason and subversive activities in favor of the restoration of the Slovak Independent State. The Communist Party hoped to isolate the Slovak Democratic Party from those Czech non-Communist parties which had opposed the more or less federal concept of the Czechoslovak State favored by Slovak Democrats. The agitation in Slovakia, coupled with several arrests of Slovak political leaders, performed by the Communist Ministry of Interior, was both a preparation and rehearsal for the subsequent coup in Prague. In January 1948 the Communist Minister of Interior, Václav Nosek, announced his intention of packing completely the Czechoslovak police force. The Communist leader of the Labor Union Council, Antonín Zápotocký, called a special convention of labor delegates to Prague for February 22, hardly veiling his intention to challenge the authority of Parliament. On February 15 Zápotocký declared bluntly: "Away with the Parliament if it does not fulfill the program of the Labor Union."

Under manifold pressures—or one may say, under intentional provocations—the democratic leaders decided to force the elections at an earlier date and through them obtain better power positions in the government. They hoped that following the weakening of the Communist Party at the polls there would be a greater prospect of success in withstanding extraparliamentary Communist pressures. It was over the question of whether the police were to become an extended arm of the Communist Party that the coalition government of the National Front broke up. Three non-Marxist parties of the coalition (National Socialist, People's Christian Democratic, and Slovak Democratic parties), although holding less than 50 per cent of the Cabinet portfolios, recalled their ministers and thus provoked a government crisis in a manner externally similar to the situations which often take place in the overthrow and re-creation of French cabinets. The hope of the non-Marxist parties was to prevent any Communist-initiated police or economic reform before the elections.

In view of the actual power situation within Czechoslovakia (and around it), this was a wrong strategy, for it took for granted, rather unrealistically, that the Communists would adhere to the constitutional framework of a parliamentarian democracy and accept the verdict of free elections, even if it were to be in favor of the enemies of Communism. In the worsening international situation—and on the eve of a showdown with Tito—Moscow could hardly afford to gamble with free elections in Czechoslovakia, the result of which could have had a detrimental effect on the Soviet position in East Central Europe.

On February 19, following two weeks of major tension in Czechoslovakia, Soviet Deputy Foreign Minister Zorin arrived in Prague. The indication of Soviet interest in the outcome of the Czechoslovak political crisis could not have been made clearer. Simultaneously, Moscow's *Pravda* spoke of "the support of two hundred million Soviet citizens for the cause of the fight against domestic and international reaction in Czechoslovakia." In the middle of an open political clash between the forces of democracy and Communism, the presence of a high Soviet official symbolized Soviet military might, Soviet economic power, secret police and Siberian camps, and the probability of Soviet support of any lawless or violent action the Czech Communists might commit.

On February 24 the Labor Union Council proclaimed a general strike. Rather than being an effort to paralyze the life of the nation, it was meant as a demonstration of the political strength, discipline, and unity of the proletariat under the leadership of the Communist Party. The key positions in the government, Communist-held since 1945, overnight became revolutionary headquarters directing the seizure of power. The positions not previously held by either Communists or fellow travelers were within a few days taken over by the so-called Action Committees. With the help of Workers' Militia (armed then by the Communist Party), the Action Committees were able to prevent the anti-Communist forces from access to any positions of power from which to strike back. The Action Committees were composed of Communists familiar with the workings of the agency which they were ordered to seize. Thus, the Action Committee in the Czechoslovak Ministry of Posts and Telegraphs was composed of two high officials of the ministry, two lower rank officials, three typists, one janitor, and one driver—all prominent members of the Communist cell in that Ministry. Their first task was to oust the Minister and his staff from the Ministry and assume the positions of command.

When on February 25 President Beneš was forced to consent to the creation of a Cabinet under full control of the Communist Party, the country and its administration were already in the hands of the Communists. While February 25, 1948 is the official date of the Communist *Putsch,* in reality that day represented the consummation of a very long process started before the end of the second World War. The Communist coup could not have succeeded in February 1948 had certain strategic positions not been in Communist hands since 1945. The relative ease with which the Communists seized power cannot be analyzed without the realization that the non-Communist forces, although numerically superior, were in their actual political and economic power, unity of purpose, outside support, and boldness inferior to the Communists. The previous Communist infiltration of the key positions in the Czechoslovak Government was the *conditio sine qua non* of the February coup.

For more than two years preceding the coup, Czechoslovak Communists controlled the following agencies of major importance:

1. *The majority of units of local government* (Regional, District, and Local National Committees). Their infiltration occurred while the Red Army was still in the country and therefore with its more or less open help.

2. *The Ministry of Interior,* which the Communists were able to obtain in exchange for their agreement to leave the Presidency, Foreign Ministry, and Ministry of Foreign Trade in the hands of non-Communists. In a unitary form of government like that of Czechoslovakia, the Ministry of Interior is an agency of overwhelming power because of its control over the national police and investigating services.

3. *The Ministry of Information,* which controlled all mass communication media (broadcasting, news distribution, and film) and allotments of newsprint to the Czechoslovak newspapers. The scarcity of newsprint in postwar Europe increased the physical control of that ministry over the press, which in the Czechoslovakia of 1945–1948 was relatively free in content.

4. *The Central Labor Union and the Ministry of Agriculture,* which meant power over the workers and influence over the peasants, respectively.

5. *Premiership of the Government.*

On the non-Communist side the positions of strength (more symbolic than real) were as follows:

1. *The Presidency of the Republic,* which according to the Czechoslovak prewar and postwar constitutions was a position of great prestige but little actual power. The Czechoslovak pattern of government had followed the French rather than the American model. The great popularity and personal prestige of the first two

presidents of Czechoslovakia, the elder Masaryk and Beneš, had obscured the constitutional weakness of the Presidency in Czechoslovakia.

2. *Ministries of Foreign Affairs and of Foreign Trade,* which under normal conditions could have been classified as positions of major influence, but not so in a prerevolutionary situation. In addition, the pre-eminent influence of the Soviet power in East Central Europe had limited the scope of Czechoslovak foreign and trade policies to such an extent that the importance of these positions became more symbolic than real.

3. *The majority in Parliament:* again a very powerful factor under normal conditions, when a parliamentary majority vote represents the consensus of an integrated society; it loses its importance when parliamentary institutions are bypassed by extraparliamentary methods of a determined and well organized minority. As soon as a political conflict shifts from the floor of a parliament to the pavements of the streets and public squares, the relationship between a majority and a minority ceases to be a problem of vote counting. It is transformed into a physical contest for power, in which the armed might of a minority makes right against the outraged protest of an unarmed parliamentary majority.

4. *The majority of the people;* a decisive factor in free elections, when votes are scrupulously counted, but certainly not a decisive factor when a determined, well organized minority mesmerizes the disorganized and surprised majority into inactivity by a display of force.

The only position of physical strength on the side of the non-Communists in the February clash for power was the army. Although the Ministry of National Defense, headed by the former commander of the Czechoslovak units in Russia (created within the framework of the Red Army), General Ludvík Svoboda, as well as several high commanding positions, was strongly infiltrated by the Communists, many high ranking generals, as well as a good portion of the officers corps and rank and file, were decidedly anti-Communist and pro-Western. With the police and workers militia at their disposal, the Communist leaders preferred to keep the army neutralized, relying on the assistance of the fellow traveler Minister Svoboda and the unwillingness of President Beneš to plunge the nation into a civil war.

President Beneš as Commander in Chief perhaps could have

ordered the army to restore civil order, at the price of a civil war in which the Communist side might conceivably have been supported by "volunteers" coming from the Soviet-held neighboring countries. No similar help would have been forthcoming from American-held Bavaria. President Beneš was decidedly not the sort of leader who would admit that even the most desperate civil war for the moral survival of a nation might sometimes be preferable to submission in the face of overwhelming force. During the Munich crisis of 1938, President Beneš was of the opinion that under uncertain international conditions a certainty of massacre could be and should be avoided. He reasoned in the same way in 1948. For this over-caution he may be criticized—as he is—by his compatriots. On the other hand, it may be said that in 1938 as well as in 1948 President Beneš simply refused, when unaided by Western democracies, to fight a battle which was not only his but that of the Western democracies as well.

From the previous account it is clear that the infiltration of the essential key positions (local government, national police, and labor unions) had occurred three years before the actual execution of the Communist coup. Technically, it seems, the Communist seizure of power in Czechoslovakia had been possible in the winter of 1945–1946. In the opinion of some, the Czechoslovak Communist leaders actually believed that, thanks to their control of key positions acquired in 1945, they would be able to demonstrate for the first time in history the establishment of Communism in an industrialized and democratic country through regular parliamentary elections. Some statements made by the Communist leaders in 1947 seem to indicate that this idea had a definite appeal to them. Other observers explain the Kremlin's postponement of the seizure of power in Czechoslovakia in the light of Soviet and American policies after Potsdam. In a dynamic international situation, which in Czechoslovakia led the Communists to flirt with the Marshall Plan,[12] Moscow decided not to let the Czechoslovak Communists try to prove that Communism under special circumstances could be established through free elections.

[12] The Czechoslovak Government under the Communist Premier Klement Gottwald accepted the joint British-French invitation to participate in the preparatory conference of the Marshall Plan on July 4, 1947. It was only under direct pressure from Stalin himself that five days later the Czechoslovak Government withdrew its publicly announced participation. This, in the opinion of some observers, was the real beginning of the Communist coup.

The downfall of the Czechoslovak democracy is certainly a good lesson in political strategy, but it has a limited relevance when applied to the American political scene. A parallel between the fall of Czechoslovakia and the risk of a similar fall of the United States could be made only if one were to visualize the United States as sandwiched between a Nazi Mexico with a population of approximately one billion and a Communist Canada with a population of over 2.5 billion; if at the same time the United States Congress contained two hundred senators and representatives affiliated with a Canada-led Communist Party, if forty-seven governors as well as a majority of the mayors of major towns were Communist, the AFL-CIO Communist-directed, the American Farm Bureau Federation under Communist leadership, J. Edgar Hoover a member of the Politburo, General Motors and Ford and Dupont run by Washington, D.C., and in addition the American people only half awake after six years of a cruel Nazi-Mexican oppression. This parallel is certainly not meant to advocate any complacency concerning the possibilities of American Communism or to emphasize that "what happened in Czechoslovakia cannot happen here." Its purpose is to stress the importance of the peculiar factors of geography and power distribution, which proved decisive in the case of Czechoslovakia.

Seven Years of Totalitarianism

Following the February coup, the regime paid, for a while at least, a hypocritical tribute to the democratic reputation of Czechoslovakia by pretending to be a continuation of its democratic traditions rather than their violent interruption. An effort was made to keep a democratic façade so long as the Soviet Government and the Communist Party of Czechoslovakia were worried about a possible international reaction to the coup and the Soviet role in it. In order to solidify its hold, the new regime was perhaps also in need of some breathing spell, following the Communist blitz-like seizure of power.

Outwardly the multiparty system was maintained. The former coalition of the National Front was renamed "Regenerated National Front." This "regeneration" of the coalition consisted in replacing the leadership of the non-Communist parties with fellow travelers. The pre-*Putsch* leaders of the non-Communist parties either were arrested or fled into exile. Both President Beneš and Foreign Minister Masaryk were induced to keep their respective positions in the new government and thus lend a certain degree of respectability to the revolutionary setup. However, this hypocrisy did not last long. Two weeks after the coup, on March 10, Jan Masaryk's body, with a broken spine, was found on the pavement under the windows of his apartment. President Beneš kept on performing the social and decorative functions of the Presidency until May 1948. He resigned after his refusal to sign the new Communist constitution of Czechoslovakia, a copy of the Stalin constitution of 1936. He died four months later on September 3, 1948. President Beneš's death, as well as that of Jan Masaryk, seemed to close a chapter of Czechoslovak modern history, so markedly shaped by those two names. Symbolically at least, the way seemed clear for a complete streamlining of Czechoslovakia according to the familiar Communist pattern. The differences which had distinguished Czechoslovakia from its neighbors began to disappear. Although some outward symbols of the political link with the pre-*Putsch* past have been intentionally kept until the present (e.g., the flag, the Presidency, and even the illusion of a multiparty system [13]), Czechoslovakia has become a typical totalitarian state with one party as the only source of political authority.

The leadership of the Communist Party of Czechoslovakia has always reflected all major movements of the weathervane on the Kremlin. In the period of the Soviet fight against Titoism, the Communist regime of Czechoslovakia staged a trial which, on the basis of the usual trumped-up charges of high treason in general and Titoism in particular, sent eleven top Communist leaders, most of them of Jewish origin, to the gallows.[14] Though it was one of the most propagandized purges, its spectacular character should not conceal the fact that in reality the Titoist anti-Soviet revolt had had very few important imitators in Czechoslovakia. The struggle for power among the Czechoslovak Communists and their purges seemed to evolve around the question who would serve Moscow more slavishly, rather than around the problem who could do it more intelligently.

While the Communist leaders were able to adhere to the rigid

[13] Czechoslovakia's People's Democracy is nominally still a multiparty system. Besides the Communist Party there are three non-Communist parties: Czechoslovak Socialists, Catholic Populists, and Slovak Renovation Party. Their leadership is appointed, and their organization and membership quota are controlled by the Communist Party. The non-Communist parties of Czechoslovakia fulfill the role of specific "transmission belts," that is, mass organizations *sui generis*.

[14] During the trial, which had lasted from November 20 to 27, 1952, eleven of the fourteen defendants were sentenced to death and the remaining three to life imprisonment. Among the eleven were the former Secretary General of the Party, Rudolf Slánský, and the former Foreign Minister, Vlado Clementis.

Stalinist line without any hesitancy, the softer line of the new Soviet duumvirate which followed Stalin's death was adopted somewhat reluctantly and belatedly. This is certainly not to be interpreted as an indication of some independent thinking on the part of the Czechoslovak Communists, but rather as a sign of the insecurity of a regime which feels safer when applying terror than in a period of relative relaxation when the boundaries between the dogma and temporary tactics are often blurred.

The Communist Party, having assumed its monopolistic position of power on February 25, 1948, has been concentrating on solidifying its hold over Czechoslovakia ever since. Between 1948 and 1949 the administrative apparatus was thoroughly purged. Organizations and institutions which had not been previously under Communist control were deprived of their leadership and transformed into agencies of the Communist Party and State. This was the golden age for fellow travelers. The purpose and spirit of all institutions were transformed to fit the needs of the new totalitarian society in the making. This process was almost immediate in some cases (trade unions, army and air force, youth organizations and sport clubs) and slower and spasmodic in other cases (peasant co-operatives and the Catholic Church, whose rightful leaders, such as Archbishop Josef Beran of Prague, were definitely silenced only in 1950).

In the economic sphere the Communist Party proceeded with vigor and skill. According to the Leninist dogma, Czechoslovakia, a small country but a major industrial power, was to be industrialized even further, especially its eastern part, Slovakia, while agriculture was to be collectivized. In accordance with the Soviet pattern, the Communist Party planned and executed a marked shift from the traditional light and consumer goods industries of Czechoslovakia to heavy and especially machine tools industries.

The Czechoslovak concentration on heavy industry was in line with both Kremlin dogma and current Soviet political offensives. Czechoslovakia was to become, as she is today, one of the main suppliers of heavy machinery and technological skills to Communist or uncommitted underdeveloped areas. The role of Czechoslovakia as a workshop and political agent at the same time should not be underestimated, especially in the framework of the Soviet plans for penetration into Asia and Africa. In countries like India, Burma, Afghanistan, or Indonesia a fear may subsist that the Great Powers, kicked out of the front door, may restore their colonialism through the back door under the guise of technical assistance. In this respect, the small size of Czechoslovakia coupled with her favorable technological reputation may prove a considerable asset to the Soviets.

The Communist Party has not pursued its economic goals for their own sake only. Industrialization and collectivization of agriculture were supposed to yield an important political dividend: liquidation of the urban and peasant middle classes, the backbone of liberal democracy.

While in 1956 the urban middle classes may be considered virtually liquidated, a great majority of independent peasants have thus far survived. Only one third [15] of the land may be classified as collectivized, although the farmers have been under constant collectivization pressures for the past seven years. The Communist failure in this sector cannot be explained by their lack of zeal or their abhorrence of violent means of coercion; the explanation should perhaps be found in their apprehension that the constant crisis in food production might be even worse as the result of additional collectivization.

Forces of Opposition

Prewar Czechoslovakia was often described as a nation with a minimum of social friction. Today, under the banner of a "classless socialist society," Czechoslovakia has been split into two classes: the privileged few (a new elite made up of party officials and appointees) and the dissatisfied masses. However, their dissatisfaction should not be equated with the potentiality of a successful revolution. Although Czechoslovakia did witness a serious rebellion of the workers,[16] it is important to note that the Communist regime after a few hours of panic was able to quell the Pilsen revolt with ease and efficacy. The Communist monopoly power over the means of coercion and communications again proved that the concept of a revolution in which a sheer weight of numbers is supposed to crush an

[15] The Czechoslovak Minister of Agriculture, V. Krutina, as quoted by *Zemědělské Noviny,* Prague, on November 26, 1955, admitted that only 26.4 per cent of the land was under a full or partial form of collective ownership. To this figure one should add the approximately 10 per cent belonging to state farms.

[16] On June 1, 1953 the workers of the famous Škoda Works (now Lenin Works) in Pilsen staged a mass demonstration against the regime and its currency reform proclaimed on the previous day. The demonstration culminated in the seizure of the administrative center of the city, so that for half a day the city of Pilsen was in the hands of the rebellious workers.

armed minority is outdated. In a modern totalitarian society a successful revolt without a split inside the power apparatus is hardly thinkable.

Although the Communist minority has certainly not succeeded in transforming the Czechs and Slovaks into convinced Leninists—there are probably fewer convinced Communists in Czechoslovakia today than there were on the eve of the coup—the Party is able to rule over Czechoslovakia without any serious opposition to its plans. Being the sole job distributor, the Communist State is able to maximize its power over life and death for millions whose first aim is necessarily to survive. Most Czechs and Slovaks are either direct employees of the State or employees of enterprises controlled by the State. In addition, almost every Czechoslovak is bound to be a member of one of the numerous mass organizations which the Party had created and now fully controls. Thus, only those who are very old or who had escaped abroad may claim to have succeeded in dodging the ever-present tentacles of the totalitarian state. Under such conditions the Communist power over the life and death of its subjects is bound to have some results: although mass indoctrination coupled with occasional terror cannot teach the people to like the system, it can at least minimize their active opposition to it.

The Western powers have no physical means to limit or challenge the overwhelming power of the Communist State over jobs, food, housing, education, and recreation in Czechoslovakia, as well as its ultimate power to determine the percentage of citizens who are to spend their lives in forced-labor camps.

The only possible challenge which the West has been able to offer so far is that to the indoctrination and propaganda pressures of the Communist regime. This is being done both in words and in print. Every day millions of Czechs and Slovaks, including members of the Communist Party, listen to broadcasts from abroad. Czechoslovakia with a population over 12.5 million has over three million registered receiver sets. Almost every Czechoslovak family possesses a receiver set, more than 90 per cent of them equipped for short wave. Thus, Czechoslovakia has become one of the major targets of radio warfare. The news and views of the Czechoslovak and Soviet Communist radio stations are constantly challenged not only by the Voice of America, Radio Free Europe, the B.B.C., Radio Paris, Radio Rome, and Radio Vatican but also by Radio Madrid and Radio Belgrade. The last had a considerable audience in the period of the Yugoslav-Soviet rift.

In addition, the Western challenge to the Communist dogmas has been lately reaching Czechoslovakia in the form of a regularly distributed air magazine.[17] In 1954 the Free Europe Committee developed a revolutionary device in mass communication: controllable hydrogen-filled balloons which twice monthly distribute one-and-a-half million copies of the Czechoslovak air magazine. Each issue of the anti-Communist semimonthly contains eight pages of text and photographs.

There is no doubt that the United States with its spoken and printed messages can and does reach Czechoslovakia on a regular basis. Now, when Czechoslovakia is enslaved, the American interest for its fate appears to many Czechs and Slovaks more conspicuous than it was when they were still relatively free.

However, one word of caution should be added: the impressive technical devices which allow unprecedented daily communication between the United States and enslaved Czechoslovakia by radio and by air balloon do not simultaneously solve the problem of the contents of this constant flow of spoken and printed messages. The question must be asked: how long can the Czechs and Slovaks be effectively advised by their Western friends to oppose the system and keep their faith in the possibility of their final liberation?

Hobson's Choice?

Czechoslovakia, in spite of her previous democratic record and political and diplomatic skill, has become a rather eloquent proof of the fact that in the postwar interdependent world a small land-locked nation, when it lives in the shadow of a dynamic totalitarian super-power, can only under a set of very exceptional circumstances be sovereign master of its destiny. At best, the national leaders may help to co-shape the fate of their nation. At worst, they are prisoners or puppets. In the case of a small power living well inside a great power's sphere of immediate interest and influence, the choice of alternative policies is severely limited. Czechoslovakia, with the Communist armies present on four fifths of her boundaries, resembles a prisoner whose life, outlook, and even death are predeter-

[17] The Free Europe Committee, on the basis of its experience with Czechoslovakia, has been using identical devices with respect to Poland and Hungary.

mined by the four walls of his cell. He can sit, or stand, or lie down. He may side with the fellow prisoners or with the guards. He can walk from left to right or pace up and down. But he cannot go beyond his four walls. Even if he wants to die, his choice is limited: he can only commit suicide by breaking his head against the wall. Only in the case of a balance (or absence) of the interests of the great powers or in the case of their self-restraint is the boldness or faintheartedness, the foresight or foolishness of the national leaders allowed to play a decisive role.

Czechoslovakia's destiny was largely predetermined by the developments of the second World War. These made it almost inevitable that the Western Allies invade Europe from Normandy rather than through the Balkans (or through Austria in 1944, instead of the Allied invasion of southern France). Russia was to play the determining role in the area, and the only countermove which could be made within the context of a global balance of respective powers was to force Russia to play its role with circumspection and self-restraint, or simply to hope, rather unrealistically, for a change in the character of Soviet foreign policy.

Czechoslovakia's democratic leaders had little choice but to reiterate American hopes for the best and fears for the worst. Their errors and wishful thinking were neither much greater nor smaller than those of the American policy. Czechoslovakia attempted to be a symbol of something that did not exist: harmony between the Soviet and non-Soviet worlds. This is why the outcome could not have been but tragic. The basic assumption of the Great Powers concerning their postwar cooperation was the cornerstone of Czechoslovak politics. As this assumption was wrong, the cornerstone became a tombstone.

Chapter 9

Hungary

STEPHEN D. KERTESZ

THE PERIOD between the world wars was an unprecedented experience for Hungary. She had become one of the small "succession" states which replaced the Habsburg Empire. For the first time in modern history no great power existed in the Danubian region, and the new era found Hungary in a most precarious predicament. The Treaty of Trianon attached more than three million Hungarians to neighboring states.[1] Moreover, it generated a whole series of economic difficulties. Most of the factories and industrial areas remaining in Hungary were deprived of their markets and were cut off from their sources of raw materials within its newly created neighbors. These and numerous related issues generated a strong desire in Hungary for revision of the *status quo,* the maintenance of which was the chief aim of her neighbors. Revisionism persisted throughout the interwar period and made impossible a sensible compromise and cooperation between Hungary and her Danubian and Balkan neighbors. Revisionism and anti-Bolshevism became the leitmotiv of Hungarian foreign policy. In the 1930's a pro-Axis orientation was almost inevitable.

On the eve of the second World War Hungary, however, followed a cautious policy. Her desire for a *rapprochement* with the Little Entente became manifest through the Bled Agreement of August 23, 1938. The turn of European events nonetheless defeated this conciliatory course, and the Munich Conference made it clear that the Western democracies intended to remain aloof from Central European affairs. The subsequent Hitler-Stalin deal of August 1939 caught the whole Danubian area between the upper and nether millstones.

[1] Harold Temperley, "How the Hungarian Frontiers Were Drawn," *Foreign Affairs,* VI (1928), 432–447.

With the outbreak of hostilities, Prime Minister Paul Teleki sought to maintain a nonbelligerent status and some measure of independence for Hungary, despite initial territorial readjustments obtained with the help of the Axis powers. Teleki rejected German demands to use a Hungarian railroad line to attack the Polish Army from the rear. But such an energetic manifestation of Hungary's independence could not last for long. Geography, revisionism, and the weakness of the Western democracies soon influenced Hungarian foreign policy; Teleki committed suicide when German troops crossed Hungary's boundaries to attack Yugoslavia; and the Hungarian Government decided to cooperate with Germany. In Winston Churchill's words, Teleki's suicide was "a sacrifice to absolve himself and his people from guilt in the German attack upon Yugoslavia. It clears his name before history. It could not stop the march of the German armies nor the consequences." [2]

Although Hungary's limited participation in Hitler's war against the Soviet Union eventually caused a state of war with the English-speaking powers, Hungarian contingents did not fight against American or British troops. After the calamitous defeat suffered by the Hungarian Army at Voronezh in January 1943, military help for Germany in Russia was reduced to a badly equipped token force. Soon afterwards emissaries of the Hungarian Government contacted British and American representatives to secure the earliest possible armistice. But, despite some preliminary agreements, this policy could not succeed, because it was based on the assumption that Europe would be invaded from the southeast. Limited cooperation between Hungary and the English-speaking powers nevertheless resulted, and the Western powers did not bomb Hungarian territory until Germany occupied the country in a surprise move on March 19, 1944. Three days before the German occupation a United States military mission was parachuted to Hungarian soil. The members of this mission soon became German war prisoners, and American army personnel trained for occupation duty in Hungary never were used.

At the end of hostilities geography proved decisive in the misfortune of Hungary, which was situated in the inner circle of the

[2] Winston S. Churchill, *The Grand Alliance,* Vol. III of *The Second World War* (Boston, 1950), p. 168. For Hungary's wartime policy, see Stephen D. Kertesz, *Diplomacy in a Whirlpool: Hungary Between Nazi Germany and Soviet Russia* (Notre Dame, Ind., 1953) and Nicholas Kallay, *Hungarian Premier* (New York, 1954).

German power sphere. Regent Nicolas Horthy's ill-prepared endeavor to conclude an armistice failed. His armistice proclamation, read over the Budapest radio on October 15, 1944, had little effect. Most of the ranking government officials left the country with the retreating German troops and the remainder of the Hungarian Army. When news spread about the behavior of the invading Red Army, even lesser officials fled. The country was first ravaged by the Germans, then systematically looted by the Russians. Because of all these circumstances, in no other Axis satellite state were the physical destruction and the vacuum of political power and administrative authority so extensive as in Hungary.

Western and Soviet Policies at the Close of Hostilities

While Budapest and Western Hungary were still in German hands, a provisional National Assembly was organized in Debrecen, the chief town in northeastern Hungary. In the "liberated" areas representatives to the Assembly were elected by acclamation. The Assembly then elected a provisional National Government, and authorized it to conclude an armistice with the Allied Powers.

In point of time Hungary was the last of the Axis satellites to conclude an armistice agreement with the three major Allies (January 20, 1945). The agreement contained obligations of a military, political, economic, and financial nature, and reduced Hungarian sovereignty to a minimum. It established an Allied Control Commission under Russian chairmanship. The Chairman was Marshal Klementy Voroshilov. Hungarian authorities were to carry out orders and instructions issued by the Soviet High Command or the ACC. In practice, Voroshilov or his deputy acted in the name of both. The ACC had American and British sections along with the Russian section but for all practical purposes was run exclusively by the Russians, who were in effective occupation of the country. Through this instrument the Russians freely intervened in Hungary's domestic and foreign affairs. In the entire armistice period the Soviet technique in Hungary was to act in the name of the three major Allies while keeping Britain and the United States from effective action.

During negotiation of the armistice agreement the Russians were unwilling to accept American proposals aiming at equal participation of the three Allied governments in the work of the ACC. Later, in Budapest, the American section prepared an elaborate plan for the operation of the ACC. An important feature of the plan was establishment of a Secretariat, which would have the function, *inter alia,* of receiving and translating all incoming and outgoing communications, and furnishing copies to each section of the ACC. Voroshilov buried the proposal with the comment that the armistice agreement said nothing about a Secretariat.

As appears from the armistice agreement, the ACC was under the general direction of the Soviet High Command during the hostilities against Germany.[3] The fact that the Soviet chairmanship was restricted to this period implied a promise for larger Western participation between the termination of hostilities and the conclusion of peace. Consequently at Potsdam in July 1945 the three Allied governments

> took note that the Soviet Representatives on the Allied Control Commissions in Rumania, Bulgaria, and Hungary have communicated to their United Kingdom and United States colleagues proposals for improving the work of the Control Commissions, now that hostilities in Europe have ceased.
>
> The three Governments agreed that the revision of the procedures of the Allied Control Commissions in these countries would now be undertaken, taking into account the interests and responsibilities of the three Governments which together presented the terms of armistice to the respective countries, and accepting as a basis, in respect of all these countries, the Soviet Government's proposals for Hungary as annexed thereto.[4]

When President Truman returned from Potsdam, he reaffirmed in a radio address to the American people the joint responsibility

[3] This was provided for in par. 2 of art. 18 in the Bulgarian and Hungarian armistice agreements. The corresponding article of the earlier concluded Rumanian armistice agreement revealed Soviet intentions more clearly; for it simply stated that an Allied Control Commission "will undertake until the conclusion of peace the regulation of and control over the execution of the present terms under the general direction and orders of the Allied (Soviet) High Command, acting on behalf of the Allied Powers." As a result of American diplomatic efforts paragraph 2 was added to Article 18 in the Bulgarian and Hungarian armistice agreements, which established Soviet chairmanship for the period of hostility against Germany. See above, pp. 66–67.

[4] There then followed a citation to "Annex I," the rather vague text of a letter sent by the Soviet Government on July 12, 1945, to the representatives of the U.S. and U.K. Governments on the ACC in Hungary. The Soviet Government promised in this letter that the President of the ACC would call conferences with the British and American representatives once every ten days or more frequently in case of need. American and British representatives were promised free movement. Moreover, it was provided that directives of the ACC on "questions of principle" would be issued to the Hungarian authorities by the ACC after agreement on these directives with the British and American representatives. These and other pledges concerning the new order of work for the ACC were not kept.

of the three major powers to establish in the liberated nations of Europe governments broadly representative of the democratic elements of the population. With particular reference to Rumania, Bulgaria and Hungary, he stated that these nations

> are not to be spheres of influence of any one power. They are now governed by Allied control commissions composed of representatives of the three governments which met at Yalta and Berlin. These control commissions, it is true, have not been functioning completely to our satisfaction, but improved procedures were agreed upon at Berlin. Until these states are re-established as members of the international family, they are the joint concern of all of us.[5]

The revised statutes of the ACC accordingly set forth that the American and British representatives on the ACC should have the right "to receive copies of all communications, reports and other documents which may interest the Government of the United States and the United Kingdom." [6] In practice, no change took place. The famous 50-50 settlement, agreed upon by Churchill and Stalin concerning Russian and Western influence in Hungary,[7] was never applied. Control Commissions in the Danubian states remained under Russian domination throughout their existence. These commissions brought pressure on the local governments and, in close cooperation with the local Communist parties, engineered the political transformation of these countries.

Contacts between Russians and the Americans and British in Hungary were, of course, only a small segment of their larger relationships. The heads of the American, British and Soviet diplomatic missions were political advisers to the ACC and were not accredited to the Hungarian Government. An American representative with the personal rank of minister, H. F. Arthur Schoenfeld, arrived in Budapest in May 1945. He functioned as the United States representative in Hungary for the general protection of American interests in addition to and separate from the ACC. Schoenfeld told Foreign Minister János Gyöngyösi at their first meeting that the American Government intended to help the reconstruction and rehabilitation of Hungary. Moreover he made it clear that the American authorities did not intend to seize as war booty the property re-

[5] *New York Times,* August 10, 1945.

[6] Art. 6.c. *Bulletin,* XVI (1947), 1161.

[7] Winston S. Churchill, *Triumph and Tragedy,* Vol. VI of *The Second World War* (Boston, 1953), p. 227. For different versions of the "percentage" agreement, see above, footnote 20 on p. 66.

moved forcibly by the Nazis from Hungary to the American zone of Germany, but intended to restore all identifiable displaced property. As for war guilt, he declared that the United States advocated punishment of war criminals but opposed application to any particular nation of the principle of collective responsibility. An American note expressed willingness to receive an unofficial Hungarian representative in Washington even before the renewal of official diplomatic relations. This offer was reiterated, but because of Soviet opposition the Hungarian Government could not accept.

The British political representative, Alvary D. F. Gascoigne, repeatedly pointed out to the Foreign Minister the shortcomings of Hungarian democratic practices—for example, the lack of freedom of speech or guarantees of personal liberties. Gascoigne particularly objected to the abuses committed by the political police. Ernest Bevin, in his first speech in the House of Commons as Foreign Secretary on August 20, 1945, had aptly characterized the shortcomings of the new regimes established in the Danubian states. In speaking of the situation in Bulgaria, Rumania and Hungary Bevin observed:

> The Governments which have been set up do not, in our view, represent the majority of the people, and the impression we get from recent developments is that one kind of totalitarianism is being replaced by another. This is not what we understand by that very much overworked word 'democracy', which appears to need definition, and the forms of government which have been set up as a result do not impress us as being sufficiently representative to meet the requirements of diplomatic relations.

Although American and British goodwill towards Hungary was displayed mainly in the form of advice and friendly gestures, there also were the humanitarian gifts badly needed in the impoverished country. One of the first American moves was a considerable gift of medicine to the Hungarian Red Cross. Later the United States granted credits totaling $30,000,000 for the purchase of surplus property. Moreover UNRRA relief supplies valued at over four million dollars were sent to Hungary.

At the first meeting of the Council of Foreign Ministers, which opened in London on September 11, 1945, Secretary Byrnes declared that the United States would not sign treaties with the existing unrepresentative governments of Rumania and Bulgaria, but was ready to recognize the government of Hungary on receipt of a pledge of free elections. This move clearly aimed at strengthening non-Communist elements in the Hungarian coalition. Molotov countered by immediate and unconditional recognition of the Hungarian Government. Thus the American and Russian missions were changed to legations, and the American and Russian diplomatic representatives to the ACC presented their credentials to the Hungarian Government as plenipotentiary ministers. Great Britain manifested a more reserved attitude. She was not willing to re-establish regular diplomatic relations with Hungary, a country still technically at war with the Allied Powers, and appointed Gascoigne as British political representative to Hungary.

But renewal of diplomatic relations did not strengthen the position of the British and American representatives in the ACC. In the course of the execution of the Armistice Agreement the Russians committed many abuses, notably in enforcing their interpretation of "democracy" and "fascism." They had a wide choice of means in exerting pressure on Hungarian authorities. Personal liberty as well as the daily bread of the population, in fact, all the necessities of life, depended entirely upon them. Devastated Hungary had to feed an occupying force of several hundred thousand men. Civilians by the thousands, including women, were deported to the Soviet Union as prisoners of war. There was no authority capable of giving protection against the Russians. The mass deportation of civilians and selected politicians was but one of the means to frighten the population into conformity with Soviet wishes. Such actions made the Russians and the Communists unpopular, but at the same time created a feeling of helplessness. The effect was cumulative, since this feeling of fear and insecurity prepared the way for subsequent Soviet political actions.

Soviet Economic Stranglehold

Besides carrying the legal burden of the armistice obligations, Hungary suffered through illegal seizures and large-scale looting. The Red Army seized a substantial part of Hungary's livestock, food supplies, means of transportation, currency, and industrial equipment. Safe-deposit boxes were forced open and their contents removed. Private homes, public warehouses, stores, government agencies, and banks were looted in the same way. Nor were the legations of neutral powers spared.

The armistice agreement authorized the Red Army to issue currency to be redeemed by the Hungarian Government. Moreover, the Soviet High Command was entitled to demand payments from the Hungarian Government to cover the expenses of the occupation. The Debrecen government had no money or any other means of meeting these and other financial obligations.

Desperate economic conditions notwithstanding, Hungary in 1945 had to begin reparations deliveries. The armistice agreement obliged the country over a period of six years to deliver commodities worth $200 million to Soviet Russia and $100 million to Yugoslavia and Czechoslovakia. A Russian-dictated bilateral agreement on the delivery of goods approximately tripled the original amount of reparation. The cost of the ACC and the occupation, added to the reparation burden, totaled some 60 per cent of the state expenditure during the last four months of 1945, and amounted to almost 40 per cent of the total expenditures during the first half of 1946. The Russians demanded and received large deliveries of manufactured goods; they paid nothing for them; but the workmen who produced the goods and the supplies of raw materials had to be paid.

In the postwar months it was impossible to proceed with the assessment or collection of taxes, and securing the necessary money for governmental administration, occupation costs, and reparation deliveries was mainly a problem of printing bank notes. As a result, Hungary experienced a record inflation, which completely disintegrated her economic system. In the last stage of the inflation, preceding the stabilization of August 1946, the monetary unit soared to 30 zeros. People sold their belongings for subsistence.

Hungary meanwhile also was forced to conclude an economic cooperation agreement with the Soviet Union.[8] The Russian-dominated ACC and the Soviet Government refused to consider reiterated American proposals aiming at inter-Allied assistance for Hungary. The Soviet Government claimed that the working out of such a plan "belongs exclusively to the competence of the Hungarian Government." [9]

The Russian interpretation of the Potsdam agreement opened further possibilities for the conquest of the Hungarian economy.

[8] *Bulletin,* XV (1946), 394–395.

[9] For the Soviet-American exchange of notes, see *Bulletin,* XV (1946), 229–232, 263–265, 638–639.

The undefined category of "German assets" in Hungary was granted to Russia as reparations, and the Russians considered as German assets all properties and rights seized by the Germans during the Nazi occupation. Thus Soviet Russia, after Potsdam, claimed to be the owner of a considerable part of the Hungarian economy. The Russians, moreover, declared that they had acquired only the net assets and credits, without any debts or liabilities whatsoever. All liabilities were left to the non-Soviet part-owners and creditors. Soviet Russia demanded from Hungary $240 million as equivalent to certain German claims in Hungary, whereas the much larger German debts to Hungary were considered null and void. After protracted negotiations the Russians settled this part of their Potsdam claims for a lump sum of $45 million, together with certain concessions and privileges for Soviet-controlled enterprises in Hungary.

Thus the combination of the Potsdam agreement and the economic cooperation agreements assured a practically free hand to Soviet Russia in the Hungarian economy. Under these circumstances Hungary agreed to establish joint companies, with theoretically equal Soviet-Hungarian participation but actually under exclusive Soviet control. The general manager in charge of the operations of each company invariably was a Soviet citizen. The Hungarian chairman was a mere front. Through these joint companies the Soviet Union after 1946 controlled Hungarian aviation, river transportation, crude oil and petroleum-refining industries, the bauxite industry, and other connected industries and enterprises. In addition to the joint stock corporations, exclusively or overwhelmingly Soviet-owned enterprises were created with the help of the former German interests in the various industrial, commercial, and financial companies. After consolidation of Communist power these façades were no longer needed. In 1952 Moscow sold sixty-nine Soviet enterprises to Hungary, and in November 1954 even the Soviet Commercial and Industrial Bank and the Soviet share in the joint companies.

In addition to such various devices, the shrewd use of Hungarian-Russian trade agreements diverted Hungarian goods from their usual markets and decreased the volume of commerce with the West. Through the trade agreements Moscow arbitrarily determined the prices of both raw materials and finished products.

Thus, during the armistice period the Hungarian economy was well prepared for further sovietization and integration with the U.S.S.R.

As a further means of crippling Hungary's economy, Russia in 1947 prevented Hungary from receiving assistance through the European Recovery Program. Instead, a bogus Council for Economic Mutual Aid was established in January 1949, through which Moscow now controls the captive states and integrates their planning, economy, and foreign trade for the sole benefit of the U.S.S.R.

Political, Social and Cultural Developments

The pivot of domestic politics in the armistice period was the "National Independence Front," a coalition established during the German occupation by the underground leaders of the Smallholder, Social Democrat and Communist parties. Later the National Peasant Party, the Citizen Democratic Party and the Christian Democratic People's Party were also admitted to the Independence Front, but the latter Party was not allowed to play a political role after the "liberation."

From the outset the strongest political element was the group of so-called Muscovites, who were Russian-trained Hungarian *émigrés,* several of them members of the 1919 Communist regime of Béla Kun. Under the leadership of Mátyás Rákosi they returned to Hungary with the Red Army and seized the key positions in the embryonic Communist Party and in the trade unions. The Muscovites advocated a coalition government, praised the principles of democracy, and preached the necessity of collaborating with the Christian churches. They emphasized that the Russians wanted only to annihilate fascism, and did not intend to interfere with domestic politics.

In the area occupied by the Red Army there immediately arose so-called "national committees," which henceforth handled all public affairs on the municipal level. These committees were formed almost everywhere through the intervention of Communist emissaries, who did their best to select as their members docile fellow travelers from the former underground parties.

Members of the provisional Government were carefully chosen in order to win confidence. The Prime Minister and two other members of the Cabinet were generals of the Horthy regime. But the Minister of the Interior became a crypto-Communist, and under his cloak and protection the Communists, from the outset, organized the police all over the country. The Communists hoped, moreover, that radical execution of a long-overdue agrarian reform, under the direction of the Muscovite Communist, Imre Nagy, would secure them the support of the agrarian population. The common sense of the Hungarian peasants defeated this calculation, as was soon shown at the national elections. The early political setup, and particularly the composition of the new government, demonstrates one of the main features of Communist politics. The pattern was to give formal authority to non-Communists, while retaining effective control in the hands of Communists or fellow travelers. In terms of real power the Communists in the new Hungarian Government had the most important positions. They controlled the police, transportation, and the execution of the agrarian reform. Later, through the all-powerful Supreme Economic Council, they directed the economic life of the country.

Evaluated in relation to this situation, the elections held in the autumn of 1945 must be seen as the zenith of democracy in postwar Hungary. It was a part of Communist tactics to hold the Budapest municipal elections on October 7, a month before the general elections. The Communists felt sure that the working-class suburbs and the city proletariat would assure a sweeping victory for the united Communist-Socialist ticket. At the elections the Smallholders obtained an absolute majority. Feverish Communist activities followed this unexpected defeat, including a single electoral ticket for the forthcoming general elections. Voroshilov himself intervened, but the Smallholders and Social Democrats refused the single ticket idea. The Communists still were optimistic; they enjoyed tremendous practical advantages: besides the support of the occupying forces, they had newspapers, posters, transportation, and other propaganda facilities in quantities not available to the non-Communist parties. It was therefore a great surprise to the Communists and the Russians when, in the general elections held on November 4, 1945, the Communists polled only seventeen percent and the Smallholders obtained fifty-seven percent of the votes cast. The Hungarian elections attracted world-wide attention. They were considered highly important because the evidence showed that the elections were free and unfettered, and they were officially recognized as such by East and West.

Despite electoral defeat, the political situation as a whole, however, remained favorable to the Communists. Land reform had liquidated the landowner classes and had also deprived the church of its main economic basis. People of the middle class lived in complete insecurity and inflation rapidly increased the difficulties. Continuance of the coalition government was secured, and the Communists hoped to rule the country conveniently behind the screen of a coalition. After the elections the Smallholder Party obtained fifty percent of the seats in the Cabinet—but not the real power positions. Although the coalition parties agreed that the Minister of Interior should be a member of the Smallholder Party, Voroshilov vetoed this agreement and a Communist became the Minister of Interior.

On January 31, 1946, the new National Assembly declared Hungary a Republic, and the provisions of the constitution corresponded to Western standards. Yet shortly afterward a law was promulgated to protect the democratic order of the Republic. This law considered as criminal activity any statements which could be interpreted as contemptuous of the democratic state order or as harmful to the international prestige of the Republic, whether the statements were true or false. And as the democratic order of the state gradually became identified with Communist tenets, this law began to be used against anyone who criticized Communist activities.

The formation of a left-wing bloc under Communist leadership, in March 1946, was the beginning of an all-out attack against the Smallholder Party. This bloc addressed ultimata to the Smallholders in the name of the progressive Hungarian people and especially demanded the expulsion of "reactionary" deputies from the Smallholder Party. Under Russian and Communist pressure the Smallholder Party expelled twenty-one deputies. Even after this initial step toward self-liquidation, the party still held a parliamentary majority. The deputies expelled from the party remained members of Parliament and formed an opposition party under the leadership of Dezsö Sulyok, which was later authorized by the ACC as the "Hungarian Freedom Party." The Smallholders played for time, in the hope that after the ratification of a Hungarian peace treaty the Red Army would evacuate the country. But the fate of Hungary was not decided in the Hungarian Parliament. The Communists, after a while, completely changed their attitude toward the Smallholder Party, because of its resolute opposition to the

Communist program, including the wholesale nationalizations and other measures aiming at "democratization" of the country. They therefore decided upon the liquidation of the existing coalition setup.

For annihilating Smallholder leadership, the well-known technique of "conspiracy" was used. The political police discovered a plot and the Russians arrested the Secretary-General of the Smallholder Party, whose "confessions" implicated several leading Smallholder politicians, including Prime Minister Ferenc Nagy. He was forced to resign while abroad. Another Smallholder leader, Msgr. Béla Varga, Speaker of the Assembly, fled Hungary to avoid arrest, and the party itself was subjected to repeated purges.

The liquidation of the Smallholder leadership was followed by new elections on August 31, 1947, and this time the Communists felt it necessary to adopt tactics different from those of 1945. In addition to the four coalition parties, six opposition parties had been authorized. A modified version of the electoral laws now assured important advantages to the coalition parties, and opened the door for disfranchisement and other abuses. Despite these efforts, and despite the calculated Communist terror during the electoral campaign, the four coalition parties received only a slightly larger proportion of votes than the Smallholders alone had in 1945. The proportion of anti-Communist votes did not change. The Communist Party polled twenty-two percent, but the five percent gain was easily explained by large-scale use of "absentee ballots" and other frauds.

After this second electoral failure the Communists embarked upon a new policy of eliminating the opposition parties and voiding the mandates of their parliamentary members. This fundamentally altered the division of political forces in Parliament. The new situation affected the composition of the Cabinet and, even more, the structure of the coalition parties. In the Smallholder Party docile fellow travelers took over the leadership. The show window, however, did not change for a while, and both the President of the Republic and the Prime Minister remained Smallholders.

The next important item on the Communist timetable was absorption of the Social Democratic Party. Socialists who were unwilling to become Communist stooges were gradually eliminated, and finally the Social Democratic Party became entirely Communist-dominated and decided to merge with the Communist

Party. The name of the united Socialist-Communist Party became the "Hungarian Workers Party." A substantial change now took place in the highest office, as the President of the Republic, Zoltán Tildy, was forced to resign (July 30, 1948) and was succeeded by Arpád Szakasits, the pro-Communist Socialist leader.

The only opposition party which managed to survive under this new Communist policy was the Democratic People's Party. In connection with the Mindszenty trial, however, the Communists decided to use this Catholic Party for their own purposes. The leader of the party, István Barankovics, refused to cooperate, dissolved the party, and fled from Hungary in February 1949.

After these fundamental transformations, all existing parties were integrated into the "Independent People's Front." New elections were held on May 15, 1949. The voters had no choice; the People's Front presented a single ticket to the Hungarian electorate; and of the votes cast at this election, 95.6 percent were for the list of the People's Front. Those voters who wanted to make a change on the electoral list had to enter a booth, and the voters favoring the People's Front simply returned the unchanged list to the electoral committee. Thus the secret ballot was in fact abolished. The new Parliament accepted the constitution of the Hungarian People's Republic, and elected the first Presidential Council in August 1949. Four years later another Soviet-brand election took place. Meanwhile the structure and legal system of the Hungarian state was entirely transformed along Soviet lines. The methods by which the Communist seizure of power had been manipulated have been repeatedly described with disarming candor by leading Communists. One of them proudly pointed out:

> We were a minority in Parliament and in the Government, but at the same time we represented the leading force. We had decisive control over the police forces. Our force, the force of our party and the working class, was multiplied by the fact that the Soviet Union and the Soviet Army were always there to support us with their assistance.[10]

With seizure of political power sovietization of the country took the usual course. The Communists did their best to establish

[10] Joseph Révai, "On the Character of Our People's Democracy." *Társadalmi Szemle* (Budapest, March–April, 1949). An English translation of the article was published in *Foreign Affairs,* 28 (1949), 143–152. Cf., Mátyás Rákosi, *The Way of Our People's Democracy,* a speech delivered on February 29, 1952, at the Academy of the Hungarian Workers Party. The National Committee for a Free Europe published an English translation of it (New York, 1952).

control over all human relations by introducing the Soviet social, cultural, and economic system and liquidating all actual and potential opposition. There was no possibility of publicly questioning Communist good faith in any way. From the outset the Communists controlled the press through a system of licenses, allocation of newsprint, and the printers' trade union, and they got hold of all the other means of communication: key positions at broadcasting stations were seized, privately owned cinemas confiscated, the film industry and film imports controlled, and theaters nationalized.

In the fields of banking, industry, and commerce the monolithic structure of the Soviet system had been achieved by nationalization. Hungarian industry, finance, export and import, wholesale trade, most of the retail trade, and in 1952 even the privately-owned apartment houses and a large category of homes were nationalized. Simultaneously with these developments, the new Communist-trained elite occupied all positions of any economic importance. Employees in enterprises were dismissed for "anti-democratic" views and the Government ordered the dismissal of "anti-democratic" civil servants.

Economic communization was greatly promoted by a three-year plan, which was followed by a five-year plan. The first plan was completed in two years and five months (August 1, 1947–December 31, 1949). It aimed chiefly at postwar reconstruction and the increase of productive capacity. The second plan (1950–1954) sought to accelerate manufacturing, primarily in the fields of heavy and machine industries. Investment in agriculture and production of consumer goods were neglected, and heavy industries were developed for which Hungary had no raw materials. The bulk of iron ore is imported from the Soviet Union and the coking coal from Poland, the Soviet Union and the Ruhr. Although Hungary possesses important bauxite deposits, lack of cheap electric power hindered development of an aluminum industry. With absolute wage-and-price control, and total disregard for the welfare of the masses, it was possible to develop Hungary's industrialization considerably, which in turn brought important changes in the social structure of the country. In 1955 the Hungarian economy was prepared for the second five-year plan to begin on January 1, 1956. In 1948–49 the functions of trade unions and other labor organizations were streamlined according to Soviet ideas. After the nationalizations the managers of the enterprises were appointed by the government and the trade unions suddenly were confronted by the all-powerful state. Thus protection of the workers against the management became impossible, and the labor organizations were also transformed into state instruments. Labor was entirely deprived of its basic rights, and could retaliate only by various forms of sabotage.

In the year of greatest change, 1948, the Communist Party announced the collectivization of agriculture. Rákosi in a speech on August 20 pointed out the advantages of collective farming, for which a drive was started. The usual three types of production co-operatives were developed, and while formation of collective farms has received substantial governmental assistance, including machine stations, cheap fertilizers, and tax remissions, the situation of the formerly well-to-do peasants, now labeled "kulaks," has become increasingly difficult. Compulsory deliveries of products, higher taxation, and denial of credit—coupled with political persecution—are only a few examples of the presently elaborate anti-kulak discriminatory policy. Ruthless pressure for collectivization has alienated even the small peasants. Because of peasant resistance, the drive for collectivization and the persecution of "kulaks" has been mitigated from time to time. For example, the effort to bring all peasants into collectives was stepped up in 1952 after a slowdown the previous year. The result was a diminishing agricultural output, insufficient even for domestic needs.

Besides peasant resistance, popular support of churches formed a serious obstacle to the totalitarian objectives of the Communists. At the outset, they asked the churches to support the regime and in return offered tolerance. First the less numerous Protestant clergy were forced to accept this policy. Those Protestant church leaders who refused to compromise were forced to resign their church offices or were imprisoned. The intimidated Calvinist and Lutheran churches accepted an ephemeral solution offered them in 1948 and thus were allowed to keep some of their schools. In 1952, however, all the Protestant bishops and church leaders who were reluctant to follow Communist instructions "resigned" and were replaced by fellow travelers.

Because of Joseph Cardinal Mindszenty's refusal to accept an agreement similar to that concluded by the Protestant churches, all Catholic schools were nationalized in 1948. The tension between the Catholic Church and the State increased until finally the Government decided to break Catholic resistance by imprisoning the Cardinal. His trial and sentence to life imprisonment in February 1949 had such international repercussions that the Government refrained for some time from further violent intervention in the affairs of the Church,[11] but in February 1950 a new anti-Catholic campaign began.

Acting under severe pressure, the Archbishop of Kalocsa, Joseph Grösz, the ranking member of the hierarchy after Cardinal Mindszenty, signed an agreement with the Government on August 30, 1950. The agreement, made in the name of the Bench of the Bishops, contained no provisions for the oath of allegiance, previously a point of bitter controversy between the Government and the hierarchy. Shortly after the signing of the agreement, the Government dissolved all but four religious orders (Piarists, Benedictines, Franciscans, Sisters of Mercy). About 9,000 monks and nuns were expelled from their monasteries and convents. Moreover, the Government enforced the formation of the "National Peace Committee of Catholic Priests." A State Office for Church Affairs was established with a Muscovite Communist as head. In April 1951 Archbishop Grösz and some other bishops refused to receive delegates of this peace committee and to sign a Communist peace petition. In June, Grösz was tried with eight "accomplices" on the charge of leading an organization aimed at overthrowing the democratic order of the state. He was sentenced to fifteen years imprisonment.[12] Several bishops were mentioned in the course of the trial, and they were threatened with similar actions. A decree was published which provided that bishops and other church dignitaries could be appointed in Hungary only with the previous approval of the Presidium of the People's Republic. The decree was to be applied with retroactive force as of January 1, 1946, and this affected the position of several church leaders. Eventually the Bench of Bishops took the oath of allegiance to the Constitution of the People's Republic on July 21, 1951. Since these events, several hundred priests have been deported or imprisoned.

There was yet another force in Hungary which cut across the

[11] On the eve of the Geneva summit meeting, on July 16, 1955, the Minister of Justice allowed the Cardinal "to interrupt" his term of imprisonment. Ever since, he has been living in confinement, allegedly in a country house of the Bishop of Pécs.

[12] Radio Budapest announced on October 13, 1955 that Archbishop Grösz would take up residence in an ecclesiastical building to be assigned to him.

different religious and social classes and hence has sorely troubled the regime. This was Hungarian nationalism. It has proved difficult to extirpate nationalism even in the Communist Party, which welcomed everybody in 1944–47. Many former Nazis saved themselves with a membership card. In 1948 this policy changed; screening of members and a sweeping purge was begun in the Communist Party; when the Cominform struggle with Tito grew more embittered, the purges became more radical. The purpose of this new policy was to eradicate all Communists regarded as potential leaders or sympathizers of a nationalist Communist movement. The execution of one of the most fanatic Communist leaders, László Rajk, and of his associates (October 1949) was the outstanding manifestation of this trend. Old-time Hungarian Communists and Social Democrats were gradually eliminated, and a new Communist elite, which has been trained according to Russian precepts, has been taking over under Muscovite leadership.

Among the many ruthless Communist actions perhaps the most cruel were the deportations, which were carried out in several drives and for different purposes. Probably the most tragic series of deportations began in May 1951, when in urban areas, chiefly Budapest, persons considered undesirable or simply useless from the point of view of the regime, were removed from their homes into concentration camps, or to remote villages. The bulk of these victims belonged to the former upper and middle classes, and there were many old people among them. In 1953 this system of deportation was abolished, but for the deportees there was no place to go. During their deportation their homes and all belongings were seized and handed over to "reliable" elements.

Measures of Sovietization and Russification also permeated the school system and the whole cultural life of Hungary. Not only did the teaching of the Russian language become obligatory in all the schools, but Russian professors were appointed in large numbers to Hungarian schools and universities. Textbooks were adopted that were partly or entirely translations from Russian. Moreover, cultural exchange between Hungary and the Soviet Union was greatly developed. Several hundred students receive scholarships for study at Soviet universities. A Soviet-Hungarian friendship month has been arranged—an annual affair during which the achievements of Soviet culture are glorified and caravans of Soviet delegates arrive to demonstrate the superiority of Russian culture in art, music, and science.

Despite all these efforts, however, one must conclude that, thus far, Russification and Sovietization have had no significant impact on Hungarian society. In the captive countries the most effective propaganda against Communism was to be found in the behavior of the Red Army, in the old colonial style exploitation practiced by the Soviet Union, in the ruthless police terror, in the suppression of freedom and decency, in the neglect of the production of consumer goods, and in the often senselessly forced industrialization. But in Hungary several special factors contributed to the lack of popular support of the Muscovite creed. Hungary is the only country which experienced a Communist regime in 1919, and the people still remember that a Russian army crushed the Hungarian forces fighting for independence in 1849. Moreover, the Hungarians are neither Slavs nor Orthodox; their language, religion and way of thinking are more an obstacle than a means of communication in Russo-Hungarian relations.

After Stalin's death the resistance of the oppressed Hungarian people brought about a spectacular reversal of Communist policies in Hungary. On July 4, 1953 Imre Nagy, who replaced Rákosi as Prime Minister, confessed the overall failures of Communist policies and outlined a new course. He promised an end both to exaggerated industrialization and to forced agricultural collectivization, and a relaxation of disciplinary measures against workers. His further promises included increased agricultural investments, more production of consumer goods, licenses for individual retailers and artisans, amnesty for minor offenses, liquidation of internment camps, better treatment of the old intelligentsia, and reforms in education.

A more satisfactory system in delivery of farm quotas was introduced. It was publicly recognized that independent peasants produce more than kolkhozes and peasants were allowed, in fact, to leave kolkhozes. More than 50 percent of the cooperative membership left the collectives, and collective farms decreased from thirty-six percent to twelve percent of the country's cultivated lands. There were reductions in retail prices, and there were even some wage increases.

For winning popular support a new political center, the "People's Patriotic Front," including Communists as well as non-Communists, was established in October 1954. At its first meeting the national anthem was sung and the national flag displayed.

But despite all such efforts Nagy's new course turned into a dismal fiasco and in eighteen months met an inglorious end. The bulk of the people considered the "new course" a sign of weakness, expected further concessions, and opposed the regime as strongly as ever. Without producing more consumer goods and agricultural products, the new policy slowed down industrialization and stopped work on certain large projects.

Although Zoltán Vas, the chief Muscovite economic planner, had in Imre Nagy's heyday denounced the five-year plan to convert Hungary into a land of iron and steel as a "megalomaniac swindle," Rákosi and the hard core of the Communist Party never had taken kindly to Nagy's liberalizing policies. As soon as Malenkov went into eclipse and *Pravda* in Moscow proclaimed reversion to the customary Soviet policy of forcing heavy industry, Rákosi immediately declared that considerations of defense compelled Hungary to develop heavy industry in harmony with the military needs of the entire peace camp (January 25, 1955).

Since Hungary after Stalin's death has traveled along the new road farther than any of the captive countries, reversal of her policies could not have been achieved smoothly, and the Central Committee of the Workers Party perforce accused Prime Minister Nagy of "duping the working class with demagogic promises." Nagy's "right-wing deviationism" was promptly characterized as an attempt to disrupt the Hungarian Communist Party. The establishment of the "Patriotic People's Front" was considered one of his major sins and a sign that he disregarded the leading role of the Party. Amid such accusations Nagy conveniently developed a coronary thrombosis and together with his close followers has dropped out of sight, whereas at the present time Rákosi, the veteran master of survival, is again riding the Communist crest. The latter recently told a party-state gathering celebrating the tenth anniversary of Hungary's World War II "liberation" that the Government was busy "undoing the damage done in the last eighteen months." Although the appointment of a new Prime Minister, András Hegedüs, a young man of peasant stock, accompanied the return to the "safe" Muscovite road, events between 1953 and 1955 have proved a serious ideological defeat for the Hungarian Communists. There has been revealed a lack of unity, insecurity and inability to cope with a mismanaged economy and hostile people.

At the Third Congress of the Hungarian Workers Party in October 1954, Rákosi disclosed that the second five-year plan will begin in 1956 simultaneously with the sixth five-year plan of the U.S.S.R. He predicted "substantial economies" in investments as a result of more integrated planning within the Soviet orbit, and a slower continuation of Hungary's industrialization, together with greater emphasis on consumer goods and further collectivization of agriculture. According to resolutions accepted by the Hungarian Communist Party's executive committee in June 1955, more than half of Hungary's farmland must be collectivized by the end of the second five-year plan in 1960. A new course for the collectivization of Hungarian agriculture has been in progress since January 1955, with all the concomitant hardship for the peasantry.

Hungarian Foreign Affairs and American Diplomacy

The foreign affairs of postwar Hungary may be divided into two periods. In the first, non-Communist political leaders tried to build up friendly relations with the U.S.S.R. but at the same time considered Hungary to be an independent member of the free community of nations and in close relations with the Western democracies. Probably the last manifestation of this attitude was the decision of the Dinnyés Government in July 1947 to accept an invitation to the Paris Conference on United States aid to Europe. But a Soviet veto prevented Hungary's participation.[13] Shortly thereafter Hungary became a member of the Soviet alliance system, and Hungarian foreign policy was integrated into the foreign political machinery of the U.S.S.R. Ever since, she has been faithfully

[13] On July 7, 1947 the Hungarian Telegraph Agency reported that great interest was being taken by the government in the Marshall offer and in the proposal for a European economic program. The communiqué added cautiously that Hungary "would have great difficulties in taking an attitude different from other southeast European ex-enemy states." Furthermore, it was reported that the Prime Minister had decided to ask the ACC for permission for his government to accept the invitation to the Paris Conference on United States aid to Europe. The Hungarian note handed to the British Political Mission in Budapest on July 10 obviously reflected the answer the Hungarian Government received for its inquiry. This note emphasized that Hungary "cannot take part at a conference on the object of which the Great Powers concerned could not come to an understanding." According to the text of the communiqué issued on the same day, the Hungarian Government could not send delegates to Paris because of the disagreement existing among the Great Powers. The reference to the "disagreement" meant the Russian veto. Prior to this veto the Smallholder and Socialist parties decided that Hungary should send representatives to Paris, and even the head of the Hungarian delegation was tentatively designated.

Almost all East Central European states desired to participate in the Paris Conference on United States aid to Europe. The local Communist parties could not have resisted this popular trend without a peremptory Russian veto. See above, pp. 140, 198, and 211.

echoing Moscow's propaganda slogans and her foreign policy is as independent as that of the Ukraine and Byelorussia. As has been described above, Soviet interferences in Hungary's foreign and domestic relations took place from the outset of the occupation, when the ACC proved a convenient channel for this usurpation of power. When the Hungarian Government, in its peace preparatory notes addressed to the three major powers, advocated close political, economic and cultural collaboration among the Danubian states,[14] international control of the Danube,[15] the internationalization of all rivers and canals in the Danube Valley, and a close collaboration of the Danubian countries to improve the Danube water system, the Russian and Hungarian Communist leaders objected on the grounds that these propositions were premature. The Danubian countries, they claimed, were still reactionary. As soon as these countries became truly democratic, cooperation would come into being.

The strong American stand at Potsdam for free elections,[16] and the fact that the final agreement reached there looked forward to an early conclusion of a peace treaty and Hungary's admission into the United Nations, favorably impressed the Hungarian public. Western representatives in Budapest strengthened the determina-

[14] See the notes of August 14 and November 12, 1945 and May 8, 1946, addressed to the United States, British and Soviet Governments. *La Hongrie et la Conférence de Paris* (Budapest, 1947), pp. 7–14, 21–36, 56–62.

[15] Cavendish W. Cannon, head of the American delegation at the Danubian Conference in Belgrade on August 13, 1948, declared:

"It is interesting to note that the postwar government of Hungary, on November 12, 1945, addressed a note to the United States, British and Soviet Governments, giving its views on the Danube question. It called attention to the great importance to Hungary of a regime which guarantees full freedom of navigation. It suggested that the prewar system of international navigation be reconstituted with provisions for changes required by new conditions. The Hungarian Government did not envisage elimination of non-riparian representation, for it suggested consolidation into one Commission of the European Commission of the Danube and the International Commission of the Danube. Both Commissions, as the Conference is aware, had non-riparian representation. There have been changes since 1946 but we believe the long-term economic interests of Hungary remain the same." *Bulletin,* XIX (1948), 283.

The Hungarian representative, Foreign Minister of the by then completely Communist-dominated Hungarian Government, did not reply other than by his one hundred per cent support of the Soviet position—which in fact denied that freedom of navigation for which the Hungarian Government had dared to raise its voice three years before.

[16] The Russians did not make a secret of their intentions in connection with the Yalta pledges and the fate of the Eastern European countries. "A freely elected government in any of these countries would be anti-Soviet, and that we cannot allow," declared Marshal Stalin at Potsdam, according to a member of the American delegation. Philip E. Mosely, *Face to Face with Russia,* Foreign Policy Association, Headline Series, no. 70, 1948, 23.

tion of non-Communist political leaders by stating that their governments would not regard elections based on a single electoral list as free elections corresponding to the Yalta Declaration. Despite such encouraging factors the Potsdam Agreement, as we have seen, in several respects further deteriorated Hungary's position. It did not change Soviet preponderance in the ACC; moreover, the undefined category of "German external assets" in Hungary, granted to Russia as reparations, opened new possibilities for Russian abuses.[17]

Furthermore, the Potsdam agreement wrongly assimilated the problem of the Germans in Hungary to the German problems in Poland and Czechoslovakia, and declared that transfer to Germany of the German populations in these three countries "will have to be undertaken." Subsequently the Allied Control Council for Germany, on November 20, 1945, put the number of the Germans to be moved from Hungary at 500,000,[18] a higher figure than the actual number of Germans in the country.

The Russians and Hungarian Communists interpreted the Potsdam text and the decision of the Council as orders addressed to the Hungarian Government by the victorious allies, and although the Hungarian Government repeatedly protested against application of the principle of collective responsibility and asked for explanations from the British and United States governments, under Soviet and Communist pressure it issued a severe decree concerning the transfer of Germans. The American reply, which supported the original Hungarian position and expressed the opinion that the decision of the Allied Council did not oblige the Hungarian Government to expel all the Germans, arrived only after promulgation of the decree. An interplay of actions and circumstances hindered an all-out transfer of the Germans from Hungary. In 1945 the Smallholder Party and the Hungarian Foreign Ministry delayed preparations; in the following year United States policy began to change, and by the end of 1946 the United States Zone of Germany ceased to accept expellees. Altogether, the number of German expellees from Hungary was somewhat over 200,000, three-fourths of them being transferred to the American zone, and the rest to Eastern Germany.[19]

[17] See above, p. 226–227.
[18] *Bulletin*, XIII (1945), 937.
[19] For the details of this complicated affair, see Stephen Kertesz, "The Expulsion of the Germans from Hungary: A Study in Postwar Diplomacy," *Review of Politics*, XV (1953), 179–208.

Moscow's support of German expulsions actually was only part of the Soviet policy of *divide et impera* which fostered hostile feelings among neighboring nations. Other examples of this policy are evident in Hungaro-Czechoslovak and Hungaro-Rumanian relations. At the close of hostilities the Prague Government announced that Czechoslovakia was going to be transformed into a national state. In harmony with this policy the Czechoslovak actions aiming at expulsion of all Hungarians from the Republic, as an introductory measure to carry out an exchange of population between the two countries, was energetically supported by Soviet Russia.[20] In addition to direct pressure Marshal Voroshilov and Soviet diplomats repeatedly alluded to the fact that Hungary might get some territorial compensation from another ex-Nazi satellite, Rumania, if she behaved well and accepted the Czechoslovak proposals. Nor were Hungarian ambitions for a boundary revision in Transylvania discouraged by Stalin, when such claims were expressed to him by members of the Hungarian Government in April 1946. Molotov himself explained on this occasion that the Rumanian armistice treaty gave an opportunity to the Hungarians to raise the issue.[21] This benevolent attitude notwithstanding, Molotov previously and subsequently opposed in the Council of Foreign Ministers an American proposal for modifying the Transylvanian boundary line in favor of Hungary.

To counteract Czechoslovak actions the Hungarian Government between April 1945 and July 1946 addressed a total of 184 notes to the ACC protesting specific cases of persecution in Czechoslovakia.[22] Because the Russian-dominated ACC could not react at all, the Hungarian Government simultaneously sent separate notes and memoranda to the three major powers. While Russia openly encouraged Czechoslovakia, the English-speaking powers remained unresponsive to Hungarian suggestions and refused to entertain requests for establishment of a Commission of Inquiry and proposals for great power intervention in the Hungarian-Czechoslovak con-

[20] During the war Beneš obtained Moscow's promise for support of the expulsion of the "guilty minority population" from Czechoslovakia. Eduard Taborsky, "Beneš and Stalin—Moscow 1943 and 1945," *Journal of Central European Affairs,* XIII (1953), 168. See above, p. 196.

[21] Ferenc Nagy, *The Struggle Behind the Iron Curtain* (New York, 1948), pp. 209–210. It should be noted that during the second World War German diplomacy exploited Hungarian and Rumanian territorial claims concerning Transylvania.

[22] For the list of these notes, see *Hungary and the Conference of Paris,* Vol. II (Budapest, 1947), pp. 155–163. For the anti-Hungarian discriminatory laws and decrees, see *ibid.,* Vol. IV, pp. 176–186.

flict. Although the United States opposed collective punishment of ethnic groups, she approved population transfers when those took place in accordance with international agreements and "in an orderly way." [23]

Eventually, continued persecution of Hungarians in Slovakia, together with Russian pressure and the negative Western attitude, compelled the Hungarian Government to conclude a population exchange agreement with Czechoslovakia in February 1946.[24] This treaty, containing a series of unilateral benefits for Czechoslovakia, was the price for a Czechoslovak pledge that the bulk of the Hungarians in Czechoslovakia could remain until the decision of the Peace Conference. In the course of the population exchange 60,000 Slovaks left Hungary and the number of Hungarians who were exchanged or forced to leave Slovakia was about 93,000. These events greatly deteriorated the relations between the two countries, and the large-scale deportation of Hungarians to the Sudetenland caused further resentment in Hungary.[25] Thus cooperation between two Western-minded states was prevented before the Communist seizure of power.

Before the peace settlement, in April and May 1946, a Government delegation under the leadership of Prime Minister Ferenc Nagy visited Moscow, Washington and London and asked the three major powers for support. This open appeal to the West by a country occupied by the Red Army clearly showed that the postwar regime of Hungary wanted to maintain close relations with the Western powers. Hungary's position improved in the West, but friendly feeling for her and some economic help could not change the realities of power politics along the Danube. Nor did the process of peacemaking have the expected favorable impact on the fate of Hungary.

In the Council of Foreign Ministers and at the Paris Conference (July–October 1946) Hungarian proposals for reorganization of Danubian Europe on a cooperative basis and for settling other fundamental issues of the Danubian states were not even considered. The United States delegation did submit to the Conference a proposal to reduce the total amount of reparations to be paid by Hun-

[23] These exchanges of notes were published in *Hungary and the Conference of Paris,* Vol. II, pp. 1–29, 50–55, 90–91.

[24] For the agreement and preceding negotiations see *ibid.,* pp. 30–49, 56–90.

[25] *The Deportation of the Hungarians of Slovakia,* published by Hungarian Society for Foreign Affairs (Budapest, 1947).

gary from $300 million to $200 million, but the Conference did not accept this proposal.[26]

The greatest direct threat to Hungary at the Peace Conference was a Czechoslovak proposal, openly sponsored by Soviet Russia, to insert in the peace treaty a provision authorizing expulsion of 200,000 Hungarians from Czechoslovakia. Determined Hungarian opposition to this proposal would have been futile without the support of the United States and other Western delegations. The Czechoslovak proposal was defeated, and Article 5 of the peace treaty instructed Hungary to enter into negotiations with Czechoslovakia for the solution of the problem of the Hungarians in Czechoslovakia. The conflict was easily solved by repeal of the anti-Hungarian discriminatory measures as soon as the Communists seized power in both Hungary and Czechoslovakia.

The Paris Conference obliterated Hungarian endeavors for a territorial revision in Transylvania. Czechoslovakia obtained three Hungarian villages on the right bank of the Danube opposite Bratislava. Otherwise the Trianon frontiers were re-established. Generally speaking, the peace settlement did little more than recast the harsh terms of the armistice agreement in a peace treaty which authorized the Soviet Union to keep armed forces in Hungary for the maintenance of the lines of communication with the Red Army in Austria.

President Truman, upon ratification of the peace treaties, expressed regret that the Yalta commitments remained unfulfilled in Hungary, Rumania and Bulgaria.[27] On March 17, 1948, in an

[26] *Paris Peace Conference 1946*. Selected Documents. U.S. Government Printing Office (Washington), 1123, 1153, 1194–1195. For the full text of the declaration of the American Delegate, Willard L. Thorp, see *Bulletin,* XV (1946), 746–748. For Hungary's preparations for, and position at, the Peace Conference, see Kertesz, *op. cit.,* pp. 163–187.

[27] In the statement released to the press by the White House on June 14, 1947, the President declared:

"At the time of ratification of the treaties establishing peace with Hungary, Rumania, and Bulgaria, I feel I must publicly express regret that the governments of those countries not only have disregarded the will of the majority of the people but have resorted to measures of oppression against them. Ever since the liberation of these countries from the Nazi yoke and the commitments undertaken by the three Allies at Yalta, I had hoped that governments truly representative of the people would be established there. Such governments do not exist today in those three countries.

"It is, however, in the interests of the Hungarian, Rumanian, and Bulgarian peoples to terminate the state of war which has existed between their governments and the United States for over five years. The establishment of peace will mean that all occupation forces (not including Soviet units needed to maintain lines of communication to the Soviet zone of occupation in Austria) will be withdrawn from these countries and armistice Control Commissions terminated." *Bulletin,* XVI (1947), 1214.

address before a joint session of Congress, he stated that

> The agreements we [the Allied victors in the second World War] did obtain, imperfect though they were, could have furnished the basis for a just peace—if they had been kept. But they were not kept. They have been persistently ignored and violated by one nation.[28]

Although American diplomacy in Hungary itself has always been friendly and helpful, in the period following the close of hostilities it has reflected Western aloofness from political realities. Secretary Byrnes's actions as late as December 1945, in Moscow, stemmed from the hope "that the Soviet Union and the United States had a common purpose." [29] When Hungarian politicians, in view of flagrant Russian interferences and encroachments, asked for the support of the other signatories of the Yalta agreement, they received baffling answers. As the American Minister to Hungary put it, the representatives of the Western Allies

> were frequently sounded out as to how much help they would provide to the non-communist political groups. When our invariable reply was that American diplomatic practice excluded the possibility of such interference in the internal political affairs of foreign countries, there was bewilderment at what seemed so unrealistic an attitude compared with that of the Russians.[30]

The same American policy was expressed even more directly in the following passage of a letter addressed by Minister Schoenfeld to Joseph Cardinal Mindszenty, December 27, 1946:

> It is noted that your letters of December 12 and December 16, touching on internal political problems of Hungary, requested the assistance of the United States Government in altering certain conditions which Your Eminence deplores. In this connection you are of course aware of my Government's long standing policy of non-interference in the internal affairs of other nations. This policy has proven over a long period of time and through many trying situations the best guarantee of spontaneous, vigorous and genuine democratic development. It will be clear to Your Eminence that it necessarily precludes action by this Legation which could possibly be construed as interference in Hungarian domestic affairs or which lies outside the normal functions of diplomatic missions.[31]

[28] *New York Times,* March 18, 1948.

[29] James F. Byrnes, *Speaking Frankly* (New York, 1947), p. 255.

[30] F. A. Schoenfeld, "Soviet Imperialism in Hungary," *Foreign Affairs,* XXVI (1948), 558.

[31] A photograph of this letter was published in the Yellow Book of the Hungarian Government: *Documents on the Mindszenty Case* (Budapest, 1949), p. 54. There are probably many forgeries in this volume, but this particular letter was not disavowed.

Although this reserved American attitude corresponded to the traditional precepts of diplomacy, it seemed strange to the Hungarians, in view of the tripartite Yalta agreement and Russian interventions in domestic affairs of Hungary. In reality American diplomatic caution may have been only the refuge of impotence. Decisive factors in Hungary were the Red Army, Soviet leadership in the ACC, and the key power positions seized by the Hungarian Communist Party, which operated as a disguised branch of Soviet administration. These conditions hardly could have been changed or influenced on a purely diplomatic level without the threat or application of forceful measures.

The first Western protest to the Hungarian Government took place against the expropriation of the landed properties of British and American citizens. Although such seizures violated article 13 of the armistice agreement, the protests of the "imperialistic capitalist" powers opened up propaganda possibilities to the Communists. When Soviet bad faith became altogether too conspicuous, American policy slowly underwent a change,[32] and as time went on American protests increased in number, became stronger in tone, and embraced a variety of political and economic problems. In Hungary the first really energetic political action took place almost simultaneously with enunciation of the Truman doctrine: the United States proposed concerted action to investigate political conditions and the alleged political plot by the Smallholder Party in Hungary. The acting Chairman of the ACC promptly refused, because the investigation "would appear to be an open intervention into the internal affairs of the Hungarian Republic." On the other hand, he considered American concern with regard to the arrest of the Secretary General of the Smallholders "as an attempt to infringe on the legal rights of the Soviet occupation authorities to defend their armed forces located on Hungarian territory." [33]

As we have seen above,[34] the conclusion of the peace treaty did not bring a change for the better in Hungary. The Hungarian Government simply disregarded the provisions of the treaty concerning

[32] Secretary Byrnes stated that the firmer attitude toward the Soviet Union began in February 1946. *Op. cit.,* p. 255. Russia's refusal to evacuate Northern Iran and Stalin's speech on February 14, 1946, in which he advocated further development of heavy industry and armaments, opened the eyes of the American policy-makers.

[33] *Bulletin,* XVI (1947), 584.

[34] See Introduction, pp. 10–12.

human rights and fundamental freedoms, rejected English and American protests, and refused to participate in the creation of a commission provided for by the Peace Treaty for the solution of disputes. Although the peace treaty limited the Hungarian Army to 70,000 men, Hungary at the present writing has over 300,000 men in various military establishments. The army has been practically integrated into the Red Army, through its high command, armaments and general organization. The establishment of a unified military command for the U.S.S.R. and the captive countries by the Warsaw treaty on May 14, 1955 was only the formal recognition of conditions which existed in Hungary since 1948. Hungary not only became part of the Soviet alliance and economic system in Europe, but she ostentatiously developed friendship and intercourse with such Asiatic Communist countries as China, North Korea and North Vietnam.

Diplomatic relations between the United States and Hungary since 1947 have consisted of a sorry chain of incidents, characterized by arrest and imprisonment of American citizens, seizure and confiscation of American property, charges and measures against American diplomatic representatives including restriction of their movement and their practical isolation, closure of the United States information center in Budapest, jailing and sentencing of four downed American fliers and refusal to submit the case to the International Court of Justice, and denial to American representatives of access to arrested American citizens like Paul Ruedemann and Robert A. Vogeler.[35] The long list of American diplomats declared *persona non grata* in Hungary included Selden Chapin, Minister to Hungary in 1947–49. Briefly, Hungary, like the other Soviet satellites, has disregarded accepted diplomatic standards. Protection of American citizens and interests has become increasingly difficult. The arrest of Hungarian employees of the United States Legation and correspondents for the Associated Press and the other

[35] The *Bulletin* published the notes and other official documents concerning these cases. Cf. *Report on the Maort Sabotage,* Hungarian Ministry of Home Affairs (Budapest, 1948); Paul Ruedemann, "I Learned About Communism the Hard Way," *Saturday Evening Post,* May 28, 1949; *Standard Oil Company and Oil Production in Hungary by Maort,* European Gas and Electric Company, (1948); *R. Vogeler, E. Sanders and Their Accomplices Before the Criminal Court,* Hungarian State Publishing House (Budapest, 1950); Robert A. Vogeler, *I Was Stalin's Prisoner* (New York, 1952); *Documents on the Hostile Activity of the United States Government Against the Hungarian People's Republic,* Hungarian State Publishing House (Budapest, 1951).

American news agencies has been a frequent occurrence. The United States repeatedly retaliated, as in the invalidation of American passports for travel to Hungary, closure of Hungarian consulates in New York and Cleveland, and travel restriction on Hungarian Legation personnel in Washington.

Since Stalin's death some improvements have taken place in formal contacts between the United States and Hungary. For example, travel restrictions on diplomatic representatives have been liberalized. Such changes, however, are but a small segment in the large picture of Soviet-American relations. Their substantial elements and the totality of Hungaro-American relations depend on further developments in great-power politics.

Chapter 10

Rumania

ROBERT LEE WOLFF

Rumania Before 1944

THE RUMANIANS emerged from the peace settlements which followed the first World War in possession of virtually all the territories to which they had claim. From Russia they acquired Bessarabia, between the Pruth and the Dniester, which had changed hands several times during the nineteenth century, and had a mixed Rumanian-Ukrainian-Jewish population. From Austria-Hungary they obtained not only the Bukovina, with a mixed Rumanian-Ukrainian-Jewish-German population, which had been ruled from Vienna since 1775, but also Transylvania, a province with a Rumanian majority, but with a large Magyar population (as well as Germans and Jews), where the Hungarians had long oppressed the Rumanians. Rumania was thus a "satisfied" nation, but its people were soon to learn that the mere possession of territories long desired did not imply good government or a sound economy.

The large landowners of Rumania, whose political organ had been the prewar Conservative Party, lost much of their land as the result of a major agrarian reform, and with it some of their political influence. But, even as owners of smaller estates, the gentry, together with the small business and professional class in the cities, formed a new ruling group. The Liberal Party, traditionally led by the Bratianu family, expressed its political views. It favored industrialization, but tried to exclude foreign capital, and operated by state subsidy to favored industries and individuals. These in turn made heavy political contributions. The Liberals' policies neglected or actively hurt the peasants, about 80 per cent of the Rumanian population.

The peasant point of view was allegedly represented by the National Peasant Party, formed in 1926. This was a fusion of the Peasant Party of the Old Kingdom, led by Ion Mihalache—an outgrowth of radical populist movements of the early twentieth century—with the National Party of Transylvania, led by Iuliu Maniu, a distinguished lawyer who had sat in the Hungarian Parliament as a Rumanian deputy. The Transylvanians had favored land reform largely because the landowners in their province had been Hungarian. But none of the Transylvanian politicians was himself a peasant. Their movement was nationalist and conservative. Although Mihalache continued to attend Bucharest cocktail parties in long white woolen peasant trousers, most of his colleagues were city people, and the party, though very popular, did not adequately represent peasant interests.

Industry grew rapidly in the interwar years, but urban workers remained a small minority of the population. In Latin Rumania, with a long memory of past Russian invasions, Russia and Communism did not attract support, as they did in Bulgaria and Yugoslavia. A tiny Communist Party (Bolshevik), descendant of earlier Social Democratic formations, continued to exist. Though outlawed in 1924, it fomented strikes. But dictation from Moscow forced it to favor the detachment of all the provinces just acquired, and this helped make it desperately unpopular. A legal Social Democratic Party also functioned in Rumania, but was ineffectual.

While the left was weak, Rumania produced a powerful right-wing movement in the Iron Guard. The corruption and incompetence of the moderate political groups led to popular disillusionment with parliamentary processes. The depression produced large-scale misery and discontent, which could not express itself on the left. Strong nationalist sentiments were already present in full measure. So was anti-Semitism, since virtually all Rumanians, no matter what their origin or education, hated the Jews. Though the Iron Guard borrowed its trappings from Mussolini and Hitler, it was a native, not an imported movement, and commanded great popular support. The 1930's were punctuated by Guardist assassinations of politicians who had opposed them. Though King Carol's governments fought the Guards, the King himself took over more and more of its doctrines.

As Hitler moved from one easy triumph to the next, in the years before the final assault on Poland in 1939, Rumania found its diplomatic position gravely undermined. Depending on the Little Entente (Czechoslovakia and Yugoslavia) and on France, Carol saw Czechoslovakia destroyed and Yugoslavia flirting with the Axis, while France did nothing. He created a royal dictatorship in 1938, outlawing all political parties except his own, emphasizing heavy industry, especially armaments, and attempting to balance his country between the Axis and his traditional French and British allies. The Hitler-Stalin Pact of August 1939 caught Rumania between the giants. Though the country was temporarily spared full-scale war, its old enemies soon began to present territorial claims.

The secret annexes to the German-Soviet Pact "called attention" to Russian interest in Bessarabia, which the U.S.S.R. had never formally abandoned. In June 1940, the Russians delivered an ultimatum to the Rumanians, demanding Bessarabia, and, in addition, the northern part of the Bukovina, which had never been Russian. Carol was forced to accede. The Bulgarians then demanded the southern Dobrudja, a province taken by Rumania in 1913, but one where the Rumanians had never had a majority, and about which they did not care very deeply. Again, Carol had to surrender. The severest demand of all was the Hungarian claim for Transylvania, which Hitler and Mussolini finally "arbitrated" in August 1940 at Vienna. The so-called Vienna Award gave Hungary northern Transylvania, and a long salient thrusting into the geographical center of Rumania. In about two months, Rumania had lost more than one third of its territory and about a third of its population. A political crisis now forced the abdication of King Carol, who fled into exile. His son, Michael, succeeded to the throne. Real political power was in the hands of Marshal Ion Antonescu, a competent officer with strong Iron Guard sympathies. He proceeded to tighten the dictatorship. Though the Iron Guard formed part of his government, its more radical members none the less indulged in savage outbreaks against the Jews.

The territorial dismemberment of Rumania led to the first major disagreements between Hitler and Stalin, foreshadowing the German attack on the U.S.S.R. of June 1941. When this took place, the Rumanians cheerfully marched against the Russians, side by side with their German allies. The Rumanian armies recovered the lost provinces of Bessarabia and northern Bukovina, and pursued their eastward advance across the Dniester into lands which had never been Rumanian. This territory, including the major port of Odessa, the Rumanians called Transnistria. They put it under a special military administration, systematically plundered it, used it as a dumping-ground for Jews deported from Rumania, and committed atrocities against the Jewish native population. Rumanian forces participated in the German campaigns in the Crimea and at Stalingrad.

Maniu and Bratianu, who acted as leaders of a "tolerated opposition" all during the war, opposed the extension of hostilities beyond the Dniester, but public opinion on the whole supported it until the casualties began to mount alarmingly in 1942. Antonescu never had a real opportunity to withdraw: Germany's hold was too strong and Rumanian oil and grain, in addition to manpower, formed too valuable a contribution to the German war effort. Moreover, Rumanians hoped that by outdoing the Hungarians in loyalty to the Germans they might prevail upon Hitler to reverse the Vienna award. Deep in Russia their armies fought for Transylvania, and hoped to get the opportunity to turn on the Hungarians.

As American power began to be felt (the first air raid on the oil refinery center of Ploeşti took place in August 1943) and it became clear that Hitler would lose the war, Rumanian diplomats in neutral capitals put forth a series of peace feelers. Hoping for an Anglo-American landing in the Balkan region, or at least for Western protection from the Russians, the Rumanians strove to surrender to Britain and the United States alone. But the Western Allies refused to hear of separate negotiations, and reported to Stalin all Rumanian approaches. For their part, the Russians insisted on retaining Bessarabia and northern Bukovina, but were willing to restore northern Transylvania. As Soviet armies penetrated into Moldavia, King Michael took matters into his own hands. Though the major Rumanian defenses had not yet been breached, he decided to withdraw from the German alliance by surrendering to the Allies. On August 23, 1944, he summoned Marshal Antonescu to the palace, informed him of his dismissal, had him temporarily locked in the safe where Carol had formerly kept the royal stamp collection, and proclaimed the surrender and a new government of national union with the nonpolitical General Sanatescu as Premier. With this act Rumanian postwar history may be said to begin, though the Rumanian armies now changed sides and fought against the Germans.

While Soviet troops moved into complete occupation of the country, negotiations took place in Moscow, which culminated on September 12, 1944 with the signing of the armistice between Rumania and the three great powers. It restored northern Transylvania and required Rumania to pay $300,000,000 in reparations in six equal annual installments, as well as the entire cost of Russian operations on Rumanian territory. Rumania was to free all pro-Allied persons, to repeal anti-Semitic legislation, to ban "fascist" groups, and to assist in arresting and trying war criminals. An Allied Control Commission, with British, American, and Russian representatives, was to sit in Bucharest. But the text of the armistice made repeated reference to this body as under the direction of the "Allied (Soviet) Command," and it was evident that the Russians were to have the major role in Rumania.

This Soviet preponderance, so important for the future of the country, arose in part from the fact that American and British strategic planners had chosen not to make landings in the Balkans, and the Red Army thus played the sole military role in Rumania and Bulgaria. Political decisions also played a major role. Despite the fixed policy of the United States not to allow the wartime marking-out of future spheres of influence in Europe, Churchill and Stalin in October 1944 reached a secret understanding whereby the Balkan countries and Hungary were divided into precisely such spheres. In Rumania the Russian "say" was appraised at 90 per cent, the Western Allies' at 10 per cent. Though the agreement was specifically limited to wartime, it was inevitable that it should affect the fate of Rumania long after military operations had ceased. It amounted to a resignation of British and American influence, in keeping with the harsh military facts. In the spring of 1944 the American State Department had opposed any such arrangement. Although President Roosevelt then privately overruled his Secretary of State, and consented to try a Balkan division for three months, no Anglo-Russian agreement was in fact concluded. It was not until October 9, 1944, almost a month after the Rumanian armistice, that Churchill and Stalin actually reached their "percentages" agreement. When they did, the United States never assented formally. But Roosevelt's temporary yielding in June 1944 permitted the arrangement to be made in October. Churchill's overriding motive was his wish to keep Greece out of the Communists' hands. He seems to have hoped that the 90 per cent "say" which the "percentages" agreement gave the Western powers in Greece would enable them to prevent a Communist uprising there. In order to save Greece, he wrote off Rumania, and, as we shall see, Bulgaria, no doubt in part out of a belief that the Western powers could in any case do nothing there in opposition to the Russians.

In December 1944, the Greek Communists made their effort to take over Greece, and brought on a war with the British forces. Whatever moral support their effort may have had from Stalin, Churchill himself believed that the Russians had lived up to the "percentages" agreement in not intervening, and in permitting the British to put down the Greek Communist uprising. When the Greek civil war was virtually over, and the big three met at Yalta in February 1945, Roosevelt produced a "Declaration on Liberated Europe" disavowing spheres of influence. The Russians regarded this as window dressing, and continued to rely on the "percentages" agreement, while the British were embarrassed because they had already taken advantage of the "percentages" agreement in Greece, and now appeared to be either abandoning their bargain or signing a document which was meant from the first to be ignored. It is against this background that the momentous events of the months following the Rumanian surrender must be considered.

The Communists Take Over

Between the surrender of August 23, 1944 and the spring of 1948, the tiny Rumanian Communist Party, relying on Soviet backing, ousted, destroyed, and replaced the opposition, transformed the monarchy into a republic, and made itself ruler of Rumania, in the face of ineffectual opposition from the Western powers. It even conducted a modest purge of its own.

During the war, the Rumanian Communists had engaged in a certain amount of clandestine opposition to the Germans, although their claim to have led a resistance movement is absurdly exaggerated. They tried to ally themselves with Maniu and Bratianu in a "united front" against the Germans and Antonescu. But, as devout Stalinites, they could not support the national effort to recover Bessarabia and northern Bukovina, on which Maniu and Bratianu insisted. Having failed, the Communists formed their own "front" organization of fellow-travelers, called the "Union of Patriots," and published a clandestine newspaper. The leading Communist in the country was Lucretiu Patraşcanu, a Western-educated lawyer, who had often defended Communists on trial for subversion. The most important fellow-traveler was Petru Groza, a wealthy Transylvanian businessman and politician, who had founded a left-wing organization of peasants called the "Ploughmen's Front." Educated in Budapest, Groza was an apostle of Hungarian-Rumanian reconciliation. Personally, he was an opportunist and a buffoon.

After the surrender there returned to Rumania from the U.S.S.R. various Rumanian Communists who had been in exile there. Ana Pauker, daughter of a Moldavian rabbi, had been active in forming and indoctrinating pro-Communist Rumanian units among prisoners of war in the U.S.S.R. Vasile Luca, partly of Szekely origin, had served the Russians as civil official in northern Bukovina and was an officer in the Red Army. Emil Bodnaraş, a half-Ukrainian from the Bukovina, had been a deserter from the Rumanian armies, and had served as a Soviet spy. He now organized armed squads of toughs, including many former Iron Guardists, to help the Communists in their drive for power. All of these three suffered from the liability of belonging to the minorities. The only true Rumanian among the leading "Muscovites" was Gheorghe Gheorghiu-Dej, a former railway worker and fomenter of labor disturbances in the 1930's.

The Communists began the postsurrender period with one Cabinet post: the Ministry of Justice, held by Patraşcanu. In addition to the Union of Patriots and the Ploughmen's Front, they organized the so-called "Patriotic Defense," ostensibly a social welfare organization raising funds for wounded soldiers and the like, but actually a paramilitary organization with its own militia. They also used the newly-founded Society for Friendship with the Soviet Union (ARLUS) as a means of blackmailing businessmen and others into contributing money for Communist purposes. They began active organizational work among the Trade Unions, now revived and headed by Gheorghiu-Dej's old associate, Gheorghe Apostol.

The presence of Soviet troops in the country and the active support given them by Moscow were indispensable for the Communists' political successes. But they were also inadvertently assisted by the National Liberal and National Peasant leaders, who were still counting on the British and Americans to assist them against the Russians. Failing to realize that the West could give them little help, they did not push for the punishment of war criminals, and some of them tried to evade the Russian demands for material assistance against Germany.

As a result, in October 1944, the Communists split from the coalition, and took with them their front groups and the Social Democrats, forming a National Democratic Front (FND). Early in November, a second Sanatescu government took office, with Gheorghiu-Dej as Minister of Communications, Groza as Vice-Premier, and several other FND leaders as ministers. Not content with this gain, the Communists now concentrated their attack on the key Ministry of the Interior, which controlled the police and rural gendarmerie, and the appointments of local prefects and mayors. Accusing the National Peasant Minister of the Interior, Nicolae Penescu, of police terrorism, and demonstrating against him in the streets, the Communists brought about the fall of the second Sanatescu government early in December 1944.

The new Prime Minister, General Nicolae Radescu, had shown opposition to the Germans during the war. He himself took over the Ministry of the Interior, but had to accept a Communist Under-Secretary, Teohari Georgescu. There was a brief lull; but the Rumanian Government was actually helpless against the Communists. The Russians had ousted the officials sent out by Bucharest to northern Transylvania, on the charge that they were persecuting the Magyars. In Moldavia too, the Radescu regime was powerless. In January 1945, Ana Pauker and Gheorghiu-Dej apparently obtained Moscow's permission to push for an all-FND government. The FND now hinted that the only way to get the right to govern northern Transylvania was to install an FND central government. It demanded a new distribution of land, to be confiscated from war criminals and those who owned properties larger than fifty hectares (one hectare is approximately 2.5 acres). Through its control of the printers' union, it prevented the publication of the Liberals' and Peasants' newspapers.

When Radescu found that he could not get one of his statements into print, he announced that he would make it publicly at a theater; and when the Communists packed the theater, he moved to another one, and broadcast his speech. On February 24, 1945, there was an FND demonstration in Bucharest, after which several people were killed. The Communists charged that Radescu had ordered the troops to fire on the crowd; Radescu declared that the bullets had come from the guns of a truckful of Communists. The bullets were not Rumanian army issue. In a final broadcast Radescu referred to Pauker and Luca as "horrible hyenas" and "foreigners without God or country," while the Communist press referred to Radescu as a murderer.

At this juncture, Soviet Deputy Commissar of Foreign Affairs Vyshinsky came to Bucharest. In a stormy interview, he pounded the table, and insisted that King Michael dismiss Radescu and appoint Groza Premier; and Groza presented a solid FND list of ministers. To the King's initial refusal to accept the ultimatum Vyshinsky responded that this was an act unfriendly to the U.S.S.R., and that Rumania might cease to exist as a sovereign state. It was by this sensational intervention of the Soviet Union at the end of February 1945 that the Communist-dominated FND came to power. The new government included Teohari Georgescu as Minister of the Interior. It included a few opportunists who had been members of the Liberal or Peasant Parties, and who now called themselves "dissident" Liberals or Peasants, and collaborated with the FND. Chief among these was Gheorghe Tatarescu, who had served as Premier under Carol, and who was known for his earlier pro-fascist record. The rest were FND members. To show their approval of the new regime, the Russians within three days restored northern Transylvania to Rumanian administration. In May, the chief Rumanian "war criminals," including Antonescu, were tried and condemned to death. Testifying at their trial, the aged and courageous Maniu shook hands with them when leaving the courtroom: a gesture which he intended as a simple act of Christian charity, but which the left instantly seized upon to blacken Maniu as a "fascist."

The Soviet intervention in Rumania violated the Yalta declaration on Liberated Europe. But Churchill was now, as he says himself, "hampered in his protests" by the "percentages" agreement. If he pressed Stalin now, he feared that Stalin would say " 'I did not interfere with your action in Greece; why do you not give me the same latitude in Rumania?' " [1] The United States deplored the Soviet action, but felt that any protest would only elicit the response that action had been necessary to protect the Russian armies. The Vyshinsky intervention in Rumania, however, was the beginning of major disagreements between the U.S.S.R. and the Western Allies,

[1] Sir Winston Churchill, *The Second World War,* VI, p. 420.

just as it had been Rumania which had provided the first open rift between Stalin and Hitler.

At the Potsdam Conference held in July–August 1945, after President Roosevelt had died and the war in Europe had ended, Stalin indicated to Churchill his dismay at finding that the United States had not considered itself bound by the "percentages" agreement. American charges that Russia had violated the Yalta agreement in Rumania were met with Russian complaints about British behavior in Greece. The United States and Britain made it clear that they would not recognize the Groza government. The powers agreed, however, to conclude peace treaties only with "recognized democratic governments." The Russians recognized Groza at once; the Western Allies of course did not.

Taking his cue from the Potsdam agreement, King Michael demanded that Groza resign, since his government was not a "recognized democratic government." Groza refused, and obtained full backing from the U.S.S.R. King Michael refused to sign any decrees. The Soviet press and the Rumanian left wrongly accused the United States and Britain of supporting the King. The impasse continued for months. It arose from the fact that any free election in Rumania, held according to the Yalta promise, would have returned an overwhelmingly anti-Soviet regime to power. The Russians were relying on the "percentages" agreement, not on Yalta. The United States did not accept the "percentages" agreement. But it is clear that we did not raise sufficient objections to it at the time. The British never made it clear whether the "percentages" agreement still held good.

A special fact-finding mission to Rumania, headed by Mark Ethridge, editor of the Louisville *Courier-Journal,* reported in December 1945 that our official information on Rumania had been accurate. Shortly afterward, the three foreign ministers, meeting at Moscow, reached an apparent compromise which was in fact a Soviet victory. The Russians agreed to join in advising the King to appoint one National Peasant and one National Liberal representative to the Cabinet. As reorganized, the government would announce the holding of free elections as soon as possible. The United States and Britain would then recognize it. But recognition was to precede the actual holding of the elections. The new Liberal and Peasant ministers were not necessarily to hold portfolios. As it turned out, they were appointed but ignored. Early in February

1946, the Western Allies recognized the Groza government. The U.S.S.R. had won another round.

Now, instead of free elections, which would have swept the left out of office, the Rumanian Communists proceeded to conduct a campaign of intimidation and brutality. They virtually forced a split in the Social Democratic Party, and induced one faction to run a common list of candidates with them. All Western protests against these practices met with rejection. All the old Balkan tricks of rigging elections were brought into play, together with much violence. On November 19, 1946, a National Assembly was elected which included thirty-two Peasants, three Liberals, and 369 leftists. In February 1947, the Peace Treaty with Rumania only confirmed the existing state of affairs. Though one article required the Rumanian Government to guarantee to its citizens fundamental human rights and freedoms, this remained a dead letter.

In 1947, with Soviet backing, the Groza government moved against its political opposition. During the summer, the National Peasant Party leaders were arrested and the party outlawed. In November, Maniu, Mihalache, and others were brought to trial on charges of conspiring with American intelligence officers to organize clandestine activity against the regime and to set up American air bases on Rumanian soil. While the Peasant Party certainly regarded the Groza government as illegal, and looked to the United States for sympathy, and while members of the party may have had contact with the American officers, the charges were absurd, and were an attempt to blacken the United States as well as the defendants. Maniu and Mihalache received life sentences of imprisonment. Toward the end of 1947 also, the "Muscovites" assumed political office: Ana Pauker became Foreign Minister, Luca Minister of Finance, and Bodnaraş Minister of War. By the spring of 1948, the Communists had dissolved the Social Democratic Party, and imprisoned its leader, while absorbing the fellow-travelers into their own "United Workers' Party."

Meanwhile, they also forced the abdication of King Michael (December 30, 1947). In March 1948 they held elections for a new assembly with the task of approving a constitution transforming Rumania into a republic. This was done on April 13. The new Constitution of the Rumanian People's Republic (RPR) was modeled on the Soviet Stalin Constitution of 1936. Though it guaranteed civil liberties, it declared that "citizens enjoy the right of association . . . if the aim is not directed against the democratic order established by the constitution." It thus left to the state all power in deciding what was and what was not subversive. Even before the RPR had been officially proclaimed, the Communists had held their own first purge: that of Patraşcanu, accused of Menshevism, befriending war criminals, and "detaching himself from the masses." He was imprisoned in February 1948, but not tried until April 1954, when he was condemned to death and executed. In June 1948, when Tito was expelled from the Cominform, Bucharest became its headquarters.

Political Developments Since Mid-1948

Because the Rumanian Communist Party could count on virtually no popular support, and because Soviet depredations long delayed economic recovery, the Communists took longer in Rumania than elsewhere in Eastern Europe to consolidate their power. Yet the Russians had a stronger natural strategic interest in the Danube delta and the Black Sea area than in any other part of the Balkan region. Thus it became necessary for the Communists to create in Rumania by fiat institutions which had elsewhere sprung up naturally or with a little encouragement. Chief among these were the local "people's councils," organs of state power in the villages, towns, districts, and counties, which bore a strong resemblance to the Soviets in the U.S.S.R. Set up during the war by the Yugoslav Partisan guerrillas, and to a lesser extent in Albania and Bulgaria, they had not existed in Rumania until decreed in January 1949. It was interesting also that the first members were appointed by the regime, rather than elected by the people.

By September 1950 the regime had redistricted all of Rumania, abolishing prewar county boundaries and so far as possible linking agricultural regions to the nearest town, in order to make industrial workers' votes weigh as heavily as possible. Accompanying this move went an electoral decree providing for the first elections to "people's councils" and excluding various "class enemies" from candidacy and from voting. Elections on the Soviet single-list principle were held in December 1950. The population elected 109,311 members of the "people's councils."

Major new political changes came with the summer of 1952, when a new constitution was presented: Rumania had reached a new stage in "socialism," the regime declared, and had outgrown the 1948 constitution. The preamble to the new document declared that the RPR owed its origins to the glorious victory of the Soviet armies, and the U.S.S.R., as ally, guaranteed its sovereignty and prosperity. The constitution provided for a Grand National Assembly to be elected every four years, with one deputy to each 40,000 inhabitants. It would elect its President, form the government, amend the constitution, approve the budget, declare war, and make peace. The President of its Presidium had considerable power, on paper at least. As in all Communist states, the Public Prosecutor (Attorney General) wielded enormous powers. Candidates for election to office might be named only by the "Workers Party" and its mass organizations. Indeed, the constitution specifically declared that members of the Workers Party were "the most active citizens and those with the greatest conscience." It once more redistricted the entire country. The most sensational innovation was the creation of an "autonomous Magyar region" in the Szekely districts of Transylvania, clearly an attempt to apply Soviet nationality policy to Rumania. After much "debate" (rather indoctrination) the new constitution was adopted on September 24, 1952. Elections for the Assembly were held in November 1952 and for the "people's councils" in December 1953, when 135,220 members were elected.

The "autonomous Magyar region" was not the only reflection of Soviet nationality policies. Hungarian cultural activities received much encouragement. The Russians had deported about 50,000 of the most able-bodied Germans over Allied protests in 1945, and others had fled to the West with the German armies; but in 1949 those who were left began to be given their own schools, newspapers, and cultural societies, all Communist. Similar treatment was accorded the Tartar, Ukrainian, Armenian, Greek, Bulgarian, Turkish, and Gypsy minorities. It was possible to interpret this attention even to the smallest minority groups as evidence of a Soviet plan to destroy the national consciousness of the Rumanians themselves. Such a conjecture received support also from the deliberate efforts of the regime to propagate the false doctrine that Moldavians and Wallachians are separate peoples. The Communist-sponsored publicity campaign to create a specifically "Moldavian" national consciousness was obviously connected with the fact that the Russians had a "Moldavian" Soviet Republic of their own, immediately across the frontier and including much of Bessarabia. They seemed at least to be toying with the plan of preparing to annex Moldavia to the U.S.S.R. At the same time they put on a propaganda drive designed to convince all Rumanians that they were really Slavs.

Two minorities, however, received different treatment. The Yugoslavs, both Serbs and Croats, were persecuted after the break between the Cominform and Tito in June 1948, and in 1951 many of them, together with others, were deported from their homes in the Banat along the Yugoslav frontier, and dumped into concentration camps. The approximately 370,000 Jews who had survived the German extermination efforts, and who had become in large number strongly Zionist, encountered Communist persecution for that reason. Arrests were made frequently, and anti-Israel propaganda was constant.

State instruments of control extended their power everywhere. The death penalty was established for crimes against the state or the national economy. In January 1949 a new militia was created, incorporating all former police forces. It watched the movement of all citizens, and managed the brutal forced deportation of unwanted inhabitants from the cities to make room for new workers, whose allowance of living space was limited to eight square meters. It arrested and took away children of "unreliable" parents, a practice which President Truman properly but ineffectively referred to as outrageous. Another Rumanian organ similar to its Russian prototype was the Union of Working Youth. The Communist sports organization had its own paramilitary body called "Ready for Defense and Work." The army, limited by treaty to a force of 120,000, was illegally expanded to more than 300,000. A virtually constant series of trials of "enemies" of the regime edified the public. "Terrorists," "kulaks," "agents of the imperialists," employees of foreign-owned oil companies in the pre-Communist era, appeared before the courts, and vanished into prisons or lost their lives.

That the regime was not only cruel but also incompetent was attested by the multiplication of ministries and their recombination, which took place in the years after 1948. At one time, there were more than forty posts of cabinet rank. Purges removed some of the most important Communist leaders. The most dramatic came in the months after March 1952, when Vasile Luca was removed from office as Minister of Finance, following a drastic currency reform, and later expelled from the Central Committee of the Communist Party. Teohari Georgescu was ousted from the Ministry of the

Interior, and most surprisingly, Ana Pauker from the Foreign Ministry. Lesser figures also suffered.

Among the mass of charges leveled at those scheduled to be purged, perhaps the most significant was that Pauker, Luca, and Georgescu had "indulged in separate discussions among themselves with the aim of establishing a policy of their own." It seems plausible that they had become alarmed over the mounting economic difficulties, and had consulted together. The greatest beneficiary of their disgrace was Gheorghiu-Dej, who became Premier on June 2, 1952, while Groza, who had served his Communist masters well for more than seven years, was kicked upstairs into the presidency of the presidium of the national assembly. The continued role of the Jewish Josip Chişinevschi rendered implausible the explanation that Pauker's disgrace was due to anti-Semitism. Figures reaching new prominence were Alexander Moghioroş, Miron Constantinescu, and Chivu Stoica.

The death of Stalin in March 1953 and the purge of Beria in June led to political and economic changes in the Soviet Union which were reflected in the satellites. In Rumania, Pauker, Luca, and Georgescu were not tried, and Gheorghiu-Dej on one occasion told the foreign press that Pauker was still in Bucharest. Rumors of a comeback naturally circulated widely. The trend toward the multiplication of ministries and the division of function sharply reversed itself, as ministries were recombined and the power and responsibilities of cabinet officials thus increased. Amnesties were granted to persons serving sentences of less than five years in jail, except for those guilty of offenses against the state.

Most striking was the Rumanian imitation of the "collegiate" government which Malenkov, Molotov, and Khrushchev had installed in the U.S.S.R. In April 1954, the Rumanian Communist Party abolished the post of Secretary-General of the Party, hitherto held by Gheorghiu-Dej, and created a new post of first secretary to the Central Committee's four-man secretariat: Apostol as first secretary, and three lesser figures as his assistants. Gheorghiu-Dej himself proclaimed that "all manifestations of the personality cult" must now disappear. He explained the new changes as necessary to relieve the busy men who had hitherto been active simultaneously in the Politburo and the Cabinet. But it was notable that they had not noticed their fatigue in their double role until Moscow pointed it out to them. During 1954 and 1955, the scheduled Party Congress was repeatedly postponed. The draft statutes set new and more difficult standards for admission to the Communist Party, and referred openly to party control over the trade unions and the army.

Rumanian foreign relations developed normally for a satellite. Intimacy with the Soviet bloc grew ever stronger: Rumania concluded agreements with East Germany in 1950, and for the first time North Koreans in numbers appeared in Bucharest. Hostility toward the West manifested itself at every turn: the repeated American and British protests at the violation of the peace treaty went unanswered or were rudely rejected. The Rumanian Government forced the closing of the United States Information Office, curtailed the rights of American diplomats to travel in Rumania (the United States reciprocated), and bitterly denounced the provisions of the Mutual Security Act of 1951 which appropriated funds for the support of anti-Communist activities within Communist states. The scurrilous "germ-warfare" charges against the United States were given great publicity, and many of those charged with espionage were tagged with the label "agent of the American imperialists."

The Rumanian press showed much solicitude for Mr. and Mrs. Rosenberg, executed in the United States for treason, and for their unfortunate children. But the Rumanian regime did not hesitate to use two other little boys, then in Rumania, the sons of Mr. and Mrs. V. C. Georgescu, in an effort to blackmail their father, now an official of the Standard Oil Company, into "collaborating" with the RPR authorities. Mr. Georgescu, realizing what the consequences to his children might be, none the less refused to be intimidated, and told the State Department the entire story. The First Secretary of the Rumanian Legation, Christache Zambeti, who had acted as blackmailer for the RPR, was expelled from the United States, and the Voice of America gave wide publicity to the whole affair, putting the children in the "trust" of the Rumanian people. Eventually, the RPR did set the boys free, and on April 13, 1954, they rejoined their parents in the United States. The State Department announced that President Eisenhower and Secretary Dulles had taken a personal interest in the negotiations which led to this fortunate ending of an episode thoroughly disgraceful for the RPR.

The Rumanian Economy

Although the Rumanian economy suffered losses during the war, as the result of German demands and the damage inflicted by air raids and by the fighting in Moldavia and Transylvania, the country emerged from hostilities not gravely damaged, and with productive capacity actually increased. But Soviet occupation did produce economic misery. The Russians arbitrarily valued the goods given them as reparations at the extremely low level of 1938 world prices. They thus obtained between two and three times as much as the $300,000,000-worth to which the peace treaty entitled them. They seized much Rumanian property in addition, on the plea that it had been removed from Bessarabia or northern Bukovina. They stripped the country of foodstuffs to feed their armies. They claimed all German assets, but ignored German liabilities. Anything else they wanted they took and called it "war booty." Total depredations may have reached two billion dollars.

In the oil industry they began by dismantling and exporting vital installations. In January 1945, a Soviet-Rumanian commercial treaty reserved all the oil output to the Russians and gave them as German assets eleven French and Belgian firms which had previously been seized by the Germans. These confiscated firms they put up in July as their share of the assets in a new "joint" Soviet-Rumanian company called SovRomPetrol. This company enjoyed government favor, and the firms outside it—American, British, and Dutch—were the victims of discrimination and persecution.

In December 1947 and June 1948, all the oil firms except SovRomPetrol were nationalized. Production, which had reached a high of 8,700,000 tons in 1936, ranged about the figure of 4,000,000 tons in these years. Without investing anything except firms confiscated from the Germans, the U.S.S.R. thus obtained control over the richest single industry in the Balkans. Similar SovRoms were founded in the field of water transport, timber, civil aviation, highway transport, tractor production, and natural gas. A SovRomBank controlled the financing of all. By 1948, the Russians had penetrated and taken over the Rumanian economy.

With recovery beginning in 1948, the state proceeded to the nationalization of all enterprises, and set up the first State Planning Commission. This produced one-year preliminary plans for 1949 and 1950, and in 1951 the first Soviet-style Five Year Plan, to be completed in four years. Production of industrial raw materials in the years before 1949 in most cases did not exceed the levels reached in 1938. Meanwhile, a disastrous inflation had set in: taking 100 as the 1939 price level, the 1947 level was 483,248. The drastic currency reform law of August 15, 1947 required the exchange of 20,000 old lei for one new leu; but limited the amount exchangable to a maximum of $1.67. Thus savings were wiped out, and while goods remained in short supply, hardship prevailed.

In agriculture, the regime put through a "land reform" on March 22, 1945, confiscating without compensation all estates over fifty hectares in size, and a variety of other categories of property. About 1,500,000 hectares were seized; about 1,000,000 distributed to claimants, with preference to sufferers from the war and those peasants with dwarf-holdings. The effect of the reform was to multiply the number of uneconomical small properties. Inexperienced and incompetent gypsies were given valuable former German properties in Transylvania. The aim of the division was to lay the groundwork for eventual collectivization, although the regime did not mention its intentions before the summer of 1948. By then it was clear that industrialization at forced draft was to be pursued at all costs; that among the branches of industry heavy industry was to take the lead; that the Communists intended to mechanize agriculture in order to feed their ever-swelling urban population; and that collectivization would be the first step.

Beginning in the second half of 1948, the regime began to preach the importance of "cooperatives" or joint peasant partnerships for the harvesting of a given crop, and to found Machine Tractor Stations. In March 1949, a further confiscation of all remaining estates of fifty hectares or more produced a further half million hectares to serve as the nucleus for the Sovkhoz type of state model farm. Graduated income taxes hit the well-to-do peasant, the kulak, called *chiabur* in Rumania, and by spring 1950 the regime openly proclaimed class warfare in the countryside. A system of compulsory deliveries of virtually all agricultural and dairy products was also manipulated to hurt the *chiabur*. Although joining a collective was supposedly voluntary, brutal methods of "persuasion" were often used. By the end of 1951 there were 1,089 collectives, with 75,065 families, and well over a quarter of a million hectares of land.

In an effort to speed up the process, the Communists authorized the formation of so-called TOZ-type "cooperatives," in which the participants did not have to surrender their property rights in land and cattle, as they did in the full-fledged kolkhoz- or artel-type collective. The TOZ had been common in the U.S.S.R. in the late nineteen twenties, and has disappeared only under Stalin's furious collectivization drive of the early nineteen thirties. 1952 was a year of rapid increase in collectivization in Rumania. By the end of the year there were 1,795 collectives, with 165,411 families. In April 1953, the regime's draft statute for collectives regulated the amount of property (the homestead, a small plot of land, a few animals) which the entrant might keep for himself, and prescribed the Soviet system of "labor-brigades." By the summer of 1953, all forms of cooperative or collective agriculture probably still totaled less than fifteen per cent of Rumanian arable land. Food production showed disastrous lags behind the Plan, and shortages kept the townsmen hungry.

This was the summer in which the satellites, in varying degrees, followed the lead of Malenkov, and embarked upon the "new course," in which the tempo of industrialization and collectivization was (temporarily) to be slowed, and greater investment devoted to agriculture and the production of consumers' goods. The slow-down came for Rumania at a time when the private peasant still bore the main burden of feeding the country. Accordingly, he received some alleviation of his lot: tax and insurance rates and compulsory delivery quotas were lowered, and a variety of other favors extended.

The publication of the agricultural plan for 1953–54 revealed that the regime was at last making a serious effort to diversify agriculture by cutting back the area devoted to grain crops, and sowing more land to fodder and industrial (cotton, sugar-beets, oilseeds) crops. It had not, however, achieved the necessary rise in grain yields; so that shortages remained. The regime also called for great efforts at increasing the number of livestock. Reclamation and irrigation plans aimed at raising the area under cultivation. In the Dobrudja, a major effort was made with Soviet assistance to plant shelter-belts of trees, a project parallel to a similar one sponsored by the Russians across the frontier in the Bulgarian southern Dobrudja.

It was, however, heavy industry into which the Communists put about forty per cent of their total investment. Even the new course, though it relaxed the tempo, and abandoned the insistence on completing the Five Year Plan in four years, dropped the level of investment in heavy industry only to about thirty per cent of total investment. Despite difficulties, it seemed probable that by 1954 a substantial amount of progress had been scored toward the production goals laid down in the plan. Large-scale electrification was under way, though the Bicaz station, one of the biggest projects, failed to reach completion. The Danube-Black Sea Canal, grave of thousands of forced laborers and political prisoners, was abandoned far short of completion in 1953 after several frenzied years of effort. The government claimed that the oil industry had reached and overtaken the 8,700,000-ton figure of 1936, though Western authorities were skeptical. Despite the efforts of SovRomCarbune, founded in 1949, coal remained a major bottleneck, and almost all coking coal was imported. The iron and steel industry expanded, and new plants produced finished goods, such as electric motors and freightcars, poor in quality by Western standards and enormously expensive to turn out. The chemical industry increased its output of caustic soda and fertilizers. Textiles rose in output to double the prewar figure. The rolling-stock position remained tight, and highway transport perhaps even worse.

The continued absence of consumers' goods from the market and the consequent excess purchasing power led to continued inflationary pressure. The currency "reform" of January 27, 1952, again called in old lei, and provided for their exchange at rates varying from one to twenty to one to 400. The purchasing power of the public was cut by two thirds, and the U.S.S.R bound the leu to the ruble, so that it could sell to the Rumanians dear and buy from them cheap. The widespread misery which this "reform" precipitated led, as we saw, to the arrest of Luca, although it had been Soviet experts who prepared the measure. On February 1, 1954 a third currency "reform" pegged the leu to the ruble at a rate of one and a half to one.

The Rumanian state budget showed an annual surplus, partly as the result of this constant robbing of the public. A sales tax, like the Soviet "turnover" tax, brought in almost half the state's revenue. Profits and income taxes helped swell the total. The state spent its income for the economy and other usual purposes: defense expenditures were often concealed as "cultural." Available figures on wages and prices helped to re-enforce the impression that the Rumanian standard of living was miserably low.

Except for the year 1948, the Rumanian balance of trade was unfavorable in all the years since the war for which figures were available. Exporting oil, timber, and vegetables, the country had to import grain because of the bad harvests and the disastrous

Communist agricultural policies. From a grain-exporter Rumania became an importer to the extent that grain was the largest single item in 1947. Roughly eighty per cent of foreign trade was with the other Eastern bloc states. Fourteen state corporations handled the trade, specializing in various types of product. The U.S.S.R. and the more advanced satellites (Czechoslovakia, East Germany, Hungary, and Poland) did deliver large amounts of industrial equipment and finished goods. To them Rumania exported raw materials. With the less advanced satellites (Bulgaria, Albania) and China the relationship was reversed: Rumania exported petroleum products and finished goods, and received raw materials.

In the autumn of 1954, the U.S.S.R. arranged for the sale to the Rumanian government of the assets of all the SovRom companies except for the most important, SovRomPetrol, and the most mysterious, SovRomQuartz (which was exploring for uranium). No doubt the sale reflected the confidence of Moscow in its secure control over the Rumanian economy. The last two SovRoms were turned over in 1955.

Religion, Education, Culture

In Rumania, as everywhere, the Communists were hostile to religion as such. Their policies varied from faith to faith, but their aim was to make it impossible for the churches or clergy of any faith to oppose them politically, to enter on any undertaking independent of the state, to play an independent role in education, or to maintain links to the West. Constitutional guarantees of freedom of religion were pure window-dressing.

The regime found the Orthodox Church comparatively docile. The first Minister of Cults, Burducea, a former Iron Guardist, founded a "Union of Democratic Priests" to collaborate with the Communists. In 1947 the state passed laws empowering the ministry to pension any priest it might choose to retire, and to redistribute sees. These permitted the purge of about thirty per cent of the parish priests, and the appointment of Communist puppets to high ecclesiastical posts. In November 1947 three "people's hierarchs" took over as Metropolitan Archbishops, and in May 1948 Justinian Marina, hand-picked instrument of the regime, became Patriarch. He signed all Soviet-sponsored "peace appeals," and loaned his name to the accusation that the United States had used germ warfare in Korea. He presided over a reorganization of the hierarchy, and emerged as chairman of various interfaith committees of collaborationist clerics. Under this safe management, the Orthodox Church kept its three theological schools, and seminaries for monks and nuns. Justinian fully earned the award of Star of the Republic, first class, which his Communist masters bestowed on him in 1953.

The Communists regarded the Uniate and Roman Catholic Churches as agents of the Vatican and of American imperialism, and thus as their greatest enemies. They determined to suppress the Uniate Church altogether, and force its faithful to "return to the Orthodox faith of their ancestors." Finding a few priests who would "revert" to Orthodoxy, it convened them at a so-called "Congress" at Cluj in October 1948. This packed meeting accepted "re-entry into the bosom of the Rumanian Orthodox Church and the definitive severance of ties with papal Rome." Thereafter the Communists employed violent persecution against those Uniate priests who clung to their faith. Police arrested them; their churches were closed; their salaries were stopped. In December 1948, a new law put an end to the existence of the Uniate Church. Forced labor camps and prisons, torture and execution awaited those clerics who resisted. Preferment in the Orthodox Church awaited those who capitulated.

The Roman Catholics, who were Magyars and Germans, could not be forced to become Rumanian Orthodox. But the regime determined to cut them off from Rome, and to take control over their faith. In 1947 there began the dismissal of priests, the closing of schools, hospitals, and orphanages, the suppression of church publications, and the arrest and trial of leading priests. During 1948, the regime revoked the Concordat with the Vatican, removed all but two Bishops, and legally closed all church schools. In the summer of 1949, it arrested the two remaining Bishops, and so many priests that only about one quarter of the priesthood remained at liberty.

In April 1950, the Communists launched their effort to create a "national Catholic Church." A so-called "Catholic Action Committee," whose head was soon excommunicated by the Vatican, tried to rally the remaining clergy to "join the forces for peace." In July, a new statute left to the papacy only authority on questions of dogma and morals, while the state took over complete administrative jurisdiction over the Catholic Church, whose priests might henceforth communicate with Rome only through the Ministry of Cults. The Papal Nuncio was expelled soon afterward, and a further link with the West was smashed. In September the Catholic Action Committee called a congress to establish an "autonomous" church. For this purpose the regime made use of the "Status Catholicus" of Transylvania, a traditional parliament of priests and laymen who managed the affairs of the Church in that province. Infiltrating it with their puppet priests, and extending its role to the whole of Rumania, the Communists called a session in March 1951. The announcement that four disloyal priests had been arrested was the only indication to reach the outside world of the bitter opposition to the foundation of a schismatic church, creation of which was abandoned for the time being. Many Catholic prelates and priests suffered death or imprisonment, as the Communists destroyed their church organization.

The Protestant churches suffered no comparable persecution. The Magyar Reformed Church (Calvinist), the Unitarians (Magyar), and the Lutherans (Germans), as well as the Baptists (Rumanians) and smaller sects, seem to have collaborated without much struggle. The tiny Muslim minority in the Dobrudja made no difficulties. There were also some Jewish religious leaders who accepted the domination of the regime; but, as we have seen, the Zionists suffered persecution. The "Society for the Dissemination of Science and Culture," a body devoted to the propagation of atheism, held many public lectures, printed dozens of pamphlets in all the languages of the country, and received the blessings of the Communists.

In the field of education and cultural life generally, the Communists imitated their Soviet masters. They virtually forced the population to read their controlled press. They waged a campaign against illiteracy, fostered minority-language schools, and modeled their curriculum on the Soviet example, in which the students received a narrow technical education on a foundation of Marxist-Leninist ideological indoctrination. Everywhere mass programs of Russian-language instruction were undertaken. Anti-Communist teachers were purged. In scholarship, the Rumanian Communists fostered "collective" research, which had to advance the cause of "socialism," and, when successful, was rewarded by state prizes. In many fields, where the results of the research are available, they are often puerile, sterile or simply wrong.

"Scânteia House," the huge new press building in Bucharest, ground out a huge number of newspapers, books, and pamphlets. *Scânteia* (The Spark) was the Rumanian *Pravda,* closely modeled on its Soviet prototype; so were the papers for the trade unions, the army, the youth organizations, the "people's front," and the peasantry. Provincial papers were modeled on those in the capital with additional local news. Specialized weeklies, corresponding to those in the U.S.S.R., dealt with politics, literature, economics, and humor. "Radiofication"—the installation of wired receivers which broadcast official programs only—became a major project.

Optional day-nurseries "educated" children between the ages of three and seven. Then began the compulsory elementary school for ages seven to fourteen, after which the four year "middle school" was available for the reliable children. At the top were the Universities and technical schools, completely reorganized by the government, which spread the prewar academic resources of the country extremely thin, founding nine new "university" centers where prewar Rumania had had four. One hundred and sixty faculties replaced the former total of forty-five. At Bucharest, a Moscow-style University "city" was planned. Many of the new provincial centers had only one faculty apiece, usually technological in a special field. The emphasis was on quantity and ideology rather than quality, which had fallen below prewar levels. The reorganized Rumanian Academy directed research in all fields.

Art, music, and literature concentrated on revolutionary and ideological subjects. Rumanian novels were didactic, exposing the evils of the former Western influence, the viciousness of "Titoism," the menace of the *chiabur,* and the vileness of former regimes. Theater "collectives" called "Artistic Agitation Brigades," sponsored dramatic work in factories to arouse enthusiasm for higher levels of production. The classics, safer than many a contemporary drama, were edited for Communist consumption. Caragiale, a witty nineteenth-century dramatist, whose work had strong overtones of social satire, was adopted by the regime as its favorite. A movie industry was founded, and one of its productions won a prize in 1952 in a competition among the satellite states.

The Society for Friendship with the Soviet Union had a huge membership, allegedly about a quarter of the total population of the country. It kept up a barrage of propaganda of all sorts about the Soviet Union, and sponsored conducted tours, ballet performances, sports contests, and the like. Friendship societies only a little less ever-present linked Rumania to all the other members of the "camp of freedom."

Communist totalitarianism had Rumania firmly in its grip, and dictated all aspects of its life, political, economic, and cultural. For this tragic development the United States was not without a certain responsibility. Washington had not protested effectively against the application of the "percentages" agreement which gave the U.S.S.R. so large a role in Rumania. Yet the "percentages" agreement in itself grew out of Churchill's appraisal of the relative power of the U.S.S.R. and the Western Allies in southeast Europe. The Russians, he felt, got nothing by it which they could not have taken anyhow, and which they were not determined to take. Once the Russians had asserted their authority in Rumania, the problem of diluting it became one of dislodging them, and this could not be achieved without a major defeat of Moscow, a thing for which public opinion in the United States was not prepared to pay the price.

Chapter 11

Bulgaria

ROBERT LEE WOLFF

Bulgaria Before 1944

IN CONTRAST to Rumania, Bulgaria fought the entire first World War on the German side, and emerged from the peace settlements deprived of small areas along the frontier with the new state of Yugoslavia and of its outlet to the Aegean Sea. The territorial losses were the more painful because, ever since they had been freed from the Ottoman Empire in 1878, Bulgarians had longed to obtain Macedonia and Thrace. The Russian-dictated Treaty of San Stefano had awarded these lands to Bulgaria, but the Congress of Berlin reversed this decision. Long years of rivalry with Serbs and Greeks had culminated in the second Balkan War of 1913, which had cost Bulgaria most of the gains scored in the first Balkan War. Thus the World War losses only inflamed old wounds.

A country of small peasant proprietors, without great landowners or a feudal tradition, Bulgaria was eighty per cent agricultural. Its ruling group, mostly sons of peasants, consisted of men who had obtained higher education, and stayed in the cities to enter the civil service, the professions, and politics. Law and university teaching were the gateway to political advancement. The Bulgarian Democratic Party represented the views of the small commercial middle class, moderate and generally conservative. But political parties were often a matter of personal following rather than of program. Those who had not succeeded in obtaining posts in the overcrowded professions often became unemployed intellectuals, spoiled for the farm by their education and their pride, bitter in their disappointment, and ripe for political extremism.

Speaking for the peasants was the Agrarian Party, founded by

Alexander Stamboliisky, a passionate lover of the peasantry and hater of the cities, who came to power in 1919. He instituted compulsory education, a progressive income tax, and a labor law requiring all Bulgarians to give one year's service to the state. Personally incorruptible, Stamboliisky had many followers who were intoxicated by power, and engaged in dishonest practices. He favored close relations with Yugoslavia, as the first step toward a Balkan federation, a position unpopular so soon after Bulgaria's defeat. Indeed, he sponsored an International Bureau of Agriculture, with offices at Prague, often called the "Green International," which strove to initiate widespread cooperation among European peasant parties. Stamboliisky's enemies, the urban classes, the Macedonians, tens of thousands of whom lived in Bulgaria and opposed all reconciliation with Yugoslavia, the army, and the new King of Bulgaria, Boris, all opposed his efforts. A *coup d'état* in 1923 ended in his murder. Thereafter, most of his followers went into exile or hiding, though a conservative wing of the Agrarian Party continued to operate openly. When allowed to return in 1933, Stamboliisky's followers founded a newspaper called *Pladne* (Noon), but played no significant role in Bulgarian political life until the second World War.

Tied to Russia by bonds of national sentiment, language, and religion, the Bulgarian people tended to look to Moscow, no matter what the color of the regime there. Moreover, Marxism had got an early political start in the country, with a Social Democratic Party founded in 1891. This soon split into two factions, the narrows (*tesni*), and the broads (*shiroki*). The former opposed reformism, and thus corresponded roughly to Lenin's Bolsheviks, although they did not accept Lenin's thesis on the revolutionary usefulness of the peasantry. Opposed to the first World War, the *tesni* had deputies in the parliament (*Sobranie*). One of their leaders was a printers' union leader named Georgi M. Dimitrov. After the war, they became affiliated with the Third International in Moscow, elected forty-four deputies out of a Sobranie of 236, and fomented strikes, which Stamboliisky put down.

When he was murdered in 1923, the Communists stood idly by. They later bitterly condemned their own failure to "form a common front with the peasantry" and resist the "forces of reaction," which now took over the country. Too late, the Communists tried an uprising after the Agrarians had been crushed, and in their turn were suppressed. In 1924, the party was banned, losing its members in the Sobranie. Its leaders fled abroad, where Dimitrov and Vasil Kolarov became high officials in the Comintern. Dimitrov received world-wide publicity through the Reichstag Fire trial in Berlin in 1933. Inside Bulgaria, the party sponsored acts of terrorism such as the bombing of Sofia Cathedral in 1925. The depression and the "popular front" policy of 1935 and succeeding years loaned much strength to the Bulgarian Communists, who were able to express themselves politically, although officially outlawed. By the time of the outbreak of the second World War, Communism was stronger in Bulgaria than anywhere else in the Balkans. The Social Democrats, descendants of the moderate *shiroki,* continued during these years to exist as a legal party, and after 1935 joined the popular front "constitutional bloc" of Agrarians and concealed Communists.

The repressor of Stamboliisky, Alexander Tsankov, admired fascist principles. King Boris married an Italian princess, and was at home in Mussolini's orbit. But there was no Bulgarian equivalent to the Iron Guard. The Internal Macedonian Revolutionary Organization (IMRO), however, made up of Macedonians resident in Bulgaria and possessing powerful sympathizers in high government and army circles, had great power in Bulgarian politics. Receiving subsidies from Mussolini, who was striving to disrupt Yugoslavia, IMRO bands raided across the frontier into Yugoslav territory. One faction of IMRO favored an autonomous Macedonia as a unit in a future Balkan federation. The other favored annexation of Macedonia to Bulgaria, the official Bulgarian view. The two factions feuded with each other, and constantly exchanged shots in the streets of the capital, creating an atmosphere of terror and disorder.

On May 19, 1934, a *coup d'état* quietly brought to power a small group of army officers, banded together in a "military league," under the leadership of Colonel Demian Velchev. He was closely associated with a group of intellectuals and politicians who produced a newspaper called "Zveno" (The Link). The Zveno people were not fascists; they were rather political technicians, tired of disorder, militant patriots, given to authoritarian behavior, but representing no particular social class. They wanted friendly relations with Yugoslavia and the U.S.S.R. They abolished political parties and labor unions, and planned a variety of reforms, cracking down on

IMRO, and forcing its leaders to flee the country. But the chief beneficiary of their coup was King Boris himself, who early in 1935 ousted the Zveno men, and instituted a personal dictatorship. The tight police regime had ended a period of violence unparalleled in the Balkans. With no "class" distinctions and no serious ethnic minority problems, Bulgaria none the less had generated hatreds which produced extreme disorder.

Determined to revise the peace treaties, Bulgarians found themselves excluded from the Balkan Entente, which included their satisfied neighbors. A Yugoslav-Bulgarian pact negotiated in January 1937 did not represent a breaking of this isolation, but rather an Axis effort to draw Yugoslavia away from its Western allies. The pact was welcomed in Rome and Berlin, and looked at askance in Paris and London. Moreover, Germany and Italy had during the 1930's captured between them over eighty per cent of Bulgaria's foreign trade, absorbing its agricultural exports, and supplying its needs for finished goods. The country had become an economic dependency of Hitler. By the time the second World War broke out, it was clear that, despite pro-Russian popular sentiment, Bulgaria was tightly bound to the Axis.

It was the failure of Mussolini's attack on Greece, launched in October 1940 from Albanian bases, that brought Bulgaria to the center of the wartime stage. Uneasy at Hitler's growing interest in the area, Molotov demanded in November 1940 that the Axis recognize Bulgaria as lying within the Russian Black Sea security zone, and accept a Russian-Bulgarian mutual security pact. The Germans evaded the question, and soon afterward determined to invade the U.S.S.R. They put great pressure on Boris to join the Axis, and despite British and American counterpressure he yielded on March 1, 1941. German troops poured into the country across the Danube, Hitler having informed the Russians that his purpose was to keep the British out of Greece. Early in April came the German invasion of Yugoslavia and Greece, and on June 21 the attack on the U.S.S.R.

Unlike Rumania, Bulgaria did not go to war against the U.S.S.R. Bulgarian war aims were the long-desired Macedonian and Thracian territories in Yugoslavia and Greece. The Germans allowed the Bulgarians to occupy these lands. Instead of giving Macedonia autonomy, which the inhabitants wanted, the Bulgarians kept it tightly under control from Sofia, and founded a Bulgarian

University in its capital, Skoplye, as part of an effort toward Bulgarization. Bulgarian national aims were satisfied. Although there were many German troops in Bulgaria, Hitler never occupied the country. Boris' regime fully cooperated with the Germans economically, delivering goods long after the Germans had ceased paying for them. It also introduced anti-Semitic laws, which, though they met with very little response from the Bulgarian people, caused great suffering among the Jews. In late August 1943, Boris suddenly died after a visit to Hitler. A three-man regency was installed to act for his infant son.

The Bulgarian Communists helped organize an underground opposition. There were some Partisan bands in the country, which cooperated with Tito's forces, and fought the government police. But postwar Communist claims with regard to the resistance are greatly exaggerated. The Communists did join with the Pladne Agrarians, the Social Democrats, and Zveno in a united front organization called the Fatherland Front (*Otechestven Front,* hereafter OF). Moreover, the traditionally anti-German Democrats kept up a parliamentary opposition.

Bulgaria was at war with the United States and Britain, and late in 1943 became the target of air raids. These and the growing certainty of Hitler's defeat, together with Russian diplomatic and propaganda pressure, led to a change of government in June 1944. What the Bulgarians wanted was a promise that they could retain the Yugoslav and Greek territory they had seized, but it soon became clear that this was unrealistic. On August 30, 1944, a week after the Rumanian surrender, Bulgarian emissaries reached Cairo to negotiate with the Americans and British, who kept the Russians fully informed. Though it was clear that the new regime under Premier Kosta Muraviev, installed on September 2, was thoroughly anti-Axis, it included no members of the OF. The Russians were apparently unwilling to let moderates govern Bulgaria, or to let the United States and Britain dictate the peace alone. On September 5, the U.S.S.R. suddenly declared war on Bulgaria. Though the Bulgarians put up no resistance, and asked for armistice terms, the Soviet armies invaded the country on September 8.

On the ninth, the OF staged a coup, ousted the Muraviev government, and installed a new Cabinet. The Premier was a Zveno man, Georgiev, and Zveno people held two other posts. The Pladne Agrarians and Social Democrats also had ministries. The Communists obtained four posts, including the key Ministry of Interior (Anton Yugov) and the Ministry of Justice (Mincho Neichev). The new government declared war on the Axis. Thus the Russians forced the issue, and were able in Bulgaria to sponsor the installation of a government in which the Communists from the first held important posts. With September 9, 1944 "postwar" history began, although Bulgarian troops now joined the Yugoslav Partisans and fought against the Germans until the end of hostilities. In Moscow, the Bulgarian Armistice was signed on October 28, 1944. It required that all Greek territory be evacuated, and that Bulgaria assume responsibility for the payment of reparations. As in the case of Rumania, there would be an Allied Control Commission under the "general direction of the Allied (Soviet) High Command." And as with Rumania, the "percentages" agreement between Churchill and Stalin on October 9, had given the U.S.S.R. the preponderant "say." Though the Russians received only 75 per cent of the "say" in Bulgaria, as against 90 per cent in Rumania, in practice this made little difference. The whole agreement reflected Churchill's lack of interest in these two Balkan states, and his belief that, to get his way in Greece, he must bargain them away.

The Communists Take Over

Stronger in number and in position than their Rumanian counterparts, the Bulgarian Communists moved with greater speed to dominate the country. They began in December 1944 what proved to be the severest purge of "war criminals" in all of Europe. Not only all politicians who had held office in wartime, but hundreds of innocent people whose only fault was opposition to Communism, suffered death and imprisonment. Political scores were settled under the convenient cover of eagerness to punish "fascists." By March 1945, the official figure of those executed was 2,138.

The Communists early began the "task" of splitting the other political parties with which they were ostensibly allied in the OF. The Agrarians were the first sufferers. Their party Secretary was Dr. Georgi M. Dimitrov, whose name was the same as that of the chief Communist, then still in Moscow. The Agrarian Dimitrov was known by the nickname "Gemeto," which we shall use here for convenience. Gemeto found himself blocked by the Communists in his efforts to organize the Agrarian Party units on the village level. He objected to the intimacy of the collaboration between his party and the Communists. He soon became the target of their wrath, resigned, and was succeeded by Nikola Petkov. Petkov's father, a Liberal prime minister, had been murdered in 1906. His brother, a Stamboliisky Agrarian, had been murdered in 1924. He himself had led the Agrarian wing of the OF resistance, and strongly favored intimate collaboration with the Communists. For the Communists, however, collaboration proved not to be enough. Elections, required by the Yalta Declaration of February 1945, were in the offing, and the Communists demanded a common OF list, with a prearranged ratio of Communists to other candidates which would give them a majority. They also demanded a single "anti-fascist" youth organization, which they would dominate, while Petkov wanted to maintain the Agrarian youth organization separate. Petkov would not surrender the identity of his party.

In May 1945, in fear for his life, Gemeto took refuge in the home of the American political representative, Maynard Barnes, who gave him asylum. Four months later, as a result of strenuous American efforts, the Bulgarian Government allowed Gemeto to leave for the United States. In May 1945, the Communists produced their own Agrarian collaborator, Alexander Obbov, who headed a pro-Communist splinter-group, which the Communists declared to be the true Agrarian Party. By packing the Agrarian Congress with Obbovites and Communists, they now ousted Petkov and took over the Agrarian newspaper. They arrested Petkov's private secretary, who committed suicide in prison. In August Petkov and his followers resigned from the government and the OF. Obbovites replaced them. The overwhelming majority of the Agrarian Party supported Petkov, the Obbovites representing nobody but themselves and their Communist masters. The Communists also split the Social Democrats in much the same way. Kosta Lulchev went into opposition, while Dimiter Neikov led those who collaborated with the Communists. The campaign for the elections continued amid mounting terror.

In these circumstances, the United States and Britain protested both to the Bulgarian Government and to Moscow, after the close of the Potsdam Conference. Under pressure from the West, the Russians secured a postponement of the elections from the scheduled date of August 26 to November 18, 1945. In the interim, Mark Ethridge's fact-finding mission for President Truman visited Sofia. It found that the OF was now allowing the opposition Agrarians and Social Democrats to print their newspapers, but not to have radio time. The threat of police terror hung over the opposition. So Petkov and his fellow opposition leaders decided not to put forward their tickets, and, like the Rumanian opposition, continued to put their hopes in Western support.

In the midst of the election campaign, Georgi Dimitrov arrived from Moscow (he had hitherto been directing affairs by telegram), and made it clear to the members of the Ethridge mission that all concessions were only a temporary tactic until the Western Allies should have signed the Peace Treaty with Bulgaria. Going on to Moscow in the hope of persuading Vyshinsky that the United States would recognize no Bulgarian government elected in an atmosphere of terror, Ethridge found Vyshinsky blandly repudiating all suggestions that either the Russians or the Bulgarian Communists were acting high-handedly. The American effort to postpone the elections a second time failed. They were held, with the opposition abstaining, and produced an eighty-six per cent majority for the government. Kolarov, Dimitrov's right-hand man, became President of the Sobranie.

The United States continued to press for the inclusion of "all democratic elements" in the Bulgarian Government. At the same time that Stalin consented to "broaden" the Rumanian Cabinet by including a National Peasant and National Liberal member (December 1945), he agreed to "advise" the Bulgarian Government to add "two truly representative members of two important political parties not then represented." Because elections had already been held in Bulgaria and not in Rumania, Stalin determined to handle the Bulgarian case alone. In January 1946, as a result of this, the OF began to negotiate with Petkov and Lulchev, whom it would have admitted in person to the cabinet, had they been willing.

These brave opposition leaders wanted to roll back the Communist tide. They demanded that the elections be annulled, and that the Communists give up the Ministries of Interior and Justice. Vyshinsky himself tried in vain to persuade Petkov and Lulchev to enter the government. The OF itself actually agreed to hold new elections, to give up the Ministry of Justice, and to install Agrarian and Social Democratic under-secretaries in the Ministry of Interior. But this agreement the Russians vetoed. Thus Stalin did not persuade the OF to add two opposition ministers to the government, as he was bound to do; instead, he prevented them from doing so.

By March 1946, the high-water mark of opposition success had been reached. The ebb now set in rapidly.

In the summer of 1946, the Communists moved against Zveno, so far permitted to remain a member of the OF. Under pressure, Velchev resigned from the Ministry of War, and accepted appointment as Minister to Switzerland. The life had departed from the movement. In September 1946, a plebiscite held after a propaganda campaign ended the monarchy by a huge majority. King Simeon was only a child, and Boris' failures were still fresh in the public mind. The young King went into exile with his mother, and with $20,000,000 compensation for the royal properties. In October, there followed elections for a "Grand" National Sobranie, to enact a new republican constitution. Though the opposition candidates were often arrested, they none the less polled twenty-two per cent of the vote, and there were ninety-two Petkov Agrarians and nine Lulchev Socialists in a Sobranie of 465 members. The rest were OF members, including 277 Communists.

Though he foresaw his fate, Petkov on the floor of the Sobranie did battle with the Communists for six months, denouncing their terrorist practices, goading Dimitrov himself, fighting for political decency. All that prevented the Communists from arresting him was the fact that the Peace Treaty with Bulgaria had not yet been ratified. The Communists arrested Petkov on the floor of the Sobranie on June 6, 1947. In August, they tried him before three Communist judges, accusing him of conspiring to commit a *coup d'état*. Refusing to allow defense witnesses to testify, and accepting much contradictory testimony, they sentenced him to death. His crime was not conspiracy, but merely parliamentary defiance of Communism. The American and British governments protested against the sentence, and asked that the Bulgarian Government suspend it, and permit the Allied Control Commission to review the case. The plea was refused.

On September 23, 1947, Petkov was hanged. Again the United States and Britain protested, the British using the term "judicial murder." Late in January 1948, Dimitrov, who had survived the 1933 Reichstag Fire Trial largely because of the volume of protests from the outside world, boasted that the efforts of the West to intervene had doomed Petkov. Not long after the execution, Dimitrov produced a spurious "confession," of a kind which the Bulgarian Communists monotonously forge after each of their political executions. The Petkov case was only the most sensational of the trials of opposition leaders, which took place during 1947 and 1948. Lulchev too was tried and imprisoned in July 1948.

In December 1947, the Sobranie adopted the new constitution drafted by the Communists and modeled on the Soviet Stalin Constitution of 1936. The Presidium of the National Assembly (nineteen members and a President) wielded the real power. The familiar State Planning Commission, State Control Commission, and Committee for Science, Art, and Culture all made their appearance. "People's Councils" (soviets) had local administrative responsibilities. The National Assembly would elect the Supreme Court and the People's Prosecutor, who appointed and dismissed all other prosecutors. The guarantee of civil liberties was the usual Communist mockery.

During these years, Bulgaria's foreign policy was profoundly effected by Tito's ambitions in the Balkans. He hoped to annex Pirin (Bulgarian) Macedonia to his own Macedonian Federal Republic (Vardar Macedonia) as the first step toward a federation with Bulgaria, which would enable him to dominate the Balkan peninsula. Many Bulgarian Communists feared that the Yugoslavs would swallow them up. Negotiations began in the fall of 1944, when the Yugoslavs proposed that, after the cession of Pirin, Bulgaria should become a seventh republic of Yugoslavia. The Bulgarians wanted to join not as one republic among seven but as a joint partner with all of Yugoslavia in a dual state. The Yugoslavs refused, maintaining that Bulgaria deserved no more prestige than Serbia or Montenegro. Early in 1945, Stalin decided the dispute in favor of Yugoslavia; but the British got wind of the arrangement, and stoutly opposed a Yugoslav-Bulgarian federation, although they would have endorsed one including Greece and Turkey also. Since this would have introduced anti-Communist regimes, the Russians were not interested.

The matter hung fire until late 1946, when Yugoslav pressure for the cession of Pirin began again. Although the Bulgarian Communist Party passed a resolution acceding, they did not publish it or do anything about the matter. Meanwhile, the outbreak of the second Communist-led Greek uprising in late 1946 gave the Bulgarians renewed hope of acquiring Greek territory. Eventually, in August 1947, Dimitrov and Tito announced at Bled the conclusion of an agreement which virtually dissolved the frontier between

Yugoslavia and Bulgaria, and envisaged a customs union. Pirin Macedonia was to have "free cultural development," and its inhabitants were to be "spiritually united with the brothers in Vardar (Yugoslav) Macedonia." This initiated a frenzied movement of Yugoslav Macedonian agents into Pirin, where they propagandized for Tito to their hearts' content, infuriating many Bulgarians. In November 1947, came Tito's visit to Sofia and the signing of a Treaty of Friendship.

Indeed, as Tito embarked on a triumphal tour of eastern European capitals, he and Dimitrov had never seemed closer. In January 1948, Dimitrov gave a press interview in Bucharest in the course of which he looked forward to the formation of a Balkan federation among the "people's democracies," a term which he took to include the future Communist Greece. This interview *Pravda* published, and three days later repudiated. Stalin summoned Bulgarians and Yugoslavs to Moscow (Tito absenting himself), and on February 10, 1948 scolded them both for proceeding toward their federation without Moscow's consent. Our knowledge of this occasion derives only from the account by Vladimir Dedijer, Tito's official biographer. It seems reasonable to accept the implication that Stalin was angry at Tito for his grandiose plans of a Balkan federation, and at Dimitrov for falling in with them.

During the spring of 1948 the anger swelled, as the Stalin-Tito correspondence prepared the way for the Cominform excommunication of the Yugoslavs. Though all the members of the Cominform acted with the Russians, the Yugoslavs declared that Dimitrov on April 19 secretly advised them to remain firm. Moreover, the day after the publication of the Cominform resolution, the Bulgarian Government sent a note saying that the action "in no way alters the existing friendly relations between" [1] the two countries. But this was the last note of friendship. Thereafter, the Bulgarians became as vituperative as the other Cominform states in denouncing Yugoslavia, and as vigorous in taking over anti-Yugoslav measures. They denounced Yugoslav activities in Pirin, expelled Yugoslav diplomats from Sofia, broke their economic agreement with Belgrade, sponsored anti-Tito Yugoslav Communist groups, and staged a regular series of "border incidents." Thus the Tito-Dimitrov

[1] *White Book on Aggressive Activities by the Governments of the USSR, Poland, Czechoslovakia, Hungary, Rumania, Bulgaria and Albania towards Yugoslavia* (Belgrade: Ministry of Foreign Affairs of the FPRY, 1951), p. 78.

friendship was broken by Stalin. Anti-Tito policies remained in force until after Stalin's death in March 1953.

Political Developments Since Mid-1948

Within the Communist parties of Eastern Europe, there were individuals who had come to resent Stalin's insistence on totally controlling their countries. In the sense that "Titoism" means anti-Soviet Communism, Titoites were everywhere. Moreover, the new heresy of "Titoism" provided a convenient label for the Communists to pin on anybody they wished to purge; the truth of the charge did not matter. In Bulgaria, the case of Traicho Kostov occupied much of the year 1949.

Kostov had been a member of the Bulgarian Politburo since 1935. The police had often interrogated him, and he had once jumped out a prison window and crippled his back rather than run the risk of answering questions under torture. He had played a leading role in the resistance, and had emerged after the war as Vice-Premier and boss of the national economy. Kostov, Dobri Terpeshev, and Anton Yugov were the three leading Bulgarian Communists after the two "Muscovites," Dimitrov and Kolarov, both of whom were aging. Kostov was a leading candidate for the succession. It now seems clear that his chief rival was the virtually unknown Vulko Chervenkov, Dimitrov's brother-in-law, who had for years served as his faithful bodyguard in Moscow, and whom nobody thought of as having any brains. When Kostov showed his bitterness at Soviet economic penetration of Bulgaria, he damned himself as a "Titoite." In March 1949, denounced for economic nationalism by Kolarov, Kostov began his long road toward disgrace and death.

Expelled from the Politburo and demoted to the Directorship of the National Library, charged in May with wanting to keep economic data secret from the U.S.S.R., provided in June with a fake Trotskyist and anti-Dimitrov past and expelled from the party, he was tried in December, on an indictment containing many obvious absurdities, including a plot with Tito to murder Dimitrov. The American Minister to Bulgaria, Donald Reed Heath, so the charges said, had assured Kostov that the Yugoslavs would transmit American orders to the Bulgarians. The State Department officially declared that Mr. Heath had never had any interview with Kostov.

Kostov admitted "nationalist deviation in relation to the Soviet

Union." But on the witness stand he boldly denied the fake past with which he was being equipped. He was hustled off the stand, but not before the courtroom had seen a man brave enough to withstand everything his torturers could do. He was sentenced to death and executed on December 14, 1949. Two days later the regime published one of its favorite "confessions," obviously a fake. Both the Soviet and Bulgarian press gibed at Kostov's hunched back, acquired in resisting the police for the benefit of the men who would eventually kill him.

Before the preparation of the Kostov indictment, Dimitrov died in Moscow on July 2, 1949. The U.S.S.R. loaned the Bulgarians Lenin's official embalmer, and the canonized leader was buried in a shrine erected at top speed in the chief square of Sofia. Kolarov became Premier, and Chervenkov Vice-Premier. Kostov's actual trial was preceded by a large-scale purge of politicians and army leaders. When the trial was over, Chervenkov turned on Yugov and Terpeshev. As Minister of the Interior, Yugov should have discovered Kostov's treachery. As chief of the Planning Commission, Terpeshev knew of it but had not spoken up. Early in 1950, these two lost their important posts, and were demoted. But neither was yet clearly marked for oblivion, because the degree of Moscow's support for Chervenkov remained unknown. When Kolarov died, on January 21, 1950, Chervenkov succeeded him as Premier. He was faced at once by a crisis in relations with the United States.

After the Kostov trial, the Bulgarian Government demanded that Washington recall Mr. Heath. The United States replied that the Bulgarians must withdraw this demand or diplomatic relations would be severed. On February 20, Washington did break relations, which as of January 1956 had not been renewed. The Bulgarian Government had arrested for espionage five Bulgarians, two of whom had been employees of the American Legation. One of them, Michael Shipkov, had long ago been tortured into signing a confession that he had committed espionage for the United States. But he had then prepared an affidavit for Mr. Heath describing his treatment by the Bulgarian police. So long as there was a chance that Shipkov might be released, the United States kept the affidavit secret. But after his trial had opened in early March 1950, Washington published it, under the title *Forced Confession*. It provided us with further knowledge of Communist brutality and with an example of great human courage. Shipkov received a fifteen-year sentence; others were sentenced to death or tortured to death in jail. In its official notification of the severance of relations, the State Department put much of the blame directly on the U.S.S.R., which was striving to cut Bulgaria off from the outside world.

During 1949, elections had been held in May for the 45,000 members of the local "people's councils," the press announcing that the ballots (single list, of course) would be valid even if anti-Communist insults were scrawled on them. The last two political parties —Zveno and the small Radical Party—dissolved, while the Obbovite Agrarians announced that they were no longer interested in obtaining power for themselves, but were solely devoted to the OF. In September 1949, after the Sobranie had re-districted Bulgaria, it was dissolved, and in December new elections were held. All the deputies in the new Sobranie were Communists or their collaborators. When elections were held again in December 1953, the same results were of course obtained. Similarly, though there was a good deal of public complaining about their inefficiency, the "people's councils" had become a functioning part of the machinery, and new elections were held for them in December 1952.

Unlike Rumania, Bulgaria had only one important minority: the Turkish, numbering about 750,000 in 1950, or about ten per cent of the population, mostly peasants and mostly docile. After they had seized power in Bulgaria, the Communists initially discouraged emigration to Turkey, and began to apply Soviet nationality policies toward their Turkish population. There was still in effect, however, a Turko-Bulgarian treaty of 1925 obligating each country to allow nationals of the other to migrate freely, taking with them all movable property. In 1950, the Bulgarian Government began to permit emigration; and in August suddenly announced to the Turkish Government that more than 250,000 Turks wanted to leave Bulgaria. The Bulgarians complained at the unwillingness of the Turkish authorities to issue entry permits, and demanded that Turkey accept the whole 250,000 within three months. The Turks, reluctant to strain their economy so unexpectedly, and needing time to check on Communist agents planted among the immigrants, closed their frontier. The Bulgarians proceeded to seize their own Turkish villagers, uproot them by the thousands from their homes, and drive them across the frontier. The wretched refugees, deprived of their property, milled about in freezing weather in a kind of no-man's land.

Suddenly, on December 2, 1950, the Bulgarians consented to proceed in orderly fashion. They would not issue exit permits until the Turks had granted entry permits. And they promised to let the refugees have their property, as provided by treaty. The abrupt change of front was no doubt due to the Turkish intention of bringing the whole question before the United Nations. It seems likely that the Soviet Union did not care to have the world examine the evidence that its satellite was violating human rights and repudiating loudly proclaimed nationality policies.

The reason for the whole episode was doubtless the Communists' wish to seize the land of the Turkish peasants in question, which lay in the Dobrudja, where major reclamation and collectivization schemes were going forward. After the question was settled peacefully, about 220,000 Turks were accepted by Turkey. Bulgarian and Russian propaganda to the Turks of Central Asia tried to gloss over the brutality of the past, and the Bulgarian government resumed its Soviet-type minority policy, with Turkish schools, theaters, and participation in the national life receiving encouragement and publicity. The Ankara government again closed the frontier in late 1951, however, alleging that the Bulgarians had tried to smuggle gypsies into Turkey.

In Bulgaria, the instruments of control were the familiar ones; the "Dimitrov People's Youth Union" corresponded to the Komsomol, and the "Dimitrov Organization of Pioneers—Little Septembrists" to the Pioneers. The "Voluntary Organization for Collaboration with the Defense Forces" (DOSO) was a typical paramilitary outfit. Restricted by treaty to 85,000 men, the army was illegally built up to a force perhaps three times as big. Civil defense organizations assisted. The police governed daily life, as everywhere in the Soviet orbit. The Russians themselves made no attempt to conceal their omnipresence. A Russian could be naturalized a Bulgarian citizen without delay. The restrictions governing Bulgarians on travel, on registering, on size of domicile, on staying in one's job were specifically declared not to apply to Russians. Their salaries from the Bulgarian treasury were said to average about four times as much as those of Bulgarians doing comparable work. They had a special school in Sofia for their children. They lived in Bulgaria as colonial administrators.

Within the party, feuds continued to rage. Even the Cominform organ declared that the Bulgarian comrades had created an intolerable atmosphere. Though Yugov and Terpeshev were demoted and humiliated, they made a comeback beginning in the summer of 1952. Ministries were subdivided and began to proliferate during 1951 and 1952. Many of the individual purges, such as that of Minister of Agriculture Titko Chernokolev in June 1951, were connected with the continuing economic crisis. The Bulgarian Assembly in March 1953 passed a brutal law providing not only that all those who had left the country without permission were traitors punishable by death, but also that all relatives of such persons were subject to loss of civil rights and property, and might be sent to forced labor. Soon afterward, Stalin died, and, in keeping with the milder measures adopted in the U.S.S.R., this law was first modified and then repealed in November 1953. The escaper could now be sentenced to no more than five years' imprisonment, and his family was not subject to punishment.

The Bulgarian "new course" brought with it the consolidation of ministries. In February–March 1954, the Sixth Party Congress formally adopted "collective" leadership on the new Moscow pattern. Like Malenkov and Gheorghiu-Dej, Chervenkov remained Premier, but lost his Secretary-Generalship of the Party, and the post was abolished. Todor Zhivkov became the chief of the three Secretaries to the Party Central Committee. Chervenkov announced that the party had a total of 455,251 members, of whom 87,109 were candidate members. Only thirty-four per cent were workers. It was maintaining a large network of political schools, with 400,000 students. Despite its achievements, it had, he said, been guilty of over-ruthless treatment of former political enemies, and "bureaucratism," "formalism," "careerism," and greed.

In foreign relations during these years, we should note especially those with Greece. After Tito's closure of the Yuoslav frontier and the victories of the Greek Army ended the Greek Communist uprising in 1949, Bulgarian relations with Greece continued hostile, and were marked in the summer of 1952 by a frontier incident on a small island in the Maritsa (Evros), which might have led to serious trouble, had not the sage counsel of the United Nations prevailed. After the Yugoslav-Greek-Turkish pact had been concluded in February 1953, Bulgaria, conscious of the threat presented, moved slowly toward a reconciliation with Greece.

As a feeble effort at reconciliation with the United States, Chervenkov even said on September 9, 1953, that he saw no reason why diplomatic relations had been broken. Washington merely "noted with interest" his remarks, and reaffirmed the traditional American friendship for the Bulgarian people. With Greece, a trade agreement and an agreement on the Maritsa frontier were signed in December 1953, contributing to the lessening of tension. But talks looking toward the reopening of diplomatic relations bogged down in 1954 over the question of reparations owed by Bulgaria to Greece. Though ambassadors were not yet exchanged between the countries, chargés d'affaires reappeared in both capitals.

The Bulgarian Economy

By far the least damaged by war of all the Balkan countries, Bulgaria also found the Soviet occupiers far less rapacious than did Rumania. Bulgaria had to pay the expenses of Soviet occupying forces until the end of 1947, but owed the U.S.S.R. no reparations. Of the $75,000,000 reparations owed to Yugoslavia and Greece, the Yugoslavs remitted $25,000,000 as a "brotherly" gesture. The droughts of the postwar years were serious, but the Bulgarian economy did not have to face any serious problem of recovery. The Communist planners thus got a head start in transforming the economic system.

In 1947, they issued a preliminary two-year plan, and in December 1948, announcing that it had been completed, adopted the first Five Year Plan, for the years 1949–1953. In May 1953, after applying intense pressure, the government announced that the Five Year Plan had been completed in four years (by the end of 1952), and that a second Five Year Plan was already under way. But this was not published until the Sixth Party Congress in March 1954. Since it covered the years 1953–1957, it had officially been in effect for more than a year.

As everywhere else in the Soviet empire, the planners put their emphasis on industry, and within industry on heavy producers' goods. In the two-year plan, the ratio of the value of industrial to agricultural production was to rise from 20:80 to 30:70. This achieved, the first Five Year Plan called for 45:55.

The ratio of the value of heavy and light industry was correspondingly 24:76 in 1939, 30:70 at the end of the two year plan, and was to reach 45:55 in 1953. Of a total investment in the two-year plan of fifty-five billion leva, forty-five per cent was earmarked for industry and mining, fifteen for transport and communications, twenty-eight for building and public services, and six for agriculture. Similar proportions prevailed in the investment figures for the first Five Year Plan. The second Plan, however, adopted after the "new course," more than doubled the investment in agriculture; but industrial investment was also to be doubled. These were grandiose schemes, incommensurate with Bulgarian resources, and capable of fulfillment only with assistance from the U.S.S.R. and by depressing the already low Bulgarian standard of living. Capital, raw materials, and technical skill were all in short supply. To industrialize Bulgaria, the doctrinaire Communists determined also to collectivize agriculture.

In the first years after the war, the Communist authorities avoided the use of the word "collective," and refrained from embarking on an all-out drive to collectivize by force. When the two-year plan was published early in 1947, there were 465 "labor co-operative farms," with 40,000 families and 150,000 hectares. There were thirty Machine Tractor Stations in 1947. The following figures from various official Bulgarian announcements show the progress of collectivization: October 1948, 714 collectives, 49,000 families, 270,000 hectares; October 1949, 1605 collectives, 147,191 families, 548,016 hectares; May 1950, 1615 collectives, 161,000 families, 550,800 hectares. So far, the movement had been gradual, and it was clear that land shortage was plaguing the Communists, as the number of families was rising much faster than the number of hectares. Party fanatics were disappointed with the slow advance, but they need not have worried.

An all-out drive got under way in May 1950. By the middle of October the figure was 2,566 collectives, 570,000 families, and 1,994,600 hectares. From 11 per cent of the arable land and 14 per cent of the peasant population, the Communists had collectivized approximately 41 per cent of the land and 46.5 per cent of the peasantry in five short months. Chervenkov's own report to a plenary session of the Central Committee in October 1950 revealed that high-ranking party members had personally helped coerce the peasants into delivering their grain, and admitted that the government had often cheated the peasant in collecting it. It was seldom that a Communist inadvertently revealed the deep measure of human suffering behind the statistics.

As the forced-draft collectivization continued into 1951, came reports of peasants slaughtering their livestock rather than surrender ownership, just as they had done in the U.S.S.R. in the early 1930's during Stalin's frenzied collectivization drive. The Bulgarian authorities steadily kept up the absurd pretense that the whole movement was voluntary, until peasant efforts to withdraw forced a decree forbidding them to take their land out with them. The Soviet "brigade" system of organizing farm labor was introduced. Although the pace slackened, the drive went on.

By the end of 1953, the regime was claiming 2,800 collectives, with 553,000 families and 2,512,500 hectares, or about sixty per cent of the arable land. The slight drop in the number of families probably reflected withdrawals. The U.S.S.R. delivered the necessary tractors to Bulgaria in March 1954; the figure was 15,302 in 150 Machine Tractor Stations. While the figures might be questioned, the gross fact was clear: Bulgaria had far outstripped any other satellite in collectivization. Though sixty per cent of the grain and seventy per cent of the cash crops were in the "socialist sector," only a little over twenty per cent of the cattle had been collectivized. The second Five Year Plan recognized the cattle shortage in its great emphasis on livestock.

The Bulgarian "new course," beginning in the fall of 1953, involved lesser concessions to the peasantry than the Rumanian. Collectives obtained a remission of overdue income taxes, and various rates on insurance and drainage charges were cut. Collectives benefited greatly by cuts in compulsory delivery quotas, but the private peasant's obligation increased. In Rumania, Gheorghiu-Dej had to conciliate the private peasant, because collectivization was retarded; but Chervenkov continued to drive him toward the kolkhoz.

Electrification formed a major item in Bulgarian economic planning, to remedy the shortages of fuel and take advantage of available waterpower. Much was done in the Dobrudja reclamation project, and large dams were built elsewhere in the country: the Stalin dam over the Iskar above Sofia provided power for the capital; the Studena dam over the Struma near Pernik (now Dimitrovo) provided power for a new iron and steel center. Total electric power rose toward, if not to, the Five Year Plan's 1,800,000,000 kilowatt-hours goal. Official figures claimed a tripling of coal production over 1939 to 7,410,000 tons, probably mostly lignite, Dimitrovo (Pernik) became an iron and steel center, producing for the first time Bulgarian finished goods. A new chemical industry and cement production center rose at the new town of Dimitrovgrad in the Maritsa valley. Light industry also advanced, with 8,000,000 square meters of cotton cloth claimed for 1951, and a tripling of sugar production, enabling a substantial advance in the important food-processing industry. A new railway line connected Sofia with Varna (Stalin) and Burgas. In contrast to Rumania, the Soviet joint company was relatively unimportant in Bulgaria, although there were five, controlling civil aviation, shipyards, ores, uranium, and industrial construction. A little-developed agricultural country was proceeding at top speed toward industrialization, benefited by Soviet deliveries.

Like Rumania but far less severely, Bulgaria in these years experienced inflation and a "currency reform." In May 1952 old leva were called in to be exchanged at rates varying from one to 100 for individuals to 1.25 for state enterprises. Wages and prices were divided by twenty-five. The reform wiped out three quarters of the cash in circulation, and half to three quarters of the savings. Rationing was abolished, price cuts of ten to fifty per cent announced, and some wages, salaries, and pensions raised. The leva was pegged at 1.7 to the ruble.

The official budget figures showed an excess of income over expenditure in every year, and a drop in both in 1954, reflecting the new course. More and more, the turnover tax provided the revenue (seventy-six per cent in 1954). Graduated income taxes sharply penalizing "kulaks," who employed hired labor, helped provide the rest. State loan subscriptions (four since the war), mingling the features of a bond issue and a state lottery, raised large sums by virtually forcing the citizen to invest his savings. There were four series of price cuts after the currency reform of 1952, but these were always accompanied by measures to reduce purchasing power by increasing deductions from wages for "voluntary" savings accounts. From the inadequate data available, the observer could conclude that the individual Bulgarian, though living in a police state, and at a standard of living which would seem intolerably low in any Western country, was at least better off than the individual Rumanian.

Between eighty and ninety-five per cent of Bulgarian foreign trade was carried on with the Eastern bloc. Immediately after the war, the Russians bought 5,000 kilograms of Bulgarian rose oil at less than a third of world prices, and sold it in the world market at a profit of almost half a million dollars, a large sum in hard currency for a poor country to lose. It was this sort of treatment which led Kostov and those like him to complain. Bulgarian exports were usually agricultural products. During the drought years, food had to be imported. It is interesting to note, however, a trade agreement with India, which called for Bulgarian exports of machinery.

Religion, Education, Culture

Beginning at the end of 1947, the Bulgarian Communists moved to take control of the Orthodox Church. In September 1948, they forced the resignation of Exarch Stefan, hitherto apparently *persona grata* to the regime. His successor, Mihail, was a government appointee. One anti-Communist archbishop was murdered at the door of his church. Church property was confiscated, schools taken over, theological seminaries closed except for a single school in Plovdiv, and religious publications censored. The Ministry of Health took over all ecclesiastical welfare organizations. The government founded its own "union" of Orthodox priests, which held a Congress in 1948 and approved its actions. The union issued its own newspaper, and its chairman was in charge of propaganda to the Orthodox clergy. In March 1949 the regime took over all church buildings, forbade the clergy to maintain any connection abroad, and established prison sentences for any priest who criticized the government. The law was called, perhaps without intentional irony, "Law on the Freedom of Religion."

In May 1953 came a startling step: the election, by a National Church Congress, of Metropolitan Cyril of Sofia to be Bulgarian Patriarch, the first since 1395. The action enabled Chervenkov to pose as the friend of the church, and also as an apostle of peace. This was because the Bulgarian Church had always before taken the stand that there could be no Bulgarian Patriarch until "all Bulgarians" (meaning Macedonians) were Bulgarian subjects. In a sense perfectly understood in the Balkans, the creation of a Bulgarian Patriarch was, therefore, in itself a kind of renunciation of Macedonian territorial claims. Cyril himself, despite a Western education, and a reputation for being an anti-Communist, had recently been attending Soviet-sponsored "peace congresses," and had clearly reached an understanding with the Communists.

Because there were only about 60,000 Catholics in Bulgaria—less than one per cent of the population—the regime did not undertake to found a "national" church. It did, however, try to discredit the Roman church. In the autumn of 1952 it brought to trial Bishop

Eugene Bossilkov, twenty-seven priests—about one quarter of the Bulgarian hierarchy—and twelve laymen on charges of espionage and conspiracy. The Bishop and three priests were condemned to death, and the others to prison sentences. The regime gave full publicity to the proceedings, and enlisted its puppet clerics of other faiths to join in condemning the Catholics. The Vatican properly described the whole affair as "premeditated murder."

The Protestants were even fewer: only about 20,000, Congregational, Methodist, Baptist, and Pentecostal. But they had traditionally cherished intimate relations with Americans and Englishmen. As early as mid-1948, the regime arrested twenty pastors, and in February 1949 tried fifteen of them on charges ranging from black-market dealings to espionage. The police had extracted "confessions" from them during the long months in prison. The confessions were, as usual, full of absurdities. The leaders of the four sects received life sentences, and the others shorter prison terms. The Muslim minority suffered no religious persecution, but, as we have seen, the Turks suffered for political and economic reasons.

The Bulgarian press, Bulgarian education, and cultural life presented a similar picture to that in other satellites. *Rabotnichesko Delo* (The Worker's Action) corresponded to *Pravda,* and the provincial and specialized journals faithfully aped their Soviet originals. Russian language study began in kindergarten and continued to the grave. The "University City" in Sofia saw two of eight planned five-story buildings completed by 1954. A new institute for librarians and a special Turkish language section were innovations. Soviet translations flooded the book-market. The Bulgarian Academy proudly hailed the achievements of its Communist president, Dr. Methody Popov, who died in 1954, after years devoted to the artificial stimulation of seeds. If the claims of increased yields obtained with seed treated by his methods bore any relation to the truth, it was surprising that Bulgarian agriculture had not advanced further. Scholarly controversy, Communist style, raged, as Professor Romansky was denounced for anti-Marxist definitions in his new dictionary, and had to be rescued by Chervenkov himself. The state prize in sculpture went to the artist who had produced a statue called "The Girl of Dimitrovgrad," a muscular lady indeed, with a fierce proletarian grin. Realism and representationalism, Stalin style, dominated the pictorial arts. Literature was hortatory and didactic. Critics suffered as they tried to have a definite opinion about a work of art, but neither to praise it nor condemn it, for fear of incurring the party's displeasure. Bulgarian cultural life, like all other aspects of the national existence, was tightly compressed into a strait-jacket made in Moscow.

Chapter 12

Albania

STAVRO SKENDI

Before Mussolini's Invasion

ON APRIL 7, 1939, Mussolini's armies invaded Albania. The occupation aroused little reaction among the other nations. Yugoslavia accepted it as a *fait accompli* and Greece, not wishing to incur the Italian dictator's displeasure, made no move. Though the equilibrium in the Mediterranean had been upset, Neville Chamberlain made no vigorous protest. Only the United States raised her voice. In a statement on April 8, Secretary Hull denounced the attack as a "forcible and violent invasion" which constituted "unquestionably an additional threat to peace."

American support had greatly contributed, after World War I, to the creation of the Albanian state. At the Paris Peace Conference of 1919, Albania's neighbors endeavored to partition her territories. Greece and Italy had even concluded a secret understanding (Tittoni-Venizelos) for that purpose. Greece desired southern Albania, which she calls Northern Epirus. It was the opposition of President Wilson, as representative of the United States Government, that saved Albania from dismemberment.

Although in December 1920 Albania was admitted to membership in the League of Nations, she was still unrecognized by the Great Powers and her frontiers were not yet internationally settled. Only in November 1921 did the Conference of Ambassadors take the long-awaited decision in this matter. The 1913 boundaries of Albania were confirmed, with the exception of a few small adaptations in the north. But the final delimitation with reference to Yugoslavia did not take place until 1925, and as late as 1926 with Greece.

While Albanians were united in their determination to defend their territorial integrity, there was a conflict over political power going on in Tirana. In 1921 Albania's first political parties appeared in Parliament, the Popular and the Progressive. Their labels were derived from Western terminology but neither was a political party in the Western sense of the word. The Popularists were known as the party of reform; the Progressives as that favoring feudal tenure. At times the struggle between them was extremely bitter.

In the early 1920's foreign interests began to appear, when oil companies applied for concessions in the country. Especially active were the British, backing the Anglo-Persian Company. As there was an American oil group, Sinclair and Standard Oil, the American Government took an interest in the matter, but there was no direct intervention on its part. The American companies had already acquired an advantageous position. Apart from proposing terms more favorable than those offered by their competitors, concessions to them would not entail interference, as the United States had no political interests in Albania. In fact, the support of the American group was taken up by patriotic deputies, headed by Luigj Gurakuqi. As the rivalry between the parties, and their factions, continued—one government succeeding the other—the discussions on the oil concessions were protracted. When they were finally granted, the American companies withdrew.

In the struggle for power Zog emerged as the strong man. On June 10, 1924, however, the government of which he was the backbone was overthrown by a revolution which brought Bishop Noli to power. Zog fled to Yugoslavia. But the Bishop Premier was far too radical to command the support of the disparate coalition which had ousted Zog. Furthermore, he overlooked the fact that popular support for his radical reforms was almost totally lacking in Albania. In the meantime, Zog managed to secure foreign backing. Provided with forces by the Yugoslav General Staff, including some of General Wrangel's White Russians, and joined by discontented Albanians, he re-entered Tirana on December 24, 1924. Bishop Noli fled to Italy.

During the following years (1925–1939), Zog ruled the country as a personal dictator, first as President of the Albanian Republic and from 1928 as King of Albania. Zog's successes had been made possible by the ties established with Italy, whose assistance he needed. This entailed a gradual yielding to Italian penetration, as evidenced by a series of agreements of a political, military, and economic character. Since public opinion considered concessions to Italy as an impairment of national sovereignty, Zog sought to call a halt to them. In 1932 he rejected an Italian proposal for a customs union and dismissed some military advisers. At the same time he endeavored to improve relations with his Balkan neighbors, concluding trade agreements with Greece and Yugoslavia.

An important step in education was then taken. Up to this time, education in Albania had not been uniform and there were several private schools in existence. On April 22, 1933, however, the nationalization of education and the suppression of private schools were decreed. The measure was mainly directed against the Italians, who ran a number of schools in the country. But it also affected the few American institutions which had no political aims and had been created in order to come to the assistance of the Albanian people. The school in Korça, directed by Rev. Phineas B. Kennedy, was closed. A similar fate befell the important *Shkolla Teknike* (Vocational School) of Tirana, founded in 1921 by The American Junior Red Cross. The only American school which was permitted to function, under a new arrangement, was the Albanian-American Agricultural School of Kavaja, near Durazzo, founded in the 1920's by private American funds on lands conceded by the Albanian Government. In 1931, through an agreement with the Albanian Government, the Near East Foundation of New York took over the school. While the Albanian people ardently supported the nationalization law, they were also appreciative of the services rendered by the American schools and were sorry to see them virtually disappear.

There were no universities in prewar Albania. Students went abroad in pursuit of higher learning. Although the regime later began to fear Western democratic ideas, it could not prevent their propagation and the formation of an intelligentsia.

Zog's policy toward Italy and his autocratic rule aroused widespread discontent. In 1932 a plot against the regime was uncovered, and in 1935 the general dissatisfaction was manifested in an insurrection at Fier. The insurrection, although abortive, impelled the King to change his policy and tactics. In 1935 he appointed a new government, composed mainly of younger educated persons, and for a time Albania seemed to be oriented toward Western liberalism. But in less than one year Zog dismissed the new government, once more turning the administration over to the "old guard." By that time relations with Italy had been improved and further concessions had been made.

During the period 1920–1939 the United States Government had concluded with Albania a number of agreements dealing with such subjects as arbitration and conciliation, nationalization, extradition, and most - favored - nation treatment. American policy toward Albania was in these years that of a friendly and disinterested nation.

Axis Occupation and Resistance Movements

When King Zog was married in April 1938, the Italian Foreign Minister, Count Ciano, acted as best man. On his return to Italy, however, he proposed to Mussolini the annexation of Albania; the move would consummate Italian control over the country and Ciano thought it would be easy because of "the rupture between the court and the people, which time deepens and does not heal."

On February 6, 1939, Mussolini and Ciano decided to occupy Albania. While preparations for the invasion were in process, discussions were carried on between Rome and Tirana about a treaty which, according to Ciano, "formally and substantially violates the independence and sovereignty of Albania." On March 31 it became apparent that Zog would refuse to sign such a treaty. A week later, Fascist warships began bombarding the coast and, despite heroic resistance, Italian troops made landings at several points. Meanwhile King Zog had left the country.

Rome moved fast to put into effect its plans for the "new order" in Albania. While the occupation was still in progress, Count Ciano flew to Tirana and there set up an administrative committee under Xhafer Ypi, former Prime Minister and Inspector General of King Zog's court. On April 12, 1939, the Albanian national assembly directed Shefqet Vërlaci, the deposed King's opponent, to form a new government. At the same time the Assembly abolished the constitution of 1928 and offered the crown to the Italian monarch, Victor Emmanuel III. Throughout Albania, however, there was a considerable opposition to a personal union with Italy; it was feared that union would signify the end of Albanian independence. The foundations of the socio-political "new order" were laid on April 21, 1939, when the Albanian Fascist Party was formed. More than a month later the Albanian Army was incorporated into that of

Italy, and a new constitution was promulgated, vesting all legislative and executive power in the King, who was assisted by a Fascist corporative council. Since the Tirana government was responsible to the lieutenancy, which in turn was answerable to Rome, it therefore existed in name only. On June 3, 1939, Italy took over Albania's foreign representation. This was followed by a guarantee of equality in civil and political rights between Italians and Albanians. Italian colonizers began to enter the country, and Italian officials assumed the role of colonial administrators. Albania's "personal union" with Italy was hardly distinguishable from outright annexation.

Such a situation was ill-borne by the Albanian population, particularly by its youth, who strongly resented Italian Fascism. It provided a favorable ground for a resistance movement, and the Communists were not slow to make use of it. Before the Italian invasion, there were but few Communist groups in Albania, of which the most important was the group of Korça. They were all extremely small groups and frequently worked at cross purposes. Their contacts with Communist elements outside the country were tenuous. However, some months after the attack on Russia by Nazi Germany two emissaries of Tito, Miladin Popović and Dušan Mugoša, arrived at Tirana. They were entrusted with the task of forming the Albanian Communist Party. Carrying the prestige of a party recognized by Moscow, they succeeded in uniting almost all the Communist groups and in forming the Communist Party (November 8, 1941). They also chose the members of the Central Committee, among whom was Enver Hoxha.

It was obvious that the new party had to be dependent on the Yugoslav Communist Party. In reality it was its branch. When the Yugoslav Central Committee advised the Comintern of the formation of the Albanian Communist Party and asked for instructions, it was Tito who transmitted the reply to the Albanian Communists.

Following its creation, the Albanian Communist Party issued several proclamations. It also took immediate steps for the constitution of cells and the strengthening of its ranks with new forces among the workers and peasants. From the outset it worked for the ideological and political education of its cadres on the basis of Marxist-Leninist theory. It also set as one of its aims to develop devotion to the U.S.S.R. and popularize her role as a vanguard in the fight against Fascism. It strove to prepare the people through sabotage, demonstrations, strikes, actions, etc., both politically and militarily, for an armed insurrection.

Having established themselves as a party, the Communists then needed popular support. As the term "Communist" was undesirable, they resorted to a political stratagem. On September 16, 1942, they organized a conference at Peza, a village near Tirana, to which were invited Communists, non-Communists generally favorably disposed toward them, and some nationalists. Their aim was to represent the conference as a union of nationalists and Communists. Although the nationalists at the conference refused to sign the resolution which proclaimed the National Liberation Movement (later called the National Liberation Front), the Communists told the people that the union between them and the nationalists had been "cemented," and that they would fight the invader together. In this way the National Liberation Movement could serve as a cover name for Communism.

Though the nationalists had begun to be apprehensive of the growing strength of the Communists, it was only after the Peza Conference that *Balli Kombëtar* (National Front) emerged under the leadership of Midhat Frashëri, a veteran democratic patriot and writer. The following of the National Front was recruited from all ranks except the Communists, and its leaders enjoyed considerable prestige as patriots.

Although both resistance organizations had been active in attacking the Italian forces, the Communists were more successful in creating effective propaganda for their actions. For a time there was silence on the part of the Allies with respect to Albania. It was broken by the United States. On December 10, 1942, Secretary Hull declared: "The Government of the United States is not unmindful of the continued resistance of the Albanian people to the Italian forces of occupation. The effort of the various guerrilla bands operating against the common enemy in Albania is admired and appreciated. The Government and the people of the United States look forward to the day when effective military assistance can be given these brave men to drive the invader from their homes." Reiterating that America "has never recognized the annexation of Albania by the Italian crown," Secretary Hull made known her future policy, based on the Atlantic Charter, declaring that the American people "respect the right of all peoples to choose the form of government under which they will live; and they wish to see sovereign rights and self-government restored to those who have been forcibly deprived of them." The restoration of free Albania was inherent in that statement of principle.

Cordell Hull's statement raised the morale of the Albanian people who were fighting against the invader; it also gave great concern to the collaborationists. But when the statement by the British Foreign Minister, Anthony Eden, followed, it threw the Albanian people into a confusion. Substantially the same as that of the American Secretary of State, Eden's declaration added the reservation that the frontiers of the Albanian state after the war would have to be considered at the peace settlement, if direct agreement between Albania and her neighbors should fail. This was interpreted by the Albanians as a renewal of the Greek claims to southern Albania, especially since, during and after the Italo-Greek war, the Greeks made no secret of their demands. Molotov also expressed the sympathy of the Soviet Government with the struggle of the Albanian patriots against the Italian forces and its wish to see Albania restored to independence. The Albanian Communists gave his statement the greatest publicity.

When the Allies landed in Sicily a great attempt was made at collaboration between the National Front and the National Liberation Front (the camouflage of the Communist Party). This effort was made because of pressure on the part of public opinion, pressure exerted by the British military mission, which had arrived a few months before, and the possibility of an Allied landing in Albania. On August 2, 1943, representatives of both organizations met at Mukaj, a village near Tirana. After compromises on both sides, the two parties agreed on unity of action and on the formation of a common committee, which corresponded to a revolutionary government, called the "Committee of National Salvation," to direct the fight. But the agreement of Mukaj remained a mere document; the Yugoslav emissaries, the real "bosses" of the Albanian Communist Party, rejected it.

The hostility between the Communists and the National Front was growing day by day. It reached its peak during the occupation of Albania by the Germans, after Mussolini's fall. Nazi Germany decided on a policy of political conciliation. She recognized Albanian independence and neutrality, and allowed the formation of a parliament and the institution of a regency council. She also favored an ethnic Albania. Though mostly lip-service, this lenient

German policy attracted several good nationalists. In October 1943 the Communists seized the opportunity to launch the civil war and to brand their opponents as traitors. Formerly they had attacked the Axis' armies near villages so that the Italians and the Germans would destroy them as reprisals, forcing the destitute peasants to join the Communist ranks. Now the ruin of every village burned by the Germans was attributed to the National Front. Later the Communists attacked the Legality organization, which was founded in November 1943, and proclaimed loyalty to King Zog. Civil war suited the Germans well, for it reduced the pressure on their troops.

While the Germans were evacuating Albania, Churchill and Stalin met in Moscow and decided on the fate of the Balkan States. It was the secret understanding of October 9, 1944, between the two statesmen on England's and the Soviet Union's percentage of interests in the various Balkan countries. Albania was not mentioned. Apparently Churchill was reluctant to include her because of the Greek claims to Northern Epirus. Stalin, on the other hand, seems to have considered her within the sphere of Yugoslavia, whose Communist Party held under control the Albanian National Liberation Front, which was now marching toward victory. Anything valid for Tito would also be valid for Hoxha's Albania. For the United States the Churchill-Stalin agreement had no binding value. Cordell Hull had repeatedly made it clear, in exchange of views with the British Government, that the United States would not support spheres of influence.[1]

In the last stage of the fighting, the Communists, confident of their ability to seize power, met at Berat and proclaimed a provisional government. The State Department declared on November 15, 1944 that there were two or three resistance groups now fighting in Albania but that the U.S. Government had not recognized any single one as an Albanian authority. Emphasizing the traditional American friendship toward the Albanian people and the desire that their full independence be achieved, the statement added: "We expect that in laying the foundations for their regained independence these sturdy people will be guided by a spirit of mutual trust, tolerance, and cooperation in working out their problems."

[1] Cf. W. S. Churchill, *Triumph and Tragedy,* Vol. VI of *The Second World War* (Boston, 1953), pp. 72–81, 226–235; also C. Hull, *The Memoirs of Cordell Hull* (New York, 1948), II, pp. 1451–1459.

It was a belated move. *Balli Kombëtar* and the Legality organization had already been eliminated, partly due to broadcasts favorable to the National Liberation Front over the Allied radios. On November 28, 1944, the government chosen at Berat installed itself at Tirana as the "Democratic Government" of Albania, with Enver Hoxha as Prime Minister.

The Establishment of the Communist Regime and the Question of Recognition by the United States

As soon as Hoxha's Government came to power it strove to consolidate itself. Many opponents were brought before the people's courts to be judged as "war criminals" or "enemies of the people." Although the alleged object of the trials was to punish those who collaborated with the enemy, the true aim was to eliminate those who had influence over the people and might oppose the Communist regime. But consolidation also meant the recognition of the regime by the Allied powers.

Tito's Yugoslavia was the first to recognize the Albanian Government. She had already sent advisers for the ministries and experts for the army. The other People's Democracies and the U.S.S.R. would certainly follow suit. It fitted well into Russia's plans to have Albania, whose position as an outpost in the Mediterranean and a base for expansion was of great importance, under the control of a satellite. The difficulty would arise with the Western democracies, which stood for democratic and representative government. Yugoslav sources have revealed that some of the Albanian Communist leaders, among them Hoxha himself, were eager to obtain recognition by the West.[2] The Tirana government requested it.

Before giving consideration to such a request, the United States Government sent an informal mission, headed by Foreign Service officer Joseph E. Jacobs, to survey conditions and developments in Albania. England did the same. The American mission entered the country on May 8, 1945.

As long as Hoxha's government hoped to obtain American recognition, it tried to create the impression that it was democratic and desired relations with the West. It had already changed the name of the National Liberation Front to Democratic Front. The Communists declared that the basis of the new front would be

[2] Cf. V. Dedijer, *Il sangue tradito,* relazioni jugoslavo-albanesi 1938–1949 (Milano: Editoriale Periodici Italiani, 1949), pp. 127–133.

broadened to comprise all shades of political opinion. They were careful, however, to keep it under their own control. Literature coming from the West was distributed as freely as that from the East. A great number of American newsreels and documentary pictures assembled by OWI were shown to large civilian and army audiences. On September 7, 1945, a conference was held in Tirana for the formation of the Albanian Writers' Union, to which many non-Communist writers were invited. It wired both President Truman and Premier Attlee a request for recognition of the Tirana regime.

On November 10, 1945, the United States Government expressed its readiness, in a note to Premier Hoxha, to enter into diplomatic relations with the existing regime in Albania as her provisional government. In establishing such relations, however, the American Government requested assurances, according to the Yalta declaration on liberated Europe, that the forthcoming elections for a Constituent Assembly should be held on a genuinely free basis; that all democratic individuals and groups should enjoy freedom of speech and the right to present and support their candidates; and that foreign press correspondents should be permitted to observe and report freely on the elections and the work of the Assembly. The note stated further:

> The Government of the United States also desires that the Albanian authorities shall confirm that the treaties and agreements which were in force between the United States and Albania on April 7, 1939, remain valid. The United States Government, on its part, confirms the continuing validity of these instruments.

The Albanian Government had long been preparing the elections. It now presented the list of the Democratic Front, composed mainly of Communists. In order to give the semblance of free elections, it had made provisions for the casting of ballots for the "opposition." But there was no "opposition," for the Albanian authorities had prevented the formation of political groups or parties. There were only two independent candidates, one of whom had withdrawn his candidacy before the day of elections (December 2, 1945). Under such circumstances, it was inevitable that the Democratic Front (the peacetime camouflaged Communist Party) should win. According to official returns, its candidates received 93 per cent.

The Constituent Assembly convened at Tirana and abolished

the monarchy, proclaiming Albania a People's Democratic Republic (January 11, 1946). The Constituent Assembly was immediately changed to the People's Assembly. Having acquired the stamp of constitutionality, this People's Democratic Republic turned into an open Communist dictatorship with all the secret-police trappings, engaging in the ruthless elimination of opposition elements and adopting an anti-Western policy.

Dissatisfaction among members of the Democratic Front was growing and becoming more vocal. In February 1946, intellectuals of that front, like Dr. Gjergj Kokoshi and Dr. Suad Asllani, who favored its democratization, were ousted and later condemned for plotting against the regime. There was also discontent among members of the Communist Party and the army; they resented control by the Yugoslavs. They found a cruel persecutor in the person of Koci Xoxe, Deputy Premier, Minister of the Interior and head of the secret police, who with the backing of the Yugoslavs had become the most powerful man in the Party.

The presence of the Western missions seemed to embarrass Yugoslav control of Albania. Restrictions were imposed upon the American and British missions. Their travel was curtailed and their alien employees were being expelled, while diplomatic members assigned to their staffs were being kept from entering the country. England had recognized the Tirana regime in November 1945 but on April 4, 1946 announced that she would not send her minister-designate to his post in Tirana nor receive an Albanian envoy in London. The Albanian authorities declined—in violation of the American-Albanian agreement of April 5, 1932—to issue permits to leave the country to American citizens who were also considered citizens of Albania. Efforts by American representatives in Tirana to place certain American publications on the market failed. Sejfulla Malëshova, Minister of Education and the most capable Albanian Communist theoretician, was purged on February 21, 1946, accused of endeavoring to establish close cultural relations with the United States. The facilities of UNRRA—to which the share of the United States for 1946 was $13,052,284 for Albania—were supervised.

For nine months the Albanian Government, because of internal disagreement, remained silent on the request of the United States regarding recognition. One group was inclined to accept the United States conditions in order to secure the independence of the country and strengthen their positions. To this belonged Hoxha, Sejfulla Malëshova and Dr. Dishnica. The other group, Koci Xoxe its most prominent member, sided with the Yugoslavs, who pressed for rejection, and prevailed. The Peace Conference of the Council of Foreign Ministers was shortly to convene at Paris, and Greece was trying her best to assure support for the claims to Northern Epirus. On August 13, 1946, the Tirana Government answered the American note, indicating acceptance of the multilateral treaties and agreements to which both the United States and Albania were parties, but failing to affirm its recognition of the validity of bilateral instruments between the United States and Albania.

At the Paris Peace Conference Secretary Byrnes endeavored to bring about a European settlement by compromise on the part of all the Great Powers. In Washington, however, the Senate had adopted, on July 29, 1946, a resolution favoring the award of Northern Epirus to Greece. It was similar to Senator Lodge's resolution which was passed in 1920. But the State Department did not express an opinion about the question of Northern Epirus, except to urge that a full hearing be given to both parties to the dispute. Its desire seems to have been to see Albania within the borders of 1913, but as friendly to the West as she was to the East. As a peace-loving nation, America was interested in seeing Albania in control of her own destinies and free at last of the domination of any foreign power. When the Greek representative asked, in the conference, for the inclusion of the Northern Epirus question on the agenda of the Paris Peace Conference, Molotov, whose Government had recognized the Albanian regime since November 10, 1945, and Kardelj, Yugoslav Vice-Premier, fought strenuously against it. It was Secretary Byrnes's influence, however, that was greatly felt in the withdrawal of the Northern Epirus question from the agenda.

Yet when Prime Minister Hoxha returned from the Paris Peace Conference to Tirana and addressed the Albanian youth, he accused the United States of being the principal obstacle to Albania's claims. His country was not invited to that Conference as an allied or associated power and the Northern Epirus question was raised. The Albanian people are very touchy about Greece's claims; without southern Albania there cannot be an Albania at all. The Albanian Communist regime has exploited the Northern Epirus question to the full in order to strengthen its position, and Hoxha's address was followed by anti-American propaganda in the press.

Confronted with the hostility of the Tirana Government and an unsatisfactory reply to the terms of its note for recognition, the United States Government decided to withdraw its informal mission. On November 5, 1946, the Acting American Representative in Tirana, George D. Henderson, delivered to Premier Hoxha a note which stated that, despite its efforts, the American mission was unable to achieve the purpose for which it was originally sent, concluding: "In the circumstances, although the Government retains its sentiment of warm friendship for the Albanian people, it does not feel that there is any further reason for the mission to remain in Albania."

Immediately after the announcement of the withdrawal of the United States Mission, the Albanian authorities instituted trials of alleged Albanian saboteurs and trumped up charges that Harry T. Fultz, an officer of the mission, together with other employes of it, had instigated and subsidized sabotage activities at a drainage project on Lake Maliq, near Korça. It was a way of justifying the failure of the project and striking at the same time at opposition elements. The grip of the Communist Party was becoming stronger. As the Albanian people have friendly feelings for the United States, the Tirana regime felt compelled to mislead them in believing that the American mission had done something wrong and had been evicted rather than withdrawn. During the trials of deputies and intellectuals in September 1947, the accused were made to testify that they were in touch with, among others, members of the American mission, who conspired to overthrow the Hoxha regime and to encourage the establishment of a government favorable to Anglo-American interests. But the trials had other aims also: to eliminate intellectuals who could discredit the regime and to purge the Party of members who were "lukewarm."

When the Truman doctrine of "containment" was proclaimed (March 12, 1947), Albania had already dropped the iron curtain to the West. Under orders from Moscow she had become, like Yugoslavia, a basis for Markos' guerrillas which fought against the Greek Government. The United States could no longer pursue a friendly policy toward Albania. At the Moscow Conference, the American delegation opposed, on March 25, 1947, the Soviet Union's proposal to include Albania among the allied states which actively participated in the war. It declared that Albanian troops actively allied themselves with the Axis in "the treacherous attack on their valiant neighbor, Greece." It stressed that the Tirana regime had declined to recognize Albania's international obligations and that it had not qualified for membership in the United Nations. Some five months earlier, two British destroyers had been mined in the Corfu Channel, off the coast of Albania.

On June 5, 1947, the United States proposed the Marshall Plan for European Recovery. Although in great need, Albania refused to participate in it; but Hoxha went to Moscow in order to participate in the Molotov Plan. On July 27 Moscow announced "a small credit" to Albania for the purchase of light industrial equipment and agricultural machinery.

In the United Nations the defenders of Albania were first Yugoslavia and later the Soviet Union. United States policy toward Albania was part of a larger policy: United Nations membership of Soviet satellites. This policy oscillated between the principle of universality—a blanket acceptance of candidate states of both East and West—and admittance of a few selected states which fully qualified for it.

Already in the early part of 1948 Russia began to be more interested in Albania. In February and March Soviet advisers began to arrive. Relations between the U.S.S.R. and Tito's Yugoslavia were becoming tense. On June 28 the rupture between the Yugoslav Communist Party and the Cominform took place. It could not but have effects in Albania.

Soviet Control and Greek Guerrilla War

In the Tito-Cominform rift the Albanian Communist Party took the side of the Soviet Union; it believed that Tito would soon be overthrown. Koci Xoxe and some of his henchmen, who had ruled the Party with a strong hand since 1944, were arrested and condemned on charges of Trotzkyite and Titoist activities. Xoxe was executed. The Albanian Government denounced all the agreements with Yugoslavia, except the treaty of friendship and mutual assistance of July 9, 1946, and expelled all her experts, advisers, and representatives of companies. The Central Committee of the Albanian Communist Party declared that the Yugoslav leaders "have tried to destroy the independence of our country and our party."

As long as Yugoslavia was within the Russian orbit, Albania was of considerable strategic importance for the Soviet Union. With the expulsion of Yugoslavia from the Cominform, only the occupation of the southern tongue of that country, separating Albania from Bulgaria, could bring the U.S.S.R. in direct land contact with Albania. Although isolated, Albania was still important for Russia. If she defected, it would be a blow to Soviet prestige. She could also be used as a propaganda center in the Balkans.

In spite of the Yugoslav-Cominform break, the guerrilla war was continuing in Greece, while the United States was endeavoring to bring it to an end. The policy of the United States toward Albania was a consequence of its Greek policy. It made efforts through the United Nations to stop the assistance from the Balkan countries to the Greek guerrillas. The report (August 2, 1949) of the United Nations Special Committee on the Balkans to the General Assembly noted that Albania was the principal source of material assistance and that this was "vital to the continuance of the Greek guerrilla movement, since all the main guerrilla concentrations are found on the Albanian frontier." Three and a half months later the Assembly adopted Secretary Acheson's resolution on the embargo on arms shipments to Albania and Bulgaria.

Meanwhile a UN Conciliation Committee, headed by Dr. Evatt, was formed in order to expore the possibilities of a settlement of the differences between Albania, Bulgaria, Greece, and Yugoslavia. In the discussions the stumbling block was the unwillingness of Greece to withdraw her claims to southern Albania. On December 14, 1948, Dr. Evatt declared that the efforts of the Conciliation Committee had failed because the Greek Government refused "to treat existing boundaries between Greece and Albania as definitive." When in April 1949 the Committee resumed its discussions at Lake Success, the Northern Epirus question emerged again as the chief obstacle to a Balkan settlement.

The guerrilla war in Greece came to an end partly because of lack of support by Yugoslavia after her expulsion from the Cominform. If at any moment the United States desired the overthrow of Hoxha's regime, her policy in 1950 seemed to be that of seeing the regime continue in office without growing stronger. Hoxha was not sure of his future. In the spring of 1949 he had secretly asked Britain and the United States to grant him diplomatic recognition. It was refused. Important for the United States, however, was the fear that any move to upset the Albanian regime—whether inspired by the West or not—might be used by Moscow as an excuse to go to its rescue, to accuse Yugoslavia of expansionist aims toward her small neighbor and to take violent action against Tito. Since the West wished to avoid the possibility of a world war arising from such an action, the United States appeared wary of seeking a change in the delicate Albanian situation.

By that time the Soviet Union had strengthened considerably her grip over Albania. She had replaced the Yugoslav advisers by Russians in the ministries, in the army, in schools, and in almost all the activities of Albanian life. Mehmed Shehu, a Moscow-trained man, had become Minister of the Interior and head of the secret police, the so-called *Sigurimi* (Security). Mitya, a Soviet citizen who organized Bulgarian Security, became Shehu's close adviser. The Albanian Communists were more willing to be placed under the Russian orders. For them the Russians have a prestige which their neighbors and former comrades lacked. Besides, Albania had passed, with this change, from the state of a sub-satellite to that of a satellite. An important role in the change of control was played by the Soviet Minister in Tirana, Dimitri Chuvakhin. The Albanian Government was under his orders.

The 1949 purges were followed by others. In 1951, after the explosion of a bomb at the Soviet Legation in Tirana, several of the Central Committee of the Communist Party, among them Manol Konomi, Minister of Justice, were purged. Konomi came into conflict with Mehmed Shehu over the utter disregard the latter showed even for a semblance of justice during his persecutions. The criminal code was soon revised (effective September 1, 1952) to be harsher even than the Soviet counterpart, which is based on the concepts of class warfare and "revolutionary justice" and holds even children twelve years old responsible for crimes against the state. Other purges in the rank and file of the Party tightened Soviet control. Since July 1954 Mehmed Shehu has been the Premier of Albania.

Conmmunist Enslavement

The process of Communist enslavement in Albania begun under Hoxha's regime has progressed during the years of Soviet control.

By the agrarian laws of 1945–46 the Government confiscated the land of the landowners and redistributed it among the farmers, each family of 5 members being allowed to use 5 hectares (approximately 12.35 acres). Although deeds of ownership were issued to the farmers, they do not in reality possess any land; they get only the produce of it, and often cannot even retain what they produce. In 1946, collectivization of land was introduced, although Albania has no broad fields. But the Government seeks to make the peasant more dependent on it. Indeed, it has reduced him to a slave of the state.

In a Communist society there is no room for the "bourgeoisie." Hoxha's regime levied war taxes on the businessmen so high that they were unable to pay them. As a result their property was confiscated and they themselves were sent to prison or labor camp. As for the industrialists, their factories were confiscated by the state. Regimentation into government-controlled groups was the lot of the liberal professions. The middle-class was destroyed.

Industry was taken up by the state. Albania had a limited number of workers, living only in the towns. With the industrial expansion of the present regime, such as the Stalin Combine for textiles or the Çerrik Oil refinery, the number of workers has greatly increased. The development of industry aims not so much at satisfying the needs of the country as at strengthening the rule of the regime. The peasants are not reliable supporters; in them the desire for the possession of land is strong. Only the workers can be their true backers, for in a Communistic society they are dependent on the state.

Labor in Albania is organized within the narrow framework of state-run syndicates (later, trade unions). A network of "activists," composed of 17,049 persons, most of them Young Communist Party members, was in 1952 spread throughout the syndicates. Their functions were to control local organizations, implement directives from above, incite workers to increase output, and further their political and ideological education.

In order to inculcate more efficiently the ideology and the principles of the Party, the Communists began in 1946 the war on illiteracy. They increased the number of schools and courses. But the school must serve to bring the child under the control of the state, for in a totalitarian system youth is the property of the state. The textbooks are prepared to conform with the teaching of Stalin and Lenin. In class the ideological purpose of each lesson must be stressed. Everything in the classroom is designed to make the student identify himself with the world Communist movement and to regard the Soviet Union as the realization of the Communist ideal. Everything Russian is extolled. The Moscow-trained director of the Higher Agricultural Institute in Tirana declared at its inauguration:

> Our instruction has as its basis the school plans and programs of the higher institutes of the Soviet Union. Our task is to give to our students solid knowledge on the theory of Marxism-Leninism, the agrobiology of the USSR, and the achievements of the Soviet scholars.

Teachers are subjected to constant indoctrination, especially by political seminars. It is the aim of the Ministry of Education that the teachers should not only follow implicitly the principles and methods of Soviet pedagogy, but should also acquire the Soviet outlook. According to the Five Year Plan (1951–1955), there are 900 Albanians studying abroad, most of them in the Soviet Union. Teaching of the Russian language is not confined to the Albanian schools; courses in Russian are also given to the people.

Owing to the diversity and loose organization of the religious communities—with the exception of the Roman Catholic Church—their enslavement was easier in Albania than in other satellite countries. On May 5, 1945, the constitution of the Moslem community was voted upon in Tirana. The Moslems formed a community, but without the Bektashis. On the same day the Bektashis, an off-shoot of the Shiah branch of Islam, often considered heretical by the Orthodox Sunni, made their own charter. By this they no longer form a spiritually and executively autonomous body within the Moslem community, but constitute a community of their own. In this way the Government, while satisfying the Bektashis with their independence, divided the Moslem forces and accentuated the Sunni–Bektashi opposition. To be sure, it ran into obstacles in seeking men to put at the head of these communities. Sunni religious leaders, like the mufti of Shkodra or that of Durazzo, were persecuted. Among the Bektashis, the Government favorite Baba Faja Marteneshi was assassinated as a traitor by men of his own community.

On November 26, 1949, a law was enacted obliging the religious communities to develop among their members the feeling of loyalty toward "the people's power" and the People's Republic of Albania. According to this law, the government has the right to veto the election of the heads of religious communities.

The head of the Orthodox Christian Church, Archbishop Kristofor Kisi, refused to become the tool of the regime. In August 1949 he was deposed and a former priest who was a Communist, Paisi Vodica, was raised by the regime to head the Autocephalous Orthodox Church of Albania. During February 5–10, 1950, the Orthodox Congress held in Tirana voted the new charter of the Albanian Orthodox Church, committed to developing in its adherents the sense of loyalty to the Communist regime.

Archbishop Paisi paid several visits to Moscow. The ties between the Albanian Orthodox Church and the Russian Patriarchate became closer in the spring of 1951, when a delegation of Soviet religious leaders, headed by Bishop Nikon of Odessa, visited Tirana.

As early as 1946 the attack on the Catholic Church in Albania as an instrument of the Vatican had begun. A number of priests were brought to trial, and those who were not Albanians were expelled. The Albanian Government executed or imprisoned the most distinguished members of the Catholic hierarchy. Yet it was not until June 26, 1951, that the great transformation of the Catholic Church took place. On that date, a "general assembly" of Catholic clergymen was convened at Shkodra, the center of Albania's Catholicism. Although a rump gathering, technically it could lay claim to represent Albania's Catholics. In August 1951, the Presidium of the People's Assembly approved the "decisions" of the "general assembly," which meant the constitution of the Albanian Catholic Church.

According to the new charter, the Catholic Church of Albania has become national. It has no organizational, political, or economic relations with the Vatican. Its relations with churches outside the country may be established only through the official channels of the Tirana Government. The priests are being trained in seminaries "created and administered" with the approval of the government.

All three religious heads have been used by Moscow to make appeals in support of the Stockholm peace campaign.

The printing presses, as well as all supplies needed for printing, are owned and operated by the government; they were seized when the Communists came to power, and were officially nationalized in 1946. Four years later all state publishing houses were combined into a single one, known as "Publishing House Naim Frashëri," which was given complete charge of printing every publication in the country. Also a single distribution center, a "Central People's Bookstore," was established and authorized to handle the distribution of all publications.

The press and all other media of information and propaganda are under complete government control and have been employed to propagate Communist policies and the programs of the regime. Several publications, like *Friendship,* with the largest circulation of all Albanian periodicals, and two monthly bulletins, the *Soviet Worker* and the *Soviet Kolkhozian,* are issued by the Albanian-Soviet Friendship Society, which is Moscow's strongest and all-pervading propaganda agency in Albania. Each September the "Albanian Soviet Friendship Month" is dedicated to acquainting the Albanian people with the alleged "successes" of the U.S.S.R. in the economic, cultural, and social fields.

Forced labor has been used extensively in Albania since the present regime seized control. But it is only recently that the Western world has learned about these labor camps. Some 16,000 persons are said to have perished in them and in prisons in Albania. The labor camps stand as the symbols of the methods of enslavement which the Communists and the Soviet Union brought to Albania.

United States Policy After the Tito-Cominform Break

If the United States policy has not been in a position to prevent the enslavement of Albania by the Soviet Union—for this objective, liberation would have been necessary, which would have entailed grave risks—it has done a great deal in convincing the Albanian people that they are not forgotten. It has given them hope. On various occasions the American Secretaries of State have expressed sympathy with the sufferings of the Albanian people and a desire to see their country free and independent. The United States has supported Albanian democratic elements abroad. In August 1949 a National Committee for a Free Albania, under the veteran patriot Midhat Frashëri, was created in Paris. It met with American support and that of the West. The existence of this Committee has disturbed the rulers of Tirana and at times they have taken harsh measures against the people, but at the same time it has raised the morale of the latter.

United States policy toward Soviet-dominated Albania has been part of her Balkan policy. It has bolstered the independence of Yugoslavia in order to preclude a Soviet advance, except by conquest. It has also supported cooperation among Yugoslavia, Greece and Turkey. On February 28, 1953, these three countries signed a treaty of friendship and collaboration. In harmony with the United

States policy of "liberation" was the article in the treaty which left the door open for the satellites to join it, if they threw away their Soviet shackles. Of all the satellites Albania had the greatest possibilities for liberation because of her geographic isolation. In Athens on July 11, 1953, the Foreign Ministers of Greece, Turkey and Yugoslavia went a step further. They declared that they agreed "on the point that the independence of Albania would constitute an important element for the peace and stability of the Balkans."

The reaction on the part of the Tirana regime and the U.S.S.R. was soon expressed. On August 2, Premier Hoxha in his speech to the People's Assembly denounced the Balkan Pact as an instrument of aggression (although the aims of the Pact are peaceful) and, owing to Greece's claims to Albania, interpreted the Athens declaration of independence as a dismemberment of the country and its subjugation by the neighboring Balkan states. An official statement, issued simultaneously in Moscow and Tirana, declared that the Soviet and Albanian Governments raised their respective legations to the status of embassies. And *Pravda,* writing on August 4, 1953, maintained that the Athens Conference was held under the orders of the United States and that because the conference worked for stronger military ties between the Balkan and NATO pacts it was a threat to the "immediate neighbors of Greece, Turkey, and Yugoslavia, and in particular Albania." On May 14, 1955, the U.S.S.R. also included Albania in the Eastern "NATO," which was formed in Warsaw and put all the armed forces of the Soviet bloc under a unified Soviet command, thus strengthening the position of the Albanian regime.

Since the Athens declaration included the independence of Albania but not her territorial integrity as well, certain doubts began to arise. In order to disperse them and convince the Albanians of the friendship of the United States Government, Secretary of State Dulles made clear its policy toward Albania in a letter addressed to the President of the National Committee for Free Albania on August 26, 1953. He stated: "To the United States which has traditionally supported the right of all oppressed peoples to freedom and liberty, the tragic plight of the Albanian people is a matter of deep concern . . ." He warmly welcomed "the recent declarations by Albania's neighbors of their peaceful purpose toward Albania and their intent to support the right of the Albanian people to freedom and independence." As far as territorial claims were concerned,

Secretary Dulles declared: "The United States recognizes that the problem of future relationship between a free and independent Albania and its neighbors is a matter primarily of bilateral discussion and solution."

In early November 1954 the Albanian application for membership in UNESCO was considered. On that occasion the United States representative, Preston Hotchkis, opposed the admittance of Albania on the ground that her regime had proved unable and unwilling to fulfill the obligation of the UNESCO Constitution: "to develop and to increase the means of communications between their peoples and to employ these means for the purpose of mutual understanding and a truer and more perfect knowledge of each other's lives." He said that not only was the iron curtain sealed around Albania but that her Government had violated human rights and fundamental freedoms. Barring Albania from international organizations had been an effective policy. Her Government frequently protested this policy and denounced the United States. Obviously it felt before the Albanian people that it was an outcast in the international world. On December 15, 1955, however, Albania was admitted as a member in the United Nations during the voting of the "package" proposal for West-supported and Soviet-supported countries. The United States Government abstained from voting on Albania's admittance.

Expressing the friendly feelings of the American people toward the Albanian people, President Eisenhower on March 4, 1955 offered $850,000 worth of food in order to ease the food shortages in Albania. The food was to be distributed by the League of Red Cross Societies. It was a humane gesture which enhanced American prestige. But precisely because of this the Tirana Government turned it down, in spite of the food difficulties which exist there. The President's offer has certainly warmed the hearts of the Albanian people. If they cannot express their gratitude now, it is because of the chains they wear. The traditional friendship of the Albanian people for the United States—based on Wilson's intervention in favor of Albania, on the prosperity and gratitude of the Albanians working in the United States, and on services rendered by the American schools in Albania—is too solid to be deflected by the propaganda efforts of the Tirana Communist regime or the power of the Soviet Union.

Part Three

ON THE PERIPHERY OF THE SOVIET UNION

Chapter 13

Finland

JOHN H. WUORINEN

IN POST-1945 Europe, Finland has occupied a special, not to say unique, position. Drawn into the war by big-power aggression, this northern Republic had to accept military defeat at the hands of the U.S.S.R., but escaped military occupation. While Finnish independence had thus been saved, the situation of the country during the years immediately after 1945 appeared to many to be such as to indicate speedy and inevitable inclusion in the Soviet-dominated areas of Europe. This conclusion seemed to be substantiated, for example, in April 1948 when Finland signed, at Soviet insistence, a ten-year mutual assistance treaty in Moscow.

The treaty provided, in substance, that if Finland were attacked by Germany or "another state allied with her," or if the U.S.S.R. were attacked across Finnish territory, Finland would fight the aggressor, if necessary, with the aid of the Soviet Union "or together with it." "Mutual agreement" was to specify when Soviet assistance would be given. Because of the U.S.S.R.'s record as a treaty breaker and the likelihood that Russian interpretation would probably be decisive in the application of the treaty, it was widely seen as placing Finland in bondage. Thus the *New York Times* claimed that the treaty put Finland "firmly" into the Soviet-dominated East-European bloc, that Russian pledges of non-interference in Finnish affairs could be dismissed as meaningless, and that Finland and its democratic ways could be safeguarded only by greater support—of which there was but a "slim chance"—by the West.

The past eight years have shown that such interpretations missed the mark. Despite the growing East-West tensions since 1948, Finland has remained conspicuously outside the region blighted by Soviet control. The paralyzing economic servitude imposed on the country by the reparations burden was ended in 1952 when the last deliveries were successfully made. Economic recovery in general has been little short of amazing. Meanwhile, domestic Communism has been held in check, and no Communist has held a Cabinet post since 1948. The latest national elections, in March 1954, indicated that the minority position to which the Communists have been consigned because of their failure to recommend themselves and their cause to the majority of the citizenry will remain unchanged, and that Finnish democratic institutions continue to function in their traditional vigor.[1]

The obvious conclusion suggested by Finland's development during the past decade is that this northern Republic has managed to remain immune to Soviet subversion and penetration, and that nothing short of military conquest by the U.S.S.R. can cut Finland loose from the democratic world of the West.

In the field of foreign relations, Finland has likewise managed to carry on without imperiling her independence. Because of Soviet hostility and suspicions, Finland has displayed extreme caution in her foreign policy and has carefully avoided commitments and responsibilities that might be interpreted in Moscow as being directed against the U.S.S.R. But traditionally close relations with Finland's Scandinavian neighbors have been maintained and the Anglo-Saxon world has loomed large in Finnish intercourse with the nations of the free West. In 1955–1956 three developments in particular underscored these Finnish inclinations and preferences in foreign affairs. The first was the admission of Finland to membership in the U.N. (previously opposed by the U.S.S.R.) in December 1955. The second was the return to Finland in January 1956 of the Porkkala enclave, which had been leased (obviously under Soviet pressure) to the U.S.S.R. in 1944 for fifty years. The third was the open joining by Finland, in the same month, of the Nordic Council, which represents the most solid and extensive form of Scandinavian international cooperation today (its members are Denmark, Finland, Iceland, Norway, and Sweden). These developments have substantially increased Finland's opportunities for following her natural and traditional Western orientation, and their consequences may be expected to be reflected not the least in relations with the United States.

[1] See *Foreign Affairs,* XXXII (1954), 651–660; *Current History,* XVI (1949), 12–15; XXI (1951), 208–211; XXI (1951), 327–330; XXVIII (1955), 70–74.

Major Factors in American-Finnish Relations to 1940

The relations of the United States with Finland during the two decades before World War II, and the foreign policy on which they were based, were uncomplicated and undisturbed by serious problems or clashes of interest. A spirit of exceptional cordiality prevailed. The reasons for this happy state of affairs are not difficult to understand. They involve long-range historical circumstances as well as developments that go no further back than 1914–1918 and the years immediately after the end of the war when formal diplomatic relations between the two Republics were first established.

One of the basic circumstances can be suggested by noting that until the time when Thomas Jefferson was finishing his second term as President, Finland was an integral part of the Swedish kingdom and had in fact been the eastern half of that kingdom for over six centuries. During this long span of years the two nationalities, the Swedes and the Finns, had constituted a single state, had evolved common political, legal, religious and other institutions and ways of life, and had acquired the same traditions in government, law, administration and the like. By the early years of the last century, therefore, the past historical evolution of the Finns had made them full participants in the Scandinavian traditions of self-rule and freedom.

This fact became of utmost importance after 1808–1809, when Finland was severed from Sweden by Russian conquest. For reasons that have never been fully explained, Finland's inclusion in the Russian Empire did not turn the country into a subject province ruled by Russia, but resulted in political and administrative arrangements that spelled self-government and genuine home rule manned and led by Finnish citizens. Self-government meant, putting it broadly, an opportunity for the Finns to continue through the nineteenth century their national existence on the bases solidly laid by preceding generations of development and tradition. The fundamental laws of the land underwent no substantial change; the courts and the general administration of law and justice functioned on a national foundation; the church (Lutheran) and educational institutions continued to develop along lines characteristic of the Western nations. Economic life had come to reflect, by the end of the century, the revolution that the factory, the steamship, the railroad, the telephone, and the telegraph had initiated and carried forward. Meanwhile the political and social emancipation of the common man also had begun and culminated in such important gains as the granting of the free ballot to all adult men and women and the establishment of a unicameral national legislature, in 1906.

Change of another kind also occurred during the period. Down to the last decade of the century, Finnish self-government was not only left intact by Russia, but was even expanded in some important respects; for example, a separate Finnish currency was introduced in 1865. After 1890, however, the Imperial government pursued a Russification policy which threatened Finland's self-government and the liberties of her citizens. Despite tenacious passive resistance, the Finns' situation had become critical by 1914. Relief came only in 1917, when the collapse of the Tsarist regime gave the Finns a chance to proclaim, on December 6, an independent republic. Independence was fully secured, however, only after a brief civil war in the spring of 1918 between Finnish Reds (aided by the Bolsheviks), intent upon establishing a Soviet republic, and the defenders of the legal government. The Reds lost. A republican constitution was thereupon drafted and went into effect in July, 1919.

American foreign policy regarding Finland emerged during the developments connected with the interventionist period in the early years of the Bolshevist regime in Russia. Next to recognition and the establishment of formal relations with the Finnish Republic in 1920, the outstanding event was the granting of an $8,281,926 loan to the Finns in 1919. Frequently referred to as a "war loan," it actually represented a sum placed at the Finns' disposal for food purchases, and enabled the starving and impoverished country to live through its most trying period of postwar readjustment. It would in all likelihood never have received any particular attention had it not been for later developments unforeseen in 1920.

By the time Europe was beginning to get back on an even keel after the war, some seventeen European nations had become debtors of the United States. The list was headed by Great Britain, France and Italy (their indebtedness ranged from 1.6 to 4.2 billion dollars) and included Finland, whose debt came to the sum mentioned. After the depression of 1929 and the years following had increasingly paralyzed the economies of the debtor nations, default of payments to the United States became the policy of all but Finland. On June 1, 1934, President Roosevelt's message to Congress stated, after reviewing the failures to make payments, that Finland remained "the only foreign Government which has met all payments on its indebtedness to the United States punctually and in full." [2]

Finland followed the policy of making full and prompt payments through the thirties and in doing so gained an enviable reputation among the American people. Finnish honesty and probity were universally commented upon and often accented with special emphasis in order, it seemed, to give sharper relief to the failure of the other debtor nations—especially that of the major powers—to meet their obligations squarely and fully. The uneventful and placid relations between the two Republics during these years were in general such as to provide repeated opportunities for flattering American comment. This was shown with special emphasis in connection with Finland's participation, along with Sweden, in the observance in 1938 of the Tercentenary of the founding of the first permanent white settlements in the Delaware River valley. A substantial part of the New Sweden colony established in 1638 was Finnish, and consequently the United States invited Finland as well as Sweden to the anniversary celebration arranged by Delaware, Pennsylvania, New Jersey, and the Federal Government.[3] The occasion yielded several illustrations of the ready inclination, in Congress and out, to see in Finland and its people the embodiment of honest and admirable democratic republicanism.

By September, 1939, when World War II began, immense American good will toward Finland, and wholly peaceful and exceptionally cordial relations with this Northern republic, had thus come to be taken for granted. When Soviet demands were presented to Finland in the following month (the details were unknown at the time, but the Soviets' part in the partition of Poland, and the moves made in the three Baltic States, justified the fear that they constituted a threat to Finland), President Roosevelt gave ample evidence of American friendship and solicitude. On October 11, he stated in a message to Kalinin that it was hoped that the U.S.S.R. would make no demands on Finland "which are inconsistent with the maintenance and development of amicable and peaceful relations" or with the independence of Finland.[4] The unprovoked

[2] The message is conveniently found in *Roosevelt's Foreign Policy, 1933–1941* (published by Wilfred Funk, Inc., New York, 1942), pp. 62–67.

[3] See the resolutions and discussions in the House of Representatives in John H. Wuorinen, *The Finns on the Delaware* (New York, 1938), pp. 121–161, and the *Congressional Record,* Aug. 21, 1937, 12309–12312.

[4] *Bulletin,* I (1939), 395. The pronouncement of the President and other statements by the Government in Washington dealing with Finland during the war years appeared in and were commented on by the press. Such comment usually appeared on the day of the statement or the day after.

Soviet attack on Finland which began on November 30 was condemned, and the people of Finland were assured of the respect and warm regard of the American nation and its government.[5] The anniversary of Finnish independence a few days later (December 6) provided, in the words of President Roosevelt, "yet another welcome occasion to voice the wholehearted esteem" felt for the Finns by the United States, and he expressed the hope, undoubtedly shared by all Americans except the Communists and their fellow travelers, that the tragic days of war would soon be followed by "a happier era to permit the Finnish people to continue, untroubled, the steady development of their free political and social institutions which have aroused the admiration of the American people." [6]

The same sentiments were expressed in a White House press release in March, 1940, after the Finns had accepted (March 12) the Russian peace terms forced upon them after more than three months of heroic fighting. In the words of the press release, "the people of Finland, by their unexcelled valor and strong resistance in the face of overwhelming armed forces," had "won the moral right to live in everlasting peace and independence in the land they have so bravely defended," and had "again increased the respect and warm regard in which they are held by the people and the Government of the United States." [7] Meanwhile, American nonmilitary economic aid had been given to the Finns in the form of a $35,000,000 loan by the Export-Import Bank (in December and January), but not in amounts large enough to influence the outcome of the war. Also, President Roosevelt went on record in favor of Finnish and general Scandinavian neutrality before the Russian attack on Finland began. When Finland paid in December—the war was already raging—the installment on her debt to the United States, Roosevelt directed the Secretary of the Treasury to place the sum in a separate account pending such action as the Congress might take regarding it. In June, 1940, some three months after the Moscow Peace, the President approved a joint resolution of the Congress which gave Finland a chance to postpone payment on the December, 1940 installment. Finland took advantage of the offer and postponed payment of the installment in question.[8]

[5] *Ibid.,* I (1939), 609.

[6] *Ibid.,* I (1939), 650.

[7] *Ibid.,* II (1940), 295.

[8] *Ibid.,* I (1939), 395, 403. The essential details are in *ibid.,* II (1940), 55; III (1940), 501–503; IV (1941), 547.

Finland and World War II

By the close of 1940 a number of important developments had occurred that ultimately changed American policy toward Finland. The developments in question grew out of the course of the war and the gradual emergence of a new conception of the requirements of national security and how to meet them.

After the Nazi invasion of Denmark and Norway in April 1940, and the attack upon the Netherlands, Luxemburg, Belgium and France a month later, resulting in the collapse of French military resistance and the surrender of France in June, Hitler's successes had reached truly ominous dimensions. Great Britain, the only remaining opponent of Nazi Germany, appeared none too safe against invasion and her defeat by no means an impossibility. American security, it seemed, was increasingly threatened by Hitler's successes. It required a new and close look at the position of the United States and renewed appraisal of the policies and measures that had been evolved to increase the safety of the nation.

The effort led first to a series of modifications in the Neutrality Laws of 1937–1939. The export of planes and other war material to Great Britain was permitted while the same opportunity was denied to Germany, and other ways of favoring the opponents of Hitler were devised. Beginning in the summer of 1940 and continuing on an expanding scale till December 1941, neutrality was abandoned and a policy of undeclared hostilities against Germany was begun. The United States became increasingly the "arsenal" of the democracies and a tower of strength for them. The destroyer-naval bases deal of September 2, 1940; the Lend-Lease Act—significantly, it was called "An Act Further to Promote the Defense of the United States"—of March 11, 1941, which put the material resources of the Government of the United States at the disposal of countries whose defense the President considered vital to United States' defense; and the Atlantic Charter declaration with Great Britain on August 14, 1941—these were only the most conspicuous illustrations of the extent to which "all-out" aid "short of war" had become a fixed American policy long before Pearl Harbor.[9] By then an undeclared shooting war had in fact begun, for the American destroyer, the *Reuben James,* while on convoy duty, had been

[9] See Samuel Flagg Bemis, *A Diplomatic History of the United States* (New York, 1950), pp. 849–865; Thomas A. Bailey, *A Diplomatic History of the American People* (New York, 1950), pp. 764–789.

sunk, with heavy loss of life, on October 30, 1941, off western Iceland.

While the position of the United States was thus changing and American foreign policy correspondingly modified, Finland also found herself in new circumstances. Involved again in war with the Soviet Union—Hitler's invasion, begun on June 22, 1941, had resulted in Russian armed action against Finland and led to Finland's declaring, three days later, that a state of war existed—the policy of neutrality which had been laboriously followed since the end of the Winter War came to an end. The consequences were quickly discernible in American-Finnish relations no less than in other areas. To the extent that American policy came to see in Hitler's war a threat to democracy and independence, the anti-Hitlerite coalition of powers was seen as a defender of the just cause, and those fighting against the coalition as a whole, or, as was the case with Finland, against one member of it—the U.S.S.R.—came to be considered as potential enemies. By the time Pearl Harbor had plunged the United States into the war, this process had transformed the earlier friendly United States policy toward Finland into attitudes of cool scrutiny and critical appraisal. After Pearl Harbor critical appraisal led to an effort to persuade the Finns to withdraw from the war, culminating in the severance of diplomatic relations in June, 1944.

A few illustrations of this change of policy will suffice. During the first few months of the second phase of the Finnish-Russian war, the United States steadily refused to accept the Finnish contention that Finland's war was a war involving the country's independence, and that the effort to save Finland from Russian aggression had nothing to do with Nazism and Hitler's larger war. Washington chose instead to see in Finland a mere handmaiden of Hitler, serving the aims of the dictator. In November, 1941, for instance, Secretary of State Hull raised the question to what extent Finnish military measures meant combined operations with the Germans "vitally to injure Great Britain and her associates and to threaten the northern supply lines over which Russia is now receiving supplies and assistance from Great Britain and the United States to aid Russia in resisting the Hitler forces. . . . and to what extent that Finnish policy is a menace to all America's aims for self-defense." With exaggeration not unusual in wartime statements of this kind, Mr. Hull also contended that "every act" of the Finnish Government in the recent past had shown that "it is fully cooperating" with Hitler.[10]

If the State Department was thus inclined (while the United States was still technically neutral) to see in Finland at war a nation whose actions constituted—or came very close to constituting—a menace to the United States, it is clear that the attitude gradually stiffened after Pearl Harbor. Broadly speaking, the effort during the early part of 1942 was to prevent further Finnish military operations against the U.S.S.R. and to limit or eliminate Finnish participation in the general military offensive of Germany. Later, additional pressure was exerted. Consular commissions of Americans in Finland were cancelled, and Finnish consulates in the United States were closed, on August 1.[11] Intermittent efforts were also made to persuade Finland to withdraw from the war. They failed. The basic reason was the failure of the United States (the same also applied to Great Britain) to offer any workable alternative that would guarantee Finland's independence or to give assurances that cessation of hostilities would not mean additional and greater exposure to Soviet aggression. The efforts to take Finland out of the war appear in retrospect to have been markedly inept and unrealistic, primarily because the effort was based on claims and contentions that either underscored the unimportant and obvious aspects of Finland's part in the war and therefore had no persuasive or coercive effect, or placed the accent on vague generalities regarding the possibilities of a peace settlement without touching upon the really vital aspect of the problem, namely, the readiness of the Soviet Union to conclude a peace that would safeguard Finland's independence.[12] Without such a guaranty the Finns could see no choice but to continue fighting, especially in view of the fact that their military position remained strong until well into the second half of the war.

Typical of the basic difficulty was the American-British-Russian view put forth in a common declaration in May 1944, and the Finnish response to it. The declaration invited Finland and the other "satellites" to withdraw from the war, to cease cooperating with

[10] *Bulletin,* V (1941), 434–435; see also *ibid.* (1941), 362–363. See also J. H. Wuorinen (ed.), *Finland and World War II* (New York, 1948), pp. 135–139.

[11] *Bulletin,* VIII (1942), 632; Wuorinen, *op. cit.,* pp. 140–143.

[12] These efforts and related developments are summarized in Wuorinen, *op. cit.,* pp. 146–158.

Germany, and to resist "the forces of Nazism by every possible means." By so doing they would shorten the war, reduce their own sacrifices and contribute to the victory of the Allies. If they continued to fight, so much the worse for them. They must decide quickly "while there is still time for them to contribute" to Allied victory.[13] The "present politics" of Finland, for example, merely contributed to the "strengthening of the German war-machine, and did not aid in getting the country out of the war."

Despite the worsening position of Finland as a result of the rising tide of Russian victories over German forces, the admonition went unheeded. The reason is not far to seek. The only alternative to continued fighting that was being offered was the acceptance of Russian military conquest, which had been the dreaded prospect that had led the Finns to take up arms in the first place. To have yielded to the admonition now bearing the stamp of approval of the United States would have meant a repudiation of the effort to safeguard the democratic institutions and national independence of the country. The situation therefore continued unchanged until the United States severed diplomatic relations with Finland on June 30, 1944.

This extreme step had been implicit for some time in the gradually stiffening policy toward Finland during the preceding months. Available evidence invites the surmise that the decision to break with Finland—probably because of Soviet insistence, although specific proof to this effect has not come to the writer's attention—had been formulated earlier and would be carried through when the right moment and pretext appeared. The moment and the pretext came late in June. A new Russian offensive against Finland had been launched on the ninth. It had resulted within two weeks in the loss of the main Finnish line of defense and the threat of further Russian advance. Hasty consideration was given in Helsinki to the possibility of setting up a new government that might succeed in obtaining acceptable peace terms from the Soviet Union. Nothing came of it. Meanwhile, Nazi Germany offered sorely needed military assistance, on condition that Finland sign a treaty of alliance binding the Republic to make no peace except in cooperation with Germany. Unwilling to bind his country by agreeing to an alliance—Germany had repeatedly pressed for an alliance during the

[13] *Bulletin*, X (1944), 425.

war—President Ryti had recourse to a personal letter in which he, as President, gave the assurances demanded by Germany. The Finnish Cabinet endorsed the action taken because of the threatening military situation created by recent Russian successes.

In the action thus taken, Washington chose to see, on June 30, a formal admission by the Finnish Government "that it has now entered a hard and fast military partnership with Nazi Germany," and claimed that "German infiltration into the councils of the Finnish Government" had reduced the nation to the condition of a mere puppet of Germany. Finland having entered into a complete "partnership" with Germany, no further relations with her could be maintained.[14] The fact that President Ryti resigned as President some four weeks later (August 1), and thus freed the Finnish Government from whatever embarrassment his personal note had caused, did not lead Washington to reconsider its decision to sever relations. The status established by the note of June 30 continued till Finland withdrew from the war by concluding an armistice with the Soviet Union on September 4, 1944.

Finland after the War: Neutralism

After September 1944, United States' relations with Finland quickly returned to the friendship and cordiality of the pre-1941 period. The speed with which the return to the "good old days" was accomplished was especially noteworthy. It gave sharp relief to the fact that the wartime severance of formal relations had not been caused by profound conflict of national interests or purposes, but by short-range compulsions of war policy in which Soviet pressure had apparently played an important part.

The first definite steps leading to the resumption of normal relations were announced in January, 1945, four months after Finland had signed the armistice ending the second phase of the Russo-Finnish war, and some four months before the end of the war in Europe. On January 12, President Roosevelt assigned Mr. Maxwell M. Hamilton as United States representative in Finland, with the personal rank of Minister. Pending Mr. Hamilton's arrival in Helsinki, Mr. L. Randolph Higgs, who had served in Helsinki before 1940 and had handled Finnish affairs in the State Department during the war, was placed in charge of the United States mission

[14] Wuorinen, *op. cit.*, pp. 171–176; *Bulletin,* XI (1944), 3.

in Finland. The mission—it did not constitute a resumption of "formal diplomatic relations"—was established in Helsinki a few days later. The U.S.S.R. and Great Britain were "fully informed" regarding the assignment of Mr. Hamilton to his new post and the designation of Mr. Higgs.[15]

The next step came in August of the same year. At the Berlin Conference, the three powers had agreed that they would in due time examine, separately, the question of establishing normal diplomatic relations with Finland. The Secretary of State announced, on August 21, that the United States had acted upon this agreement, and that the Finnish Government (which had been formed after the elections in March) having been found to be "broadly representative of all democratic elements in Finnish political life," the United States Government had instructed its representative in Helsinki to propose the establishment of diplomatic relations between the two Republics. This was done, and the first Finnish postwar Minister to Washington, K. T. Jutila, presented his credentials on November 21, 1945.[16] The two Ministries were raised to Embassy rank in the fall of 1954, and Ambassador Jack K. McFall assumed his ambassadorial duties in Helsinki in January, 1955.[17]

During the decade that has elapsed since 1945, American policy toward Finland has been a part of the evolving policy that has increasingly been defined by the rising menace of Soviet-led world Communism. It has been a part of the policy of containment elaborated since 1947 and continued through to the cold war of the more recent past. Its main element may perhaps be said to have been the determination to limit Soviet expansionism in Europe by means of an armed Western alliance and other corollary undertakings, without a commitment to offensive moves designed to force the U.S.S.R. to recede beyond the boundaries of 1947 or 1939. Economic aid,

[15] *Bulletin,* XII (1945), 148.

[16] *Ibid.,* XIII (1945), 283, 483, 861. The political "means test" that Finland had to meet before relations with the United States could be normalized is an interesting illustration of wartime views in Washington. Actually, all Finnish elections since the founding of the Republic had resulted in Governments "broadly representative" of the democratic elements in the nation. The March, 1945, elections did add a new element to Finnish political life, however. They enabled the Communists, whose party had been outlawed in 1930 as treasonous, to reassert themselves, with Soviet support. They gained some 20 per cent of the seats in the national Legislature. For the next three years they rode the crest of the wave. Since 1948, however, they have been excluded from Cabinet posts and have in general been compelled to accept a minority position that corresponds to their numerical strength.

[17] Mr. McFall had been appointed Minister to Finland in September, 1952.

in order to speed recovery and create conditions that would increase resistance to Communist infiltration and Soviet advance, has been a part of the policy of containment since it was first formulated by Secretary of State Marshall in June, 1947.

Specifically, American policy has recognized the realities of Finland's position since 1944 for what they are. Finland's cautious and restrained Western foreign policy commitments and attitudes have been accepted without reading into them either indifference to American purposes or subtly disguised resolve to oppose them.

The realities of Finland's postwar situation—especially during 1945–1952—were indeed formidable. The immense war indemnity, nominally fixed at $300,000,000, imposed on the Republic by the U.S.S.R., was to be paid in commodities. This sum was reduced to some $226,000,000 in 1948. However, in reality the evaluation of the commodities and their delivery were specified by the Russians in such a way that Finland in effect paid an indemnity of well over $600,000,000. This meant that a substantial proportion of Finland's industrial capacity served Soviet economic needs until the last reparations deliveries in September, 1952. Since 1952, roughly 20 to 30 per cent of Finland's foreign trade has been with the Soviet bloc and the chances are that, barring war, the proportion will not substantially change in the near future. However desirable American policy has considered an economic boycott of the U.S.S.R. to be, Finland has not been able to participate in it.

This circumstance has been understood in Washington, where it has been seen that the outcome of the last war and the conflict between the Western democratic world and Soviet imperialism have placed Finland in a precarious position, and that it is in America's interest to assist Finland in maintaining her republican institutions and democratic way of life. It is significant that during the early and specially difficult years of fulfillment of the reparations clauses, when Finland was subjected to various political and economic pressures, American aid was extended to Finland on several occasions. During the crucial period 1946–1948, sorely needed credits were extended, through the Export-Import Bank, in the amount of more than $80,000,000. The figure ultimately came to approximately $120,000,000. Some $38,000,000 additional aid was granted in 1949–1952 through the International Bank for Reconstruction and Development. About $23,000,000 has been allocated to Finland for the purchase of war surplus materials, and additional smaller sums were made available for special purposes.[18]

Other measures were also taken to help the Finnish people "to maintain their free institutions and their national integrity" (to use a phrase from the Truman doctrine) [19] during these years. Thus the State Department announced in December, 1947, that the United States would not invoke, as it might well have done, the status of a "third-party beneficiary" under Article 29 of the Finnish peace treaty, which would have enabled the United States to avoid paying compensation for Finnish ships seized during the war. This decision permitted Finnish shipowners ultimately to collect about $4,475,000 for tonnage that had been requisitioned by the United States in 1941–1942. A commercial air service between the United States and Finland was authorized in April, 1947, and a formal air transport agreement was signed in March, 1949. The trade agreement signed in Helsinki on May 7, 1955, is only the most recent illustration of American readiness to assist in keeping Finland's economy sound. It provided for the purchase by Finland of $5,250,000 worth of American cotton and tobacco, much of which will be paid for by Finnish-made prefabricated houses. The arrangement was intended to provide a safeguard against the consequences of possible heavy decreases in Soviet purchases of Finnish industrial goods.[20]

Not the least significant illustration of this policy came in January, 1949, when the United States Advisory Commission on Educational Exchange recommended that future Finnish payments on the World War I indebtedness be used to pay for the education of Finnish citizens in the United States and for American educational materials for use in Finland. Acting upon this recommendation the Congress carried the matter forward and provided, in a Joint Senate-House Resolution of August 24 of the same year, that future payments on Finland's debt be used for a reciprocal educational exchange program between the two republics. The first funds became available when Finland paid its December 1949 installment ($264,000). Some three years later (July 2, 1952) the United States and Finland signed another agreement which ex-

[18] *Bulletin,* XVI (1947), 960; XIX (1948), 529; XXVII (1952), 866; statement from the Embassy of Finland, Washington, D.C., dated Dec. 20, 1954.

[19] See *Congressional Record,* 80 Cong. 1 sess. (March 12, 1947), 1981.

[20] *Bulletin,* XVIII (1948), 62–63; XXI (1949), 790; XVI (1947), 725; XX (1949), 466; *The New York Times,* May 8, 1955.

tended the Fulbright educational exchange program to Finland. It provided annual expenditures for five years of not over $250,000 (that is, the equivalent of this sum in Finnish currency) for study, research and teaching purposes. The program has been financed by means of certain funds made available to the United States by the sale of surplus American property in Finland.[21] By 1955, over 300 Finns had come to the United States to pursue studies financed by the funds provided by the Joint Resolution of July, 1952. This fellowship program is a most significant and continuing means for bringing the two nations together. These students have learned that the United States, where only a few years ago the inability to recognize Soviet aggression had been widespread, is now the main author of a policy which readily identifies evidences of Soviet expansionism and offers support to those who resist it. This circumstance alone means a source of moral strength for the Finns, whose survival depends upon the capacity to maintain in the years that lie ahead the individual liberty and democratic freedoms which have long been an integral part of Finnish life.

The spirit reflected in the policy of economic and related aid has also been shown in other ways. Finland has served for several years as an illustration—Sweden also belongs in the same category—of what has come to be called neutralism. Faced with the threat inherent in the Soviet policy of subversion and penetration, Finland has followed a policy of staying clear of big power groupings and has in general displayed deliberate caution in all commitments in order not to assume a posture or become involved in action that could be construed as something other than neutrality. To hold internal Communism in check and to remain in all respects fully outside the Iron Curtain have meanwhile been a prime concern. The success of this policy is amply demonstrated by the fact that the country has remained free and democratic. It has come to be accepted by Washington as unavoidable and appropriate to Finland's needs, for it accounts, in no small measure, for the significant circumstance that, while the U.S.S.R. has been able since 1939 to push hundreds of miles westward in central and southeastern Europe, the only dent in the North made by the Soviets is that represented by the southeastern and northern Finnish areas ceded in 1940 and 1944. The rest of the borderline of 1939 still holds fast and now represents a Northern dike against Communism that will not be

[21] *Ibid.*, XX (1949), 171; XXII (1950), 241, 243; XXVII (1952), 53.

easily breasted. In a word, Finnish neutralism has played a part in denying to the Soviet Union a key area which seemed, a decade ago, to be exceptionally exposed to Communist advance. It has thus served the same ends as the American policy of containment.

Finnish neutralism has obviously not been an isolated phenomenon. Leaving aside neutralist inclinations and preferences in western Europe, it suffices to note that as the West-East conflict has continued, something like a belt of neutral states—say, from Yugoslavia in the south to Sweden and Finland in the north—has emerged. This belt of states may be said to have become an area that partly insulates the West from the East. This insulation gives something of an advantage to the U.S.S.R., while it denies to the Western alliance a clear-cut demarcation line between friend and foe and therefore suggests the possibility that it might become, in a crisis situation, the source of something more than annoyance and irritation.

Finnish Independence and American Policy

President Truman, in urging the Congress, in 1947, to provide funds to be used for economic and military aid for Greece and Turkey, stated in part that one of the primary purposes of United States foreign policy "is the creation of conditions in which we and other nations will be able to work out a way of life free from coercion. . . . We shall not realize our objectives, however, unless we are willing to help free peoples to maintain their free institutions and their national integrity against aggressive movements that seek to impose upon them totalitarian regimes. This is no more than a frank recognition that totalitarian regimes, imposed on free peoples, by direct or indirect aggression, undermine the foundations of international peace and hence the security of the United States. . . . It must be the policy of the United States to support free peoples who are resisting attempted subjugation by armed minorities or by outside pressures." [22]

Since 1947 the Marshall Plan, NATO, and other developments have illustrated, in varying degree, the expansion in Europe of American commitments. Nowhere, however, have the commitments been such as to translate fully into action the extravagant idiom which Truman used in his statement in Congress. American policy toward Finland, for example, has not shown readiness to consider

[22] *Congressional Record,* 80 Cong. 1 sess. (March 12, 1951), 1981.

the precarious aspects of Finland's position—clearly the consequence of Soviet aggression and designs—a circumstance that undermines the security of the United States and should therefore be frankly recognized as a vital concern of the United States. There has been, understandably, no commitment to help the Finns "maintain their free institutions and their national integrity" against possible Soviet aggression, despite the obvious fact that Finland has been exposed, since 1944–1945, to "outside pressures" originating in Moscow.

Specific American commitment has, clearly, been limited to the Western military alliance and related undertakings. In the Scandinavian North, Denmark and Norway are within the area which, presumably, the Soviet Union can penetrate only at its own peril, while Sweden and Finland are—again presumably—outside of it. While the Truman doctrine was uncritically generous in suggesting ample limits for American interest and assistance, the post-1949 expansion of United States commitments has not been carried far enough to result in a clear-cut identification of those areas in Europe (outside NATO) which will be defended or those, if any, which will be abandoned. Finland and Sweden will be involved in the choice when it comes. Especially as regards Finland, the choice represents a serious dilemma. Both military and moral considerations suggest that Finland's eastern border be recognized as the northernmost segment of the Western defense frontier in Europe. The chances are, however, that especially if a crisis situation compelling a choice is postponed for several years, the plans to contain or reduce Soviet expansion will not thus define the Soviet border of Finland. Yet it would seem that if military readiness to meet aggression is the best way to discourage and prevent aggression—a concept which lies at the basis of the vast American defense program of the past several years—it will serve no useful purpose to abandon or to fail to make use of the defense potential of the eastern part of the Scandinavian area. If the cold war means, as many leading Americans have claimed times without number, that the two opposing worlds are engaged in a grim contest for survival, it follows that one of the objectives of our European policy must necessarily be the full utilization of the resources and potential of Finland and Sweden in the contest. The relations of the United States with Finland since 1945 have laid a firm foundation for such a policy.

Chapter 14

Austria

R. JOHN RATH

The Liberation

ON APRIL 13, 1945, Soviet troops, which had crossed the Hungarian frontier on March 29, entered Vienna. Before the end of the month they occupied large areas of Lower Austria and Styria. From Italy the British invaded, at the beginning of May, the southern Austrian province of Carinthia, while United States soldiers, coming from Germany, took over control of the Tyrol on May 3 from an Austrian resistance group led by Dr. Karl Gruber (Austrian foreign minister from 1945 to 1953 and now Austrian ambassador to the United States), which had a few days earlier ousted the National Socialists from Innsbruck. Armed with proclamations calling the attention of the newly-liberated populace to the commitments made by their respective governments at Moscow in October, 1943, to support the re-establishment of a free and independent Austria, the commanders of the three Allied armies "temporarily" assumed supreme authority over the parts of Austria held by their troops.

The Austria thus set free by the Allies in April and May, 1945, was virtually in a state of disintegration. Food depots and industrial resources not destroyed in the fighting were pillaged by retreating Germans, freed slave laborers, starving Austrians, or undisciplined Russians who, bent on wreaking vengeance on the "Germans" for their spoliation of Western Russia, treated all public and private property and all Austrian women as legitimate war booty. The orgy of looting and fire inevitably led to famine. In spite of the desperate efforts of Austrian officials to transport foodstuff to the capital, the Viennese food ration in early May was a mere 350 calories a day per person.

The Establishment of a Provisional Government

Not only was the Austrian economy in utter ruin, but the administrative machinery was also in complete disorder. The provincial and local officials appointed by the Nazis had in the spring of 1945 either been obliged to flee with the retreating German army or been suspended from their jobs by the newly-arrived Allied commanders. To fill the resulting political vacuum in Vienna a group of Social Democrats and Christian Socialists who had lived in retirement or in Nazi prison or concentration camps set up a temporary municipal government, with General Theodor Körner, a venerated Socialist political leader, as mayor. At the same time, Leopold Figl, the former director of the Austrian Peasants' Union, was appointed provisional governor of Lower Austria.

Meanwhile, the Red Army had prevailed upon Dr. Karl Renner, the first Chancellor of the prewar Austrian Republic, to take the initiative in re-establishing a democratic central government for Austria.[1] Within a few days Renner succeeded in reaching an agreement with the leaders of the chief Austrian democratic parties to form a provisional government based on the 1929 constitution. Announced on April 27, this government was recognized by the Soviet authorities two days later. To insure that the new regime would have the full confidence of all elements of the populace, as well as that of the Red Army, the new Chancellor allotted three of the most important cabinet posts to the Socialists, three to the People's Party (the reconstituted former Christian Social Party), two to the Communists, and two to nonparty men. In all the ministries except finance under-secretaries were appointed from parties other than that to which the minister belonged. Since the Communists were entrusted with the all-important Ministries of Education and Interior, they were well pleased with the arrangement. In fact, Ernst Fischer, their Minister of Education, was so exultant that he was nearly always at the point of jumping up and singing the old

[1] For an interesting account of how Dr. Renner, after going to the nearest Russian outpost to try to influence the Russians to treat the inhabitants of Gloggnitz, where he was living, less harshly, was led to higher headquarters, where he was recognized and asked to re-establish the Austrian government, see Karl Renner, *Denkschrift über die Geschichte der Unabhängigkeitserklärung Österreichs und Bericht über drei Monate Aufbauarbeit* (Zürich: Europa Verlag, 1946).

Austrian national anthem, *Gott erhalte und beschütze unsern Kaiser!*

For several months the authority of the Renner government was limited to the areas occupied by Soviet armies. Carinthia and Styria, from which the British had with difficulty ousted Tito's partisan forces and Soviet troops, were governed by British military government teams brought up from Rome. In Upper Austria and Salzburg American officers rapidly established at least a modicum of law and order. In the Tyrol and Vorarlberg, where United States occupation troops were replaced by the French early in July, the French ensconced themselves and inaugurated a policy of requisitioning which exasperated the impoverished Austrians. Communications between the different occupation zones were so difficult in the summer of 1945 that Chancellor Renner smuggled confidants into the non-Russian areas to learn what was happening in them. Not before late August did any Western Austrian political leader dare to go to Vienna, and not until late in September was the federal Chancellor in a position to consult an all-party provincial conference in Vienna about means to extend the authority of his regime over all Austria.

Conflicting Allied Policies and Practices

Highly suspicious that the Renner government was a mere puppet of the Soviet Army, the Western Powers did not grant it recognition before October 20, and then only with the proviso that it was to be under the close supervision of an Allied Council, which had been agreed upon by the governments of the four occupying powers on July 4, 1945, and which had held its first meeting in Vienna on September 11.[2] In addition, the Allies stipulated that the government was to hold free elections as early as possible.[3]

Although all four occupying powers consented, in October, 1945, to acknowledge the Renner government, the policies of the three Western Powers in regard to Austria differed vastly from those of the Soviet Union. The paramount aim of the United States Government, as well as that of its Western allies, was to sign a treaty with and withdraw all occupation troops from Austria as soon as her people were fully committed to democratic principles.

[2] The Allied Council consisted of four high commissioners (one representing each occupying power), an executive committee, and various departmental staffs. The agreement on the control machinery for Austria was made by the European Advisory Commission in London.

[3] See *American Policy in Occupied Areas,* Department of State Publication No. 2794 (Washington, D.C.: U.S. Government Printing Office, 1947), p. 27.

To accomplish this aim American authorities in Austria were instructed to turn over all administrative functions to the Austrians as rapidly as possible, to foster the re-establishment of a democratic state and society, and to direct all their efforts towards making the country economically and financially viable.[4] On the whole, the policies of the French and British coincided with those of the United States.

Notwithstanding their promises to support Austrian independence and the surprising latitude which they allowed Dr. Renner in organizing his provisional government,[5] the Russians attempted in 1945 to maneuver the Austrians into a semidependent position. To them the coalition government which they had encouraged Renner to establish was nothing but a façade admirably suited to veil the numerical weakness of the Austrian Communists and a thinly veneered facsimile of the "national concentration" governments which they had fashioned in Eastern Europe.[6] Perhaps to prepare the way for the eventual creation of a "people's democracy," the Communists ordered Renner, over his strenuous objections,[7] to assign the all-important Ministry of Interior to a tough Moscow-trained Communist, Franz Honner, who, in close cooperation with the Red Army and the MVD, installed reliable Communists in key posts in the police and gendarmerie and organized a secret political police of 1000 men, modeled closely after its Russian prototype.

The November 25, 1945 Elections and Their Results

The Russians apparently intended to fashion Austria into a Soviet satellite. If this goal proved to be too difficult to realize, they expected Austria at least to be a fertile field for economic ex-

[4] See especially *ibid.*, p. 23; *Military Government Austria. Report of the United States Commissioner* (hereafter cited as "Austria, *U.S. Commissioner Report*"), No. 7 (May, 1946), pp. 5–7; and American directive on military government of Austria, June 27, 1945, Cary Travers Grayson, *Austria's International Position 1938–1953: the Re-establishment of an Independent Austria* (Geneva: Droz, 1953), Appendix X, pp. 198–99.

[5] Renner makes a point of emphasizing this in his *Denkschrift über die Geschichte der Unabhängigkeitserklärung,* pp. 34–5.

[6] For similar evaluations of Russian intentions in Austria in 1945, see "American Migrant," "Democracy Besieged in Austria," *The Contemporary Review,* November, 1947, pp. 270–71; G. E. R. Gedye, "Austrian Recovery," *ibid.*, January, 1949, p. 8; Ernest O. Hauser, "Vienna Isn't Berlin—Yet," *The Saturday Evening Post,* November 13, 1948, p. 27; and Edgar Snow, "Behind Russian Lines in Austria," *ibid.*, August 11, 1945, p. 84.

[7] Karl Renner, *Nachgelassene Werke,* Vol. II: *Österreich von der ersten zur zweiten Republik* (Vienna: Wiener Volksbuchhandlung, 1953), pp. 233–34.

ploitation. Nonetheless, even though in 1945 the Soviet Government obviously did not desire the establishment of a truly free and independent Austria—at least not in the immediate future—the Russians surprisingly enough joined the other occupying powers in approving free elections on November 25, 1945, and made no efforts to interfere with them, even though the campaign speeches occasionally stimulated anti-Russian demonstrations. No doubt the Soviet authorities were misled by reports of imaginative Austrian Communists assuring them that they would get forty, and perhaps even fifty per cent of all the ballots cast. Instead they received a bare 174,387 votes (less than 5½%) and elected only 4 members of the National Assembly, in contrast to 85 for the conservative People's Party and 76 for the Socialists. Bitterly disappointed with the outcome, the Russians could momentarily do little more than chide the Austrian Communists for their failure and resume their traditional tactics of "boring from within" in the hope that eventually a change in the international situation would allow them to adopt a policy of direct action.

Following the elections a new coalition government was formed, with Leopold Figl (People's Party) as Chancellor and Adolf Schärf (Socialist) as Vice-Chancellor, while the venerated Dr. Renner became President of the Republic. The Communists were ousted from the key Ministries of the Interior and Education and—for public relations purposes only—granted just the relatively insignificant Ministry of Energy and Electrification.

Since the Allied Council approved all Austrian legislation prior to June, 1946, the Figl government could at first hardly call its soul its own. A new control agreement, dated June 28, 1946, in effect restored legislative powers to the Austrian parliament and required that henceforth only constitutional laws needed the unanimous approval of all four occupying powers.[8] The Russians, however, repeatedly nullified the effects of this understanding by forcing the Austrian Government to accept unilateral agreements and by frequently declining to enforce in their own zone Austrian regulations which displeased them. Although the Americans, British,

[8] All other legislative enactments were automatically to become law and could be put into effect if the Allied Council had not objected to them within thirty-one days. Before June 28, 1946, all laws and decrees had to be approved by the Allied Council before they could go into effect, and the Allied Council exercised vigorous controls over all Austrian legislation. In 1945, for instance, 248 laws and decrees of the Austrian Government were acted on by the Allied Council.

and French withdrew their military government teams from the local level in 1946, and although the Allied Council in the same year gave Austrian citizens permission to pass freely between all zonal demarcation lines, the Russians refused to permit free passage of food, goods, and raw materials from their own zone and stubbornly vetoed Western Power recommendations to abolish postal, telegraph, and telephone censorship in Austria.

Soviet Practices in Austria, 1945–47

The real threat to Austrian security, however, stemmed, not from Russian obstructionism in the Allied Council, but from the wholesale Soviet seizures of property in Austria. Immediately after the liberation the Russians loaded every eastbound train with such valuables as cattle, clothing, machinery, raw materials, office fixtures, and even furniture, all of which were sequestrated as war booty. The most profitable Russian loot, however, consisted of the so-called "German assets," thoughtlessly handed to the Russians at Potsdam in July, 1945, as indemnification for the German destructions in Russia. Since the Nazis had taken over practically everything valuable in Austria between 1938 and 1945, the Potsdam "gift" virtually amounted to bestowing upon the Russians the main industrial wealth of Eastern Austria to use in any way they saw fit.

The most important resource thus expropriated was the Zistersdorf oil fields,[9] outside Rumania the most highly prized oil reserve in non-Russian Europe. After the Austrian Government had rejected a Soviet proposal to exploit these petroleum resources by a joint Austro-Russian concern, the Russians created a special Soviet Mineral Administration to manage the Austrian fields. Refusing to supply the Austrians, even at a high price, with many needed petroleum products, the Soviets sent them either to their homeland or to the satellite countries of Eastern Europe.

The other "German assets" appropriated in Austria, comprising numerous industrial, agricultural, commercial, and financial enterprises, were placed under the management of U.S.I.A. (Administration for Soviet Property in Eastern Austria)—a gigantic monopoly which in a short time embraced approximately 300 concerns, and opened up close to 200 retail outlets, called "Uncle Joe's

[9] It should be noted that between 1949 and 1955 the Soviets put into production several oil fields located in villages near Zistersdorf. The most important of these are at Matzen, Aderklaa, and Bockfliess.

Junk Stores" by the Austrians, which, because they paid no taxes and violated all Austrian commercial regulations, became a serious threat to legitimate Austrian businesses.

Even more dangerous to Austrian security were the frequent arrests and kidnappings. In 1945 the Soviet secret service and Red Army began a systematic policy of abducting persons who had incurred the disfavor of the Communists or were considered a threat to Russian security. Austrian circles estimated that by the spring of 1946 more than 500 people had been arbitrarily arrested or spirited away, sometimes in broad daylight, occasionally in the dead of night.

The Austrian Government courageously fought all Russian machinations to undermine its security. It steadfastly refused to legalize the Russian rights to German property and issued repeated warnings that Austrians who allowed themselves to be used as a cover for unlicensed U.S.I.A. enterprises were punishable according to Austrian law. Most important of all, after the Communists lost control of the all-important Ministry of Interior in November, 1945, the new minister, Oskar Helmer, a tough-minded, intrepid Socialist, silently but ruthlessly purged the Communists and their henchmen from the police force. Then he turned his attention to the political police organized by the Russians in 1945, rapidly dismissing or transferring from it all but 150 reliable men—just enough to keep check on Communist subversion. The Figl ministry also initiated drastic steps to set its financial house in order by passing a law in November, 1945, requiring all persons to turn in all their Reichsmark holdings to Austrian banks in the next month. In exchange they were to receive 150 new Austrian schillings ($15.00 according to the arbitrarily pegged exchange rate) and to have the remainder credited to them in a special blocked account which could be used only for strictly limited purposes.

Economic Conditions, 1945–47

Although this currency conversion for a time effectively curbed a serious threat of wild inflation, it could not remove the grave handicaps which crippled the Austrian economy during the immediate postwar years: the arbitrary zonal demarcation lines, the lack of negotiable foreign exchange, the Soviet exploitation of "German assets," the refusal of the Allied Council to permit the

Austrians to resume normal trade relations with Germany, the inability to purchase essential raw materials from abroad, the lack of machinery, the severe shortages in fuel and hydroelectric power, and the absence of skilled workers. By the end of 1946 the production rate in most basic industries was barely a third of what it had been in 1937,[10] and even this slow production rate was sharply reduced by the severity of the winter of 1946–47—the coldest in many years. In 1947 there were substantial increases in some fields and significant ones in nearly all branches of industry; with the exception of hydroelectric power, copper ore, salt, and talcum, the production rate, however, was still substantially below that of prewar years.[11]

The critical food shortages continued. In March, 1946, the food ration, which had been raised to 1550 calories in the fall of 1945, had to be cut to 1200 calories, of which only 950 could actually be provided in May. It could not be increased again to 1550 before November, 1946, and only to 1700 in December, 1947. Meanwhile, the cost of living advanced from 100 (the base index rate) in April, 1945, to 165.7 in January, 1947, and to 182 in the early summer of 1947. The steady rise in prices, the critical food shortage, and the lagging production in consumer goods, especially clothing and shoes, led to labor unrest, irresistible demands for price and wage increases, and threatening inflationary pressures. To prevent runaway inflation, repair the growing disequilibrium caused by officially set prices, and soothe the anxieties of the workers over the widening gap between wages and prices, the Austrian parliament in July, 1947, passed the first of a number of wage-price decrees establishing a formula for allowing prices (particularly for food and public utilities) to rise, and increasing wages between 43 and 50 per cent. This law was followed by such extensive price and wage increases that by December the cost of

10 For the year 1946 the production of iron ore, for instance, was 31.3% of that of 1937; that of raw iron, 31.5%; that of unprocessed steel, 31.1%; that of wood products, 27.3%; and that of paper, 29.2%.—See *Österreichisches Jahrbuch 1945–1946. Nach amtlichen Quellen,* herausgegeben vom Bundespressedienst (18th ed., Vienna: Österreichische Staatsdruckerei, 1947), p. 50.

11 That of coal was 77.4% of the 1937 rate; iron ore, 46.9%; raw iron, 71.6%; unprocessed steel, 54.9%; wood products, 55.8%; lead, 43.0%; magnesite, 56.0%; graphite, 24.4%; cement, 65.7%; paper, 48.8%; and cellulose, 22.4%.—As given in the *Österreichisches Jahrbuch 1947. Nach amtlichen Quellen,* herausgegeben vom Bundespressedienst (19th ed., Vienna: Österreichische Staatsdruckerei, 1948), pp. 34–5.

living was between three-and-one-half and four times that of April 1945,[12] while wages had increased by three times.[13]

Now that the price level of various commodities had struck a more realistic equilibrium the government hastened to enact another currency reform to prevent a dangerous inflationary spiral. After paying the Soviet Union approximately 500,000,000 schillings to insure immediate Russian cooperation in carrying out the act, the government proclaimed, in December, 1947, another sweeping currency reform which reduced the amount of money in circulation by nearly 50%. The enactment had another important effect. In order to prepare the way to stage strikes and demonstrations against the currency reform, the Communists, screaming that the measure had been drawn up "on the orders of Wall Street," decided that their one minister in the government, Dr. Altmann, should resign. Thus they deprived themselves of an effective listening post within the government and were rewarded by the arrival in Vienna of a special Moscow emissary, who upbraided their executive committee for its gross inefficiency.

Allied Economic Aid to Austria and Its Consequences

Currency reforms, however, could be only a temporary palliative as long as the occupying powers levied heavy occupation costs on Austria, which amounted to 230% of the Austrian civilian budget in 1945 and early 1946 and to 15% in 1947. Even though the United States Government on July 1, 1947, renounced its claim to occupation costs, the burden of maintaining the other armies would have put a severe strain on Austria's already badly shaken economy had she not received timely assistance from a number of sources: UNRRA, post-UNRRA, emergency supplies delivered by military authorities, private gifts, credits from the Export-Import Bank, and Marshall aid. To pay for the importation of necessary foodstuffs and to supply funds for agricultural and industrial rehabilitation, UNRRA allotted more than $100,000,000 to Austria during 1946–47, most of which was actually contributed by the United States. Then followed over $100,000,000 in special

[12] The cost of living index was 357.5% of that of April, 1945, according to the index of the Austrian Institute for Economic Research, and 396.9% according to the statistics prepared by the Austrian Government's statistical office. Austria, *U.S. Commissioner Report,* No. 26 (December, 1947), pp. 126–27.

[13] 305.1% according to the calculations prepared by the Institute for Economic Research. *Ibid.,* p. 127.

post-UNRRA help from the United States, in addition to generous sums from Great Britain and other countries. Finally, came the European Recovery Program (ERP), or Marshall Plan, which the Austrians joined, notwithstanding bitter Russian protests that the project was nothing but a sinister scheme to make Austria a tool of American capitalism. The Marshall Plan became effective in April, 1948, when the United States Congress approved the first installment of the necessary funds. Under the plan, Austria received direct aid for importing essential commodities from the Western hemisphere; indirect aid, to procure necessities from other countries with which she had an unfavorable balance of trade; and counterpart funds, made up of payments from Austrian citizens for goods sent to Austria through the ERP, to use for long term industrial investments and stabilizing the currency. By June 30, 1952, a total of $909,100,000 of ERP aid had been sent to Austria.

This munificent and timely financial assistance from the United States not only warded off general economic collapse but also greatly strengthened the ability of the Austrian coalition government to protect itself against unending Russian machinations to undermine it. Except for the highly vocal Communist fragment, the Austrian people were highly appreciative of this immense and vital help, which they regarded as an unmistakable token of American friendship. Nonetheless, realizing that they could never be master of their own fatherland as long as foreign soldiers were on Austrian soil, they were impatient for all Allied troops to return home as rapidly as possible. Beginning in 1946 the almost universal cry of the populace was for a treaty which would guarantee complete political and economic independence for their country.

The Treaty Negotiations, 1947–54

Notwithstanding a Soviet offer in 1945 to conclude an Austrian treaty on condition that foreign troops remain in Austria until a definitive peace was made with Germany, and the efforts of the American State Department to include a treaty with Austria among those signed in 1946 with Bulgaria, Finland, Italy, Rumania, and Hungary, deputies of the foreign ministers of the four occupying powers did not meet before January, 1947, to initiate preliminary work for an Austrian treaty. These conversations, which were held in London, bogged down, however, over the insistent claims of the Yugoslavs to Southern Carinthia.

At the meeting of the foreign ministers in Moscow, in March and April, 1947, the most troublesome problem was the Potsdam agreement in regard to German assets in Austria, which the Russians interpreted so liberally that had their viewpoint been accepted the Soviets would have secured legal title to the vast amount of property which they had expropriated in Eastern Austria. Failing to arrive at an understanding on this and other disputed questions, the four ministers adjourned the conference after appointing a special commission to meet in Vienna to discuss the whole German property question.

Towards the end of the Vienna sessions Cherrière, the French delegate, suggested by way of compromise that, instead of continuing their fruitless efforts to define German assets, the Allies should draw up plans for Austria to turn over to the Soviet Union approximately half of her oil concessions and all possessions of the Danube Shipping Company in Hungary, Bulgaria, and Rumania, and pay a lump sum of $100,000,000 to repurchase the remainder of the German property from the Soviets. In January, 1948, the Russians made public counterproposals in which they asked for two-thirds of the oil, one-fourth of the property of the Danube Shipping Company in Austria, as well as all which was located in the countries east of Austria, and $200,000,000 in settlement for all other German assets. After the Russians made this offer, the Austrians were hopeful that a peace treaty would finally be signed at the meeting of the foreign ministers in London in the spring of 1948, but their expectations were in vain, for at London the question of Yugoslav reparations and territorial claims again disrupted the conference.

When negotiations were resumed in 1949 the Russians agreed to a United States proposal to give Russia a 60:40 division of the Austrian oil production, to grant the Soviets all former property of the Danube Shipping Company in Eastern Austria, Hungary, Bulgaria, and Rumania, and to award the Russians $150,000,000 for the rest of the German assets in Austria. Then a new deadlock developed when the Soviets insisted that before treaty talks could be continued the Austrian Government had to pay them a large sum of money for peas which the Red Army had delivered to the starving Austrian population in 1945, presumably as a gift, and for numerous other donations.

By the fall of 1949 it became clear that the Soviet Union was determined for the time being not to reach an agreement. During the numerous conferences held the next year the Russians raised angry charges about a resurgence of neo-Nazism and militarism in Austria, and insisted that the Trieste issue must be settled before further progress could be made with the treaty talks.

Negotiations did not commence again until 1952, when the American Government proposed the substitution of a new short treaty draft, comprising only eight short articles, seven of which had already been agreed upon, for the old treaty which had been debated since 1947. The new text provided merely for the recognition of an independent Austria, with the same frontiers as those of January 1, 1938, and for the withdrawal of all occupation armies within ninety days after the treaty came into force. Most important of all, it declared that no reparations whatever were to be exacted in Austria. Maintaining that the new draft seriously limited the freedom of Austrian organizations pledged to the preservation of democracy and peace, the Soviet Government angrily rejected the proposal, demanded a return to the older draft, and reverted to its former stand that the Austrian treaty could be discussed only after the Trieste question had been resolved.

In spite of the fact that the General Assembly of the United Nations on December 20, 1952, unanimously passed a resolution urging the four powers to make every effort as early as possible to reach agreement on the Austrian treaty, in 1952 and 1953 the Kremlin repeatedly obstructed the unceasing efforts of the Western Powers to arrive at an understanding. When serious four-power talks were resumed in January, 1954, the Russians balked at signing a treaty unless Austria would pledge herself never to participate in a military alliance against her or permit the erection of any foreign military establishments on her soil. Furthermore, they asked that all Western troops immediately withdraw from Vienna but that all four powers remain in occupation of their own zones (except Vienna) until a peace treaty was signed with Germany. Since neither Austria nor the Western Powers would agree to these conditions, which had deliberately been framed to promote Russian interference in Austrian domestic affairs, negotiations again broke down, amidst a barrage of accusations and counter-accusations.

Russian Tactics in Austria, 1948–55

Instead of attaining their longed-for treaty, the Austrians were constrained until 1955 to endure continual Russian exploitation of their resources and perpetual Soviet meddling in their internal affairs. During the late 1940's and the 1950's the Soviets confiscated additional Austrian businesses as "German assets" and rapidly increased the Austrian oil production rate. U.S.I.A. concerns continued to dump Russian and satellite wares on the Austrian market and operated their enterprises as extra-territorial entities which violated Austrian laws with impunity.

In a more direct and brutal fashion, the Red Army stepped up its kidnappings. After broadly hinting that they planned to extend their arrests to members of the Austrian Government, the Soviets in 1948 brazenly abducted Chief Inspector Anton Marek, chief of the police unit commissioned with ferreting out antidemocratic conspiracies; Franz Kiridus, a gendarme official associated with the Ministry of Interior; and Dr. Margarethe Ottillinger, an important member of the Ministry of Property Control and Economic Planning. Between 1949 and 1955 the Soviets arrested numerous police and customs officials, farmers, workers, and housewives, casual travelers, displaced persons, intellectuals, and businessmen. Early in 1955 they took into custody Dr. Alfred Sokolowski, liaison officer between the Vienna city government and the Russians.

The Soviets endeavored to undermine the Austrian police, refusing to allow them to be adequately armed, trained, or manned, and frequently preventing them from enforcing orders to which the Russians objected. Without consulting the Austrian Government, the Red Army submitted personal questionnaires for Austrian public servants to fill out. At times individual Russian commanders enjoined the Austrians to notify them in advance about all political gatherings or any sittings of the provincial diet or local government, so that a Russian officer could be present at the deliberations. In the fall of 1950 the Communists staged a dress rehearsal for a *coup d'état* à la Czechoslovakia. After calling a general strike, Communist storm troopers and U.S.I.A. workers, openly protected by the Red Army, engaged in violent demonstrations, seized telephone exchanges and railway stations, occupied factories and public buildings, mishandled police officers, and cut off road and rail communications to Vienna. When the Socialist workers threatened to storm all factories and public places occupied by Communist rioters, the champions of "people's democracy" called off the demonstration.

Austrian Politics, 1949–53

Instead of frightening the Austrians, the Russian tactics of obstructionism and intimidation made the Austrians more determined than ever to maintain a coalition government strong enough to ward off every possible danger. Although in the 1949 elections the newly formed rightist League of Independents elected sixteen members of the National Assembly, the Communists won only five seats (an increase of only one over 1945), while the People's Party and the Socialists maintained the same relative strength which they had in 1945. In the 1953 elections the League of Independents lost two seats and the Communists one, while the Socialists increased their representation in the National Assembly from 67 to 73, in contrast to the 74 held by the People's Party, which lost three seats. The Figl government was replaced by a new coalition ministry headed by Julius Raab (People's Party), former president of the Austrian chamber of commerce, but the composition of the new cabinet remained essentially the same as that of the previous one, and the new Chancellor continued to follow the same conservative policies which had characterized the administration of his predecessor.

Steady Economic Improvement, 1948–55

The cautious economic and financial policies of the Austrian Government, plus the substantial ERP assistance received from the United States, paid increasing dividends during the 1950's. By 1948 about half of the damaged buildings in Vienna had been put into habitable shape, and the 2100 calorie ration established in September, 1948, was easily supplemented with point-free produce readily purchased in the markets. As a consequence of the 1947 currency reform and improved business conditions, hoarded consumer goods began to appear in substantial amounts on the legal market, and many necessities of life were gradually removed from the rationed list. More important, by 1948 the government managed to balance the ordinary budget and have a small surplus.[14]

Meanwhile, industrial production, which in January, 1947, had been at the pitifully low level of 28.9% of the 1937 rate, increased to 106.9% of the 1937 total in November, 1948; to 129.6%, in November, 1949; to 131%, in November, 1950; and to 171.4%, in

[14] It should be noted, however, that although there was a surplus of 28,000,000 schillings in the ordinary budget, another 723,000,000 schillings not accounted for in the ordinary budget were spent for reconstruction and investment purposes.

September, 1951. The next year there was a slight leveling off to 167.1% of the 1937 production rate, which went up only to 169.9% in 1953. Between January and June, 1954, however, industrial production was approximately one-third greater than during the previous year, and by the middle of 1954 it was approximately double that of 1937. Early in 1955 the production rate rose to 214% of that of 1937. The greatest improvement was registered in the non-ferrous metallurgical industry, in foundry products, in machine products, and in hydroelectric power.

The rapid growth of Austrian industrial production reflected itself in the increasing financial stability of the country. By the end of 1954 the total savings deposits of the Austrian people, which were practically nonexistent in 1945, amounted to 7,500,000,000 schillings. At the same time, the foreign exchange and gold holdings of the Austrian National Bank increased from $24,000,000 at the end of 1951 to $385,000,000 on August 31, 1954. Austria's balance of foreign trade payments, excluding foreign aid, changed from a deficit of $104,000,000 in 1952 to a surplus of $71,000,000 in 1953, while the Austrian debt to the European Payments Union turned into a total credit balance of $96,100,000 in December, 1953. On account of this highly favorable trade situation, foreign economic aid to Austria was discontinued in 1953, and the Austrian Government in 1954 approved a 75% liberalization in import quotas (which was subsequently increased to 83%), sharply reduced the import duty on goods not produced in Austria, raised the travel allowance for Austrians traveling abroad, and freed foreign exchange transactions from most of the restrictions to which they had been subjected. In addition, on January 1, 1954, for the first time since the war, the government reduced taxes by approximately 10%. The results were so favorable in increasing production, savings deposits, investments, and even tax receipts that on January 1, 1955, an additional 10% tax reduction was decreed.

The Relaxation of Allied Controls, 1953–54

This remarkable melioration in economic and financial conditions was accompanied by a noticeable relaxation of occupation burdens, particularly in 1953. The four occupying powers substantially reduced the size of their military forces, and the Russians, British, and French, following the policy pursued by the United States since 1947, renounced all claims on Austria for occupation costs. On their own accord the Russians released 600 Austrians still held in Russia and freed other prisoners jailed in the Soviet Zone. Voluntarily they turned over the valuable Ybbs-Persenbeug hydroelectric works to the Austrians, abolished all controls for persons and freight crossing the Soviet demarcation lines, lifted the ban forbidding Russian soldiers from fraternizing with the Austrians, abolished the censorship in the Soviet Zone, replaced their military occupation commander with a civilian high commissioner (which the three Western Powers had previously done), and established normal diplomatic relations with the Austrian foreign office. In the same year the Russians, after withholding their approval ever since 1947, joined the other three occupying powers in removing the Allied censorship over the mail, telephone calls, and telegrams.

After making these surprising concessions in 1953, the Russians the next year again tightened their hold on the unfortunate Republic. In the provincial elections in the fall of 1954 the Red Army exerted various pressures to try to prevent the election of anti-Russian officials and instructed the Austrian police to furnish them with details about the time and place of party meetings and the speakers who were to participate in them. At the same time the Soviets again denounced the Austrian Government for allegedly encouraging anti-Soviet activities, fostering the growth of numerous fascist and military organizations, subsidizing *Anschluss* propaganda, inciting the Austrian people to war against the Soviet Union, and collaborating with the Western Powers to separate the three Western zones from the Soviet sector.

The 1955 Treaty Negotiations

Then, to the surprise of the numerous observers who had concluded in 1954 that the Soviets had no intention of voluntarily withdrawing from Austria for some time to come, the Kremlin intimated early in February, 1955, that it might be willing to remove Russian troops from and sign a treaty with Austria prior to the conclusion of a German peace treaty, provided that sound guarantees of Austria's independence and neutrality were given.

In response to a formal invitation sent on March 24, Chancellor Raab flew to Moscow early in April to explore treaty possibilities. Received in Moscow in a cordial, even comradely, atmosphere, the Austrian Chancellor obtained more concessions than he had previously even dared to expect. In return for assurances that Austria would never join any military alliance or permit foreign military bases on her territory, that she would always pursue a "policy of independence" with respect to all states, and that she would never undertake any actions that would lead either to economic or political *Anschluss* with Germany, the Soviets agreed that the military forces of all four occupying powers should be withdrawn from Austrian soil as soon as possible after the acceptance of the treaty and at the latest by December 31, 1955, and that Austrian prisoners still remaining on Russian soil would be released by the time the Soviet troops had left Austria. Instead of demanding the repurchase of the "German assets" in cash, the Russians allowed the Austrians to pay for them with $150,000,000 worth of Austrian goods. For proper recompense (reportedly $2,000,000), they relinquished the assets of the Danube Shipping Company in Austria. More important, the Soviet Union promised to surrender all its oil concessions, exploration rights, and oil refineries in Austria in return for the "delivery of crude oil in amounts agreed upon" by the two governments. This figure was set at 1,000,000 tons annually—approximately one-third of the estimated Russian production for 1954—for ten years.

Between May 2 and May 15, 1955, these Russian proposals were discussed point by point in Vienna by representatives of the Austrian, British, French, and Russian foreign offices and of the United States State Department. During these conversations the Russians consented to change several articles in the 1949 treaty draft which the Austrians and Western Powers found objectionable. They dropped the fugitive clause, which made it possible for the Russians to force the Austrians to return refugees from Communist lands to them, the article limiting the Austrian army to 53,000 men, and the part of the preamble implying Austrian war guilt. For a brief time the Russian delegates balked at including in the treaty any reference to the Austro-Soviet economic understanding made in Moscow in April. However, after Secretary Dulles refused to fly to Vienna to sign the treaty unless the Russians yielded on this point, the Soviets capitulated to the Western demands. On May 13 the representatives of all four powers agreed to the text of the treaty, which was formally signed at noon on May 15 by the foreign ministers of the four occupying powers and the foreign minister of Austria.

In the treaty the United States, Great Britain, France, and Russia recognized Austria's independence and territorial integrity within the frontiers existing on January 1, 1938. Austria was prohibited from undertaking any actions promoting "political or economic union with Germany" or the restoration of the Habsburgs, and was instructed to eliminate all traces of Nazism from her soil, to dissolve "all fascist-type" and National Socialist organizations, and to make every effort to establish and preserve democratic institutions. The Slovene and Croatian minorities were guaranteed rights equal to all other Austrian nationals in regard to their own schools, organizations, and the use of their own language. Although no limitations were placed on the size of the Austrian army, former high-ranking Nazis were excluded from it. Furthermore, the Austrians pledged themselves never to cooperate with the Germans in taking "steps outside German territory towards rearmament."

The Soviets promised to return the Austrian prisoners as soon as possible, and all four occupation powers agreed to withdraw their troops from Austrian soil within ninety days from the coming into force of the treaty "and insofar as possible not later than December 31, 1955." At Russian insistence most of Article 35 of the 1949 text was retained in the present treaty (as Article 22). This gave the Soviet Union 60 per cent of Austria's oilfields, refineries, and exploration rights and the entire property of the Danube Steamship Company. Arrangements were made for the repurchase of the other former "German assets" within six years for $150,000,000 in U.S. dollars. Annex II of the treaty, however, provided for the transfer to Austria of the above property on the basis of the arrangements made between the Soviet and Austrian governments in April. Except for religious, cultural, charitable, and educational property, none of these assets were ever to be returned to the ownership of "German juridical persons" or to private German citizens whenever the rights and interests exceeded 260,000 schillings (approximately $10,400). The Austrian Government, furthermore, pledged itself never to allow the oil fields or oil exploration rights given back to Austria by Russia to pass to foreign ownership.

Nothing was inserted in the treaty to implement the Austrian assurances in Moscow that their country would be perpetually neutral and would never join any military alliances. The Allies and Austria, however, informally agreed that after the ratification of the treaty the Austrian Government would submit to Parliament a constitutional law stipulating perpetual neutrality and then take the necessary steps to insure that this constitutional declaration obtained international recognition.

The Effects of the Treaty on Austria

Tired of not being the real master of their own country for seventeen years and indignant at seeing "privileged foreigners" housed in their best living quarters, the Austrian people were naturally enthusiastic over the prospect of becoming an independent and neutral country—a second Switzerland, which is now the goal of many Austrians.

The price which the Austrians must pay for these blessings, however, is high. Austria will be virtually defenseless. The strain of creating and maintaining an army worthy of the name will be so heavy a drain on the Austrian budget that Austrian officials have already concluded that their army will have to grow very slowly. Then, too, although the Austrian people have recently been enjoying much greater prosperity than at any time since the Republic was created in 1918, this opulence has stemmed at least in part from the substantial amount of economic assistance poured into the country by the United States and other Western democracies and from the jobs and foreign currency provided by the Western occupation forces. Now new jobs must be found and new export markets located to supply the needed foreign exchange. Also, within the next six years the Austrians will have to deliver $150,000,000 worth of goods to the Russians and an estimated $170,000,000 worth of oil during the next ten years. Out of their own resources they will need to spend large sums to renovate the former "German enterprises," many of which are now facing bankruptcy and nearly all of which require new capital for repair and modernization. Furthermore, the Germans, who have already expressed bitter anger over the severe restrictions which have made the recovery of their former property in Austria almost impossible, will probably make concerted efforts to recover at least some of it. They will be in a position to put powerful economic pressure on the Austrians to gain a satisfactory adjustment, for the Austrians must look to Germany for many of their tourists, the largest percentage of their imports, their best market, and badly needed capital.

Meeting these onerous obligations will put a severe strain upon the economy of a country with a population substantially less than that of New York City and with capital assets which are almost infinitesimal by comparison with those of the New Yorkers. To pay for their freedom, the Austrians may find it necessary sharply to increase their tax rate, borrow heavily from their former friends, and economize drastically.

In spite of these handicaps, the future of the Austrian people seems reasonably bright. Since the days of Seipel, Dollfuss, and Schuschnigg an ever-increasing number of Austrians have developed a genuine feeling of Austrian patriotism and a strong will to maintain their independence. Since 1945 the Austrian Government, which is one of the most democratic in Europe, has been supported by all elements in the population except the Communists. To the surprise of many observers of the Austrian scene, the People's Party and Socialists, under the pressure of the occupation, have usually managed to cooperate moderately well in maintaining a coalition government. The industry and highly skilled workmanship of the Austrian people have resulted in a steady rise of exports from $200,000,000 in 1948 to $610,000,000 in 1954, a high rate which may more than offset the payments to the Russians. Austria has valuable timber and mineral resources, supplies large amounts of hydroelectric power, and attracts numerous tourists. All these factors, plus the indomitable will of the Austrian people to maintain their independence, now that it has been regained, may enable the Austrians to make their little Republic, slightly smaller than Indiana, a peaceful and relatively prosperous land.

Chapter 15

Yugoslavia

ALEX N. DRAGNICH

PRIOR to her expulsion from the Cominform in June 1948, Yugoslavia was the prototype of a satellite. She was the first of the Eastern European states in which the Communists were successful in consolidating their position. In domestic politics she was the first to establish a ruthless dictatorship and to seek to follow in the footsteps of the Soviet Union. Her newly established Communist government was in the forefront in proclaiming open hostility toward the West even though, ironically enough, its success had in large part been due to Western wartime assistance. Of all the satellites, she was the most vocal in support of the Soviet position in foreign affairs, and by all odds regarded as the most devoted of the Kremlin's followers. In viewing Yugoslavia as a special case in this study, therefore, it is important to bear in mind that the possibilities of American diplomacy were severely limited from the outset. Here was an early demonstration of the futility of attempting to alter the course of events once the Communists had seized power.

Political Developments

At the end of World War II, the Yugoslav Communist Party emerged from a wartime revolution with a monopoly of political power.[1] Although initially portraying itself as a guerrilla resistance movement fighting against the Nazi and Fascist invaders, the National Liberation Front was from the outset a tool of the Communist Party. Although the Communist-controlled Liberation Front was utilized for some limited actions against the occupier, principally defensive

[1] The question of how the Communist Party seized political power in Yugoslavia, as well as other topics in this chapter, is treated in greater detail in my book, *Tito's Promised Land: Yugoslavia* (Rutgers University Press, 1954).

moves to ward off annihilation, its main function was to serve the party in its determination to seize political power at all costs. Internally, the use of the Liberation Front served to conceal the real Communist aims and to secure the active help of many patriotic citizens who believed that the movement was designed not only to help free the country of the enemy but also to bring about a "real people's democracy." In their foreign propaganda output, the Communists pointed to the Front as "proof" that the aim of the movement was not a dictatorship of the proletariat but popular democracy. By the end of the war there was no doubt about Communist Party aims; the dictatorship of the proletariat had for all practical purposes been established.

The initially decisive point in the Communist struggle for power was reached when the Western Allies decided to extend aid to Tito's partisan movement and thereby made it the chosen instrument of Allied wartime policy in Yugoslavia. The first anti-Axis resistance movement, led by Drazha Mihailovich, was abandoned primarily on the basis of Churchill's pragmatic conclusion that the Tito forces were doing the more effective fighting against the enemy. The allegation of the Tito camp that Mihailovich was collaborating with the enemy, a charge which remains without much foundation, no doubt also constituted a factor in the thinking of Western policymakers. The capstone in Western assistance to Tito was placed when King Peter II was forced first to accept as his Premier, Ivan Shubashich, who was committed to reaching an agreement with Tito, and second when he was forced to accept the agreement itself after it was "ratified" by the Big Three at Yalta.

The Tito-Shubashich agreement provided, among other things, for a coalition government, pending the election of a constituent assembly and its determination of Yugoslavia's future form of government. Ivan Shubashich, Milan Grol and other non-Communist representatives from the Yugoslav government-in-exile joined the Tito government. From the outset, they were veritable prisoners of Tito and his comrades, who saw to it that they had no real power or responsibility in the ministries which they nominally headed. Disilusioned and frustrated at every turn, and seeing that the election planned for the fall of 1945 would be a fraud, Grol and Shubashich were left with no decent alternative but to withdraw, which they did in the late summer and fall of 1945. Tito and other Yugoslav Communists have since openly admitted that they were not sincere when they agreed to a coalition government, that it was merely a tactical maneuver on their part.

Following the liquidation of the coalition government, the Communist leaders still sought to maintain the impression that the regime had a broad political base. The wartime Liberation Front became the People's Front, which the Communist leaders sought to present as the real political force in the country instead of as an adjunct of the party, which it really was. A few unimportant leaders of insignificant prewar political parties were brought into the Front, but neither they nor their so-called parties were permitted to function in the normal way. For a time they were assigned unimportant places on electoral lists, but as time passed they were moved closer and closer to political oblivion. The façade of a popular front was maintained until the expulsion of the Yugoslav Communist Party from the Cominform. Stung by charges that they had permitted their party to melt away in the People's Front, the Yugoslav leaders asserted that the party had always been the leading force in the Front and that the Front had no program but that of the party.

As was to be expected, the election of November 1945 was no different from other Communist plebiscites. The people did not have an opportunity to vote for the type of government which they desired. The agreed-to referendum on the monarchy was never held. The Communist-controlled constituent assembly did very little debating on anything. It proclaimed Yugoslavia a republic, and it went through the motions of adopting a constitution, a document virtually identical with the Soviet fundamental law, the so-called Stalin constitution.

Under this constitution, Yugoslavia became a "federation" of six constituent republics (Serbia, Croatia, Slovenia, Macedonia, Bosnia-Herzegovina, and Montenegro). Taking a leaf from Stalin's book, the Yugoslav Communist leaders thereby "solved" Yugoslavia's nationality problem with a stroke of the pen. It is widely recognized throughout Yugoslavia that, far from solving the nationality problem, the Tito regime has in some ways actually aggravated it. But no public discussion of the problem can take place, for it is a crime to maintain that the question has not been satisfactorily handled by the regime. Yugoslav "federalism," like that in the Soviet Union, does not meet the commonly accepted tests associated with a federal form of political organization.

As might be expected, the political structure under the Soviet-type constitution was modeled after that in the Soviet Union. A two-house legislature, one a federal council and the other a council of nationalities, was declared to be the supreme authority of the land. As in the Soviet Union, this legislative body chose a collegial presidium as the formal executive. Similarly, a council of ministers constituted the government. This structure was duplicated in each of the republics. At the local level people's committees were set up to correspond to local soviets in Russia. The so-called public prosecutors, people's courts and people's judges completed the structural frame.

Effective political power, however, was to be found in the hands of the Communist Party at all levels. The party organization followed that established in the Soviet Union under Stalin. The Central Committee and its all-powerful small inner circle, the Politbureau, in effect constituted the dictatorship of the proletariat. Detailed instructions and orders from this center to party organizations below flowed in a steady stream. In a sense, the party and the government were dual hierarchies. At every level of government there was a corresponding party organization through which instructions from the top were funneled. Very often, of course, the local party secretary and the head of the local people's committee were one and the same man.

Since Yugoslavia's break with Moscow in 1948, Tito and other Yugoslav leaders have talked about modifications being made in the country's political structure. Despite these assertions, however, it is important to note that there have been no really fundamental changes. Yugoslavia is still a political dictatorship of the Communist Party, although the name was changed to League of Yugoslav Communists at the Party Congress in November 1952. At the same Congress, the delegates and the world were told about forthcoming changes in the governmental structure. None of these can be regarded as profound; certainly the authority of the party and its monopoly of political power have not been undermined.

It should be noted in passing, however, that apparently at least one important Yugoslav Communist, Milovan Djilas, seems to have thought that the party should promote, or at least tolerate, considerable freedom of discussion and political activity within the framework of Marxian principles. When he made his pleas for greater freedom, through the party's official organ, he incurred the displeasure of Tito and his other close collaborators and was expelled from the Central Committee in January 1954. His was a minority voice in the top circles of the party, and his expulsion from high party positions and his subsequent withdrawal from the party itself seem to offer proof, if such were needed, that Yugoslavia remains a Communist dictatorship.[2]

Bearing the above in mind, it may be of interest to touch upon one or two of the formal revisions of the constitution proclaimed in January 1953. In the first place, the presidium was abolished and in its place the position of President of the Republic was set up, a position specifically created for Tito. Changes in the legislature consisted primarily in replacing the council of nationalities with a council of producers, although nationality representation is formally retained in the other house. Councils of producers are to be found at the local as well as the republican level. Their avowed function is to provide within the government representation for various sectors of the economy. Perhaps the most important governmental body is the new Federal Executive Council, which in a sense replaces the Council of Ministers and the Presidium. The FEC seems to have two primary functions: (1) the active supervision of the five secretariats of state (foreign affairs, national defense, internal affairs, financial affairs, and exchange of goods), and (2) the providing of guidance to the governments of the six republics and the coordination of their work.

The Tito regime has made much of these changes, insisting that they constitute a reversal of the centralist system which they had copied from the Soviets, that democratization and political decentralization would best describe the alterations in the political setup. An examination of the constitutional amendments, to say nothing of actual practice since their enactment, reveals that the central government has lost none of its important powers. In fact, it may have gained some. While there is some decentralization in the administration of governmental programs, there has been no decentralization in basic policymaking. The Communist Party continues to retain and to exercise effective political power.

Economic Developments

In the economy, no less than in the sphere of political organization, the Yugoslav Communists sought to emulate the Kremlin. Lenin's watchwords, industrialization and electrification, were adopted by Tito and his cohorts as economic symbols for the new Yugoslavia. The fact that Yugoslavia was a predominantly peasant country (over

[2] In January 1955 Djilas and Vladimir Dedijer, Tito's official biographer, were convicted of having promoted hostile propaganda against Yugoslavia, but received mild sentences.

three-fourths of the inhabitants living on the land) with no problem of large landholdings [3] did not stop the new rulers. Neither were they much influenced by the nonexistence of a sizable or discontented working class. The meager industrial capacity, and the lack of trained and capable skilled workers, did not dampen their enthusiasm. The only important consideration seems to have been to follow in the footsteps of the Soviet leaders, and, by avoiding some of the Kremlin retreats, to achieve the desired goals in a shorter period of time.

The Tito regime did not wait for formal governmental authorization before launching its economic program. Confiscation of property began even before the end of the war and was in full swing before the formal adoption of the new constitution in January 1946. Sweeping nationalization laws in 1946 and 1948 brought virtually all property under government ownership, except for dwelling units and agricultural holdings. A vast ambitious five-year plan stressed electrification and industrialization, principally capital goods and heavy industry generally. There was little or no thought of consumers' goods production.

The unreality of most of the economic goals and the accompanying economic difficulties were in evidence long before Yugoslavia's excommunication from the Cominform. When it became evident that it was in the interest of the Western Powers for the Tito regime to survive Moscow's hostility, however, it was not difficult for Tito to convince the Western policymakers that his economic difficulties stemmed primarily from the economic blockade imposed by Moscow and her satellites. In view of the nature and the extent of Yugoslavia's economic relations with the Kremlin bloc, it was not difficult to perceive at an early date that the economic blockade argument was of little substance. That something more basic was at fault in the Yugoslav economic picture is attested to by the persistence of economic difficulties despite some five hundred million dollars of economic aid from the West during the past five years.

By 1951, some three years after the break with the Cominform, the Yugoslav leaders realized that there was something radically wrong with their approach to the economy. Unwilling to admit or even consider admitting that their difficulties might be attributable to Marxian principles, they endeavored to extricate themselves

[3] Yugoslavia was, however, confronted with the problem of agrarian overpopulation.

through (1) modifications in the goals of their five-year plan, and (2) improvisations in methods and forms, which they chose to call economic decentralization. There was no rejection of ultimate goals or of the principles upon which they were predicated. As in the political organization, so in the economy, the Tito government declared that the source of its troubles was to be found in the centralist system which they had "inherited" from the Russians. Their answer, not unlike that in the political sphere, was to retain the power of basic decisions at the center while seeking to place the responsibility for operational decisions in the hands of those charged with the management of enterprises at the plant level.

Much was made of the creation of workers' councils which were to assist in the management and operation of individual economic enterprises. While it cannot be said that in some instances the workers' councils did not play a significant role in management, it should be noted that their sphere of authority was limited. The basic goals were set by someone else; the authority of the workers' councils was confined to assisting plant management in reaching them. If one is to judge by the Yugoslav press, there is an active and determined supervision from the center. Economic enterprises, their management boards and the workers' councils are frequently criticized for activities and decisions which are not in conformity with the ideas of the top economic planners.

While it may be difficult to measure its extent, it cannot be denied that economic development and growth have taken place. The costs, both material and human, are incalculable but there is no doubt that they have been high. Moreover, there would seem to be little doubt that much of this economic growth was made possible by large grants and loans from the West, and perhaps in spite of the system rather than because of it. In any case, few economists familiar with Yugoslavia would question the thesis that the country would have developed more rapidly as a free society even without such extensive assistance as the Tito regime has received.

In agriculture, as in industry, the Yugoslav leaders were bent upon copying the Soviet system. Their ultimate aim was collectivization. To achieve this aim, they embarked upon two broad fronts to destroy the independent peasant. On the one hand, they imposed crushing compulsory deliveries of grains, meats and other foodstuffs which had to be surrendered to the government at ridiculously low prices. On the other hand, they devised several types of "cooperative" farms, with the Labor Cooperative (a copy of the Soviet collective farm) being termed the most advanced and the one which Yugoslav Communists sought to establish. In other ways, too, such as punitive taxation, crop controls, outright confiscation of livestock and other methods, the party faithful sought to destroy the independent peasant.

It is not surprising, therefore, that the regime should have incurred the hostility of the peasants from the outset. The hated system of compulsory crop deliveries was finally abolished following the acute agricultural crisis of 1951. By 1952 approximately twenty-five percent of Yugoslavia's agricultural lands had been brought into the "socialist sector" of the economy, much of it in the so-called peasant labor cooperatives. Most of these turned out to be economically unproductive, due in part to poor management and to the hostility of the members, most of whom had been forced into the collectives against their will. Widespread attempts of peasants in 1951 to leave labor cooperatives caused the government to embark upon a retreat in 1952, which by 1953 resembled a rout.

The abolition of compulsory deliveries and the reforms of 1951–52 in the organization and management of collectives, which had been accompanied by a ruthless suppression of the legal rights of peasants to withdraw from the labor cooperatives, did not stem the growing tide of discontent which continued to bring in its wake a steadily deteriorating agricultural situation. Seeking desperately to salvage as much of collectivization as possible, the Titoists in March 1953 issued a decree permitting liquidation or reorganization of labor cooperatives. Peasants began to leave the collectives in droves even before the detailed procedural decrees could be issued. These developments resulted in widespread consternation among the party rank and file. Communist leaders from Tito down issued proclamation after proclamation that the intent of the decree was not liquidation but reorganization and a putting of the collectives on a more sound and successful basis. The decree had not made it easy for peasants to withdraw without considerable material loss to themselves, but this seemingly did not stop them.

Faced with numbers of jobless Communist functionaries who had been running the now disbanded collectives, and with other peasants who had brought no land into the labor cooperatives, the government in May 1953 further reduced the maximum land holdings of all peasants from eighty-five acres to twenty-five. Out of the land fund thus created, the government was to reward the faithful, not by giving them land personally but only as they became members of labor cooperatives or other collective groupings to which the land would be made available.

By the beginning of 1955, the agricultural situation in Yugoslavia was still unsettled. Over 85% of the labor cooperatives in existence at the outset of 1952 had been disbanded in less than two years. The government has continued to insist that collectivization in some form is still the party aim, and has sedulously promoted the creation of new labor cooperatives wherever possible. The independent peasants, on the other hand, have been encouraged by the government's difficulties and have in limited ways endeavored to aggravate them. The most eloquent result of more than a decade of Tito's campaign, through force, terror and other brutal means, to do away with an independent peasantry is to be found in the fact that agricultural production is still below prewar levels, in spite of the extensive use of tractors and other mechanization, select seed from the United States, technical assistance teams and other efforts to raise agricultural output.

Cultural Developments

As in other fields, the Yugoslav Communists were eager to become faithful followers of the Kremlin in the realm of cultural life. There was a veritable duplication of Soviet forms and Soviet methods. All cultural and educational activities had one focus, that of serving to further the goals of the dictatorship. Mass organizations were created; the schools were placed in an ideological strait jacket; the press, radio and other public opinion media were brought under government ownership and control and thereby mobilized in the service of totalitarianism. Already existing organizations which were unwilling to serve Communist ends and the few non-Communist publications which sprang up during the brief period of the coalition government were quickly disbanded.

The most far-reaching of the mass organizations was the People's Front, formerly the Liberation Front, and since 1953, the Socialist Alliance of the Working People of Yugoslavia. Because the people had to depend upon Front organizations for ration cards and other vitally important services, nearly every adult was obliged to belong. Through the Front's many subsidiaries, the local Communist functionaries engaged their untiring efforts in carrying out party directives. Until 1948, they did not identify themselves as party members in such groups. Members of the Front were frequently also enrolled in other mass organizations, such as the antifascist women's organization, the people's youth, veterans and other groups. All such associations fitted into a pattern and were expected to perform two principal functions. Above all else, they were to put the people in the appropriate frame of mind, to get them to see things in the way that the Communists saw them, and hence to make them want to be of assistance. Secondly, they were employed to mobilize people for the so-called voluntary work projects and other activities, and to supervise the actual efforts in these endeavors.

The rigid control over education, from the nursery school through the university, was based on long-term considerations and upon the conviction of the Communist Party that the regime's future hopes and expectations were inextricably bound up with the new generations. The ideological screening of teachers, the minute supervision over what was taught and what young minds were given to read, the concern for the "right type" of afterschool activity, the provision for summer youth projects, the establishment of youth theaters, youth restaurants, and a youth press, all constituted striking testimony of the regime's concern with youth. The more active members of youth groups served to inform on teachers and to discipline youngsters with anti-regime sympathies. In Yugoslavia, as in the Soviet Union, the "science" of Marxism-Leninism became the ideological guidepost for students and teachers alike.

In order to complete its totalitarian control over all phases of the people's cultural life, the Tito regime extended its firm grasp over all public opinion media. The press came under party control either through outright ownership by the party, the government or other instrumentality. The same was true of periodical and book publishing. The radio was directly in the hands of the government. This was also true of the theater and the movie houses. What these instrumentalities produced for the public was under direct control of the party's agitation and propaganda section. In the early days of the regime, there was much translating from Soviet sources or the direct use of Soviet-produced materials (e.g., movies and plays). And, of course, the Soviet mentors were copied in their conspicuous efforts to exclude by various means "the decadent and corrupting influences" from abroad, principally the West.

From time to time, since 1951, there have been rays of hope that the Yugoslavs might discard, at least partially, the ideological strait jacket which they had borrowed from the Kremlin. During 1952, for example, there was a lively debate in two Yugoslav literary periodicals concerning doctrinal rigidity in the fields of literature and art. The spokesmen for one group seemed to be arguing that endeavors in these fields ought to serve the positive aims of the government in its attempt to build socialism, while adherents of the other group contended that there was merit in the art for art's sake school and that anything which did not oppose "socialism" should be permitted. At the present writing this issue seems unsettled. Efforts of writers and others to break out of the ideological shell have been met with criticism from important party dignitaries, who have insisted that the added freedom which the government has accorded them has been misused. Constant reminders keep appearing to tell writers and artists that they are not realizing their full potential, that they are being misled, that they are becoming complacent at a time when the country expects great things from them.

American Diplomatic Relations with Tito's Government

Following Tito's failure to live up to the agreement he had concluded with Shubashich and his open establishment of a ruthless Communist dictatorship, the United States and other Western Powers nevertheless decided to recognize his regime. In December 1945, the United States expressed a willingness to recognize the new government but was sharply critical of its failure to provide guarantees of personal freedom, freedom from fear, liberty of conscience, freedom of speech and the press, freedom of association and assembly, which were contained in the Tito-Shubashich Agreement. It was also critical of the failure of the election of November 11, 1945, to provide for a free choice of the people's representatives.[4]

United States diplomatic relations with the Tito regime, therefore, had an inauspicious beginning and were destined to deteriorate in the years immediately ahead. A whole series of actions by the Yugoslav Government within a brief few months contributed to increased tension and hostility. Tito's attempt to seize and to hold Trieste by force even before the war ended in Europe produced suspicion and distrust. The provocative actions of his troops on the Trieste frontier in the years immediately after the war served as a continuous source of trouble. These difficulties were considerably sharpened by the deliberate shooting down of two American military

[4] See *Bulletin,* XIII (1945), 1020–21.

planes which had flown off course in their flight from Austria to Italy.[5] In one of these five American airmen were killed. Tito yielded to a stiff American note condemning these acts and demanding indemnity for the planes and payments to the families of the airmen killed, but retaliated with demands that the United States close down its Information Center in Belgrade.[6]

While the grave difficulties on the Trieste frontier continued, Tito opened a new arena of conflict and controversy with his assistance to the Communist rebels in Greece, who were determined to overthrow the Greek Government. Officially the Yugoslav Government insisted that it was in no way involved in the Greek civil war. Only after the break with Moscow did Yugoslav leaders admit that they had aided the Greek rebellion.

These difficulties were further compounded by certain domestic acts of the Yugoslav regime. Among the first of these was the capture and execution of General Drazha Mihailovich, the leader of the first guerrilla resistance movement in Yugoslavia. American pleas to permit U.S. soldiers who had served with or had been rescued by Mihailovich to testify at his trial were rudely rejected.[7] The arrest and imprisonment of Archbishop Stepinac of Zagreb, as well as other church leaders, provided dramatic testimony of the Communist concept of the freedom of religion.[8] Similar actions of the government, which snuffed out freedom in other phases of life, further impaired the already strained diplomatic relations.

The Tito regime's mistreatment of American citizens also aroused the ire of the United States Government.[9] Many were arrested with impunity and many more, mainly dual nationals, were not permitted to leave the country. Some of these had gone to Yugoslavia for brief postwar visits with relatives, only to discover that they could not obtain exit visas permitting them to return to the United States. Moreover, property of United States citizens was taken over by the government, with no indication of intent to compensate the owners.

Adding insult to injury, the Yugoslav authorities refused to accord to U.S. diplomatic representatives in their country the customary amenities. All types of difficulties were imposed. Domestic servants were hounded and arrested by the secret police (OZN, later UDB).

[5] *Bulletin,* XV (1946), 415ff., 501ff.
[6] *Ibid.,* 637, 725.
[7] See *Bulletin,* XIV (1946), 634, 669–70, 909.
[8] *Ibid.,* XV (1946), 725.
[9] *Ibid.,* XV (1946), 232, 761–64.

Local employees of the American Embassy (janitors, chauffeurs et al.) were forced to become informers for the UDB. The less cooperative ones were threatened and some even arrested. The movements of American diplomats were carefully watched and followed. It became exceedingly dangerous for Yugoslav citizens to be seen or to associate with Americans. Other impediments, such as making it difficult to obtain adequate housing and other necessities controlled by the government, were placed in the way. A systematic effort was made to build up a "bad" dossier on every U.S. diplomat from the time he reached Yugoslavia, for possible future use against him or the United States, or both.

Tito-Cominform Controversy and American Policies

Slowly, almost imperceptibly, and not without many irritating difficulties, American-Yugoslav relations improved in the years following Tito's expulsion from the Cominform family. Solutions in one form or another have been found to most of the aggravating problems discussed in the above paragraphs. The principal exception concerns the internal status of Yugoslav society itself. Despite some limited relaxations, Yugoslavia remains a Communist police state. The Communist Party retains its firm grip on political power at all levels, with little evidence that it will permit the growth of democracy or any significant expansion of freedom.

When the Tito-Stalin rift appeared, the United States decided that it was in its national interest that Tito should be able to survive the onslaughts from the Kremlin and its allies. This decision was based on several assumptions. First of all, it was assumed that since the Tito dictatorship had made it impossible for the democratic forces in Yugoslavia to maintain any form of effective organization, any struggle for power in the immediate future would probably be won by the pro-Moscow forces in Tito's party. Secondly, it was assumed that if Tito were successful in surviving, other Communist leaders in Eastern Europe and elsewhere might be encouraged to rebel against Moscow domination. Finally, it was assumed that in view of the situation in Greece and Trieste, as well as the general weakness of Western Europe, any subtraction from the potential power of the Soviet bloc was highly advantageous to the West. In view of these considerations, the American Government decided to extend limited assistance to Tito's regime and to take such other measures as would enable it to withstand Stalin's calculated campaign to destroy it.

In pursuit of this policy, which during 1951–52 was considerably extended beyond the original decision to grant limited aid, Western assistance (mainly U.S.) in grants, loans, drought relief and technical assistance has passed the five hundred million dollar mark. Military aid has also been extensive but no accurate monetary measure of the amount has been made public.

While it may be difficult to calculate the full import of this fairly extensive Western assistance, there is little doubt that without it Tito's regime could not have survived. It is probably too early to tell whether in the long run this will have been to the advantage of the free world. True, the turn of events helped settle the civil conflict in Greece, and a solution to Trieste was finally found. Yugoslavia has formed with Greece and Turkey a Balkan Pact of friendship and cooperation, supplemented in 1954 with a military alliance. The Titoist "rebellion," however, did not spread elsewhere, and it is difficult to predict what impact the Balkan alliance would have in case of Soviet aggression. Judging on the basis of various statements and actions of Yugoslav leaders, as well as by the widespread domestic hostility toward his regime, it could be argued cogently that Tito is at best an uncertain ally. Certainly, there seems to be much evidence to indicate that, despite protestations to the contrary, his regime is following basically a neutralist policy.

The "normalization" of relations with the Soviet bloc which has taken place during the past year or so, together with Soviet overtures for further improvement and Yugoslavia's cautiously favorable response, would seem to reflect a neutralist policy. Tito has welcomed normalization, for it makes it less likely that he would be forced to take sides. The last thing he wants is a war between the Soviet Union and the West, for irrespective of the victor in such a conflict his chances of political survival would not be very good. He is only too well aware of the potentialities of the domestic hostility toward his regime in such an eventuality. On the one hand, he cannot go back to the pre-1948 days, for he cannot really trust the Russians. On the other hand, he is too much of a Communist to associate himself closely with the West, for he is aware of the "corrupting influence" of such an association. But neither does he wish to cut all of his ties with the West, at least so long as he continues to receive much needed assistance from this quarter. In short, he wants to preserve the *status quo;* he supports India's policy of "active coexistence"; he wants the best of both worlds. And in no small measure, he seems to be succeeding.

This is not to suggest that the West has not benefited from Yugoslavia's being outside the Soviet orbit. Nor should the impact of association with the West upon Yugoslav internal affairs, however limited and indirect, be discounted. It may be that in the long run favorable results which are not now forseeable, from the democratic point of view, will evolve from contemporary Yugoslav-American relations. The future alone has the answer, although it seems unlikely that even the limited association of Yugoslavia and the West would fail to produce some desirable influence upon long-term domestic developments in that country.

American Policies and the Yugoslav People

When in 1948 American policymakers decided on a policy of extending limited assistance to the Tito regime, they were not unmindful of the unpopularity of the Communist dictatorship among the Yugoslav people. They were aware of the danger that even limited aid might serve to fasten more firmly upon the people a government which, it was estimated, was bitterly hated by some 85 per cent of them. In view of the considerations discussed above, however, there did not seem to be any other alternative. The risk had to be taken. Those who formulated the later decisions to increase the amount and extent of Western aid, to bring the benefits of technical assistance to Tito's Communist experiment, were seemingly less concerned with the long-range impact of these policies upon a freedom-thirsty people.

When the break with the Kremlin came, most Yugoslav citizens greeted it with guarded optimism. Tito did not become a hero in their eyes. Many said, "Long live Tito," because they hoped that his actions would undermine the whole Communist edifice in the world and that it would come tumbling down. For the first time since their enslavement they perceived the possibility of their liberation. In large measure they understood the considerations which led the West to extend aid to a regime whose downfall they hoped soon to see, but at the same time they were afraid. They hoped that the United States and the other Western Powers knew what they were doing, but considerable skepticism accompanied their hopes.

As the hoped-for day of liberation tended to recede into the unknown future, Yugoslav citizens became more openly critical of Western assistance, regarded by them as the result of American policies alone. Most of them did not think it possible that the United States would not exact some concessions from the dictatorship, particularly in view of the desperate economic straits in which Tito ound himself in 1950–52. They were convinced, too, that Tito's rmy would not be of much help to the free world in a showdown, or in such an event the Yugoslav people would also be seeking to id themselves of Communism. Failing to comprehend Western polcies, they were more and more drifting into a mood of resignation to he inevitable.

This air of pessimism which hung over the Yugoslav people was or a time partially lifted by the election in 1952 of Dwight D. Eisenhower as President of the United States, together with the election of a Republican Congress. Statements during the campaign by General Eisenhower, John Foster Dulles, and other Republican leaders raised the hopes of the people of Yugoslavia, who were by and arge convinced that liberation would come only as the result of forceul action by the West. At the beginning of 1956, however, the clouds of gloom had descended again. Hopes had been raised, only to have hem shattered. And again, an attitude of resignation, coupled perhaps with deep inward hopes, seemed to prevail.

Part Four

THE ECONOMIC FRAMEWORK

Chapter 16

Economic Consequences of a Divided World

GOTTFRIED HABERLER

FROM the point of view of technology, travel, and transportation the world is a much smaller place than it used to be only thirty years ago.* This process of physical shrinkage which has been going on for quite some time does not show any signs of slackening. The same is true of communication of ideas, dissemination of knowledge, and the exchange of persons and of works of art and literature.

But never before has there been such a sharp contrast between, on the one hand, the unification and integration of the whole globe in the respects just mentioned and, on the other hand, the deep cleavage in the economic and social order which separates the free world from the world ruled by totalitarian Communism.

True, the free world no longer lives under a regime of nineteenth century capitalism and the economic orders prevailing in the free world are far from uniform; they range from what may be described as "reform capitalism" as we know it in the United States, Canada, Belgium, Switzerland to the so-called "welfare state" in Great Britain and Norway. In contrast, the economic regimes of the various countries in the Russian orbit (including China) are becoming more alike every year. Despite the diversity of economic systems prevailing in the West the line of demarcation between East and West is quite sharply drawn, not only with regard to political order but also with respect to the economic organization, for Yugoslavia is the only country on this side of the Iron Curtain whose economic and political order resembles more the Russian model than those prevailing in the free world.

* An earlier version of this paper was delivered at Marquette University's 75th Anniversary Conference, "From Disorder to World Order," Milwaukee, November 9, 1955.

Thus none of the countries of the free world has a complete foreign trade monopoly such as *all* Communist countries have, and in all free countries a large part—in most of them, especially in the most important ones, the much larger part—of economic activity is still carried on by private enterprise, although the scope of public enterprise and of government control and regulation of private business has grown everywhere and is still growing.

In view of this it seems to me quite justifiable to contrast capitalism—"capitalism in its present form"—and collectivistic economic systems. I shall take the existence of this cleavage as my point of departure and shall investigate some of its economic consequences, without probing into the deeper social, political, and spiritual roots of this state of affairs. But even within these self-imposed limits we shall soon discover that the economic consequences of the existing cleavage in the economic order cannot be fully understood without paying attention to non-economic, that is, psychological, social, and in the last resort spiritual factors.

"Can capitalism flourish and continue to achieve a growing welfare of the nations living under it when a large part of mankind lives under a totalitarian collectivistic regime?" This is a complex question which cannot be answered categorically "yes" or "no." The answer will have to be conditional, that is to say it will depend (a) on what we can assume about the basic objectives of the Communist rulers and the ability, skill, and ruthlessness with which they pursue those objectives and (b) on the foresight, skill, and ability with which the free world countries—and especially the leading country in the free world, the United States—conduct their affairs.

As far as the Communist rulers are concerned, we have obviously to assume that their objective is not only to improve the material welfare of their peoples but also to undermine and if possible destroy the capitalist regimes abroad.[1] But the degree to which

[1] It might even be questioned whether they are at all interested in raising the standard of living of their people, except to the extent necessary for keeping the population quiet and cooperative. The remarkable and painstaking study based on Russian statistical sources by Janet G. Chapman, "Real Wages in the Soviet Union, 1928–1952," *Review of Economics and Statistics,* XXXVI (1954), concludes that the level of real wages, after taxes and bond purchases, in 1937 was at 81 and in 1952 at 90 compared with 100 in 1928. Before taxes and bond purchases the figures are 100, 82, 103. These startling results are based on a cost-of-living index using 1937 weights. This method, in fact, overstates the actual level of real wages. If 1928 weights are used, the index of real wages before taxes and bond purchases in 1952 is 73, and, after taxes and bond purchases, 63.

they are willing to subordinate the former objective to the latter, in other words, the price in terms of domestic consumption and welfare which they are willing and able to pay for disrupting and undermining the capitalist economies, is a matter for speculation.

It is evidently a demand of elementary prudence not to delude ourselves about the enemy's bad intentions nor to underestimate his skill, determination, and perseverance. But it might be equally fatal grossly to exaggerate the danger, to overestimate the strength and power of the Communist bloc. We must aim at a balanced view, although it will be safer to err on the side of overestimating the skill and power of the adversary.

In order to gain perspective and to estimate to what extent the internal social cohesion within the countries of the West, the co-operative spirit between them, and the ingenuity and skill of American leadership in the economic sphere are likely to be taxed by Communist economic aggression or subversion, let me first answer some related and preliminary questions and cite a few facts and figures which are apparently not generally known.

The virtual withdrawal or expulsion of Russia from the world market after the first World War constituted a loss for both sides. This was only partially offset by the liberation from Russian rule of Poland, the Baltic countries, and Finland and their incorporation into the world economy. Russia as well as her trading partners, especially those with whom she used to have the greatest volume of trade before 1914 (Germany and Great Britain), would have gained if they had engaged in a more intensive exchange of goods and services. Since the virtual exclusion of Russia from the world economy came at the same time as all the other structural changes and disturbances caused by the first World War (such as the destruction of the Austro-Hungarian Empire, the emergence of the United States as the world's largest creditor nation, the inflation engendered by the war, and the two severe postwar depressions, that of 1920–21 and the catastrophic Great Depression of the 1930's), it is impossible to evaluate precisely the consequences of Russia's retreat into economic isolation.

But we can say with confidence that it was not of major importance compared with the other economic upheavals created by the war, because Russia has never been one of the major trading nations, although she played a greater role in the world economy under the Tsars than under the Soviets.

One thing is certain: Russia played a quite negligible role in the world economy throughout the interwar period. The volume of foreign trade of the Soviet colossus was in the same order of magnitude of, in fact for most years smaller than, that of tiny Switzerland.

Despite the fact that fear of Russian "dumping" and of other Soviet trade machinations devilishly designed to disrupt the capitalist economies was widespread during the 1920's and 1930's, there is no evidence that Russia was ever a disturbing factor in world trade during the interwar period. Her economic weight (as measured by her percentage share in world trade—a little over 1 per cent) was too small, and most of the time she was too preoccupied with her domestic troubles and her international position was too insecure to enable her to exploit her potential nuisance value in the economic field.

Russia, the true victor in the second World War, has tremendously gained in economic power, both absolutely and relatively to the rest of the world. While before the war about 7 per cent of the earth's population lived under Communist rule, now Russia with her European satellites and her Chinese allies rules a solid land mass from Central Europe to the Pacific Ocean and the South China Sea, an area inhabited by a third of the world's population.

The economic strength of this colossus has not grown in proportion to its area and population. But although it is impossible to give any exact figures it has undoubtedly grown absolutely and relatively to that of the West—and is still growing absolutely although hardly relatively.[2]

While we are still largely tapping in the dark as far as Russian internal economic strength is concerned (despite the highly ingenious work of unraveling the "mystery inside an enigma" performed by our modern economic paleontologists, the Russian experts), we are on much firmer ground concerning the external manifestations of Russian economic strength. It is true that not only Russia but also the satellites treat trade figures as state secrets. But a rough picture of their external trade with the Western world

[2] That she has not grown relatively to the West is probably true as far as *total* output per head is concerned and is certainly true with regard to economic welfare. But this does not exclude the fact that her military potential has increased as compared with that of the West. The latter depends not only on total output but also on the percentage of it currently devoted to military purposes and on how much could be so devoted in case of war. In these two respects the West obviously labors under great disadvantages.

can be pieced together from the trade statistics of the Western countries. Obviously the peacetime influence of the Soviet bloc on the outside world depends on the volume and composition of their external trade.

Perhaps the most interesting point which emerges from a study of the relevant facts is that not only the share in Western world trade of Russia herself but that of the whole Communist bloc (including the Eastern European satellites, Eastern Germany, Bulgaria, Poland, Czechoslovakia, Rumania, and Hungary, as well as Red China) is much smaller than before the war.[3] More precisely the total exports of the countries now constituting the Soviet bloc to the Western world amounted in 1937 to about $2 billion and in 1953 to about $1.8 billion, while the total trade among the countries of the Western world has tripled since 1937, rising from $23 billion in 1937 to $68.4 billion in 1953.[4]

This decrease in the volume of exports to the West is especially marked in the case of the European satellites and is a consequence of the increasing integration of these countries into the Russian economy. In fact, according to fragmentary Russian statistics the trade between the countries of the Eastern bloc has increased to such an extent that the share of total Eastern trade (internal trade plus trade with the West) in total world trade has risen from 8 per cent to 10 per cent. The figures of intra-Eastern bloc trade, available only from Russian sources (partly in the form of alleged percentage increases over certain periods), are certainly much inflated. But that much of the prewar trade of Eastern Germany, Czechoslovakia, and the other satellites with the West has been deflected toward the East cannot be doubted.[5]

[3] The factual statements about trade are taken from reports of the U.N. Economic Commission for Europe (ECE), especially *Economic Survey of Europe in 1954* (Geneva, 1955) and *Economic Bulletin for Europe,* VII, No. 2 (Geneva, August 1955).

[4] Since these sums represent *current* (undeflated) dollars, and prices have risen substantially, the *real* value of trade has *not* tripled, although it is greater than it was in 1937. But the real value of the Soviet bloc's trade with the West is half or less than half of what it used to be before the war. ECE computed a *volume index* of the "General Level of Trade between Eastern and Western Europe." (Not of the *total* trade of the *whole* Communist bloc. See the August 1955 *Bulletin,* p. 35.) According to that table imports from Eastern Europe into Western Europe fell from 305 in 1938 to 85 in 1952 and then rose again to 106 in 1954. The corresponding figures for exports from Western Europe to Eastern Europe are 205, 91, 126.

[5] This fact makes it impossible for these countries, so long as they remain under Russian domination, to play the role they played before 1939 as suppliers of materials or markets for Western industries. Those who speak hopefully or nostalgically of the importance of Eastern markets—and such views are frequently

It is possible to draw a few conclusions from these broad facts. According to accepted principles of international trade the decrease of East-West trade undoubtedly constitutes a loss to all parties concerned, especially for those countries in the West which before the war had close trade connections with the East because of geographical location or complementary economic structure. For example, before the war, of Austria's exports 28 per cent went to Eastern Europe and 32 per cent of her imports came from there, while in 1954 the percentages were 9.4 and 9.1. For Germany the change was certainly as drastic, but a precise figure cannot be given because in the prewar period trade data are available only for the whole of Germany, not for Western Germany alone.[6]

Now, however great the loss due to the drastic reduction of trade with the East, it did not prevent capitalism in the Western countries from achieving "a growing welfare of the nations living under it." This is especially true of the two countries hardest hit—Germany and Austria. Both these countries have achieved a remarkable recovery. They have managed, with massive American aid (which by now has largely been discontinued), to find substitutes in the West for lost Eastern markets and supplies. For example, the volume of exports of Western Germany, which goes almost entirely to the West, is greater than the volume of the whole of Germany before the war.[7]

Altogether "Western capitalism in its present form" has shown tremendous recuperative power, adaptability, and vigor. True, there have been difficulties, mainly in the form of acute balance-of-payment crises. Europe, in particular, has had substantial dollar

---

expressed even by people who are far from being sympathizers of Communism or fellow travelers—completely delude themselves on this point.

[6] In 1934 for the whole of Germany the share of Eastern European trade was about 13 per cent in exports and in imports. This, however, does *not* include the prewar trade between Western and Eastern Germany. For Western Germany in 1954 the percentage of Eastern European trade (including trade with Eastern Germany) was 1.9 in imports and 1.5 in exports. ECE *Bulletin,* August 1955.

[7] It is therefore simply not true that Germany "needs Eastern trade." Developments since the end of the war conclusively demonstrate that she can do very well without it—at least so long as the Western World does not suffer from a severe depression. (More on this aspect of the problem presently.)

It will perhaps be objected that Germany improved her trade position at the expense of other industrial countries, especially of Britain. This objection overlooks the fact that Britain too has improved her trade position. True, she is at present (1955) suffering from mild balance-of-payments difficulties. But the cause of this indisposition is clearly a mild spell of internal inflation. Moreover her balance-of-payments crises in 1947 and 1949, before Germany's reappearance on the world markets, were much more severe than those of 1951 and 1955.

deficits which were covered by Marshall Plan aid and similar devices. These deficits were very large immediately after the war but have since, especially during the last three years, greatly diminished and for some countries entirely disappeared. At the time of their occurrence, the acute balance-of-payments crises looked threatening, and many economists were misled to diagnose them as the effects of deep-rooted structural maladjustments in the Western world economy. The theory of the secular dollar shortage, allegedly due to the dominant position and superior productive power of the American economy, became popular. An alarmist view of the consequences for the non-dollar part of the West of the virtual disappearance of the Eastern bloc from the world market is a logical corollary of the theory of the chronic dollar shortage.

However, events of the last five years have fully vindicated those economists who refused to be stampeded by acute postwar difficulties into scrapping all the classical principles of international trade. It is clear, or should be clear by now, that these difficulties were the natural consequences of war destruction and dislocation and of inflationary policies, which during the first years after the war may have been unavoidable; they are not the ineluctable result of a permanent structural malformation of the world economy due to the overwhelming size, superior productivity, or too fast growth (compared with the rest of the world) of the American economy.

To summarize, Western capitalism in its present form (or forms) has shown great adaptability and vigor. Moreover, it has been definitely demonstrated that capitalism can flourish and achieve growing welfare even though a large part of mankind lives under a regime of totalitarian economic collectivism. The economic separation of Eastern Germany (which includes a large part of Central Germany), Czechoslovakia, Poland, Hungary, etc., has added greatly to the dislocations caused by the war and to the difficulties and economic cost of repairing war damage and rebuilding a workable peacetime world economic system. But it has not prevented economic recovery. It has not even greatly slowed up the process of recovery. This can be inferred from the remarkable fact that economic reconstruction after the second World War was just as speedy as that after the first World War, despite the greater damage caused by the second World War as compared with the first World War.

However, these optimistic conclusions should not make us complacent. Let us not forget that the Great Depression after the first World War did not start until eleven years after the end of hostilities. From 1918 to 1929, economic recovery proceeded quite satisfactorily (apart from the short but sharp depression of 1920–21)—or so it looked at that time. It is easy to foresee that a similar catastrophe now, or even a depression much milder than the terrible slump of the early thirties, would tremendously increase for many countries of the West the attractions of trade with the East. If the United States market were to shrink, as it certainly would in a serious depression,[8] many countries would try to find compensations in trade with the Soviet bloc. And the East would be eager and, up to a point, able to offer outlets for exports and supplies to imports partially offsetting the losses in United States trade. The propaganda value would be enormous whatever the size of such a substitution of East-West trade for international Western trade lost in a depression.[9]

This is an impelling reason, in addition to many others, why a severe United States depression simply must be avoided. Can it be done? Will it be done? My answer is yes, it can be done, and I think the chances are very good that it will be done. But lack of time compels me to confine myself to this dogmatic although carefully considered statement. However, avoidance of severe depression in the United States, or, to put it differently, maintenance of high level of employment, although a necessary condition, is not sufficient to prevent the emergence of serious disequilibria in Western world trade which would give the East an opportunity to gain a dangerous position in the trade of certain Western countries—a foothold which it would strive to enlarge into a stranglehold.

By indulging in inflationary policies, even in comparatively mild ones, any country can easily develop balance-of-payments difficulties which can then be conveniently blamed on the American tariff

[8] It is true that the mild recession of 1953–54 contrary to widespread alarmist views—"a sneeze of the United States economy," it was said, "causes pneumonia abroad owing to the huge size of the U.S."—did not lead to a widening of the dollar gap. But this would not be true of a more serious setback.

[9] Interestingly enough, it was only during the depression in the thirties that Soviet trade amounted to a substantial factor for some Western countries and industries. For example, in 1932 the U.S.S.R. took 11 per cent of German exports. In 1931 Russia accounted for 55 per cent of all machine tools exported from the U.S. In 1932 she took 81 per cent of all British machine tool exports, and 74 per cent of German export of machine tools. In 1931 Russia imported 90 per cent of the aggregate world exports of tractors. See A. Gerschenkron, *Economic Relations with the U.S.S.R.* (New York, 1945), p. 20.

or the superior productivity of the American economy. It would be easy to cite contemporary examples. If, then, such a country, instead of correcting the basic trouble by resolute anti-inflationary policies and adjusting the exchange rate to a realistic level, clings to a rigid exchange rate and introduces or tightens exchange control, it may well maneuver itself into a position where offers of trade from the East would seem a promising way out of the difficulty.

It is primarily the task of other countries of the free world rather than of the United States to guard against this particular danger. But there are certain things the United States can do and other free countries can do to make it easier for any Western country that may have gotten into trouble to extricate itself from such predicaments, whether due to carelessness or the force of external circumstances.

The best method to prevent too close trade entanglements with the East, to enable a country to resist trade blandishments, and to reduce trade ties with the East, lest they later be used for economic exploitation or political blackmail and extortion, is to keep the market of the free world as free as possible and to remove artificial impediments to the free flow of goods and services, such as tariffs, quotas, excessive customs red tape, and exchange control. Needless to say, any rise in the tariff, any new customs classifications (of which there have been quite a few in recent years) which make it harder for foreign countries to sell in the United States market and to earn the dollars necessary for buying necessary supplies from us, increase the temptation to trade with the East. Our protectionists who agitate for higher tariffs and try to block any attempt to negotiate mutual reductions of trade barriers are playing right into the hands of the Communist bloc.

Japan, for example, is in a very difficult position owing to the loss of Formosa and Manchuria, cessation of trade with China, and trade discrimination against her in many parts of the world, including some members of the British Commonwealth. (Inept internal policies of an inflationary nature have greatly aggravated the Japanese trade and balance-of-payments position, although there has been a marked improvement in the last two years.) Here is a country for which the attractions of trade offers from the East are very strong indeed. In order to counteract these attractions the State Department has proposed to enter into trade negotiations with Japan with offers to open the United States market a little bit more for the import of Japanese goods. Even apart from the political aspect emphasized above, any such reciprocal tariff reduction (I would argue even a unilateral one on the part of the United States) is in the long-range general economic interest of this country, although some particular interests will be hurt temporarily. The agitation of our protectionists, especially the academic ones (who more than anyone else should put the common weal above special interests), for higher duties and against concessions to Japan are shortsighted, reckless, and irresponsible.

This admonition to keep the channels of trade free within the Western world applies, of course, not only to the United States but also to other Western countries. For example, some European countries and certain members of the British Commonwealth have pursued and are still pursuing highly protectionist and discriminatory policies against Japanese exports, while at the same time lecturing the United States on the duties of a creditor nation and blaming her for not sufficiently opening the American market to foreign goods.

In the case of a few Western countries the share of Eastern European trade has recently gone up sharply. For example, in 1953, 30 per cent of Finnish exports went to Eastern Europe, compared with 15.5 per cent in 1948 and 2.3 per cent in 1937. For Iceland the figures are 0.8 per cent in 1947 and 24.7 per cent in 1954. In 1954, Turkey sent 16.5 per cent of her exports to countries behind the Iron Curtain, compared with 9.5 per cent in 1948. Similarly Greece has come to rely more on Eastern Europe for the export of tobacco, Denmark for the export of its butter and meat, and Norway for the export of fish products and marine fats and oils.[10]

Some of these increases can be traced directly to protectionist policies in the West, for example, narrowing of the British market for Icelandic fish and for Danish butter and bacon. When this happened Eastern countries recognized their opportunity and bought some good will along with fish, butter, and bacon.

These developments are not yet alarming. For nineteen Western European countries (including Yugoslavia) the share of Eastern Europe in 1954 was 3.2 per cent, compared with 3.7 per cent in 1948 [11] and 7 per cent in 1937; for imports the figures are 2.9

[10] See ECE *Bulletin,* August 1955, p. 37.

[11] For 1948 Yugoslavia's trade is not included. Yugoslavia's trade with the East fell from 49.8 per cent (exports) and 43.3 per cent (imports) in 1948 to practically nothing during the next few years. In 1954 the share in exports was again up to 2.6 per cent and in imports to 1.2 per cent.

per cent, 4 per cent, and 8.5 per cent respectively. These percentages are not large and they do not provide much of a leverage for exerting political influence. Averages can, of course, be very misleading. For countries near the Iron Curtain the importance of Eastern trade is much greater. Fortunately, proximity to the danger increases awareness of its implications, and countries along the Iron Curtain seem to have developed some immunity to infection by the Communist virus as the examples of Finland, Turkey, Germany, and Austria clearly demonstrate.

It is possible, or even probable (although nothing is quite certain in these matters), that East-West trade will increase during the next few years, even if no depression or increased protectionist tendencies in the United States or elsewhere make trade with the East appear more attractive to some countries of the free world. The tactics of Soviet policy have certainly changed even though their basic objectives remain the same. Moreover, in Russia as well as in the European satellites discussions have been going on in recent years which definitely show greater awareness of the *economic* advantages of international trade for them.[12] We should be prepared to see Russia and her satellites making increasingly attractive trade offers to individual Western countries and to see the actual volume of East-West trade go up.

This raises several important questions. First, how much trade can a country, especially a small country in the vicinity of the Iron Curtain, safely engage in? At what point do trade ties with the East become dangerously close? There is, second, the technical question: how should the West organize its trade relations with the East? What kinds of trade treaties and arrangements would minimize the dangers of too close entanglements? Third, there is the political question for the United States: what should be our attitude toward other free world countries' trade relations with the East? Should we actively discourage our allies from trading with the Soviet bloc? Or, should we follow a hands-off policy? Let me suggest tentative answers to these questions in turn.

To the first question—how much truck can a country safely have with the devil without exposing itself to the danger of blackmail and extortion? I would answer that it depends primarily on the internal political stability, spiritual strength, national pride, and will to remain free and independent. On the whole, I believe that

[12] On this see ECE *Economic Survey of Europe in 1954*, pp. 125–135.

the American public and American policy are inclined greatly to overestimate these dangers to the independence of Western countries resulting from peaceful trade so long as it is not backed up by military threats. I do not believe that any country in the free world is close to a dangerous dependence on trade with the East. So long as the Western world market is kept reasonably free, any single country or group of countries could in an emergency, if it were threatened by Russia with being cut off from supplies or markets, find substitutes in the West. In 1948 Yugoslavia depended on the East for almost 50 per cent of her trade. After her break with the Soviet bloc in 1948 trade ceased almost completely; her economy was undoubtedly hurt but not fatally.[13]

No free world country has at present such intimate trade ties with the East as Yugoslavia had until 1948, and, let me repeat, precisely those countries that have the largest volume of trade with the East (Finland, Turkey, Austria) are fully aware of the possible dangers. I would conclude that even if East-West trade doubled or tripled during the next few years—which is unlikely—there would be no cause for alarm on *economic* grounds, except if such an increase had been caused by a depression or protectionist policies in some parts of the West. In these two latter cases the situation would be different for two reasons: (a) because it would give the Soviets a tremendous propaganda advantage, and (b) because in the case of shrinking Western markets due to protection or depression there would be little hope for finding outlets for exports and supply of imports in the West to resist Soviet blackmail.

I come now to the second question, which is of a more technical nature. What kinds of trade arrangements are suitable for trade with collectivist countries which is conducted on their side by exclusive state trade monopolies?

It is clear that the ordinary methods which have evolved in the Western world for trade between the more or less competitive capitalistic countries are not applicable for trade with government monopolies. The Russians would, of course, like to be accorded most-favored-nation treatment with respect to tariffs and other matters. Quite a few countries have actually done that. They accord *de facto* most-favored-nation treatment to Russia, that is, they tax imports from Russia like imports from elsewhere (or possibly a little heavier) and impose no other restrictions.

[13] Yugoslavia did, of course, receive substantial American aid, mainly in the form of grants for military purposes.

During the war and immediately after the war, when the problem of postwar trade organization was discussed and the plan for an International Trade Charter and an International Trade Organization was negotiated at numerous international conferences, much thought was given to the problem of fitting Soviet Russia and her state trade monopoly into the proposed International Trade Organization (I.T.O.). The Havana Charter for World Trade (which did not become law because it was never ratified by the U.S. Congress) adopted as a solution the so-called "commercial consideration" principle. This means that, while the capitalistic countries promise non-discrimination and most-favored-nation treatment, countries that engage in state-trading pledge themselves to be guided in their foreign trade operations "solely" by "commercial considerations, including price, quality, availability, marketability, transportation, and other conditions of purchase or sale, and shall afford the enterprises of the other member countries adequate opportunity, in accordance with customary business practices, to compete for participation in such purchases or sales" (Article 29 of the Havana Charter).

To regard this clause as a solution of the problem is incredibly naive for two reasons. First, even if scrupulously observed as to the letter and spirit, the "commercial considerations" clause is no safeguard against discrimination comparable to the most-favored-nation clause in trade treaties with non-collectivist countries, for the simple reason that discrimination may actually be based on eminently "commercial," that is, "economic," considerations. In other words, any degree of economic discrimination is entirely compatible with the letter and spirit of the "commercial consideration" clause, so long as it is based on economic ("commercial") rather than on political considerations. Second, it is often extremely difficult to prove that a state monopoly has, in fact, engaged in discriminatory practices, and it is utterly hopeless to demonstrate in such cases that an alleged or admitted act of discrimination was based on political rather than "commercial" or "economic" considerations.

Many countries, especially all those whose foreign trade is carried on under strict control of imports and payments (exchange control), have resorted to bilateral methods, or to outright barter deals, in their trade with the East. This system provides, of course, maximum protection against encroachment and economic aggression on the part of the Soviet bloc, but is not conducive to maximizing benefits from trade for either side. It also violates the principle of freer, multilateral, non-discriminatory trade, which is one of the principal objectives of American foreign economic policy.

Within the Western world much progress has in fact been made in the last few years towards realization of that ideal. Trade has been liberalized and multilateralized, and currencies have been made more easily convertible. It is to be hoped that this trend will continue. But we should not pursue these ideals in a doctrinaire fashion to such an extent that the enemies of our economic order are given a chance to engage in disruptive and subversive trade practices. The countries of the free world should not accord to countries of the Soviet bloc the *right* to most-favored-nation treatment—surely not in exchange for a worthless "commercial considerations" clause.

On the other hand, in view of the small magnitude of Eastern trade, much is to be said for the policy of some Western countries, for example, the United Kingdom, which accord *de facto* equality of treatment to Soviet bloc countries (excepting, of course, restrictions on trade in military and strategic commodities), and do not stipulate that trade be balanced bilaterally. But countries for whom trade with the East is of great importance should be left to deal with the problem as they deem fit as long as they do not discriminate against American exports in favor of exports from the Soviet bloc countries.

The third question which I posed above concerns the attitude of the United States towards the trade of other countries in the free world, especially our allies, with the Soviet bloc. Should we bring pressure upon them to keep their trade with the East at a minimum or should we adopt a hands-off policy? Let us postpone for a moment consideration of trade in strategic materials, which evidently poses special problems.

I think it would be a great mistake to bring pressure upon our friends and allies not to trade or to cut down their trade with Soviet countries. The reason is not so much that by dissuading them to accept trade offers from the East we would deprive them of the benefit which they could derive from such trade; the reason is rather that we thereby offer the Russians a golden opportunity to make greatly exaggerated claims about the possibilities of trade and of their potentialities as suppliers of needed commodities and market for the free world's surpluses. Their potentialities are in reality quite limited.[14] The most effective way to expose such exaggerations is to call the bluff. Every country should, if it so wishes, have an opportunity to find out for itself.

It was no mere chance that the Russians held their "trade conferences" in Moscow and elsewhere during the hottest period of the cold war. At these gatherings they offered with great propaganda wonderful bargains, markets for Western industries, and cheap supplies of raw materials. Many gullible Westerners including a few *bona fide* business men were deceived by these "Potemkin trade fairs." Soviet propaganda at that time was aided by the fact that they could pretend that only American pressures prevented Western Europe from taking full advantage of the splendid trading opportunities offered by the Soviet bloc.

When the cold war cooled off and official and unofficial restraints on trade with the Soviet bloc were relaxed, East-West trade expanded only a little, much less than trade within the Western world during the same period. This quickly caused disillusionment among those who expected a great expansion of East-West trade. The trade bluff has, in effect, been called and exposed for what it was.

The situation is not really much different regarding trade restrictions on military and strategic grounds. It should be noted, however, that I am speaking of peacetime conditions only and do not discuss military and political problems such as Soviet bloc arms deliveries to Egypt at bargain prices, maintenance of secrecy of military equipment, and the like.[15]

A policy of withholding from Soviet countries strategically important manufactured goods (machinery) or raw materials is probably doomed to failure. The Communist world is too large, its economies too diversified, its armament industries too highly developed (think of Czechoslovakia and Eastern Germany), and

[14] In the theoretical literature much has been made of the advantages enjoyed by centrally planned economies to exploit in monopolistic and monopsonistic fashion competitive markets in the rest of the world. Unorganized buyers and sellers are always at the mercy of a monopolist or monopsonist. There is, however, ample evidence that the "theoretical" advantage is in practice outweighed by the clumsiness, inefficiency, and slowness of the bureaucracy of a planned economy. The theory of the private monopolist in a competitive society cannot readily be applied to the government trade monopoly of a planned economy.

[15] Moreover, it should be noted that I am not speaking here of the delivery of military end items. If, as has been reported a few years ago, the sale of jet planes to Russia has enabled her to copy them and to save precious time in the development of these machines of war, we have here an inexcusable mistake.

there are too many neutral and neutralist countries in the world to make a trade boycott an effective weapon of economic warfare in peacetime, except perhaps for a short period in such a case of acute tension as existed during the shooting war in Korea.

There remains one question to which I have not yet addressed myself: "Can collectivist economic systems prevail in the long run in a great part of mankind when capitalism flourishes in the rest?"

From an economic point of view I am afraid the answer is "yes." Experience seems to show that they can. In fact economic life is made much easier for the collectivist countries by the existence of capitalism in the rest of the world; they profit from trade with the capitalist countries and partake in the fruit of technological progress which is much more rapid under capitalism.

From the political and psychological point of view the situation may be different in the long run. We can confidently expect a growing gap in the standard of living between the two worlds.[16] And the growing standard of living in the capitalist world compared with that of the people living under a collectivistic regime will perhaps lead to dissatisfaction and unrest. But the limited experience we have on this problem certainly does not warrant highly optimistic expectations.

This is, however, a problem of political science and social psychology, and the economist may be pardoned if he refrains from making categorical statements on this issue.

Let me briefly summarize my main conclusions.

Capitalism has shown tremendous recuperative power and great vigor. This proves that "capitalism in its present form can achieve a growing welfare of the nations living under it even though a great part of mankind lives in a collectivist form." The broad conclusion can be drawn that at present the Communist bloc plays a minor role in world trade as a supplier of raw materials and as a market for the export industries of the West. It also follows that it has not much of a leverage for economic exploitation or political blackmail by means of threats to close its market or cease to supply badly needed raw materials.

But this optimistic conclusion should not make us complacent. It has to be somewhat qualified inasmuch as averages are always

[16] Let me repeat the warning that larger output and higher standard of living do not necessarily imply greater military strength.

misleading. While total Soviet bloc trade is negligible for the West as a whole, it is not negligible for every Western country. For example, in 1955 and 1954 about 30 per cent of Finland's trade was with the Soviet bloc, and Turkey's exports to the East jumped from 5.6 per cent in 1952 to 16.5 per cent in 1954. In the case of Austria it is in the neighborhood of 10 per cent, while in 1954 for Western Germany Soviet bloc trade was still negligible.

These figures are not yet alarming especially for the following reason: we find the closest trade ties with the Soviet bloc in countries near the Iron Curtain; and, fortunately, proximity to the danger increases awareness of it and seems to confer a certain immunity from infection by the Communist virus. This favorable picture could, however, change quickly—not so much because of a determined trade drive by the Eastern countries, but because of economic changes and mistakes in economic policies within the Western world.

There are two principal dangers which would greatly strengthen Soviet economic power and make Soviet trade offers perilously attractive to Western countries. These twin dangers are depression and highly protectionist policies.

Depressions are always accompanied by outbursts of high protection. When the home market shrinks and unemployment and excess capacity become widespread, the clamor for protection from foreign imports becomes practically irresistible. But we are all familiar with the fact that the pressure for protection is strong even in the absence of a general depression.

It is clear or should be clear that the protectionists in this country as well as in other parts of the free world are playing right into the hands of the Soviets. Some of the recent increases in East-West trade can, in fact, be traced directly to protectionist policies in the West. For example, Iceland's market for fish in Great Britain was closed (due to a dispute on fishing rights) and the share of the East in Iceland's exports jumped from 7 per cent in 1952 to 25 per cent in 1954. Similarly, when Denmark's exports of butter and bacon to Great Britain were curtailed by British protectionist measures the Russians took advantage of the situation and bought some good will along with butter and bacon. A much more important case is that of Japan. Japan literally must export or die. If the West does not take her products she will be driven into deals with the East. Our protectionists who agitate against tariff concessions to Japan and urge additional impediments against Japanese imports are playing with fire.

This applies also to other members of the free world. Several European countries and members of the British Commonwealth of Nations actively discriminate against Japanese imports while at the same time lecturing the United States on not sufficiently opening the doors of the American market to foreign imports.

My general conclusion then is this: the free world need not fear Soviet economic aggression, and even if the present volume of East-West trade doubled or tripled in the next few years there is little danger of economic exploitation or political blackmail, as long as no severe depression is allowed to develop and the channels of trade within the West are not blocked by highly protectionist policies. Russia and her satellites once tried to apply economic blackmail with disastrous results for themselves. They thought they could force Tito, after his break with Moscow, into submission by economic boycott. But Tito with American aid survived. The Yugoslav economy was hurt but not fatally. So long as the Western economies, especially the U.S. economy, are reasonably prosperous and the channels of Western world trade are kept open, and if we stand ready to assist with special measures (including freer access to our market) any country that has become dependent on Eastern trade, the Soviets will have no chance for blackmail and exploiting.

The lesson of all this applies especially to the leading economic power of the West—the United States. Liberal trade policies and maintenance of a high level of employment are the surest method of preventing Communist economic encroachment. If we follow this line and persuade others in the Western camp to do the same, we need not be alarmed if the volume of East-West trade goes up, even substantially, compared with the present low level.

If all that sounds rather optimistic, let me repeat that I discussed only one aspect of the problem and that from a purely economic standpoint. I did not discuss the actual and potential military economic strength of the Soviet bloc. If I expressed confidence that material output and economic welfare are growing faster under capitalism in the West than under collectivism in the East, it does not necessarily follow that the same is true of military economic power, either in case of war or during peace. Nor did I discuss the dangers of dissolution and decay threatening the capitalist society from within. I confined myself to a discussion of the external threat, resulting in peacetime from the existence of a hostile totalitarian collectivist regime which rules one third of the world's population.

But let me end on a somewhat comforting note. The very existence of a powerful totalitarian enemy should make it easier for the West to keep in check those internal forces of dissolution and decay. If there is anything in Toynbee's theory of challenge and response in history, here should be an application. Will the West rise to the challenge? I for one believe that I can see many signs that this will not be a vain hope.

Chapter 17

Problems of East-West Trade and Economic Trends in the European Satellites of Soviet Russia *

NICOLAS SPULBER

The General Framework

THE PROBLEM of East-West trade is an extremely controversial one. Usually the approach to it is charged with emotionalism and the discussion deals more often with a series of "myths" rather than with facts. The object of this chapter is to present, as far as it is possible, the facts. We shall try to determine the effects on the economic relation between the Soviet bloc in Europe and the outside world of both the "strategical embargo," which is intended to prevent the flow of strategical goods toward the East, and of the new economic and trade relations developing between Soviet Russia and its East European satellites.

We propose to consider in turn two distinct periods: 1) the period 1948–1953, which corresponds broadly with the first planned quinquennium in Russia's satellites in Europe and coincides with the establishment and expansion of the Western strategical controls on East-West trade; 2) the period from 1954 to the present, which corresponds to the policy called the "new course" and also coincides with the "streamlining" of the previously existing international strategic controls. We shall examine this second period briefly, and only as a necessary introduction to the drawing of the perspectives for the future.

Two basic trends are apparent as far as the total *trade turnover* of all these countries is concerned, for the period 1947–48 to 1953. One is the generally declining trend of their trade with the countries

* A slightly shorter version of this text (excluding notably the appendix) has appeared in "Economia Internazionale," *Revista dell'Istituto di Economia Internazionale* (Vol. VIII, #3, August 1955), 597–617.

outside the Soviet bloc; the other is the strong intensification of the intra-bloc trade.

On the basis of unadjusted data [1] concerning the extra-bloc trade of Soviet Russia and of her European satellites, it can be noted that over the period considered, the yearly imports (f.o.b. of the bloc) oscillated from $1 billion to $1.4 billion—the highest point, $1.434 billion, being reached in 1948, the lowest, $1.080 billion to $1.090 billion, in 1950 and 1953 respectively. The exports (unadjusted data c.i.f.) oscillated from $1.0 to $1.5 billion—the highest point, $1.518 billion, being reached in 1948, and the lowest (excepting 1947) in 1950 and 1953 (see Table I).

TABLE I: Extra-bloc Trade of Soviet Russia and of Her East European Satellites, 1947–1953. Unadjusted data in thousands of US dollars.

Extra-bloc exports to Soviet bloc (unadjusted bloc imports)	1947	1948	1949	1950	1951	1952	1953
U.S.S.R.	477,249	533,479	436,902	293,189	386,458	480,856	415,731
Europ. Sat.	856,328	901,253	918,647	787,331	852,408	672,319	677,780
Total	1333,577	1434,732	1355,549	1080,520	1238,866	1153,175	1093,511
Extra-bloc imports from Soviet bloc (unadjusted bloc exports)							
U.S.S.R.	271,295	491,770	272,128	252,007	396,666	462,343	377,733
Europ. Sat.	732,974	1026,705	1090,124	940,064	959,846	778,790	794,565
Total	1004,269	1518,475	1362,252	1192,071	1356,512	1241,133	1172,298

Source: Value Series, Free World Exports and Imports to and from Soviet Bloc; compiled by U.S. Department of Commerce, International Economic Analysis Division, Bureau of Foreign Commerce.

The extra-orbit trade of Soviet Russia and of her satellites not only failed to develop after World War II, as many economists thought it would, but since 1950 has remained more or less "stabilized" at a low level. The total free world (extra-bloc) turnover (i.e., exports plus imports) including Soviet bloc trade with it, amounted to $108.5 billion in 1948 and to $148.2 billion in 1952. Hence, the trade of Soviet Russia and of her East European satellites with the free world was only 2.7% of the total transactions in the extra-orbit markets in 1948 and 1.6% of this total in 1952.

Concomitantly with the failure of development of the extra-bloc

[1] Unadjusted data in current prices of *exports* (excluding transportation cost, that is, f.o.b.) of extra-bloc countries = unadjusted imports of the bloc. Conversely, imports of extra-bloc countries (imports including cost, insurance, and freight—c.i.f.) = exports (unadjusted) of the bloc. Normally, the import figure of the bloc, including c.i.f., would be larger, while the export figure, usually f.o.b., would be smaller. No *detailed* data is available, however, from Soviet bloc sources in this respect.

trade of Soviet Russia and of her satellites, their intra-bloc trade increased at a rapid pace. As can be seen from Table II, the intra-bloc trade (excluding China) probably [2] amounted to $2.3 billion in 1948 and to $7.8 billion in 1952—that is, it more than trebled in that period. In percentages, the share of intra-bloc trade in the total trade turnover of the countries considered increased from 44% in 1948 to over 76% in 1952.

TABLE II: SOVIET BLOC: Estimated Total Foreign Trade Turnover and Bloc Trade in 1948 and 1952. Based on derivative data. Millions of US dollars in current prices.

Country	Total trade 1948	1952	Total bloc trade 1948	1952	Percentage increase 2 ÷ 1	4 ÷ 3
	1	2	3	4	5	6
Czechoslovakia	1,216	1,406	365	998	15	173
Poland	1,053	1,589	358	1,065	51	197
Hungary	292	564	99	400	93	304
Romania	341	578	242	491	69	103
Bulgaria	163	302	121	269	85	122
Soviet Union	2,181	4,716	1,156	3,772	116	226
East Germany		1,018	(a)	804		
Total	5,246	10,173	2,341	7,799	193	333
China		2,265	(a)	1,631		

(a) countries not included at that time in that market.

Sources: Basic data as in Table I combined with percentages from *Probleme Economice* (Bucharest, #5–6, 1952); and *Vneshniaia Torgovlia* (Moscow #10, Oct. 1952, and #11, Nov. 1953).

More and more, the Soviet bloc countries refer to their intra-bloc trade as the embodiment of "new economic relations," which are forming a "second world market." Let us note, however, in this respect that the total value of the transactions occurring in this so-called "second world market," if related to the total trade of the "first" world market in, say, 1948 and 1952 (i.e., a total trade value of $105.6 billion and $145.2 billion if we exclude the transactions in the world markets of the Soviet bloc itself), would be equal to *less than 5% of the latter in 1948 and to 8.5% in 1952*. Thus, the "second world market" represents a far more limited market than its geographical size might suggest.

[2] We use the word "probably" since these figures are derived figures from official *percentages*. As already stated, no detailed absolute figures are released by these countries on their trade turnover.

Let us now examine concretely, and without losing sight of the central object of this symposium, the following questions:

a. the conditions and forms of the decline in the extra-bloc trade of the countries considered;
b. the nature and forms of the intra-bloc trade increases;
c. the perspectives.

Soviet Versus Satellite Shares in Extra-bloc Trade

If we consider the respective shares in this extra-bloc trade of Soviet Russia on the one hand, and of her satellites on the other, we notice, as far as the former is concerned, a *decrease* of her share up to 1950, followed by an *increasing* trend afterward (see Table III).

TABLE III: Extra-bloc Trade of Soviet Russia and of Her East European Satellites, 1947–1953. Percentages.

Extra-bloc exports to Soviet bloc	1947	1948	1949	1950	1951	1952	1953 †
U.S.S.R.	35.79	37.18	32.23	27.13	31.19	41.70	38.02
Europ. Sat.	64.21	62.82	67.77	72.87	68.81	58.30	61.98
Total	100.00	100.00	100.00	100.00	100.00	100.00	100.00
Extra-bloc imports from Soviet bloc							
U.S.S.R.	27.01	32.39	19.98	21.14	29.24	37.25	32.22
Europ. Sat.	72.99	67.61	80.02	78.86	70.76	62.75	67.78
Total	100.00	100.00	100.00	100.00	100.00	100.00	100.00

† Provisional.
Sources: As in Table I.

It has sometimes been inferred from these figures that Soviet Russia was "shifting toward her a larger size of the satellite trade." This is true, but only up to a certain point; it does not explain the increasing trend in the Soviet extra-bloc trade since 1950. To see this point more clearly, let us follow the shifts in the relative shares of the satellites during the period considered.

It must be noted from the outset that the trade of each of the satellites with the outside world has not followed strictly the same pattern.[3] For instance, a systematic decrease can be observed in the imports of Czechoslovakia and Poland from the outside world. The reverse is true for Eastern Germany, Rumania and Bulgaria, while Hungary occupies an intermediate position. A steady decline can also be noticed in the exports to the extra-bloc countries, especially of

[3] See Table A in the Appendix.

Czechoslovakia (which fell from $467 million in 1947 to $205 million in 1953). A very fluctuating, but generally decreasing trend of exports from Poland ($361 million in 1948, around $270 million in 1953) is also noticeable. On the other hand, a steady increase is registered in the exports of Eastern Germany (from $9.8 million in 1947 to $168 million in 1953), as well as Rumania and Bulgaria. Again, an intermediate position is occupied by Hungary. The explanation of these varying patterns is rather obvious. Czechoslovakia and Poland were thoroughly engaged in world trade in 1947 and 1948. After 1948, instead of securing new positions, they lost the ones already acquired. Czechoslovakia—more than Poland—had to turn increasingly toward the intra-bloc trade and its demand. Contrariwise, Eastern Germany, Rumania, and also Hungary, mortgaged after the war by reparations to Soviet Russia, could turn toward the extra-orbit markets only after 1948–49, that is, after the reparation burden had started to decrease. Thereafter their extra-orbit trade turnover increased from year to year, but remained generally at low levels.

If we consider now the changes in the relative shares of each of these countries in the total satellite extra-orbit trade, we can notice the following trends. For instance, with reference to Czechoslovakia's exports to the extra-bloc countries, its share fell from close to 50% in 1947 to around 20% in 1953, while her share in the imports of the extra-bloc countries (satellite exports) fell from over 64% in 1947 to 25% in 1953 (see Table IV). These large displacements are certainly not due to the fact that the satellites have "shifted toward themselves" some of Czechoslovakia's extra-orbit trade, but to a series of more complex factors, such as the changes in the structure of Czechoslovakian foreign trade since 1948. The table further indicates that the foremost trading position among the satellites is held by Poland whose relative share in their total extra-orbit turnover has been, year in, year out, relatively the same size—one-third of the total. These trends do not suggest that Soviet Russia (or, say, Poland) has replaced some of the satellites on the world market (that is, it has shifted larger and larger parts of the latter's trade to itself) but rather that these countries have succeeded in maintaining some of their own positions, losing relatively less than Czechoslovakia for instance, and have done so partly because of the very nature of the products they had to offer on the world markets.

TABLE IV: Extra-bloc Trade of the East European Satellites of Soviet Russia, 1947–1953. Relative share of each country.

Years	Czecho-slovakia	East Germany	Poland	Hungary	Rumania	Bul-garia	Albania	Total
Extra-bloc exports to East Europe (bloc imports)								
1947	48.67	0.59	37.02	8.05	3.30	1.48	0.89	100.00
1948	43.43	1.35	37.02	10.43	5.65	2.06	0.06	100.00
1949	37.96	2.39	38.49	13.98	4.60	2.56	0.02	100.00
1950	31.76	14.44	31.15	14.93	5.62	2.07	0.03	100.00
1951	32.19	11.85	38.00	10.84	6.24	0.87	0.01	100.00
1952	25.34	17.00	35.40	12.10	7.78	2.37	0.01	100.00
1953	19.68	23.40	31.28	12.10	9.31	4.21	0.02	100.00
Extra-bloc imports from East Europe (bloc exports)								
1947	63.79	1.35	23.68	6.87	1.65	2.62	0.04	100.00
1948	44.82	3.28	35.24	9.63	4.68	2.33	0.02	100.00
1949	39.16	3.76	36.87	14.15	4.09	1.97	(.)	100.00
1950	36.84	16.23	31.14	10.97	3.44	1.38	(.)	100.00
1951	33.63	11.77	38.54	10.30	4.55	1.20	0.01	100.00
1952	30.50	15.48	36.80	10.56	4.43	2.22	0.01	100.00
1953	25.77	21.10	33.86	7.65	7.99	3.61	0.02	100.00

(.) less than 0.01%.

Sources: Based on *Value Series,* U.S. Department of Commerce, International Economic Analysis Division, Bureau of Foreign Commerce. For underlying data see Appendix, Table A.

Let us now turn specifically to the structure of the foreign trade of the countries considered and to the shifts which occurred in these structures during the period under review.

Structural Changes in the Foreign Trade of the Satellites

Notwithstanding the enormous Western aid extended from 1945 to 1947 to Soviet Russia, Czechoslovakia, and Poland and the favorable international political climate which followed the war, Soviet Russia systematically tried to establish firmly its hold over the whole of East Central Europe and to prevent any too friendly *rapprochement* between such countries as Czechoslovakia and Poland, and the West. The Prague *coup d'état* of February, 1948, broke the contacts of Czechoslovakia with the West and opened a period of "compartmentalization" of both world politics and world trade. The Western world tried to cement its unity while the Eastern world attempted to solidify itself into an apparently "monolithic" bloc.

The whole period from the end of 1948 to the end of 1953 coincided broadly with the period of the first five-year plan of development in each of the East European countries.[4]

All these plans were drawn on *parallel lines,* and for each and every country aimed to attain "all-round" development in the framework of the national economy whatever its size and its budget of resources. Each engaged in the creation of heavy industrial capacity, each country drew ambitious production programs for supplying the national market with a large variety of home-made products and the intra-bloc market with various types of manufacturing goods. Apparently, it was assumed that the "second world market" had an unlimited capacity for absorbing manufactured goods. Each country built its plan around the same center: the metal-working industry, and again, in the metal-working industry, each plan focused on the heavy engineering sector.

As a consequence of this policy, a country like Czechoslovakia, for instance, proceeded to wide structural changes in her industrial machinery, in order to shift the emphasis from light to heavy industry goods. Countries like Poland, Hungary, or Rumania started to develop new centers of heavy industry far more important than any of the previously existing ones. Even little Bulgaria started to build its first steel mills. The unfolding of the plans and new and even higher targets of "industrialization" resulted in substantial changes in the volume and composition of both the exports and the imports of the countries considered.

In percentages, the proportion of manufactured goods to the total value of the Czechoslovakian exports increased from around 72% in 1937 to 82% in 1948 and probably to more than 85% in 1953.[5] Out of these totals, textiles and clothes, for instance, accounted for 25% in 1937 but represented only 16% in 1948, and only 10% in 1953. In contrast, machinery and vehicles increased

[4] While some plans were launched at the end of 1948 (Czechoslovakia, Bulgaria) and others at the end of 1949 (Poland, Hungary) or even 1950 (Rumania), the period January, 1949, to December, 1953, can be considered as the period of the first quinquennium in the area, because at the latter date substantial changes in the pattern of allocation of resources were envisaged and the ensuing two years (up to the end of 1955) have been treated as "preparatory years" for a second quinquennium to start simultaneously in nearly all the countries of the area. The second quinquennium is scheduled to extend from January, 1956, to the end of 1960.

[5] For some of the underlying data, cf. A. Chistiakov, "Razvitie Economicheskogo Sotrudnichestva Stran Sotsialisticheskogo Lageria" (Development of the Economic Cooperation between the Countries of the Socialist Camp) in *Kommunist* (Moscow, Vol. XXXI, #15, October, 1954).

from 6.8% in 1937 to 20% in 1948 and 40% in 1953. In the Polish exports, the shares of transport equipment and machinery increased from 3.9% of the total exports in 1949 to 12% in 1953. For Hungary large increases occurred in machinery, transport equipment, electrotechnical products, etc. In the Rumanian exports, the share of manufactured goods increased from below 2% in 1938, to close to 18% in 1953. On the other hand, the substantial changes undergone by the countryside (land reforms and the collectivization drive) affected adversely both the amount and the nature of the so-called "traditional" agricultural exports of some of these countries. After the land reform, in the case of Hungary, for instance, the staple products of the larger estates fell off and were replaced by products of small holdings such as poultry, goose liver, eggs, feathers, seeds, oilseeds, vegetables, game and fish, bowels and bladders, etc.[6]

The collectivization drive failed for its part to reorganize the countryside as forecasted by the plans and to secure, on a reduced sown area, higher and higher yields and outputs. The collectivization drive brought about, in fact, a further reduction in agricultural output. A country like Rumania, for instance, which in the prewar period used to produce 7,920 thousand tons of grain per year (average 1934–1938), produced only 4,530 thousand tons yearly during the period 1949 to 1953 and far less up to 1949.[7]

While these changes were reducing both the nature and the amount of exportable surpluses, the industrialization, as well as the structural modifications in agriculture, brought about substantial shifts in the nature and the volume of the demand for imports. A larger emphasis started to be placed on industrial raw materials (coal, steel, ores, etc.) along with a larger demand for heavy and light machinery, transport equipment, and the like. Contrariwise, the demand for consumer goods, textiles, shoes, household goods, etc. fell off sharply. The demand for foodstuffs increased rapidly up to 1948 because of the postwar disruptions, structural changes, and some severe drought years, but started to taper off toward the end of the period considered.

Only a country like Poland—with its "stable" exportable sur-

[6] See: "Foreign Trade of Hungary Since the Introduction of the Florin Currency," *Monthly Bulletin of the National Bank of Hungary* (new series, 3rd year, #3–4, March–April, 1947), 55ff.

[7] The grain area has been substantially reduced relative to its prewar extent, because of territorial losses; however, official targets for 1954 were 8,880 thousand tons of grain. Cf. the Report of Gh. Gheorghiu-Dej. of August 22, 1954 in *For a Lasting Peace, for a People's Democracy* (Bucharest, August 27, 1954).

pluses of coal—or a country like Soviet Russia, with the period of structural changes in agriculture already past, could maintain a larger stability in the structure of their exports. Hence, they could and did secure a more stable position in their extra-orbit trade and fared better, from this point of view, than the other countries of the area. Rumania might have been in the same position as far as oil is concerned but a large part of the latter was mortgaged to Soviet Russia (following the reparation obligations and the formation of the joint Soviet-Rumanian Oil Company). Thus, Russia secured its favorable position first and foremost thanks to the more stable nature of its exportable surpluses; in a secondary way, however, it also increased its surpluses by mortgaging certain outputs of the satellites or by playing the role of "middleman" for them.

East-West Trade and the "Strategical Embargo"

The Prague *coup d'état* marked dramatically the break of the Soviet area with the West and the consolidation of the Soviet hold on Eastern Europe. From that moment on, the United States and some of the Western powers started to build up, in regard to the flow of East-West trade, what can be called a system of "security export control." From the beginning, this implied the application of *selective* controls with the stated aims: 1) of *denying* to the Soviet bloc the goods which could imperil Western security (i.e., applying an "embargo" in respect to goods of primary strategical importance, not only arms but also specialized machinery for the production of armaments, machine-tools, transport equipment, etc.); 2) of *limiting* the exports of goods which could be turned rapidly from civilian to military use (i.e., fixing "quantitative controls" in respect to a series of goods of secondary strategical importance, as specialized machinery and the like); 3) of *establishing* a *surveillance* list for certain key commodities (such as rubber, etc.).

The emphasis was thus placed from the beginning on the *composition* and not on the *volume* of this trade. Time and again, Washington stressed that for certain Western countries the traditional commercial interchanges with Eastern Europe were necessary, even indispensable, and that no security principles required that this trade should be cut off completely.

The United States initiated its exports controls in March, 1948. Some other Western countries established for their part their own controls over certain war materials. Through the Economic Cooperation Act of 1948 (cf. Section 117d as amended) Congress directed the ECA administrator to prevent the shipment to the Soviet bloc of ECA-financed products which were banned for export to the Soviet bloc by the United States itself. In the beginning of 1950, the United States, Canada, and the Western European powers—some of which had already established tighter security controls on their trade with the East—established together an informal committee for determining the areas of controls and of agreement, and for common action.[8] One of the official reports to Congress stated:

> The setting up of controls acceptable to all allied nations has been a difficult process. Roughly, it has involved the specific definitions of commodities which they wished to embargo, which commodities shipments they wished to restrict in quantity, and which should be kept under surveillance. In addition, the experts have had to agree on effectiveness of enforcing these controls.[9]

The continuing discussions resulted in a steady expansion of the lists of commodities agreed for control. At the same time, the Congress adopted the Battle Act providing for the determination of an embargo list, which the U.S. Government "believes the free world should withhold from the Soviet bloc," and for the maintenance of some sort of controls (either quantitative controls or surveillance) concerning other goods.[10]

By the end of 1953, besides munition and atomic energy items, 260 items were placed on the international embargo list; 90 items figured on the quantitative control list; 100 were placed on the surveillance list.[11]

[8] The Consultative Group (C.G.) of the fifteen powers concerned formed a working committee (COCOM). The latter never issues communiques as the participants "have always believed that they could work most effectively without publicity." The details of their discussions are not revealed. (Cf: "The Revision of Strategic Trade Controls—Mutual Defense Assistance Control Act of 1951" (The Battle Act), *Fifth Report to Congress* (first half of 1954, Washington, 1954), p. 16.

[9] The lists established by the COCOM have to do with exports to the European Soviet bloc only, not to Communist China. The embargo concerning the latter is carried out under another control system, based on a United Nations' resolution.

[10] If a country which is receiving military, economic, or financial aid from the United States "knowingly" permits an item on the Battle Act embargo list to be shipped to the Soviet bloc, the President must decide whether to cut off such aid or order its continuance.

[11] At the end of that period the Battle Act embargo list approximated the combined lists of items accepted for embargo by the Consultative Group mentioned above. As stated, this list concerns potential exports to the bloc from countries other than the US. The United States' *own* export lists, unified now in a "master export security list," comprise: the *munitions list,* compiled and administered by the Department of State; the *atomic energy list,* compiled and admin-

Step by step, a vast network of export controls were thus established by the countries participating in the COCOM. However, though the aims were clearly defined, varying tendencies were bound to manifest themselves in the West in respect to the trade with the Soviet bloc, following the immediate interests of the countries involved, the changes in the international political situation, the economic difficulties at home, the conditions prevailing in the world market, etc.

For its part, the Soviet bloc counteracted the embargo by a series of measures. Essentially, it tried to deepen any real or imaginary conflicts among the Western powers, promoted "international trade conferences," participated lavishly in international trade fairs, invited to Soviet Russia trade missions of "honest businessmen," and finally resorted to contraband systematically and on a large scale.

Let us now follow the *combined* results of both the changes in the trade structure of the Soviet bloc countries and the Western controls in respect to the total trade of Eastern Europe with the world markets up to the end of 1953.

Pattern of Extra-orbit Trade 1948–1953

By 1953, the registered trade of extra-bloc Europe with Soviet Russia and her European satellites represented but 31% of the prewar volume of the former's exports to the bloc, and only 22% of the prewar volume of the former's imports from these sources. Given, however, the even sharper shrinkage of the trade of the bloc with other main trading areas (e.g., the United States, Canada, the Far East), the *relative* share of extra-bloc Europe in the total nonorbit trade of Russia and of the satellites appeared to increase during the period under review.

In 1948, less than 60% of the Soviet imports from nonorbit sources were coming from extra-bloc Europe. In 1950, the relative share of the latter increased to 63% and in 1953 to 81% (see Table V—and for the underlying data, Appendix, Table B). For the satellites, this share increased from 68% in 1948 to 76% in 1950 and 80% in 1953. In the falling volume of bloc imports from outside sources, a decisive effort has been made by these countries to secure a *relatively*

istered by the Atomic Energy Commission; and the *export security list,* compiled and administered by the Department of Commerce. See: "Hearing before the Sub-committee on foreign economic policy of the Committee on Foreign Affairs of the House of Representatives, 83rd Congress, Second Session, on East-West Trade" (Washington, February 16, 1954).

larger share of machinery and equipment—even if of a "secondary" strategical value. In 1938, the share of equipment and other producers' goods amounted to 53% of the bloc imports from Western Europe; in 1948 this share represented 57%; in 1950, 65%; in 1951, 61%.[12] To illustrate the correct significance of these shifts, let us examine concretely the trade with Britain. This trade has fallen sharply in value from 1936–38 to 1948; it has remained rather constant since then, except for a dip in 1950. If we distinguish between Soviet and satellite trade, we can note that from 1948 on this trade has tended to *increase* with the former and *decrease* with the latter. The United Kingdom's exports (including re-exports) to Russia had risen from $28.5 million in 1950 to $39.3 million in 1950, $66.6 million in 1951, $104.9 million in 1952. They fell sharply in 1953, namely to $34.3 million; but some goods previously bought as re-exports through London were then either purchased directly (e.g., wool from Oceania) or eventually became obtainable from other sources as well (e.g., rubber). On the other hand, the United Kingdom trade with the satellites fell from $91.5–92 million in 1948 and 1949 to half that total and below from 1950 to 1953 included.

TABLE V: Pattern of Imports of the Soviet Bloc in Europe, 1948, 1950, 1953. Based on derivative data: i.e., extra-bloc exports to bloc. Percentages by main trading areas.

	Soviet Union % of total imports from extra-orbit areas			East Europe satellites % of total imports from extra-orbit areas		
Exporting areas	1948	1950	1953	1948	1950	1953
United States	5.25	0.25	(.)	10.57	3.30	0.26
Canada	0.02	0.06	(.)	2.07	0.47	0.07
Europe (extra-b)	58.84	63.13	80.91	68.43	76.17	80.27
of which U.K.	5.35	13.57	8.26	10.15	7.26	6.02
Finland	27.53	22.10	35.00	1.40	2.08	4.19
Near East & Africa	11.99	11.38	9.11	4.11	3.77	5.79
Far East	15.10	15.90	1.95	3.93	3.06	4.49
Oceania	6.47	8.91	7.95	1.98	5.43	5.62
Latin America	2.33	0.37	0.06	8.91	7.80	3.50
Total	100.00	100.00	100.00	100.00	100.00	100.00

(.) less than 0.01%.
Sources: As in Table I. For underlying data see Appendix, Table B.

[12] Computed from: U.N.-ECE *Economic Bulletin for Europe,* Geneva, III, 2, table 4 and IV, 3, table 6—underlying data in constant prices, exports of eleven Western countries, f.o.b.

In the Soviet imports from the United Kingdom, the *value* of such "secondary" strategical goods as non-ferrous metals, machine tools, electrical generators, and other machinery fell below prewar levels; but in the structure of imports their *relative* share became much more substantial. In 1951, out of the total imports from the United Kingdom (excluding re-exports), the relative shares of electrical generators represented 21.6%, that of machine tools 27.0%, other machinery 21.6%. In 1953, the largest relative share in the Soviet imports from the United Kingdom (excluding re-exports) was represented by electrical goods, namely 33.3% (i.e., £1.1 million) while electrical generators, machine tools and other machinery accounted for 18% (£0.6 million). The satellites also obtained machinery of secondary strategical importance, some of which figured probably only on the quantitative control lists. The *relative* share of electrical apparatus, electrical machinery, other machinery and vehicles, while increasing as compared to prewar, remained, however, at a total not exceeding £4.5 million.[13]

These figures are quite *small:* they do not purport to show that they represented a major deal for the bloc, or that the United Kingdom was "breaking" the embargo. What they do suggest is, in the first place, that the "quantitative restrictions" might often hit harder not Russia itself but its satellites. This distinction is meaningful so long as these countries remain economically "autonomous" units—as long as each is supporting its own burden of trade deficits, investment problems, and the like. In the second place, they show concretely that the system of controls implied constantly limited adjustments in specific cases. The Western nations "marched always together but not always in perfect step." [14] The necessity of adjusting the controls to specific cases found its expression in the official United States acceptance of certain limited exports of even *primary strategical* goods from certain countries receiving American aid. During 1952 and 1953, the first two years of the Battle Act, the total amount of Battle Act *embargo* items knowingly permitted by countries receiving United States aid was in the neighborhood of $15 million—actually a small sum in regard to the total exports to the bloc.[15]

[13] Data computed from: "East-West Trade," British Information Service, Reference Division, New York, August, 1954.

[14] Cf: "The Revision of Strategic Trade Controls. Mutual Defense Assistance Control Act of 1951" (The Battle Act): *Fifth Report to Congress* (first half of 1954, Washington, 1954), p. 1.

[15] "East-West Trade Trends, Mutual Defense Assistance Control Act of 1951" (The Battle Act). *Third Report to Congress* (first half of 1953, Washington, 1954), p. 59.

It is the relative modesty of these totals which explain the bloc's sustained efforts to enlarge the contraband imports. Often the contraband has consisted in the purchase by a neutral agent of certain goods for a fictitious destination, the shipments of these goods to a free port and then their transfer to a bloc destination. This procedure has been strongly hampered by a control system called "import certificate-delivery verification" (I.C.D.V.).[16] However, the condition of success for contraband is evidently the continuous renewal of the devices employed. Evidently, numerous firms, especially from the border countries—such as Western Germany, Austria, Italy—have cooperated with agents of the bloc.[17]

Whatever the real volume secured through contraband, one thing is certain: contraband is a very expensive item; and in this case, it might be added that the larger its scale, the *more* expensive it is. Hence, also, the decisive efforts made by the Soviet Union in 1952 to break the embargo and to present at the so-called "International Conference" meetings of April, 1952, in Moscow, vast perspectives for the expansion of the East-West trade flows.

Before returning to this point, let us first have a look at the pattern of the bloc exports toward the extra-bloc countries during the period considered.

The main commodities exported by Soviet Russia outside its orbit were as usual grain, wood and timber, hides and skins, and nonferrous metals. The satellites exported raw materials, agricultural products, timber as well as light manufactures and other goods.

As far as the Soviet Union is concerned, the striking characteristics of changes in the pattern of exports from 1948 to 1953 were the sharp fall in the exports to the United States as well as the loss of

[16] Under this system "a government, before granting an export license may require the exporting firm to present an import certificate executed by the importing firm and certified by *his* government. After the goods have been shipped, the exporting country may further require that the exporting firm produce a "delivery verification" in which the importing country verifies that the goods were really delivered to the country for which they were originally licensed." Cf: "Worldwide enforcement of Strategic Trade Controls. Mutual Defense Assistance Act of 1951" (The Battle Act). *Third Report to Congress* (first half of 1953, Washington, 1953), p. 13.

[17] See for instance a strongly dramatized but interesting report by David Douglas Duncan: "To Messrs. Dulles, Stassen, Conant: A Memo on Western Aid for Red Build Up," *Life,* Vol. 34, No. 4, January 26, 1953, 23–33. Actually, the official reports to Congress also contain a series of examples where the contraband did not succeed. (See for instance "The Revision of Strategic Trade Controls," *op. cit.,* pp. 25 ff.) At a certain moment, not less than 87 West German firms were blacklisted for "improper trade" with the orbit. (Cf: *New York Times* of June 4, 1952).

some other positions, notably in the Far East (see Table VI). Following these shifts, the relative share of the European extra-bloc outlets increased from 69% in 1948 to 71% in 1950 and 88% in 1953. Two countries, the United Kingdom and Finland, took over 53% of the total extra-bloc exports of Russia.[18] The changes were less spectacular as far as the satellites are concerned. The latter continued to maintain a wider distribution than Russia over the main trading areas of the world. In the case of the satellites, Great Britain and Finland, while representing again the main customers, each accounted, however, for less than 12% of the total trade of the group. While some of these commodities were often essential to the importing countries (e.g., grain for the United Kingdom), the total value of this trade accounted only for a small percentage of the trade of most of the importing countries. As far as the United Kingdom is concerned, the imports from the Soviet Union and the satellites accounted in 1953 for 3.5% of the total United Kingdom imports. Generally the bloc countries have tended to build up balances in London (as well as in the United States) for payments to other countries.[19]

TABLE VI: Pattern of Soviet Bloc Exports to Nonorbit Countries, 1948, 1950, 1953. Based on derivative data: i.e., extra-bloc imports from bloc. Percentages by main trading areas.

	Soviet Union % of total exports to nonorbit countries			East Europe satellites % of total exports to nonorbit countries		
Exporting areas	1948	1950	1953	1948	1950	1953
United States	17.66	15.20	2.86	2.56	4.50	3.21
Canada	.	0.03	0.23	0.48	0.63	0.51
Europe (extra-b)	68.81	70.88	88.24	84.29	78.15	81.83
of which U.K.	22.23	38.04	29.58	9.78	8.60	11.96
Finland	10.41	9.39	23.73	4.03	4.90	11.47
Near East & Africa	10.14	11.04	7.32	6.04	6.93	7.74
Far East	3.16	2.36	0.83	1.70	2.89	2.92
Oceania	0.04	0.48	0.50	1.42	1.66	0.75
Latin America	0.19	0.01	0.02	3.51	5.24	3.04
Total	100.00	100.00	100.00	100.00	100.00	100.00

Sources: As in Table I. For underlying data see Appendix, Table C.

[18] The United Kingdom obtained from the Soviet Union in 1953, for instance, wood and timber (34% of the Russian deliveries), non-ferrous metals (24%), hides and skins (16%), grain (9%), and other produce. The share of grain, very large in 1951 or 1952 (from 45 to 60% of deliveries), fell sharply in 1953. From the satellites the United Kingdom obtained mainly meat (48% of the deliveries), wood and timber (16%), and grain (6%).

[19] In 1953, except for Finland and Austria in Europe and Iran and Hong-

At the 1952 Moscow Conference, the bloc indicated the possibility of exporting yearly, over the period 1953–55, two or three times as much as previously (see Table VII). Actually these exportable surpluses did not at all materialize. East-West trade, by and large, stagnated in 1953 at the previous levels.

TABLE VII: Soviet Bloc in Europe: East-West Trade in 1952, and Level Proposed for 1953–55 by the Moscow Conference. Millions of dollars, and percentage increases.

Country	Estimated turnover in 1952	Eventual yearly turnover, 1953–55 (Moscow Conference estimates)	Percentage increase
Czechoslovakia	408	900–1,000	+120 or +145
Poland	524	700– 800	+ 34 or + 53
Hungary	164	300– 400	+ 83 or +144
Romania	87	200– 300	+130 or +245
Bulgaria	33	100	+203
Soviet Union	944	2,500–3,300	+165 or +249
Total	2,160	4,700–5,900	+118 or +173

Sources:

1952—See above Table II.

1953–55—Data grouped in *Economic Bulletin for Europe,* IV, 3, on the basis of the data released at the Moscow Conference of April, 1952.

Pattern of Intra-bloc Trade

The drive toward industrialization in each and every national economy of the orbit, as well as the embargo itself, shaped together the new characteristics of the intra-orbit pattern of trade. Two of the basic characteristics must be noted, from the outset: 1) the central position of Soviet Russia (see Table VIII) as the main supplier of industrial raw materials in exchange of manufactured goods; 2) the tendency of each unit, including Soviet Russia, to try to provide this restricted and isolated market with substitutes for the key industrial equipment and produce denied by the West.

From 1948 to 1952, 70 to 90% of the trade of each country of the orbit was carried on with the other "people's democracies" (including China). In the total turnover of each of the countries considered, the share of the Soviet Union increased from around 10–25%

Kong in Asia, the imports of the nonorbit countries trading with the Soviet bloc (including China) usually accounted for from 1 to 3% of their imports from the whole world, and at the most, 5 to 6% (e.g., for Sweden and Iceland). See Appendix, Table D.

TABLE VIII: EASTERN EUROPE: Shares of Soviet Union and of Soviet Bloc Countries in Total Trade of Each Country, 1937, 1948, 1952. Percentages.

	Soviet Union			People's Dem.			Combined share			Rest of world		
Country	1937	1948	1952	1937	1948	1952	1937	1948	1952	1937	1948	1952
Czechosl.	1	16	35	10	14	36	11	30	71	89	70	29
Poland	1	22	32	6	12	35	7	34	67	93	66	33
Hungary	—	11	29	13	23	42	13	34	71	87	66	29
Romania	1	25	58	17	46	27	18	71	85	82	29	15
Bulgaria	—	54	57	12	20	32	12	74	89	88	26	11
Albania	—	. .	57	. .	. .	43	5	38	100	95	62	0

Sources:

1937—*Probleme Economice* #5/6, 1952, p. 66, corrected with "The Network of World Trade," League of Nations, Geneva, 1942.

1948, 1952—*Probleme Economice, ibid.,* and *Vneshniaia Torgovlia,* #10 (Oct. 1952) and #11 (Nov. 1953).

For Albania, 1951, *New Times,* Moscow, #5 (January 28, 1953) p. 10.

in 1948 (excepting Bulgaria) to around 30–60% in 1952 (cf. Table VIII). While remaining, as before 1948, the main supplier of raw materials for all these countries, the Soviet Union also started to deliver to them fully equipped plants and heavy equipment, not to speak of armaments. If up to 1948 the investment goods represented an insignificant part of the Soviet exports to the bloc, henceforth they attained every year around 15% to 20% of the total commercial value of these exports. Although this percentage might not appear very large, in many countries the very core of the plan, capital construction of steel facilities, became strictly dependent on Russian deliveries (e.g., the Polish steel mills of *Nowa Huta,* etc.). On the other hand, the launching of the development plan in each and every country, the reorientation and diversification of their outputs, allowed a substantial increase and diversification in the exports of the region to the Soviet Union. These exports increased in variety, not only as far as aggregates (fully-equipped plants, notably from Czechoslovakia), heavy machinery, locomotives and transport equipment were concerned, but also in the range and importance of textiles, footwear, light-metals-industries products and appliances, foodstuffs, tobacco and mass-consumer goods, as well as in the range and importance of raw materials and semi-finished products.

Basically, the structure of this trade in the period considered appeared to be as follows (see Table IX). It is indubitable that the Soviet Union exported the aggregates in question in order to help the increase in the outputs *in which she remains interested for a long*

TABLE IX: EASTERN EUROPE: Structure of Soviet–Eastern European Trade, 1948–1953.

Soviet Exports								Soviet Imports							
Goods	C	EG	P	H	R	B	A	Goods	C	EG	P	H	R	B	A
Fully equipped plants	+		+	+	+	+	+	Fully equipped plants	+	+					
Heavy Machinery	+		+	+	+	+		Heavy Machinery	+	+	+	+			
Agric. Machinery			+	+	+	+	+	Ships	+	+	+	+			
								Locomotives	+		+	+			
								Transport equipment	+		+	+	+		
								Light metal ind.			+	+			
								Chemicals		+	+	+	+		
								Textiles	+		+	+	+	+	
								Footwear	+						
Oil & oil products	+		+			+		Oil & oil products					+		+
Steel					+			Cement	+		+		+	+	
Coke		+		+	+			Coal & coke			+				
Pig iron & Cast iron				+	+		+	Metals			+			+	
Iron ore	+		+	+	+			Ores						+	+
Other ores	+		+												
Non-ferrous metals	+	+	+	+	+		+								
Cotton	+	+	+	+	+	+		Tobacco						+	
Wool	+		+	+	+	+									
Rubber	+		+	+	+										
Timber	+			+				Timber					+		+
Grain	+	+	+				+	Sugar	+		+				
Other foodstuffs	+	+						Other foodstuffs				+	+	+	+

Sources: The trade agreements for the period 1948–1953.

period, such as steel, cement, oil. Furthermore, it is equally evident from the experience during the period up to 1948, that she provided the region with the bulk of raw materials, *part of which were to return to the Soviet Union as finished goods.*

The industrialization effort and the pressing necessity of coping with the Western controls brought about a certain degree of specialization as among the various countries of the area insofar as their intra-bloc trade was concerned. This specialization, while not eliminating the duplication and waste implicit in the all-round planning attempts of each unit, insured, however, some degree of substitutability for the products denied by the West.

Thus, Czechoslovakia started to export all types of aggregates, even electric power stations (e.g., the key Hungarian power station, *Inota*), heavy transformers, turbines and boilers, machine-tools, building machinery and materials, transport equipment, as well as limited amounts of coke and coal. (In 1951 for instance, 75% of the exported industrial products were sold to the U.S.S.R. and the People's Democracies as compared to 55% in 1949). In turn, Czechoslovakia obtained from Eastern Germany various types of machinery, chemical installations and equipment, as well as precision instruments, chemicals and fertilizers. Furthermore, Eastern Germany sent some fully equipped chemical aggregates to Poland and Rumania and exported heavy building machinery, machinery for the light industries, and appliances. Poland remained basically the supplier of coal, iron, and steel, cement and some chemicals. However, it also exported mining and drilling installations, especially to Czechoslovakia. To the smaller countries of the orbit it sent such commodities as railway rolling stock, machine tools and metallurgical goods. Hungary supplied this market with such key products as engines (sent to Eastern Germany), motor trucks and trailers (mainly for Poland), Diesel trains (for Czechoslovakia) and transformers. Rumania provided mainly oil products and drilling installations. Bulgaria furnished non-ferrous ores and Albania, small quantities of chrome, ores, and bitumen. Along with these efforts to substitute for the "strategical goods" unobtainable from the West, the countries considered also exported consumer goods—such as textiles, shoes, appliances—as well as agricultural produce.

If we take as a base the figures given at the Moscow Conference of April, 1952, we could assume as "desirable" an inflow of imports from non-orbit sources, for the area as a whole including East Germany, of, say, \$3.0–3.6 billion. If we further make the conservative estimate that 30% of this total would be, as in 1948, earmarked for equipment and machinery, the needed inflow of equipment from non-orbit sources could be placed at between \$1 and 1.1 billion. It is doubtful that the area could cope with all its needs and substitute successfully for the "missing" imports from the non-orbit sources.[20] The embargo has thus placed a serious limitation to the over-ambitious industrialization schemes of the area.

The New Course and the "Streamlining" of the Embargo

At the close of 1953, and the beginning of 1954, substantial changes were enacted by the Soviet bloc in respect to the pattern of allocation of resources, the ratio of investment in heavy industry versus light industry, the ratio of investment in industry versus agriculture, etc. In respect to intra-bloc planning and trade, the period from the end of 1953 to the beginning of 1956 was designed as the period of a "new course" aiming to end both some of the policies of self-sufficiency in the framework of each national economy and the drive toward super-industrialization. The new course was to prepare both a real division of labor in the area and a better lot for the consumer in general. Briefly, "more butter than guns."

Following the "new course," the Soviet Union increased its demand in the Western markets for food (of which precisely butter became the biggest item along with meat, fish, citrus fruit), textiles (a larger demand than in any recent years) as well as ships—notably fishing vessels. It exported, on the other hand, such key products as manganese and petroleum (for which it accepted commitments far larger than before) and finally sent to the Western markets between

[20] In regard to this needed inflow of imports over and above what the intra-bloc market can offer, the imports of machines and equipment from the West reached in 1953 a total of probably not more than \$250–300 million—even if we assume that they represented over 40% of the *total* imports of the satellites from these sources. (See Appendix, Table A.) Soviet Russia, for her part, as stated officially by the Russians, "exported to the people's democracy in 1953, machines and equipment for a total of about 800 million roubles," i.e., at the official rate of exchange, \$200 million worth of goods. Assuming that Czechoslovakia and East Germany each contributed an equal amount of "strategical commodities," while the other also made up together some \$200–300 million worth of goods of this type, we arrive at a total of some \$900 million worth of machinery and equipment —i.e., a figure *below the minimum deemed necessary to be obtained from the West, over and above a given level of trade in the orbit itself.*

Additional Soviet exports of machinery *on credit* might have to be added to the figure given above. This total would not, however, exceed some additional \$150 million per year.

$100–200 million worth of gold. The satellites, for their part, increased their demand for consumer goods both outside and inside the bloc. Outside the bloc, this implied an increased demand for such products as wool, cotton, leather, and fertilizers.

Inside the bloc, this implied not only an increased demand for agricultural produce by countries like Czechoslovakia and East Germany, but also a larger demand in the whole area for mass consumption goods such as bicycles, radio sets, and sewing machines. Supplementary exports and imports in excess of those previously signed were drawn between Czechoslovakia and East Germany, for instance, for the exchange of Czechoslovakian furniture, leather goods and motorcycles, against German cameras, photo equipment, watches, etc.[21]

The pressures for an increased East-West trade were felt at that moment more strongly in the West than at any other moment since 1947. It is perhaps as a consequence of these pressures that it was felt that "the large process of expanding the international control lists has gone just about as far as it could go under current world conditions." [22] Hence, in the first half of 1954, the West undertook the difficult mission of overhauling the existing international controls. The "streamlining" of the international control lists—deletion of some items, re-definition of some others, etc.—reduced the embargo list to 170 items (instead of 260), the quantitative control list to 20 (instead of 90) and the surveillance list to 60 items (instead of 100).

As a result of the increased bloc demand for consumables and of the sharper distinction between the controlled items and the rest of the goods susceptible of entering into the East-West trade flows, the latter showed a tendency to increase in 1954. Western Europe's exports rose by probably one-third over 1953, while the imports from the bloc increased by some 10%. These figures are, however, far below the stated targets of the Moscow Conference of 1952 and do not substantiate at all the rather common illusion in some Western European countries that any relaxation of controls would automatically condition the "swelling" of East-West trade flows. Actually, the trade increases of 1954 might well be of a short-run nature and not indicative of a further rising trend. The decisive fact which might again

[21] See for instance, R. Dvorak, "Economic Cooperation of Countries of Socialistic Camp" in *For a Lasting Peace, for a People's Democracy,* Feb. 12, 1954.

[22] "The Revision of Strategic Trade Controls—Mutual Defense Assistance Control Act of 1951 (The Battle Act)," *Fifth Report to Congress* (first half of 1954, Washington, 1954), p. 2.

keep the bloc trade at about the low levels of the 1948–1953 period is the unceremonious discarding of some of the tenets of the "new course," such as the former emphasis on the increase of the share of consumption versus the share of "accumulation" (investment) in the national income. The renewed emphasis on heavy industry—this time along with the stressing of the necessity of the development of agriculture but with limited investments—affirmed since the opening of 1955, might again condition a decrease in the demand for consumables and an increase in the demand for such "strategical" goods as heavy equipment, machinery, and vehicles. It is as a function of this policy that Soviet Russia and the satellites will shape the new quinquennium to extend from the beginning of 1956 to the end of 1960, in most of the countries of the area. This renewed emphasis can and probably will again raise a host of questions in the Western alliance about the *extent* of the strategical controls. For the satellites, who one after another have cracked under the strain of their first round of stepped-up industrialization, the second planned quinquennium with its increasing demands for equipment and heavy goods is susceptible to a new cycle of strenuous efforts and of interior crises.

Concluding Remarks

In conclusion, it appears to us that the "strategical embargo" has extended, from 1948 on, to all the extra-orbit trading areas dealing with the Soviet bloc. It has thus *become as effective as possible,* since "marching together" has not necessarily meant "marching in the same step." [23] In becoming effective, the embargo has not necessarily "hit" the seat of power in the bloc but often its periphery. The structure of the Soviet exports has frequently enabled Soviet Russia to fare better than most of the satellites and to obtain from extra-bloc sources, even through normal trade, some non-negligible items of strategical interest. In other words, the countries of the bloc disposing of different types of commodities, some of which are in more pressing demand than the others, have tried and succeeded in varying degrees in cutting through the embargo lines.

The policy of the embargo, with its emphasis on security and long-range perspectives, is perhaps less responsible for the present low levels of East-West trade than is the lack of exportable surpluses of

[23] A crude attempt to evaluate these various increases and decreases in the volume of East-West trade by countries up to 1952 has been made by the author in "Effects of the Embargo on Soviet Trade," *Harvard Business Review* (November 1952).

the bloc itself. What the embargo policy has actually prevented is the further development of the Soviet industrial machine on the basis of Western deliveries of heavy equipment, vehicles, etc. on long-term credit.

By its very scope or nature, the embargo has probably indirectly facilitated the strengthening of the central position of Russia in regard to the satellites, given the latter's increased dependence on Russia's deliveries of industrial raw materials and of even limited capital equipment, not obtainable from outside sources. Under the assumption that each satellite, whatever its actual political and military dependence toward Russia might be,[24] is still treated as an "autonomous" unit in respect to its trade deficits, investment problems and so on, this fact is not deprived of importance.

The idea that the East-West trade could increase abruptly if the strategical controls were lifted—and *that without credits from the West*—appears as a myth more than a reality. Actually, the lifting of the controls would be more liable to condition a shift in the bloc imports from nonorbit sources, toward more producers' goods, rather than an increase in the total volume of this trade. Given the framework in which this trade is bound to flow—determined as it is in its structure by both planned requirements and embargo limitations—the prospect seems to be for *spasmodic increases and decreases* in this trade not far above the general trend followed since 1952–53. These spasmodic increases remain implicit in the fact that the vast nonorbit world is itself subject to circumstantial shifts in the trade position of one country or another, over a long period of "cold war."

[24] There are present and potential different *degrees* in this dependence, as the case of Yugoslavia, and the situation of a country like China, would prove.

Appendix to Chapter 17

TABLE A: Extra-bloc Trade of the East European Satellites of Soviet Russia, 1947–1953. Unadjusted data in thousands of US dollars.

Years	Czechoslovakia	East Germany	Poland	Hungary	Rumania	Bulgaria	Albania	Total
Extra-bloc Exports to East Europe (unadjusted EE's imports)								
1947	416,686	5,132	317,018	68,905	28,271	12,659	7,657	856,328
1948	391,397	12,170	333,625	93,985	50,949	18,576	551	901,253
1949	348,664	21,926	353,507	128,453	42,337	23,528	232	918,647
1950	250,047	113,682	245,295	117,541	44,266	16,271	229	787,331
1951	274,417	101,011	323,905	92,373	53,216	7,411	75	852,408
1952	170,330	114,325	237,990	81,384	52,315	15,902	73	672,319
1953 *	133,410	158,638	211,923	82,036	63,086	28,513	174	677,780
Extra-bloc Imports from East Europe (unadjusted EE's exports)								
1947	467,567	9,836	173,611	50,361	12,089	19,231	279	732,974
1948	460,201	33,667	361,794	98,872	48,006	23,909	256	1,026,705
1949	426,925	40,960	401,889	154,235	44,587	21,497	31	1,090,124
1950	346,374	152,545	292,700	103,167	32,276	12,938	64	940,064
1951	322,813	112,964	369,897	98,818	43,659	11,549	146	959,846
1952	237,545	120,589	286,568	82,216	34,475	17,314	83	778,790
1953 *	204,789	167,674	269,045	60,739	63,475	28,722	121	794,565

* Provisional.

Sources: (based on) *Value Series,* U.S. Department of Commerce, International Economic Analysis Division, Bureau of Foreign Commerce.

TABLE B: Pattern of Imports of the Soviet Bloc in Europe, 1948, 1950, 1953. Unadjusted data for extra-bloc exports. In thousands of US dollars.

Exporting areas	Soviet Russia 1948	1950	1953	East European satellites 1948	1950	1953
United States	28,004	752	19	95,239	25,949	1,757
Canada	112	168	4	18,671	3,717	461
Europe extra-bloc	313,911	185,082	336,363	616,750	599,675	544,060
United Kingdom	28,528	39,789	34,344	91,482	47,131	40,811
Finland	146,914	64,802	145,522	11,490	16,081	28,388
Near East and Africa	63,987	33,364	37,895	37,071	29,664	39,249
Far East	80,559	46,612	8,112	35,400	24,104	30,418
Oceania	34,479	26,121	33,071	17,818	42,801	38,087
Latin America	12,427	1,090	267	80,304	61,421	23,748
Total	533,479	293,189	415,731	901,253	787,331	677,780

Sources: (based on) *Value Series,* U.S. Department of Commerce, International Economic Analysis Division, Bureau of Foreign Commerce.

TABLE C: Pattern of Exports of the Soviet Bloc in Europe, 1948, 1950, 1953. Unadjusted data for extra-bloc imports. In thousands of US dollars.

Importing areas	Soviet Russia 1948	1950	1953	East European satellites 1948	1950	1953
United States	86,840	38,300	10,791	26,298	42,285	25,532
Canada	4	74	855	4,954	5,946	4,050
Europe extra-bloc	338,407	178,612	333,326	865,396	734,678	650,211
United Kingdom	109,318	95,853	111,722	100,454	80,824	95,001
Finland	51,207	23,676	89,647	41,395	46,082	91,141
Near East and Africa	49,885	27,814	27,641	62,015	65,185	61,477
Far East	15,517	5,949	3,172	17,438	27,196	23,226
Oceania	214	1,216	1,878	14,605	15,598	5,979
Latin America	903	42	70	35,999	49,176	24,090
Total	491,770	252,007	377,733	1,026,705	940,046	794,565

Sources: (based on) *Value Series,* U.S. Department of Commerce, International Economic Analysis Division, Bureau of Foreign Commerce.

TABLE D: Imports of Nonorbit Countries from Soviet Bloc (including China). Expressed as percentage of their total imports from the world.

	From whole of Soviet bloc			From European satellites
	1948	1950	1953	1953
	1	2	3	4
Argentina	1.2	3.0	1.8	1.8
Austria	25.6	14.8	11.0	10.8
Belgium-Luxemburg	4.3	2.3	2.0	1.0
Brazil	1.1	.8	.8	.8
Canada	.3	.4	.1	.1
Ceylon	.4	.6	13.5	.5
Denmark	11.8	6.1	4.1	3.0
Finland	19.0	18.0	34.4	17.2
France	2.2	1.3	1.3	.6
Germany—West	1.9	6.6	4.3	3.1
Greece	2.1	.3	1.3	1.2
Hong Kong	20.8	23.1	22.1	—
Iceland	8.6	9.6	8.6	6.2
India	1.2	1.0	.7	.3
Indonesia	3.3	1.1	.9	.6
Iran	3.5	6.3	.9	.6
Italy	3.1	4.2	2.2	1.5
Japan	4.0	4.5	1.6	.2
Malaya	6.7	3.7	3.8	.6
Netherlands	4.3	3.1	2.9	.9
Norway	9.0	5.8	4.8	2.6
Pakistan	6.8	8.3	1.2	.3
Portugal	.4	.5	.3	.2
Sweden	11.1	7.1	3.9	3.2
Switzerland	6.2	5.8	4.3	2.6
Turkey	8.7	7.9	5.5	5.5
United Kingdom	2.9	2.8	2.5	1.0
United States	3.3	2.6	.3	.2
Yugoslavia	45.9	none	none	none

Source: *Col. 1 and 2:* "World Wide Enforcement of Strategic Trade Controls. Mutual Defense Assistance Control Act of 1951" (The Battle Act), *Third Report to Congress* (Washington, 1953), p. 85.
Col. 3 and 4: "The Revision of Strategic Trade Controls." *ibid., Fifth Report to Congress* (Washington, 1954), p. 74.

Part Five

AMERICAN IDEAS FOR A FREE EAST CENTRAL EUROPE

Chapter 18

Post-Liberation Problems

ALVIN M. BENTLEY

Introduction

THE TASK of discussing problems which may arise following the liberation of East Central Europe is not an easy one. For one thing, the nature of the problems which might be anticipated would depend greatly upon the amount of time intervening between the present and the date of liberation. Obviously, if liberation is only two or three years away, the post-liberation problems would be very different from those which might ensue following an additional decade or two of Communist control.

The manner and type of the liberation itself will also greatly influence the problems which would thence ensue. If freedom comes to East Central Europe through gradual stages of peaceful development, there would be one set of problems. If freedom comes as the result of a violent revolution or internal upheaval, new problems would arise. And if freedom should come during the course of a new world war by means of an anti-Communist invasion from without, such post-war problems would again be very different, especially if the war had been waged with atomic and thermonuclear weapons.

It is not the purpose of this essay to speculate as to the form which liberation may take or as to the amount of time which may occur before it is accomplished. The author does not even believe it to be his function to discuss the multitude of problems which might occur in each and every contingency. Discussion will rather be limited to those problems which might be expected to arise following *any* type of liberation at *any* given date in the reasonable future. Particular attention will likewise be paid to current American thinking regarding these particular problems and their possible solutions.

The geographic area which this study encompasses consists of the Baltic states of Estonia, Latvia and Lithuania; Poland; Czechoslovakia; Hungary; Rumania; Bulgaria and Albania; in other words, those countries now popularly regarded as Soviet satellites. Although Yugoslavia does not now belong in this category, it is to be expected that liberation in any of the satellites would greatly affect developments in that country as well. The Soviet Zone of Germany presents special problems which lie outside the scope of this paper and will not, therefore, be included.

Certain of the Soviet republics within which nationalistic or pro-independence aspirations have been manifested in the past, especially Ukraine, Armenia, and Byelorussia, may very well be influenced by post-liberation developments in East Central Europe. To the extent of such influence, they may also be considered as within the scope of this study.

Views of U.S. Government

The United States Government, as could naturally be expected, has been extremely cautious about making public pronouncements regarding any possible post-liberation developments in East Central Europe. However, the desire and hope of this government for such liberation has been underscored on repeated occasions. On February 20, 1953, President Eisenhower sent a draft resolution to both houses of Congress with the purpose of putting the Federal government on record against such conditions of Communist enslavement as exist at present. The resolution stated in part:

> That the Senate and the House . . . join in proclaiming the hope that the peoples who have been subjected to the captivity of Soviet despotism shall again enjoy the right of self-determination within a framework which will sustain the peace; that they shall again have the right to choose the form of government under which they will live, and that sovereign rights of self-government shall be restored to them, all in accordance with the pledge of the Atlantic Charter.

This government thereby asserted its hope and belief that the nations of East Central Europe would, following liberation, have the right and the opportunity for self-determination in choosing their own form of government. The President also appeared to envisage their ultimate membership in the United Nations or some comparable organization whose purpose would be to "sustain the peace."

In a speech on April 16, 1953, President Eisenhower seemed, however, to look at the future more from the standpoint of regionalism when he said:

> We are ready not only to press forward with the present plans for closer unity of the Nations of Western Europe but also, upon that foundation, to strive to foster a broader European community, conducive to the free movement of persons, of trade and of ideas. This community would include a free and united Germany, with a government based upon free and secret elections. This free community and the full independence of the East European nations could mean the end of the present unnatural division of Europe.

These remarks would appear to contemplate post-liberation participation by the people and nations of East Central Europe in a broadened version of one or more of the present regional organizations of West Europe.

Secretary of State Dulles and Assistant Secretary Robertson participated, on July 17, 1953, in a Joint Report to the Nation which further emphasized the concept of an expanded European Community. Speaking of the recent Foreign Ministers' meeting, Mr. Dulles said:

> We particularly emphasized that the unity of Europe was necessary in itself and that its consummation should in no way be dependent upon the existence of tension with the Soviet Union. If there were no Soviet tension at all, the uniting of Europe would still be essential for lasting peace. That unification is not directed against Eastern Europe or Russia, as the three Ministers pointed out. The European Community is open to others, provided only that they are free. If, for example, liberty were restored to Czechoslovakia, it could become a member of the European Community and enjoy the vast economic and security benefits which are available to the Community members.

But with the exception of a belief in the value and necessity of an expanded European Community, the State Department seemed anxious to preserve a hands-off policy toward a liberated East Central Europe. At least this was the line of reasoning followed by Assistant Secretary Merchant when he declared in a public address on May 14, 1954:

> In our diplomatic moves on behalf of the peoples behind the Iron Curtain, we do not attempt to prescribe what shall be the way of life of these people once they regain their freedom and independence. . . . For the future of this region, all we can legitimately expect is that the form of government and economic system to be established will correspond to

> the freely expressed will of the people. Thus, we feel that in such states of the future, each individual should enjoy the protection of due process of law, and the right to work, to live and worship in accordance with his own conscience and belief. We further expect that each nation will live in peace and harmony with its neighbors. Since no nation's security and well-being can be lastingly achieved in isolation, each nation should cooperate fully with its neighbors in establishing full and friendly exchange of ideas, persons and goods within an acceptable international framework.

This pronouncement by Mr. Merchant seems to represent the fullest extent to which official U.S. government thinking has gone with respect to the post-liberation future for the captive peoples of East Central Europe. This government feels that the liberated nations should eventually merge with an expanded version of the European Community. Each nation should meet its political and economic problems with solutions which are in the best traditions of democracy (in the Western sense of the word) among which the principle of self-determination is foremost. It is a known fact that the State Department contemplates liberation as the end result of an internal movement of a peaceful nature. There could, of course, be no public pronouncements regarding liberation by any other means.

Although the U.S. Government thus officially comes very close to proclaiming a complete hands-off policy so far as the future American attitude towards the liberated nations is concerned, it is unofficially hoped and felt in many government quarters that the program of military and economic assistance to Yugoslavia which has been carried on since 1948 would encourage the satellite governments to expect similar treatment if they likewise declared and maintained their independence of Moscow. It is, moreover, noteworthy that this assistance has been forthcoming on a sizable scale even though the premises contained in Mr. Merchant's speech can hardly be said to have been completely fulfilled by the Tito regime.

Economic Problems

It is manifestly evident that, under Soviet control, the captive nations of East Central Europe are being subjected to a process of economic integration which is based on uniformity and totalitarian regimentation. It is also evident that the area is in large part being forcibly diverted from its erstwhile predominantly agricultural economy to one which embodies a large and rapidly-growing amount of industrialization. This industrialization is accompanied by an overwhelming predominance of state capital in industry and by strict governmental and police control of the trade unions.

The urgent post-liberation need of this area for some form of federation is no less clear in the economic than in the political field. As an example of successful West European functionalism, the eyes of the liberated peoples will be drawn to the Coal and Steel Community as established under the Schuman Plan. Some form of co-operation or integration between the Community and the freed countries would seem to be highly desirable. However, the problem in this field will be whether adherence will be as individual countries or as a group. The question of adherence will, of course, have to be decided in the light of the very real problems that will face the countries of East Central Europe after liberation.

The present harsh attitude of the satellite governments toward labor and the lack of adequate technical and organizational progress in hard coal extraction have created a serious bottleneck that jeopardizes plans for all forms of industrial production. This situation has probably been partially responsible for the recent reduction in the rate of expansion of heavy industry and a resultant increase in the production of consumer goods. Even if projected targets in the output of hard coal, coke, brown coal and lignite are reached, it is still doubtful that the expected target in steel and steel products can be attained. Therefore, the rate of development of the coal and steel industries of the captive countries at the time of liberation and the urgent necessity to maintain this production during the immediate post-liberation period represent a very real economic problem to be faced at this time.

The question of oil and electric and water power, fortunately, does not present such difficulties, owing to the fact that captive Europe traditionally is an exporter of its surplus energy to Western Europe and has an adequate power supply on hand. Although oil production under the Communists has been unsatisfactory, the production of electric power based on lignite and low grade coal has so far been sufficient for most purposes. However, even without a serious dislocation of order in this field following liberation, there still will be a serious under-supply of electrical energy for private consumer purposes owing to the rapid expansion of industries requiring power. It has also been reported that some of the older plants now in operation are uneconomical because of obsolescence and overwork. It is probable, therefore, that any large expansion of hydroelectric energy would require outside assistance to build and equip the needed hydroelectric plants. The necessity for new laws and regulations governing the power industry, the question of integrating European power on an inter-regional basis and the part that atomic energy will play in the future of the European power industry are all problems that will have to be met at this time.

The greatest post-liberation problem that will arise in the field of transport will probably be the fact that standardized railway rolling stock now being built in East Central Europe differs greatly from that in use in Western Europe. The fact that, in the captive area, railroads form such a preponderant majority of all freight transportation (as compared with highways and waterways) will probably result in a very long lapse of time before international transport arrangements can be satisfactorily implemented. This, of course, will limit East-West freight traffic to a possibly critical degree during the post-liberation period and will complicate the problems of reconstruction and readjustment.

One of the most immediate post-liberation needs will be for the liberated countries to import raw materials to replace those which they now receive from the Soviet Union. This will be essential in order to maintain production levels permitting maximum employment as well as essential exports, and will in turn pose the problem of how these imports are to be financed and how credit facilities are to be obtained. In other words, there will be an urgent need for these credit facilities to finance the necessary imports that cannot be counterbalanced by proceeds from foreign trade and other assets abroad.

It must also be assumed that there will be an equally pressing need for investment capital, since the existing domestic sources of capital will not be adequate for new investment. Communist financial policies have effectively dried up almost all accumulated savings, and other sources of capital accumulation are likewise expected to yield little or nothing. New compulsory state loans can hardly be considered in a post-liberation period and any expansion of banking credits might open the gates to inflation. Therefore, the foreign capital market will have to meet this need for long-term investments, since the capital resources of the liberated countries themselves will probably be insignificant. This, of course, will present a multitude of problems and the question will logically arise whether or not to continue some forms of Soviet planning for the time being in order to escape economic and financial disruption, or worse.

The question of overall financial stability in the liberated countries will also pose several serious problems, not only to keep the various currencies stable but also to maintain their respective purchasing power and to re-establish normal financial incentives. The need for government and private investment capital will also enter here in order to stabilize economic and financial conditions. Agricultural production must be increased and the food-processing industry expanded. Improved housing will be a vital necessity, not only for present occupants but also for those returning from forced labor and labor camps and all others who have been displaced by the Communists. There will be a need for industrial expansion to absorb unemployment and to produce for export. New investment capital, therefore, which will be required in these fields, will also be making its own contribution to economic and financial stability. The problem of attracting this capital, from both government and private sources, will be one of the greatest of the post-liberation period.

The reduction of existing trade barriers will also be one of the immediate problems of the post-liberation era, and not only the barriers that exist to the movement of trade but also those to movements of people and ideas. But let us examine the matter of trade for a moment. There has been in the past a real lack of much natural wealth in East Central Europe and, thanks to the Iron Curtain, Western Europe has been forced to obtain much of its foodstuffs from elsewhere. However, the former economic nationalism among the countries under discussion here has to some extent been replaced by a series of economic treaties and other inter-satellite agreements. This raises the post-liberation question as to the future of these treaties and agreements. Should they be continued in some form, should they be abandoned, or is there some other alternative?

As might be expected, the trade of this area has been subjected to severe economic dislocation and the traditional commercial and trade relationships between Western Europe and Central and Eastern Europe have been violently disrupted. Before World War II Western Europe was predominantly an industrial region while Central and Eastern Europe were essentially agricultural. The nationalization which has been forced by the Communists on both trade and industry is bound to have lasting effects and to force a complete change in the traditional relationships of the two parts of the continent.

It is probable that after the liberation the system for exchanges of goods which now exists among the satellites will have to be maintained, at least for the time being, to prevent total economic disruption of the area. Since the area is completely dependent at the present on industrial products and raw materials which come from the Communist orbit, including the Soviet Union and China, and since these sources will probably be lost at the time of liberation, it will be necessary to find new trade channels to obtain these raw materials.

On the other hand, it is probable that at least for a time the liberated countries will be unable to offer sufficient quantities of marketable goods in exchange for the needed raw materials. Contact, therefore, must be re-established between the liberated markets and the free world markets on an entirely new trading basis. It is also probable that the liberated countries will not have sufficient international confidence to induce trade except on a cash basis; that is, other countries will be reluctant to extend them credit terms. This will present a very real problem to be met in the post-liberation period.

It seems that a continuation of close economic cooperation, at least among the countries of the Danubian Basin, will be needed following liberation. Perhaps this will take the form of a customs union with common economic planning for adequate development in this field. The regional economic cooperation which has already developed under Soviet control will undoubtedly have to be continued in view of the rapid industrialization which has taken place. Because of this industrialization, because of the degree of integration in fields such as electrification, transport, etc., and because of the fact that industrialized people will not wish to revert to a peasant status, the existing situation at the time of liberation will have to be met on the basis of the facts as they are at that time.

In this respect, it is encouraging to read the declarations made at Philadelphia on February 11, 1951, and at Williamsburg, Virginia on June 12, 1952, by representatives of ten of the enslaved peoples. The former specifically stated that the movement of goods and services should be free, that individual initiative should be stimulated and that the choice between private and public enterprise should be determined on the basis of merit. The Williamsburg Declaration essentially confirmed this by declaring that all forms of political, social and economic organizations should be chosen by the people, in such a manner that social justice would be established.

Agricultural Problems

The two most important post-liberation problems in the field of agriculture in East Central Europe will probably be the reorganization of land tenure and a necessity to improve present agricultural methods. The future status of collectivism is, of course, highlighted by the fact that agricultural production is definitely on the decline in this part of Europe and by the common assumption that, following liberation and presupposing a united East Europe, some regions should be industrialized and others remain agricultural. The importance of solving these agricultural problems is emphasized when one considers that the peasantry is the backbone of peace and order in Eastern Europe and will exert tremendous influence in the settlement of all problems in this part of the world.

The agricultural problem overlaps the problem of surplus population which is also very considerable here. Solutions to this latter question will probably include emigration, land reform and the improvement of agricultural output as well as other methods of reconstruction of a non-agricultural nature.

The signers of the Philadelphia and Williamsburg Declarations recognized the importance of dealing directly with these problems. The former document specifically stated that "the land shall be owned by the peasant as his private property in accordance with the desire of the whole peasantry, which forms a major part of our populations and the backbone of our nations." It went on to say: "Cooperatives and other forms of association voluntarily entered into by the peasants for economic ends shall be free from government interference. Advanced scientific methods and modern implements will help to raise the standard of living of the rural and urban populations." The Williamsburg Declaration was similar except that it pledged the restoration of the right of private ownership of land and added that "land and other property taken from the peasants for collectivization shall be given back to those who till the land." Whatever form of integration may have developed by the time of liberation, a question will arise as to whether it should be maintained, adopted or dismembered.

We should, then, re-examine for a moment the two major post-liberation problems in the field of agriculture—the need to restore the land quickly and equitably to private ownership and the need to maintain at least the existing nutritional standards and to improve them rapidly so as to attain a level comparable with at least the minimum in Western Europe.

A program for the restoration of collectivized land to private ownership must be based on the urgent need to increase agricultural production as well as a moral obligation to provide some sort of compensation to former owners. Land should not necessarily be restored to private hands, merely because of a previously existing title, if full and efficient production cannot be obtained thereby. The early post-World War II programs of land reform were in many cases disruptive of the agricultural economies of the individual countries since they split large well-run farms into holdings so small that the new owners were unable to provide decently for themselves even if they had been versed in the newest methods of scientific agriculture, which most of them were not.

It should not be thought that this writer is advocating a return to the large feudal estates of pre-war days. However, it is a well-known fact that many of these estates were well and scientifically managed, and provided a much more stable existence for the tenant farmers than was the case following their breaking up into small subdivisions. This fact should be carefully borne in mind when a program of land restoration gets under way.

Most of these large estates were confiscated or expropriated with little or no compensation to the former owners. If the question of original restoration is not to be taken into consideration, some overdue form of compensation should be forthcoming in such instances. This problem promises to be one of the most vexing that East Central Europe will face in the post-liberation period, although, fortunately, it is not one of the most immediate.

In the field of nutritional requirements, it must be recognized that, at present, general nutritional standards are very low. Following liberation, it is essential that further decline be prevented at all cost and that the present trend be reversed. This, in turn, will pose another wholly new set of questions, and it is probable that any drastic alteration or change from collectivization to private ownership will have to be deferred or at least must proceed slowly and cautiously. It is also probable, in any case, that emergency food relief will have to be sought abroad in order to supplement local stocks.

If there is to be future European agricultural integration, educational efforts in modern farming methods will have to be undertaken without delay. In order to increase production, the peasants will have to be made acquainted with such technical methods as are now in use in Western Europe. Further, since it is evident that a continued shortage of financial and material resources will limit the peasant's ability to raise his yields, some form of purchasing and marketing cooperatives, such as are now established in Western Europe, may have to be introduced in the liberated areas.

If agricultural production is to be improved in the immediate post-liberation period, some form of assistance will be seriously needed and must be forthcoming, probably from abroad. It also seems that farm rents will have to be guaranteed and that some basis for compulsory agricultural insurance will have to be laid. If foreign credits are forthcoming for these and other related purposes, the agricultural economies of East Central Europe can be rejuvenated and enabled to take their rightful place in European markets and even eventually in an integrated European farm economy.

Social and Related Problems

The post-liberation status of organized labor will present one of the most interesting problems to be dealt with in this period. It is, of course, assumed that all forms of forced labor will be immediately abolished, as will punitive laws relating to labor discipline. The Williamsburg Declaration specifically stated in this connection:

> Free and independent voluntary trade unions and labor organizations shall be the guardians of workers' rights and interests. The workers shall be free to choose their employment and the places where they wish to live and work. The rights and dignity of the worker shall be truly protected, and his opportunity for social and economic progress, including the right to ownership of property, shall be inviolate.

The earlier Philadelphia Declaration added the following expressions of thought:

> The workers, manual and intellectual, shall be protected against exploitation whether by public or private enterprise and shall be free from the fetters of arbitrary and competitive forced standards in work as from repressive labor laws. . . . There shall be responsibility on the part of the public authorities and private administrators that technological and scientific resources be employed to increase output and improve levels of

> living. The workers shall be entitled to a just share in the profits earned by their industries. Before the interest of the machine comes the interest of man.

In the post-liberation period the restoration of free trade unionism, which has been deliberately destroyed by the Communists, will not be an easy task. A rather considerable bias existed in many of the East Central European countries prior to World War II against strong labor organizations, and in the minds of many persons they were responsible for nurturing Communist and allied Socialist movements. If this bias continues after liberation it will prove a formidable barrier to the continued existence of any trade unionism at all. The fact that free trade union leaders were among the inevitable victims of the Communist tyranny is, of course, disregarded by anti-labor elements in these countries.

Because of the strong disruptive economic tendencies that will exist in many of these countries following liberation, it will probably prove impossible to restore the full rights of organized labor for some time to come. The compelling need for full industrial production, for reasons explained above, will also serve to relegate trade union demands for wages, hours and working conditions to a secondary position. During this transitional period, organized labor will have to concentrate upon the issue of mere survival and probably must forego bargaining opportunities for a later, more stable time.

Another complicating factor lies in the feeling of industrial workers themselves. Trained as they have been to regard the Communist-dominated unions as agencies of the state and of nationalized management, they have probably achieved such a stage of resentment that the original concept of unions as representing labor and the rights of the individual working man have been all but forgotten. The historic traditions and fundamental aims of free trade unionism are almost unknown to this new generation of workers. Even among rural workers, the forced collectivization and mechanization of agriculture may have created a new type of outlook and mentality which is very different from that of the conservative East European peasant of the past. Finally, especially among the industrial workers of the large urban centers, the problem of overcoming the mass effect of Communist indoctrination may prove a harder task than among any other single stratum of the population. These factors, coupled with the aforementioned necessity to restrict temporarily such union rights as free collective bargaining, will not only cause the future of trade unionism in East Central Europe to be extremely unsettled for a time but will also present problems which must be met and overcome before the question of labor integration with the organizations of Western Europe can possibly be considered.

Communist barriers to the free movement of labor must, of course, be eliminated, but if such restrictions were abruptly removed immediately following liberation, something approaching economic chaos would result. A widespread desire to migrate westwards in search of higher wages and better working conditions would drain the freed countries of a large part of their industrial manpower. Even within the liberated areas themselves complete freedom of movement will have to come in a gradual and cautious manner.

This question truly will represent one of the great problems of liberated Europe. Even without the desire for economic betterment, there will be other strong and compelling motives which will influence toward a disruptive and unsettling movement of labor. For example, there will be those frontier and agricultural workers who will immediately wish to resume their traditional seasonal migrations across existing boundaries in search of temporary employment. There will be those industrial workers, both of a specialized or technical and those of a general nature, who have been uprooted from their homes and sent to new places to work by the Communists. These people will be endeavoring to return once again to their former homes and, in many cases, to their families. And finally, but by no means of least importance, there will be the hundreds of thousands of displaced persons, exiles and refugees who, following liberation, will be wishing to return to their homelands or, conversely, will be trying to leave East Central Europe entirely behind them. To these must be added the innumerable multitudes of persons freed from slave labor camps who will be motivated by the same feelings. The solution to these problems must be found, but it will require the talents of a genius.

The matter of social security benefits will probably also have to be postponed during the immediate post-liberation period. In speaking of this social insurance, of course, the three types of health insurance, accident insurance and old age or pension insurance are understood to be included.

Communist-organized social insurance has been markedly conspicious for its centralization and degree of Party control. Noticeable also has been the tendency toward uniform benefits among all the captive countries, a factor which will be of considerable interest in future implementation of integration with the system of Western Europe. As might be expected, there has also been considerable discrimination, since certain groups have been specifically and completely excluded from coverage and other groups have been covered, from a variety of political motives, regardless of whether they were gainfully employed or not. Then, too, there is a marked difference of premium rates among different groups, and all insured persons do not receive insurance benefits on an equal basis. Although there has recently been a slight tendency toward reducing such discriminatory practices, they still persist to a considerable extent. Political and related reasons, of course, govern almost all examples of discrimination such as have been noted above.

Given these considerations regarding the present operation of social security in Communist-dominated Europe, it can readily be perceived that many social advantages have been promised by the Red regimes which are completely unfulfilled in fact and in practice. The Communist methods of applying these policies have, in many cases, aggravated long-standing social injustices and wrongs and even assisted in creating new ones. Finally, it should also be recognized that the so-called "new social order" will have social claims of its own which must be considered in the post-liberation period.

Immediately following liberation, there will unquestionably be a pressing need for social assistance in the freed countries. Such a need will probably require that the present social security systems be left unchanged, at least for a temporary period, and administered in their present forms, although unfair discriminatory provisions should be removed as soon as practicable. There will also be the pressing question of whether or not contributions to the systems from both workers and employers alone will be sufficient to maintain these systems or whether in individual cases the state will have to assume a partial financial responsibility and take on at least a part of the burden.

Eventually, the question of integration with the social security systems of Western Europe must also be considered. In this connection, the present regional uniformity may have to be maintained to a certain degree in order to facilitate such integration.

Lastly, there will be the problem of how to obtain the necessary foreign credit facilities which will be needed to cover the immediate emergency needs. The question of maintaining social stability concurrently with financial stability will be an important one, and a balance must be found. It is doubted that even the most generous foreign financial creditors would extend assistance to a social security system which was unrealistic and out of line with the financial resources available at that time. This, of course, emphasizes the need for achieving a balance between monetary soundness and full employment.

Post-liberation problems in the fields of health and education may also properly be considered at this time. As was mentioned earlier, those segments of the population, such as forced laborers, inmates of labor camps, deportees and others, who have been displaced from their usual places of residence by the Communists, will be attempting to return to their homes. Transportation arrangements and food provisions of an emergency nature will have to be made. Then there will be the legal question of settling rights in connection with housing, compensation, etc. An emergency housing condition will surely be present, and will call for prompt action because of the aforementioned expected movements of large parts of the population as well as the general slowness and insufficiency in residential housing construction in these countries during the period of Communist domination. A general food shortage in the area can be anticipated following liberation, and it is probable that large stocks of relief food supplies will have to be found and brought in from abroad, at least until the freed countries are able to increase their own agricultural production. In this connection, expert advice will be needed to establish a diet that will satisfy requirements for minimum standards of nutrition. Finally, under the Communists, the countries of East Central Europe have been relatively backward in acquiring techniques and practices of modern medicine as well as the supplies of the latest medicines and drugs themselves. With the possibility of mass epidemics in the immediate post-liberation period, the likely shortage of medicines and experienced medical help will necessitate urgent assistance from abroad in these fields. Other related problems include the reorganization of national Red Cross societies on a humanitarian basis, and the possible temporary evacuation of younger children abroad to relieve any short-range crises in food and housing.

The Iron Curtain has been particularly effective in creating barriers between the cultures of the captive peoples and those of the free world. Following liberation, it will be extremely desirable to re-integrate, insofar as possible, the cultures of Western and Eastern Europe as a necessary preliminary to the establishment of a European community itself. Furthermore, textbooks, especially history texts, will have to be vastly improved and a thorough revision of all publications, as well as films and other media of mass communications, will have to be undertaken in order to remove bias and distortion. New teaching staffs will have to be created and expert assistance in educational, agricultural and professional fields will be needed from abroad. Youth organizations, especially, will have to be reactivated in accordance with their original concepts. It is hoped that East European exiles will be given an opportunity here to play their part in the reconstruction of public administration and general education. A general exchange program of educational, scientific and cultural personnel between West and East Europe would probably prove to be of considerable benefit at this time.

As might be expected, the problem will not be one of educating the liberated peoples to be against Communism; little or no work of this kind is required for those who have actually lived under such a system. But the need for modern medical assistance to restore health and physical vitality, and the need for education to teach the freed peoples the concepts and beliefs of the Western world regarding human freedom and material progress, are very real indeed. Such needs can obviously not be met by the liberated peoples of East Central Europe alone—they must receive cooperation and assistance from the free world.

Perhaps the question of education deserves even a further word. As was found to be true in Germany after the end of World War II, even half a generation of totalitarian thought control is enough to mould the minds and thinking of hundreds of thousands of young people. It is not enough to revamp a national literature which has been prostituted to the service of the Communist state, it is not enough to purge the libraries of their atheistic and anti-national propaganda, it is not enough to enlist the service of teacher cadres for future education in a truly democratic manner. The problem of the school children who have been educated under Communism and who have been poisoned with Communism will be one of the most difficult problems of the post-liberation period, but there will be no more important problem to solve, not only for the present but also the future of the liberated countries. And, if liberation is extended beyond the so-called satellites to parts of the Soviet Union itself where Communism has been in control for a full generation or more, such as Ukraine, the problem will be two and three times as difficult to solve. But it must be solved for the future of the entire region itself.

Legal and Related Problems

The legal problems of the post-liberation period would almost require a separate study at least the size of this present paper. Suffice it to say that so-called socialist law has replaced common and civil law in every one of the captive countries. Each country has seen the provisions of its constitution changed and altered to fit the aims of its Communist masters, and each has seen its politico-administrative structures revamped with the same purposes in mind. The problem of eliminating these perversive characteristics and of restoring the tenets of justice for all and special privileges for none will pose a tremendous task. Not only the concept but also the organization of so-called people's justice and the "people's courts" must be erased from the legal structures of East Central Europe. Communist-dictated concepts of civil and criminal legislation will have to be altered. The various problems involved are many and complex and years may pass before they are finally settled.

The Philadelphia and Williamsburg Declarations were, however, quite specific on these points. The former assured the restoration of the right of *habeas corpus* and added: "The machine of mutual extermination shall no longer roll through our countries. Crimes against humanity shall be dealt with by the regular process of justice and on grounds of personal responsibility for definite acts. Eastern European democracy cannot be revived through vengeance. 'Thou shalt not kill' is the basic commandment for us." The Williamsburg Declaration amplified these expressions in many respects, quoting extensively from the principles to be found in the Virginia Bill of Rights (1776), and also pledged the abolition of secret police, concentration camps, forced labor, trial by torture and intimidation, extortion, unwarranted arrest, genocide and deportation.

This, of course, raises the question as to what should be done with the local Communist parties, the local secret police, the local satellite armies and the local units of government, both as to the organizations themselves and the individuals who participated therein, either willingly or unwillingly. The trends and popular feelings for vengeance will be very strong in East Central Europe following liberation. Everyone who served the Communist state will be marked for revenge.

Experiences following World War II have clearly demonstrated the futility, as well as the danger, in the assumption of collective responsibility. Those government leaders who acted as willing stooges of the Kremlin should be brought to justice if they are apprehended and survive the actual period of liberation itself. Persons responsible for individual acts of atrocity must also be punished for their individual crimes. In this connection, source material collected by refugee organizations and other interested groups regarding individual perpetrations of crimes and atrocities should be of tremendous value.

But outbreaks of mass vengeance or other popular attempts at collective revenge will merely add to the bitterness and resentments that have so long plagued this region. Whatever law enforcement authority may be available at the time of liberation should strive to do all in its power, not only to punish the guilty, but also to protect the innocent. In such cases of political and social upheaval it is a simple thing to pass from one extreme to the other; it is much more difficult to preserve a balance of justice and order. It will be especially difficult because of the likelihood of individual denunciations made on a basis of individual spite and rancor rather than on a foundation of truth. But this balance must be preserved if *vendettas* and feuds are not to leave their scars behind for untold years. And the danger will not lie only with individuals; nationalistic disputes of an irredentist origin must be solved through calm negotiation rather than by the applications of all available physical force and pressures.

Political Problems

As was mentioned in the introduction to this essay, individual boundary and population problems that may exist in East Central Europe following liberation will find no solution here. It would be a brave man indeed who would attempt to decide the future of Slovakia, Croatia, Transylvania or many similar areas of this region. Such a person would not only be brave but indeed foolhardy if he speculated in writing on the outcome of the Oder-Neisse line, the cities of Memel or Teschen or Bratislava, the status of the Banat or Carpatho-Ukraine, among a host of others. The scope of this paper should be limited to a survey of the political problems of East Central Europe as a whole, and that limitation will be strictly adhered to in what follows.

Let us take a final look at the Philadelphia and Williamsburg Declarations from which quotations have previously been drawn to exemplify the best thinking of exile and refugee leaders in the United States. At Philadelphia it was stated categorically that the people of Central and Eastern Europe were firmly resolved, upon their liberation, to join the community of free nations. It added:

> The peoples of Central and Eastern Europe are eager to take their natural place in the great movement of free peoples towards better relationship and closer union. They are desirous of establishing among themselves strong ties of a federal character and of joining in the formation of a United Europe. Such a fraternal federation must prize and respect the distinctive values of each nation, for the common good of our European civilization and for the cultural heritage of mankind throughout the world.

Similar sentiments were echoed at Williamsburg the following year.

Before this question of federation can be further considered, however, some very real questions must first be posed. In the first place, it is a truism that the liberated peoples must enjoy the right of self-determination with respect to the governments and the social and economic institutions of their own future. It then follows that at the present time it is impossible to know the feelings and thoughts of the captive peoples themselves in these matters. No individual exile, no association of refugee leaders, regardless of past prominence or influence, can truthfully presume to speak for the people of their native land today. As a matter of fact, it is the firm conviction of this writer that the future leaders of the liberated countries will almost exclusively come from among the persons who literally stayed behind. Without intending to minimize the importance of the work carried on today by prominent refugee individuals and organizations, I do not believe that they will be able to return to their former roles of influence and prestige following liberation. The likelihood is, rather, that the future leaders of the freed countries will come from the ranks of those who remained and somehow survived the Communist terror. The majority of prominent exiles with whom this writer has discussed the question are in agreement with this thesis.

The peoples of East Central Europe have always been regarded as among the most nationalistic in the world. Such tendencies were forced upon them by geography and by their own historic developments. In order to survive, not only politically but also economically and culturally, in the face of larger and more powerful neighbors, they had to imbue themselves with a fiercely nationalistic spirit which would enable them to resist even in the face of prolonged foreign domination and occupation. It is that spirit of nationalism in East Central Europe which is today providing the Communists with their greatest problems as they try to strengthen their control over the captive countries.

If we assume that some form of federation or integration is indispensable for post-liberated East Central Europe, it is clearly the course of wisdom to attempt to prepare the captive peoples for receptivity toward such an idea, even before liberation is an accomplished fact. Such a course, however, immediately encounters two obstacles among people who have always looked askance at any such form of mutual participation and cooperation. The first is the degree of forced integration in many fields which has been imposed upon this region by the Communist domination. The natural anti-Communism of the people themselves has been extended to all forms of Communist-imposed institutions and it is likely that intra-regional cooperation is included. In other words, to the degree that the Communists have forcibly imposed integration among these countries and with the Soviet Union, to that degree opposition may be expected, following liberation, to cooperation on a voluntary basis with each other or future integration with Western Europe or any organization.

As was said earlier, the existing spirit of nationalism is the greatest obstacle to communization of the area. It is, or should be, a part of "cold war strategy" to encourage this nationalistic spirit in order to make the task of the Communists more difficult and to keep the hope of freedom alive among the captive peoples. At the time of liberation, therefore, the feeling of nationalism may properly be expected to be at a peak. It will be an immeasurably difficult task to reconcile this resurgent nationalism with any trend toward regional federation or eventual integration with Western Europe, especially in view of the antipathy toward federalism that will already exist because of experiences with the Communist version of it. And yet the reconciliation must be made, since some form of regional cooperation on all planes appears to offer the only hope for the political future of East Central Europe.

Proponents of federation for this area point to the relative stability that existed under the former Austro-Hungarian Empire. While they can in no sense be termed monarchists or Hapsburg legitimists, they do favor some sort of regional grouping along lines similar to that of the Empire, especially for the people of the Danubian Basin. They point out, for example, that, since the Empire was broken up by the victors of World War I into several small independent countries, nationalism has been rampant in this part of Europe, and no political cohesive defense organization could be maintained against either Germany or Russia.

The problem of the future political organization of these countries, therefore, is very likely the greatest of all problems that must be met and solved in the post-liberation period. Such an organization can in no sense be a reversion to the past but must instead be based on enlightened twentieth century principles and must, furthermore, provide a real hope of economic and social improvement to the peoples of its member states. Regardless of the possible menace from outside ideologies, the liberated nations must offer their citizens a genuine opportunity for future betterment, else they will again divide between extremist movements of both the right and the left.

Naturally the political institutions of the various countries involved cannot be expected to achieve too great a degree of similarity. They must be recast along democratic lines, but such a transition will be governed to a great degree by the political maturity or immaturity of the various countries themselves. What supranational organs of government may be created within the region, or, for that matter, within Europe as a whole, must be shaped so as to permit the maximum degree of national consciousness which is consonant with opportunities for free and equal exchanges of goods, services, people and ideas within a general association of nations. If these political problems can be surmounted, the greatest barriers to federation will have been removed. The whole question is that of integration without amalgamation.

Given the assumption that for the future East Central Europe must be considered as a political and socio-economic entity, not for the protection of some of its members against others but for the protection of all against outside influences, we should realize that the future status of this region will depend to a very great extent upon the status of Germany and Russia. An examination of this aspect, of course, lies outside the scope of this essay, but it is only being realistic to recognize that the matter of East Central European minorities residing outside their natural homelands, whether it be in Germany or Russia or even within another member state, will be a difficult one. Conversely, there is the question of German or Russian minorities within the member states. Some have advocated population transfers as the answer to this problem, but the bitterness engendered by the operation of such a policy following World War II would make this seem an unlikely solution.

Such difficult nationality problems in this area will be bound to make the problem of federation in part a constitutional one. And right here it must be emphasized that whatever form of federalization is eventually arrived at must be a voluntary one. Concerning the question of the rights of these religious and national minorities, the prospective member states will have to learn that autonomy granted as a privilege will prove no solution to the problem, and that it is almost impossible to guarantee such rights without some form of federalism. It should also be shown that federalism can open the way toward a higher standard of living for all concerned, although there is a legitimate question as to how far its territorial extension should go.

It is to be hoped that this future East Central European federation might eventually be integrated with some all-European system as a whole, thus enabling friendly relations to be cultivated with the great powers of Western Europe. As has already been mentioned, there would have to be autonomy and self-government for all national minorities, and all nationalities in this mixed area would have to be assured of cultural autonomy, freedom and equality. Many authorities also advocate an equalization of social patterns, social justice and social security as well as a customs union and a common economic plan for adequate mutual economic development.

By way of comparison, it should be pointed out that those forms of Western European integration which have already taken place, such as the Schuman Plan creating the Coal and Steel Community, have been based on democracy and diversity, while the captive nations have been forcibly subjected to integration based on uniformity and totalitarian regimentation. As has been mentioned earlier, the whole area is undergoing a rapid process of industrialization and an involuntary form of regional economic cooperation has developed within the Soviet bloc.

It is this forced integration and cooperation under Communist pressure that, paradoxically enough, may make the problems of post-liberation federationists more difficult. Although it will indeed be a hard task to persuade the nationalistic elements in the freed countries, who will be desirous of abolishing everything that smacks of Communist planning, to retain the desirable features of Soviet-bloc integration, these features will almost certainly have to be the foundation for East Central European federation.

In a final review of this question of federation, we have seen that, because of the presence of Germany and Russia, a high degree of military defense effectiveness is essential for the countries of East Central Europe, and this in turn will require a combination of all their defense potentials. Such a grouping would prepare the way for a close integration of these countries in a united Europe. Similar arguments have been put forward as the economic, agricultural, legal and social problems of the post-liberation period have been examined, and all seem to point to federalism or some form of intergovernmental organization as the answer, with regional, not national, autonomy as the best safeguard for minority rights.

If we assume, therefore, that the liberated countries of East Central Europe must be included in an all-European integration, but that possibly some interim form of regional cooperation and organization may first have to be found, we cannot help but look upon the Council of Europe as the logical vehicle for such progress. Several resolutions of the Council's Consultative Assembly have confirmed the fact that its ultimate goal is to extend its activities over all European countries which have played a part in creating European culture. Political independence, military capacity for self-defense, social stability and economic soundness are all evident goals of the Council, and clearly the fulfillment of these basic objectives demand the cooperation of Eastern and Central Europe with Western Europe. Future Russian or Soviet pressure, whatever form it may take, can only be resisted by a Europe united in some effective form of cooperation, just as only a unified Europe will continue to merit and receive the support and confidence of the United States of America. The empty seats at the Council of Europe, in symbol if not in fact, are clear-cut evidence that the captive nations are expected to resume their rightful and lawful places one day within the European family.

pressure from outside is severe enough may make the problem of post-liberation federation more difficult. Although it will indeed be a hard task to persuade the nationalistic elements in the freed countries, who will be desirous of abolishing everything that smacks of communist planning, to retain the desirable features of Soviet planned integration, these features will almost certainly have to be the foundation for East Central European federation.

In a final review of this question of federation, we have seen that, because of the presence of Germany and Russia, a high degree of military defensive cooperation is essential for [illegible] grouping would prepare the way for a close federation of these countries in a united Europe. Similar arguments have been put forward as the economic, agricultural and social problems of the post-liberation period have been examined, and all seem to point to federation or some form of intergovernmental organization as the answer, with regional, not national, autonomy as the best safeguard for minority rights.

If we assume, therefore, that the ultimate solution of East Central Europe must be included in an all-European integration, but that possibly some interim form of regional cooperation and organization may first have to be found, we cannot but look upon the Council of Europe as the logical vehicle for such progress. Several resolutions of the Council's Consultative Assembly have confirmed the fact that its ultimate goal is to extend its activities over all European countries which have played a part in creating European culture. Political independence, military capacity for self-defense, social stability and economic soundness are all evident goals of the Council, and clearly the fulfillment of these basic objectives demand the cooperation of Eastern and Central Europe with Western Europe. Future Russian or Soviet pressure, whatever form it may take, can only be resisted by a Europe united in some effective form of cooperation, just as only a united Europe will continue to merit and receive the support and confidence of the United States of America. The empty seats in the Council of Europe, in symbol if not in fact, are clear evidence that the captive nations are expected to assume their rightful and lawful places one day within the European family.

INDEX

INDEX

30 20

EUROPE

Pre-World War II state boundaries

Boundary between Eastern and Western Germany

Countries under control of the U.S.S.R. — so-called Iron Curtain countries

Territorial gains of Yugoslavia from Italy

Territorial gains of Poland from Germany, and of Bulgaria from Rumania

Territorial gains of the U.S.S.R. from Finland, Poland, Czechoslovakia, Germany, Rumania, Baltic States

States treated in book

0 100 200 300
MILES

Dublin

ATLANTIC

OCEAN

10